HOUSING, URBAN GOVERNANCE AND ANTI-SOCIAL BEHAVIOUR

Perspectives, policy and practice

Edited by John Flint

First published in Great Britain in July 2006 by

The Policy Press
University of Bristol
Fourth Floor
Beacon House
Queen's Road
Bristol BS8 1QU
UK

Tel +44 (0)117 331 4054
Fax +44 (0)117 331 4093
e-mail tpp-info@bristol.ac.uk
www.policypress.org.uk

British Library Cataloguing in Publication Data
A catalogue record for this book is available from the British Library.

Library of Congress Cataloging-in-Publication Data
A catalog record for this book has been requested.

ISBN-10 1 86134 684 0 paperback
ISBN-13 978 1 86134 684 1 paperback
ISBN-10 1 86134 685 9 hardcover
ISBN-13 978 1 86134 685 8 hardcover

Cover design by Qube Design Associates, Bristol.
Front cover: photograph supplied by kind permission of
www.third-avenue.co.uk
Printed and bound in Great Britain by MPG Books, Bodmin.

Contents

List of tables, figures and photographs   v
Acknowledgements   vi
Notes on contributors   vii

Introduction   1
John Flint

**Part 1: The definition and construction of anti-social   17
behaviour in the UK**

one   Housing and the new governance of conduct   19
           John Flint

two   Governing tenants: from dreadful enclosures to   37
           dangerous places
           Pauline Card

three   Labelling: constructing definitions of anti-social behaviour? 57
           Helen Carr and Dave Cowan

four   Anti-social behaviour: voices from the front line   79
           Judy Nixon and Sadie Parr

five   Spaces of discipline and control: the compounded   99
           citizenship of social renting
           Rowland Atkinson

**Part 2: Legal techniques and measures utilised by   117
social landlords to address anti-social behaviour**

six   Tenancy agreements: a mechanism for governing   119
           anti-social behaviour?
           Diane Lister

seven   The changing legal framework: from landlords to agents 137
           of social control
           Caroline Hunter

eight   Social landlords, anti-social behaviour and   155
           countermeasures
           Hal Pawson and Carol McKenzie

Part 3: The emerging mechanisms of addressing   177
anti-social behaviour in housing governance

nine   Evaluating the Shelter Inclusion Project: a floating   179
support service for households accused of
anti-social behaviour
Anwen Jones, Nicholas Pleace and Deborah Quilgars

ten   Tackling anti-social behaviour: an evaluation of   199
the Dundee Families Project
Suzie Scott

eleven   Policing and community safety in residential areas: 219
the mixed economy of visible patrols
Adam Crawford

twelve   Gated communities: a response to, or remedy for,   239
anti-social behaviour?
Sarah Blandy

Part 4: Studies of housing and anti-social behaviour   257
from an international perspective

thirteen   Housing and anti-social behaviour in Australia   259
Kathy Arthurson and Keith Jacobs

fourteen   Testing urban forms: city, control and 'urban violence'   281
in France
Olivier Ratouis and Jérôme Boissonade

fifteen   Residential stability among adolescents in public housing: 301
a risk factor for delinquent and violent behaviour?
Timothy O. Ireland, Terence P. Thornberry and Rolf Loeber

sixteen   Conclusion   325
John Flint

Index   335

List of tables, figures and photographs

Tables

3.1   Lists of ASB   61

7.1   Number of ASBOs taken out from April 1999 to September 2004   148

8.1   Use of ASB legal countermeasures by local authority landlords (England) (2002/03)   164

9.1   All households in Shelter Inclusion Project, by type by gender of key service user (current and former cases)   182

15.1   Descriptive statistics (%)   308

15.2   Prevalence of property and violent crime among those always, sometimes and never in public housing (%)   310

15.3   Prevalence of property and violent crime among those never, transiently and always in public housing (%)   312

15.4   Prevalence of property and violent crime among those always, sometimes and never in large developments or high-rise buildings (Pittsburgh only) (%)   313

15.5   Prevalence of property and violent crime among those never, transiently and always in large developments or high-rise buildings (Pittsburgh only) (%)   314

Figures

i.1   Front page of *The Sun*, 3 August 2005   3

5.1   The politicisation of fear. Cover of *Putting Our Communities First* (Scottish Executive, 2003)   106

8.1   Trends in recorded crime (raw figures) (England and Wales) (1998/99-2003/04)   160

8.2   Trends in perceived 'serious problems in the neighbourhood' (England) (1994-2004)   160

8.3   Changes in social landlords' organisation of counter-ASB functions (2000-03)   163

10.1   Map of partnership relationships   210

Photograph

3.1   ASB poster   62

Acknowledgements

We are grateful to the Department of Urban Studies, University of Glasgow, and the ESRC (Economic and Social Research Council) Centre for Neighbourhood Research for their contribution towards this publication. We wish to acknowledge Rowan Alcock for providing the photograph in Chapter Three. John Flint would like to thank Emily Watt, Philip de Bary, Natasha Ferguson, Laura Greaves and the anonymous referees at The Policy Press for all their help in preparing the typescript.

Notes on contributors

Rowland Atkinson is Director of the Housing and Community Research Unit, School of Sociology and Social Work at the University of Tasmania, Australia (www.utas.edu.au/sociology/HACRU/Rowland_Atkinson.htm).

Kathy Arthurson is a senior research fellow in the Urban and Regional Planning Group at the University of South Australia (www.unisanet.unisa.edu.au/staff/homepage.asp?Name=Kathryn.Arthurson).

Sarah Blandy teaches property law at the School of Law, University of Leeds (www.law.leeds.ac.uk/lawstaff).

Jérôme Boissonade is an assistant professor in the Institut des Mers du Nord at the Université du Littoral Côte d'Opale, Dunkirk, France (www.univ-littoral.fr/).

Pauline Card is a lecturer in housing in the School of City and Regional Planning at Cardiff University, UK (www.cf.ac.uk/cplan/staff/card_p.html).

Helen Carr is a lecturer in law at Kent Law School, UK (www.kent.ac.uk/law/people/carr_h.htm).

Dave Cowan is Professor of Law and Policy in the School of Law at the University of Bristol, UK (www.law.bris.ac.uk/staff/staffmember.html?person_code=013702).

Adam Crawford is Professor of Criminology and Criminal Justice and Director of the Centre for Criminal Justice Studies at the University of Leeds, UK (www.law.leeds.ac.uk/leedslaw/StaffProfile.aspx?TabID=1&MenuID=7&SubMenuID=144&Username=crawfordad).

John Flint is a senior research fellow in the Centre for Regional, Economic and Social Research at Sheffield Hallam University, UK (www.shu.ac.uk/research/cresr/staff/j-flint.html).

Caroline Hunter is Senior Lecturer in Housing Law in the Centre for Social Inclusion at Sheffield Hallam University, UK (www.shu.ac.uk/research/csi/c_hunter.html).

Timothy O. Ireland is an associate professor and Chair of the Department of Criminal Justice at Niagara University, New York State, US (www.niagara.edu/crj/).

Keith Jacobs is a senior lecturer in the School of Sociology and Social Work at the University of Tasmania, Australia (www.utas.edu.au/sociology/HACRU/Keith_Jacobs.htm).

Anwen Jones is a research fellow in the Centre for Housing Policy at the University of York, UK (www.york.ac.uk/inst/chp/Staff/jones.htm).

Diane Lister is an associate professor in the Centre for Peace Studies at the University of Tromsø, Norway (http://uit.no/cps/3325/45).

Rolf Loeber is Professor of Psychiatry, Psychology and Epidemiology in the Western Psychiatric Institute and Clinic in the School of Medicine at the University of Pittsburgh, Pennsylvania, US (www.psychology.pitt.edu/people/faculty/loeber.php).

Carol McKenzie is studying for a PhD in the School of the Built Environment at Heriot-Watt University, Edinburgh, UK.

Judy Nixon is Senior Lecturer in Housing Policy in the Centre for Social Inclusion at Sheffield Hallam University, UK (www.shu.ac.uk/research/csi/j_nixon.html).

Sadie Parr is a researcher in the Centre for Social Inclusion at Sheffield Hallam University, UK (www.shu.ac.uk/research/csi/s_parr.html).

Hal Pawson is a senior research fellow in the School of the Built Environment at Heriot-Watt University, Edinburgh, UK (www.sbe.hw.ac.uk/staff/res/pawson.htm).

Nicholas Pleace is a senior research fellow in the Centre for Housing Policy at the University of York, UK (www.york.ac.uk/inst/chp/Staff/pleace.htm).

Deborah Quilgars is a senior research fellow in the Centre for Housing Policy at the University of York, UK (www.york.ac.uk/inst/chp/Staff/quilgars.htm).

Olivier Ratouis is an assistant professor in the Institut des Mers du Nord, at the Université du Littoral Côte d'Opale, Dunkirk, France (www.univ-littoral.fr/rech/labo/imn.htm).

Suzie Scott is the Policy and Research Manager of the Glasgow Housing Association, UK.

Terence P. Thornberry is Professor of Sociology and Director of the Research Program on Problem Behavior in the Institute of Behavioral Science at the University of Colorado, Boulder, Colorado, US (www.colorado.edu/ibs/pb/thornberry/).

Introduction

John Flint

On the morning after New Labour's re-election in the UK in 2005, Prime Minister Tony Blair set out the government's priorities. In his speech he said:

> I've been struck again and again in the course of this campaign by people's worry that in our country … there is a disrespect that people don't like. And whether it's in the classroom or on the street, or our town centres on a Friday or Saturday night, I want to focus on this issue. We've done a lot so far with anti-social behaviour and increased numbers of police, but I want to make this a particular priority for this government – how we bring back a proper sense of respect in our schools, in our communities, in our towns, in our villages. (Blair speech, 6 May 2005)

Blair was correct to state that since 1997 'a lot has been done' with anti-social behaviour (ASB), if this is taken to mean the political priority given to the issue in rhetoric, discourse, legislation and policy development. Tackling ASB is now embedded in a new organisational architecture of governance at central and local government, and increasingly community and neighbourhood, levels. In 2003 an Antisocial Behaviour Unit (ASBU) was established (in the Home Office) within the traditional crime and policing remit of the Home Office along with a new Respect Task Force (see www.respect.gov.uk). Local authorities in the UK have been given enhanced powers and responsibilities and encouraged, through Crime and Disorder Reduction Partnerships (CDRPs), to prioritise tackling ASB. In Scotland local authorities are required to develop anti-social behaviour strategies and are encouraged to establish ASBUs (Scottish Executive, 2003). The Home Office-led TOGETHER campaign and action plan (a resource for practitioners working to tackle ASB across England and Wales: see www.together.gov.uk) has maintained the high profile given to tackling ASB, translated into action through funding and intervention in 50 communities designated as TOGETHER Action

Areas. Increasing emphasis is given to strengthening neighbourhood tiers of governance and incorporating citizens and communities as part of the wider policing family coupled with policing reforms aimed at delivering neighbourhood policing (Home Office, 2004). This governmental focus on ASB is also reflected in, and influenced by, the increased profile given to the issue by professional groupings and agencies, for example the Social Landlords Crime and Nuisance Group[1].

Legislation including the 1998 Crime and Disorder Act, the 2002 Police Reform Act, the 2003 Anti-social Behaviour Act and the 2005 Serious Organised Crime and Police Act have introduced a range of new legal mechanisms which enhance the powers of state and other agencies to extend the scope of governance and to exert social control over both individual and collective behaviour, in both public and private spaces. These include Antisocial Behaviour Orders (ASBOs) that prohibit individuals engaging in specified behaviours. Breaching an order is a criminal office. After a slow initial take-up, ASBOs have become increasingly used by local authorities and registered social landlords and have been extended to an ever-widening range of behaviours and age groups. Dispersal Orders and Curfew Orders (although successfully challenged in court) enhance the state control of public space by giving the police powers to disperse groups in areas which have experienced ASB, and extend the scope of intervention to individuals, and entire groups such as those aged under 16, who may not actually be engaged in ASB at the time of contact with the police. Electronic monitoring increases the surveillance of individuals whilst the use of Acceptable Behaviour Contracts (ABCs) and Parenting Orders intensifies the supervision and responsibilities of individuals and families. An increased state social control function is also apparent through an enhanced presence of visible authority figures. There are record numbers of police officers, increasingly focused on high visibility 'reassurance' policing (Home Office, 2004), complimented by community support officers and neighbourhood wardens.

Housing is increasingly central to the contemporary governance of ASB. Social landlords are now firmly embedded within local CDRPs and ASB strategies and have been provided with new legal mechanisms of social control including strengthened powers of eviction, injunction and probationary tenancies. Social landlords increasingly utilise a range of sub-legal mechanisms including good neighbour agreements and tenant reward schemes to promote desirable and required conduct among their tenants. While this enhanced role for social landlords is often portrayed as essentially disciplinary and punitive, housing-based interventions also extend to the promotion of community relations and regulation of interaction, through, for example, mediation schemes and the provision of a range of preventative interventions, including tenancy support services and rehabilitation and resettlement projects. The role of housing in governing ASB is not confined to the social rented tenure. Increasing government attention is given to incorporating private landlords into regimes aimed at tackling ASB (Home Office, 2003), and the emergence of gated communities and the purchase of additional security mechanisms by residential communities illustrates the need to include owner-occupied areas within studies of housing and ASB.

The concept of ASB, its causes, extent, manifestations, perpetrators and solutions are constructed through a discourse involving policy makers, local residents, housing practitioners and the media. Government White Papers such as *Respect and Responsibility* and *Building Communities, Beating Crime* (Home Office, 2003, 2004) set out the rationales for government policy and explicitly link proposed action with wider conceptualisations about how society should function and the problems it faces. This policy rhetoric may be seen within a wider predominant discourse (Figure i.1).

Figure i.1: Front page of *The Sun*, 3 August 2005

This discourse of a 'lawless Britain' conflates a number of risks, and identifies key themes that will be returned to throughout this book. A 'yob culture' is identified, now extended from problem estates to town centres, and is linked to fears at the neighbourhood level, including 'kids scared to go out' and paedophiles 'living next door'. The alleged abuse of the welfare state and legal system, including benefit fraud and legal aid to the 'undeserving', is part of a long tradition of problematising the recipients of welfare, including social housing tenants. There is criticism of authority, and the suggestion that traditional sources of protection such as the judiciary and the police can no longer be relied on to secure our safety. After the July 2005 London bombings ASB is related to fears of terrorism, conflated with immigration. Thus ASB is cast as part of a spectrum of risks and fears, and a symptom of a nation in transitional crisis, in which achieving safety and security and protecting the traditional through undefined norms and values of 'the majority' becomes key.

Such discourse may be defined as part of a process of 'moral panic' famously identified by Cohen (2002; see also Cooper, 2005) based on the 'labelling' of 'outsider' individuals or groups whose conduct is conceived as being outwith constructed norms and values posited to exist in the majority of what the Home Office repeatedly terms 'ordinary people' (Home Office, 2003). Further legitimisation for the intensive disciplinary surveillance and control of disrespectable groups occurs through 'deviancy amplification' (see Cooper, 2005) that exaggerates both the extent and scale of problematic behaviour among 'outsider' groups and the adherence of the majority to respectable and required conduct. Such moral panics are not new. For example, in recent times the list of 'folk devils' (Cohen, 2002) listed by Seabrook (1984) 20 years ago replicates almost exactly those identified in the figure above (with the exception of terrorism). Concepts of the underclass (Murray, 1990) represent recent labelling and deviancy amplification processes, which in their contemporary manifestation crystallise around ASB. All of this amounts to a discourse in which 'society must be defended' (Foucault, 2003). How the norms and values of that society and its contractual and relational basis of citizenship are constructed, who they are to be defended against, how they will be defended and who will do the defending are questions that lie at the core of this book.

What is anti-social behaviour?

A central problem emerges in defining what is actually meant by anti-social behaviour. The range of conduct it encompasses, from nuisance to serious criminality, may preclude a single definition (SEU, 2000). The 1998 Crime and Disorder Act defines ASB as 'behaviour that caused or was likely to cause harassment, alarm or distress to one or more persons not of the same household as the perpetrator'. Increasing attempts are being made to operationalise ASB in legal terms and to quantify its occurrence, through, for example, the Home Office's one-day count exercise and the British Crime Surveys, although evidence about increasing incidences of ASB is ambiguous (see Chapter Eight, this volume).

Perhaps the most comprehensive definition to date is provided by Millie et al (2005, p 3), who define ASB as behaviour that:

> causes harassment, alarm or distress to individuals not of the same household as the perpetrator, such that it requires interventions from the relevant authorities; but criminal prosecution and punishment may be inappropriate because the individual components of the behaviour:
>
> – are not prohibited by the criminal law or
> – in isolation constitute relatively minor offences.

This definition usefully identifies the role of authorities in constructing ASB through decisions about when intervention is appropriate. It also separates ASB from more serious criminal activity and recognises the importance of the cumulative impact of incidents. However, such clear differentiation is uncommon in policy discourse and practice. The Local Government Information Unit (1997, p 5) defined ASB as:

> Behaviour that causes harassment to a community; amounts to antisocial criminal conduct, or is otherwise anti-social; disrupts the peaceful and quiet enjoyment of a neighbourhood by others; intimidates a community or section of it.

This elastic definition represents a blurring between criminal and non-criminal conduct, providing an ambiguity open to wide interpretation and offering wide discretion in enforcement (Scraton, 2005). One consequence of this blurring of criminal and non-criminal behaviour is an emphasis on how objectionable conduct is to particular groups, rather than whether or not it is unlawful (Rowlands, 2005), resulting in examples of ASBOs being used to tackle non-criminal behaviour including being sarcastic, feeding birds in a garden or political protesting. These examples have often involved vulnerable individuals, such as a suicidal woman who was banned from watercourses, railways and loitering on bridges (see Rowlands, 2005). Thus the range of behaviours subject to surveillance and intervention have been extended, as have the populations subject to ASBOs, most notably to children aged 10 or over (see Squires and Stephen, 2005).

However, these broad definitions of ASB also include criminal acts, resulting in criticism that new measures such as ASBOs, with their lower evidence requirements and procedural emphasis on the powers of local authorities and social landlords (see Chapter Seven, this volume), are being used to bypass the safeguards of the traditional criminal justice system (Rowlands, 2005; Scraton; 2005; Squires and Stephen, 2005). This conflating of criminal and ASB measures is epitomised in so-called Criminal ASBOs or 'CRASBOs', which are made against an individual at the point of their conviction and extend the prohibitions on an offender beyond the period of their sentencing.

As several contributors to this book point out, definitions of ASB are important if we are to find 'solutions'. But, as Helen Carr and Dave Cowan argue in Chapter Three, it is the fact that ASB is not defined that invests the label with such power. As a number of chapters illustrate, ASB acts as a vehicular idea, in which concepts are enshrined about crime and government, what constitutes ethical behaviour and the causes of social problems and the relative responsibilities of individuals, the state and wider society. The definition of ASB previously developed by the Chartered Institute of Housing as 'behaviour that opposes society's norms and accepted standards of behaviour' (CIH, 1995, p 3) may be so vague as to preclude its technical efficacy in intervention strategies, but is useful in illustrating that definitions of ASB are part of much wider and contested debates about its individual and societal causes and appropriate solutions.

Housing, urban governance and anti-social behaviour

This book focuses on the role of housing in the governance of ASB for a number of reasons. Firstly, the emergence of public housing was integral to the public health discourse around the condition and behaviour of the poor that led to the emergence of state urban governance in the 19th century. Secondly, since the early 19th century the building and management of housing has been at the forefront of attempts to regulate community relations and construct accepted norms of required behaviour (Ravetz, 2001). Thirdly, housing has, far more than other pillars of the welfare state such as education and health, been premised on conditionality of access linked to conduct, involving the moral classification of individuals as 'deserving' and 'undeserving'. Furthermore, through the mechanism of the tenancy agreement, social housing provides the most long-standing example of how acceptable and unacceptable behaviour, rights and responsibilities and conditionality in welfare are defined and governed, debates that lie at the heart of the contemporary ASB agenda.

Social housing is, of course, managed housing, providing the governance infrastructure and legal scope for government intervention, and has therefore been the predominant site of attempts to define, regulate and change the conduct of particular groups of citizens. Social housing management has always been concerned with policing and reforming the behaviour of its tenants, and, as Brown points out, the contemporary conceptualisation of ASB is in part a product of housing management itself (Brown, 2004). It is also the case that the residualisation of social housing has resulted in a concentration of social problems including ASB largely, but not exclusively or uniformly, in this tenure (Murie, 1997).

The role of housing in governing ASB also provides a lens for examining wider developments in urban governance, including the emergence of community and neighbourhood governance, ambiguous developments which simultaneously empower individuals while making them subject to greater disciplinary control, and the continuing reconfiguration of the roles and responsibilities of the state and other actors. These trends in contemporary governance extend across housing tenures, for example in the rise of gated communities and the mixed economy of policing. And they are not confined to the UK. (These trends have also been discussed extensively in criminology; see, for example, Crawford, 1997; Hope, 2000; Garland, 2002.)

This book has five aims. Firstly, it seeks to bring together contributions from a range of academic disciplinary, national and theoretical perspectives in order to link social theories to policy, practice and empirical research, recognising the equal validity and value of these approaches and the importance of comparative international research.

Secondly, it presents the findings from a large number of recent empirical research studies, many undertaken by the contributors themselves. It thus seeks to contribute to the relatively limited knowledge and evidence base about both the causes of ASB and what interventions and policy responses, from small-scale local projects to much wider and more fundamental governmental and societal reforms, may be required to begin to alleviate the very significant negative impacts that ASB has on its victims, witnesses, and indeed, perpetrators. Thirdly, in such a fast changing field, this book aims to identify further research areas and questions.

The book's fourth aim is to demonstrate the centrality of housing to the study of ASB and to wider studies of contemporary and historical governance and to illustrate how seeking an understanding of housing functions may illuminate much broader trends in contemporary governance and society. Finally, the book aims to link the study of ASB to broader issues and to widen the debates about ASB beyond narrow technical definitions and measurement of the efficacy of individual pieces of legislation, policy interventions or projects. Rather, underlying assumptions about values, conduct and the roles and responsibilities of actors need to be constantly assessed, challenged and negotiated. There is, in short, a need for a wider politics of behaviour (Field, 2003), and this book seeks to contribute to such a politics.

The structure of the book

This book is structured in four parts. Chapters One to Five examine the definition and construction of ASB in the UK, and in particular, the role of social housing in ASB governance. The second part (Chapters Six to Eight) provides evaluations of a range of legal techniques and measures being utilised by social landlords (and in some cases private landlords) to address ASB. The third part of the book (Chapters Nine to Twelve) explores emerging mechanisms of addressing ASB in housing governance, including intensive resettlement projects, a mixed economy of policing services and gated communities. The fourth part of the book (Chapters Thirteen to Fifteen) includes studies of housing and ASB from an international perspective. These chapters do not provide a comparative overview of ASB and housing policy in their respective countries. Rather, they offer new empirical research evidence from Australia and the US and a critical account of how concepts of urban disorder have been developed in housing and urban policy in France.

The first five chapters of this book are largely concerned with the construction of ASB. Chapter One links the governance of ASB to wider processes of governance in advanced liberal democracy centred on concepts of self-regulation and responsibility. It demonstrates that the role of social housing management in regulating behaviour has a long historical precedent, and indeed many of the discourses and techniques about how to address 'deviant behaviour' date back to the birth of social housing in the 19th century. However, there are contemporary elements emerging in which housing plays a central role, most notably the shift to community governance based on local neighbourhoods, the rise of contractual governance and an increased 'mixed economy' of policing ASB across all tenures, which also forms the subject of Chapter Eleven.

Pauline Card builds on these ideas in Chapter Two by describing the different roles that have been assigned to council housing since the early 20th century. She argues that these roles are linked to changing political rationalities, in which translation discourses define the behaviour of both individual tenants and council estates as problematic, and facilitate new ways for governments to govern the conduct of tenants. The chapter reveals how the contemporary problem of ASB, based around concepts of underclass and social exclusion, represents the latest in a continual reconfiguration of the welfare state, involving notions of the deserving and undeserving and resulting in social landlords' increasing use of legal measures to 'protect' communities.

Chapter Three, by Helen Carr and Dave Cowan, explores the epistemic underpinnings of ASB. It assesses attempts to define ASB, but makes the point that obscurity is an important tool of governance, and the fact that ASB remains largely undefined invests it with a conceptual power that is used to label groups as problematic and in particular to amplify conceived ethical differences between tenants and 'entrepreneurial' owner-occupiers. A central theme running through this chapter is the role of vernacular and technical language in constructing and legitimising intervention. The chapter importantly extends the governing coalition of ASB to incorporate housing professionals and various housing management mechanisms, increasingly deployed beyond the social housing tenure, and in particular the judiciary, who provide an 'interpretative ventriloquism' which reinforces the predominant political and social 'common-sense' discourse around ASB, limiting debates around the social circumstances and vulnerability of the perpetrators of ASB.

How these constructions of ASB and categorisations of individuals actually play out at local levels is the subject of Chapter Four. Judy Nixon and Sadie Parr begin by critiquing contemporary political and media discourses which result in the reaffirmation of normality attributed to powerful majority groups and the demonisation of 'deviant' groups categorised as 'other'. They describe how, in their recent research, witnesses of ASB constructed the causes of the problem around the characteristics of the alleged perpetrators. Commonalities emerge between these individual and local discourses and predominant national rhetoric, including the construction of individuals as 'other', a focus on dysfunctional families and bad parenting and the emphasis on individualised deficiencies. The chapter then provides a platform for the voices of the alleged 'neighbours from hell', and reveals that, far from constituting the 'other', these individuals shared the concerns and values of their neighbours, were often the victims as well as perpetrators of ASB, and their behaviour was largely attributable to personal and family vulnerability and very difficult social circumstances.

In Chapter Five Rowland Atkinson argues that the ASB agenda has been shaped by particular representative, contextual and class filters. He makes the point that affluent residential areas are not unproblematic spaces, but rather through processes of seeking security, may act to displace risks including ASB to deprived neighbourhoods. The chapter identifies how ASB interventions have been extended from housing estates to 'iconic' city centres to 'tackle' begging and homelessness, and links this expansion in scales of intervention to neoliberal discourses of city competitiveness. Atkinson also criticises the current policy emphasis on informal mechanisms of social control, where residents in deprived communities are regarded 'as their own saviours' when other social forces such as increased residential mobility and workplace practices and a declining presence of various authority figures undermine social control. The chapter introduces the notion of 'compounded citizenship' whereby, in spite of these processes, residents in deprived areas have to endeavour to tackle local social problems, and the chapter ends by calling for policy solutions aimed at addressing the powerful social forces that give rise to the social geography of ASB.

The following three chapters in the second part of the book explore in detail how landlords attempt to govern ASB. In Chapter Six Diane Lister assesses the extent to which tenancy agreements offer a mechanism for governing ASB. She regards the increasing emphasis on tenancy agreements as symptomatic of a wider contractualisation of social relations, including neighbourliness. Like Atkinson, she identifies how such processes attempt to achieve social control in the absence of trust and legitimate expectations among neighbours. Based on research in the private rented sector, she argues that while tenancy agreements have potential to prevent ASB through civil law rather than disciplinary sanctions, their utility is limited by the assumption that parties are aware of and understand the legal framework and their obligations, necessitating a more proactive role for landlords in utilising tenancy agreements to positively influence behaviour. Lister also identifies how the use of good neighbour agreements represents a process through which the landlord–tenant relationship is extended to include wider neighbourhood governance functions.

In Chapter Seven, Caroline Hunter outlines how the numerous changes to legislation since 1996 have increased the social control function of social landlords in two ways. Firstly, the legal powers of social landlords have been strengthened as Hunter illustrates through a discussion of introductory and starter tenancies. Secondly, the legal framework has shifted the scope of social housing management beyond the regulation of individual tenants to include the governance of non-tenants and indeed entire localities or neighbourhoods. However, through an examination of injunctions and ASBOs, Hunter illustrates the enormous variation between landlords in their willingness and capacity to use such enhanced powers, indicating that the role of social housing in governing ASB cannot be easily generalised.

Hal Pawson and Carol McKenzie use Chapter Eight to offer a wide-ranging assessment of the legal and non-legal techniques social landlords use to tackle ASB. They challenge the assumption that ASB is increasing, but identify nonetheless the growing expectations on landlords to address the problem. The chapter describes the growth of specialist ASB teams within housing management structures, and provides evidence from national surveys about how social landlords have utilised evictions, ASBOs and injunctions. While the chapter identifies how landlords have sought to increase the effectiveness of these legal measures, one of its important findings is that landlords are not exclusively using punitive sanctions to address ASB, but are also engaging in preventative approaches including mediation, the use of ABCs and tenancy support to vulnerable households, although there remains scope for improvement in these practices.

In the third part, the next four chapters provide studies of emerging forms of housing governance linked to ASB. In Chapter Nine Anwen Jones, Nicolas Pleace and Deborah Quilgers evaluate the Shelter Inclusion Project based in Rochdale, an intensive resettlement and rehabilitation service for households at risk of homelessness because of ASB, and Suzie Scott in Chapter Ten provides an evaluation of a similar initiative in Scotland, the Dundee Families Project. Both chapters illustrate the very high levels of vulnerability within the referred families, including the problems faced by children. The projects provide a wide range of practical, emotional and social support and the evaluations suggest that they have been relatively successful in addressing ASB and in preventing homelessness. While the longer-term and community-wide impacts of both projects are not known, these findings indicate the efficacy of addressing the complex support needs of such families, preventing further exclusion through homelessness, and the importance of supportive interventions within ASB strategies.

Adam Crawford in Chapter Eleven links housing to an increasingly mixed economy of policing in which the increasing demand for security patrols in residential areas in all tenures is delivered through various forms of police officers, neighbourhood wardens and private security firms. In addition to critiquing the effectiveness of this mixed economy in ameliorating communities' fears of crime and ASB, Crawford argues that these developments symbolise an emerging form of community-based but parochial governance through which differential access between neighbourhoods to either government or market resources may result in a 'patchwork' distribution of security and risk, which may exacerbate social inequality and exclusion. Crawford identifies the need to address the coordination between 'plural policing personnel' and to ensure adequate accountability and regulation in this mixed economy.

These themes of devolved community governance and privatised security occurring across housing tenures are picked up in Sarah Blandy's study of gated communities in Chapter Twelve. She identifies such residential developments as illustrating the move towards more formal and contractual forms of social control, to be achieved both through physical gating and defensive walls but also through the regulation of many aspects of residents' conduct. The chapter argues that while gated communities are in part driven by a response to crime and ASB, the evidence is ambiguous about their potential to act as a remedy for these problems and to foster the communitarian endeavour and collective efficacy which are promoted in current ASB discourse, suggesting caution in transferring their features into social housing. Blandy concludes with the important insight that the tensions within and around gated communities are analogous to the tensions that exist in government housing and urban policies in relation to ASB.

In the last part of the book, the final three chapters explore aspects of housing and ASB in other countries, and include useful international perspectives on the situation in the UK. The emergence of ASB as an important issue in Australian policy discourse and housing management practice is the subject of Kathy Arthurson and Keith Jacobs in Chapter Thirteen. They argue that ASB is not as established a concept in Australia as it is in the UK. They also describe how policy discourse in general, and the actions of housing managers and other professionals, have been less focused on punitive legal sanctions than is the case in the UK, but rather are characterised by community-focused interventions aimed at addressing complex causal factors. Furthermore, tenants' discourse around ASB identified the lack of opportunities for young people, rather than personal or family dysfunction as the most important causal factor, in stark contrast to the UK evidence presented in Chapter Four. However, the chapter also indicates that Australian housing and ASB policy is at a critical juncture, which may result in a change in discourse, policy and practice.

Writing from a French perspective in Chapter Fourteen, Olivier Ratouis and Jérôme Boissonade begin their discussion of conceptions of urban violence with a detailed account of the portrayal, marginalisation and subsequent cultural responses of young excluded people. The chapter continues by describing city housing policy responses and the objectification and problematisation of the behaviour of residents of France's Priority Urban Development Zones (ZUPs) that mirror similar processes with UK council housing estates. In identifying a conceptual shift from 'urban violence' to 'incivility' the chapter argues that French cities are increasingly characterised by spaces of control subject to surveillance in order to secure them as corridors of movement for individuals between privatised spaces, rather than by public spaces that act as sites for urban interaction and promote both diversity and wider social cohesion.

Chapter Fifteen reports on research in the US by Timothy O. Ireland, Terence P. Thornberry and Rolf Loeber. The chapter begins by outlining how, as in the UK, public housing developments are regarded as high-crime areas and have been subject to a range of interventions. It reveals the ambiguous conceptual position, again analogous to the UK, whereby, on the one hand, public housing is conceived as both a 'dangerous' tenure which individuals should be encouraged to leave to reduce their risk of offending and victimisation and, on the other hand, the promotion of residential stability and community ties that are regarded as reducing levels of ASB, linked to the promotion of responsibility and reduced welfare dependency. The research findings suggest that adolescents who experience transitory residence in public housing, rather than those who live in the tenure for a sustained period of time, are more likely to be involved in offending, but also that rates of offending between tenures is closer than may be expected.

The conclusions for the book (Chapter Sixteen) identify the key themes that have emerged from the contributions, and offer suggestions for a future research agenda on housing, urban governance and ASB.

Note
[1] 'The Social Landlords Crime and Nuisance Group (SLCNG) is the leading housing-based group focusing on nuisance and ASB. The group grew from a housing conference in 1995 where a method for sharing ideas and lobbying on nuisance and ASB was identified. The local authority working group on ASB was then formed, with a core group of 20 members and an administrator appointed to recruit affiliate members. Originally the lobbying element was achieved with the assistance of the local government association' (www.crimereduction.gov.uk/antisocialbehaviour3.htm, accessed 25 January 2006).

References
Brown, A. (2004) 'Anti-social Behaviour, Crime Control and Social Control', *Howard Journal of Criminal Justice*, vol 43, no 2, pp 203-11.
CIH (Chartered Institute of Housing) (1995) *Neighbour Nuisance: Ending the Nightmare*, Coventry: CIH.
Cohen, S. (2002) *Folk Devils and Moral Panic*, London: Routledge.
Cooper, C. (2005) 'Places, "Folk Devils" and Social Policy', in P. Sommerville and N. Sprigings (eds) *Housing and Social Theory: Contemporary Themes and Critical Perspectives*, London: Routledge, pp 69-102.
Crawford, A. (1997) *The Local Governance of Crime: Appeals to Community and Partnerships*, Oxford: Clarendon Press.
Field, F. (2003) *Neighbours from Hell: The Politics of Behaviour*, London: Politico's.
Foucault, M. (2003) *Society Must Be Defended*, London: Penguin.
Garland, D. (2002) *The Culture of Control: Crime and Social Order in Contemporary Society*, Oxford: Oxford University Press.
Home Office (2003) *Respect and Responsibility: Taking a Stand Against Anti-social Behaviour*, London: Home Office.
Home Office (2004) *Building Communities, Beating Crime: A Better Police Service in the 21st Century*, London: Home Office.
Hope, T. (2000) 'Inequality and the Clubbing of Private Security', in T. Hope and R. Sparks (eds) *Crime, Risk and Inequality*, London: Routledge, pp 83-106.
Local Government Information Unit (1997) *Community Safety: Consultation in Advance of the Crime and Disorder Bill*, London: Home Office.
Millie, A., Jacobson, J., McDonald, E. and Hough, M. (2005) *Anti-social Behaviour Strategies: Finding a Balance*, York: Joseph Rowntree Foundation.

Murie, A. (1997) 'Linking Housing Changes to Crime', *Social Policy and Administration*, vol 31, no 5, pp 22-36.

Murray, C. (1990) *The Emerging British Underclass*, London: Health and Welfare Unit, Institute of Economic Affairs.

Ravetz, A. (2001) *Council Housing and Culture: The History of a Social Experiment*, London: Routledge.

Rowlands, M. (2005) *The State of ASBO Britain: The Rise of Intolerance*, ECLN Essay No 9, European Civil Liberties Network (available at www.ecln.org).

Scottish Executive (2003) *Putting Our Communities First: A Strategy for Tackling Anti-social Behaviour*, Edinburgh: Scottish Executive.

Scraton, P. (2005) *The Denial of Children's Rights and Liberties in the UK and the North of Ireland*, ECLN Essay No 14, European Civil Liberties Network (available at www.ecln.org).

Seabrook, J. (1984) *The Idea of Neighbourhood: What Local Politics Should Be About*, London: Pluto Press.

SEU (Social Exclusion Unit) (2000) *Anti-Social Behaviour*, Report of Policy Action Team 8, London: SEU.

Squires, P. and Stephen, D.E. (2005) 'Rethinking ASBOs', *Critical Social Policy*, vol 25, no 4, pp 517-28.

Part I
The definition and construction of anti-social behaviour in the UK

ONE

Housing and the new governance of conduct

John Flint

Introduction

Anti-social behaviour (ASB) has emerged in recent years as a predominant concern for government, media discourse and social housing management in the UK, and a plethora of new legislation and management techniques have been introduced in order to tackle the problem. This chapter has three aims. Firstly, it seeks to place the governance of ASB within the wider context of emerging forms of governance in advanced liberal democracies in order to link studies of housing interventions to policy developments in policing and crime control. Secondly, the chapter aims to assess the extent to which current developments represent a 'new' housing governance of conduct rather than a continuation of historical housing management practices. Thirdly, the chapter sets out three central themes that underpin the 'housing' governance of ASB: the emergence of community and neighbourhood governance, the rise of contractual governance and the new mixed economy of governing ASB.

The governance of conduct

A defining characteristic of contemporary governance in advanced liberal democracies including the UK is the conceptualisation of subjects as active, autonomous and rational agents (Foucault, 1991; Rose, 1999). Subjects, as consumers or citizens, are identified as being agents and nodes of power through which governmental objectives are to be achieved; less through direct acts of state intervention, but rather by reshaping the behaviour of autonomous citizens. In this 'governance at a distance', the self-regulation of individuals is utilised as 'technologies of the self' to achieve governmental aims, combined with enhanced roles for non-state actors and organisations (Dean, 1999;

Hope, 2000; Garland, 2002). Subjects become identified as individuals desiring autonomy and responsibility for their own life outcomes and are to be empowered to have the capacities, opportunities and responsibilities to do so (Foucault, 1991; Rose, 1999; Forrest and Kearns, 2001).

Such empowerment and freedom are not limitless, but rather operate within a framework of bounded autonomy (Etzioni, 1995) built on a moral dominant discourse shaped by government and other forces such as the media, of what constitutes required, appropriate and 'correct' behaviour (Dean, 1999). These discourses construct 'grammars of living' (Rose, 2001) which establish rules for conduct based around norms and values. Rose (2001) argues that governance increasingly utilises what he terms 'ethopower' to shape conduct through the values, beliefs and sentiments thought to underpin responsible self-government and obligations to others. This discourse is imbued, therefore, with notions of ethical behaviour, duty to others, civility and responsibility, with ASB defined as the antithesis of required conduct.

Jacobs et al (2003) describe how social problems, their causes and the assigned responsibility for their resolution are constructed within policy narratives. The recognition that what constitutes appropriate behaviour is in itself subject to conflict and negotiation and interpretation indicates that such debates constitute a politics of conduct (Rose, 1999). Influential commentators such as Frank Field (2003) have argued that this 'politics of behaviour', based on defining what is good and acceptable conduct and what constitutes civil society, represents the central contemporary issue of government and citizenship, demonstrated in the emphasis on and prioritisation of ASB within government. In this governance of conduct the capacity and behaviour of individuals are observed and classified in a framework that explicitly links conduct to moral judgements of character. However, this contemporary governance has ambiguous and conflicting elements (Dean, 1999). On the one hand, there is an increasing empowerment, capacity building and presentation of opportunities for individuals to become more autonomous and responsible for their lives. On the other hand, contemporary governance extends the scope and extent of the surveillance and classification of individuals, as famously set out in Bentham's notion (Bentham, 1995) of panoptic governance providing technologies for the constant and permanent monitoring of behaviour and increasing the range of disciplinary interventions and punitive sanctions applied to those who do not behave acceptably (Dean, 1999).

Housing and a 'new' governance of conduct?

One of the central arguments of this chapter is that housing policy, including the provision and management of state housing, has always played a very important function in urban governance. Indeed, the tackling of social problems, particularly health conditions and deviant behaviour, linked philanthropy and later the state provision of housing to the very emergence of local municipal state governance during the 19th century (Damer, 2000; Ravetz, 2001). Throughout the 20th century housing was both symbolic of, and at the forefront of, the welfare state and its subsequent evolution and reconfiguration (Malpass, 2004). In turn, municipal housing governance has always been influenced by wider debates about the responsibility that the state, and other sections of society, have towards the poor, linked to questions of the causation of poverty and criminality and appropriate solutions (Ravetz, 2001). Similarly, new conceptions of the nature of poverty and social problems and how they manifest themselves in urban environments have seen social housing management increasingly incorporated into wider policy practices aimed at securing urban regeneration and neighbourhood renewal (Ravetz, 2001).

Do contemporary forms of housing governance represent a break from the historic role of housing in governing conduct? Ravetz (2001) makes the important observation that the purpose of council housing and its predecessors was always as much about changing the behaviour of the poor and shaping their conduct towards middle-class defined norms of acceptability as it was about the provision of affordable and quality housing. For Damer (2000), the emergence of public health departments within British cities in the 19th century and the subsequent evolution of a public housing management profession represent a long-standing systemisation of the surveillance, control and moralisation of the working class. Helen Carr and Dave Cowan (see Chapter Three, this volume) and other contributors to this book identify the social control function of social housing management dating from Octavia Hill's early governance measures in the late 19th century. This disciplinary aspect of housing management has been linked to the contemporary social control function of social landlords in relation to crime and ASB (see Chapter Two, this volume).

Haworth and Manzi (1999) point out that morality and assessments of tenants' ethical conduct have always been a defining feature of social housing management practice and discourse. Such processes act to classify tenants as deserving or undeserving based on moral assessments of their conduct in order firstly to ration access to housing (Cowan,

1999; Haworth and Manzi, 1999), and secondly to secure the conformity of a tenant's behaviour to constructed social norms through tenancy agreements and a range of reactive and punitive sanctions (Card, 2001). Such sanctions have been extended in recent years, including strengthened grounds for eviction, injunctions and new governance techniques such as demoted tenancies and Antisocial Behaviour Orders (ASBOs), as discussed in Chapters Six, Seven and Eight.

In one sense then the current techniques used to tackle ASB represent a continuation of what Octavia Hill herself termed the 'tremendous despotism' of housing management (Ravetz, 2001, p 30). However, a relatively neglected element of Hill's management style was her attempts to 'bring out the powers of the people, treating them as responsible for themselves within certain limits' (quoted in Ravetz, 2001, p 30). This attempt to encourage autonomy and self-regulation is an important dimension within the contemporary politics of behaviour. It involves an understanding of tenant responsibility being framed as a proactive and empowering process within housing management, and the conceptualisation of the responsible and responsive tenant as an increasingly central figure in the organising mechanisms of housing governance (Flint, 2004a). A key characteristic of these attempts to achieve housing governance aims through the behaviour of tenants is the broadening out of tenant responsibilities to incorporate the promotion and facilitation of positive behaviours, rather than merely preventing prohibited conduct. These behaviours include engagement in community activity, volunteering, involvement in the strategic decision making of housing organisations, and a more active role in the governance of ASB (Flint, 2004b). What we are witnessing in relation to the housing governance of ASB is the continuing reconfiguration of the identities of social housing tenants from passive and dependent welfare recipients into autonomous, empowered and responsible individuals, a process with legislative underpinnings since at least the 1980 Housing Act (and 1980 Tenants' Rights Act in Scotland). What these disciplinary and empowering notions of responsibility share is an increasing range of interventions being taken in order to achieve them, both in terms of the aspects of individual behaviour governance seeks to influence and in the number of housing management techniques being deployed.

The linking of the provision of housing to individual behaviour is not new, nor is the role of housing management in promoting moral and ethical frameworks for appropriate conduct. The longevity of such processes is illustrated by Robert Owen's Clydeside community of

New Lanark in the early years of the 19th century, where situated next to the workers' houses and large mills was the community centre, called 'The New Institution for the Formation of Character' (Ravetz, 2001, p 28). This demonstrates how social housing governance has always sought to reform the culture and behaviour of its inhabitants, and how housing has always been linked to wider community development. New Lanark also had nurseries and schools, mirroring the current conceptualisation of social housing being linked into wider community development and neighbourhood renewal processes. It also illustrates the links between housing, communitarianism and the building of self-governing communities that were the guiding principles of model villages such as Bournville and Port Sunlight in the 19th century. Such communitarianism has re-emerged as a driving element in current governance and housing policy in the UK, particularly in relation to ASB.

There are striking echoes of the contemporary rationales and techniques of governance in the earliest years of public housing and its predecessors. Damer (2000, p 2012) quotes a doctor in Victorian Glasgow, writing in 1887, as describing how:

> We are living under moral government ... there is a disciplinary element ... it [problematic behaviour] must be remedied through the householder, by constant pressure upon the man as a rational and responsible human being.

This mirrors the key features of contemporary housing governance, including its moral and disciplinary element, the focus on governing through the conduct of tenants, the application of constant techniques of government and the emphasis on rationality and responsibility. Similarly, the Chief Medical Officer of Health in the same Scottish city wrote a paper in 1933 whose title posed a question with startling contemporary resonance: 'Can the Undesirable Tenant be Trained in Citizenship?' (Chalmers and Mann, 1933). Not only does this paper indicate the very long history of concerns within housing government about undesirable or anti-social behaviour, but the question he poses remains central to debates about ASB policy in the UK today. To what extent do the state and other agencies seek to reform individuals and address the underlying causes of their behaviour? Alternatively, to what degree has policy and intervention increasingly become based on an actuarialism that limits the aim of governance to the removal of ASB from the public realm? Such questions provide the wider context for discussions about the appropriate balance between supportive and preventative measures and reactive, disciplinary enforcement measures within ASB policies in the UK (Millie et al, 2005).

Recent studies have suggested a blurring of the boundaries between policing, crime control and social housing management (Crawford, 2003; Brown, 2004). Crawford (2003) described how new forms of governance amount to policing through housing opportunities, whereby housing management techniques including tenancy agreements and Acceptable Behaviour Contracts (ABCs) are used to regulate ASB. Brown (2004) describes a 'coming together' of policing and social housing management in a process that results in social landlords rather than the police being the main agency for controlling certain forms of behaviour and deploying instruments such as ASBOs. Brown (2004, p 203) discerns a 'changing constellation of care and control professions' as ASB becomes an increasingly important element of the social housing profession, and argues that the definition of ASB is in part a product of social housing management itself. However, this policing function for housing governance and its focus on the conduct of anti-social tenants is not in itself new, but is, rather, recast from its previous manifestations. The current rationales and techniques of housing governance have many historical precedents, so that we are witnessing a reconfiguration and evolution of the governance of conduct, rather than a revolution of new approaches. However, three emerging elements of the governance of ASB, while having their roots in the history of housing, represent a shift from the more recent past: the emergence of community and neighbourhood governance, the rise of contractual governance and the new mixed economy of ASB management.

Community and neighbourhood governance

Housing and neighbourhood governance

A defining element of New Labour's Third Way is the identification of community as both the location and process of governance (Rose, 2001), and the promotion of communitarianism with its emphasis on localised collective action and mutual rights and responsibilities (Giddens, 1998). Community governance acts as a mechanism for re-engaging citizens with government and linking the participation and self-regulating capacities of individuals and communities to the achievement of government aims. It aims to create 'citizen governors' with the capacity to regulate their own behaviour and to fulfil their obligations as members of local communities and to act collectively to form 'self-governing communities' (Local Government Association, 2004).

The community as the arena of governance is usually equated with local neighbourhoods, resulting in a 'new localism' within urban policy as neighbourhoods are increasingly conceptualised and identified as the appropriate sites for policy intervention, improving the delivery of services and promoting active citizenship (Forrest and Kearns, 2001; SEU, 2001; ODPM, 2005a). The rise of neighbourhood governance combines the concept of community with a long-standing emphasis in UK urban regeneration policy on area-based regeneration to tackle the spatial concentration of localised social problems. This concept is reframed as neighbourhood renewal, targeting the most deprived communities through holistic, multiactor programmes of intervention aimed at simultaneously tackling environmental degradation, substandard housing, poor health, low educational achievement, weak economic activity and high levels of ASB (SEU, 2001). Housing is identified as one of the key elements driving neighbourhood decline and therefore a key component of local renewal strategies (SEU, 2001). Housing management is also identified in government discourse as having a broader contemporary scope that includes 'key elements of neighbourhood management such as tackling crime and anti-social behaviour' (ODPM, 2005b, p 6).

There is a shift from the local state as the key provider of core services towards a facilitating and enabling role in which central and local government aims to increase the involvement of the private, voluntary and community sectors, including local residents, in determining policy priorities and service delivery mechanisms (SEU, 2001). This limiting of the role of the state and the enhanced roles given to private, voluntary and community actors is particularly evident in crime policy in the UK (see Hope, 2000; Garland, 2002). This multiagency approach and the diluting of a local state role in favour of the empowerment of non-state actors is evident in the plethora of locally based partnerships which are the central mechanism for determining urban policy interventions, for example, Crime and Disorder Reduction Partnerships (CDRPs) aimed at tackling ASB, in which registered social landlords have statutory rights and obligations to participate.

Similar processes are also evident in housing policy which seeks to replace council-owned properties either by the transfer of ownership of housing stock to quasi-public housing associations or to establish 'arm's-length management organisations' (ALMOs) which also serve to reduce the direct housing provision and management role for local authorities (Bramley et al, 2004). One important element of the stock transfer discourse is the facilitation of tenant participation in the management of their homes and local communities, and indeed in Scotland stock transfer is explicitly promoted as a means to achieving 'community ownership' of both housing and local service delivery mechanisms. These processes of devolution and localism are also apparent at the sub-local authority and neighbourhood level. An emerging model of local governance is neighbourhood management whereby a collation of agencies and providers as well as community representatives are empowered to deliver locally defined and controlled services under the auspices of a neighbourhood coordinator. Research by Power and Bergin (1999) suggests that neighbourhood management is an increasingly prevalent model of local governance and is usually led by a local housing agency. Housing is also often the lead agency in Antisocial Behaviour Units (ASBUs) that seek to coordinate a holistic, multiagency approach to tackling ASB.

A further element underpinning the rise of neighbourhood governance is the emergence of the social exclusion paradigm within urban and housing policy (see Chapter Two, this volume, for a more detailed discussion). Social exclusion, partly influenced by communitarianism, broadens out the previous emphasis on material poverty to include culture, moral behaviour and social interaction as explanatory factors in disadvantage (Levitas, 1998). Firstly, this increases the focus on the capacities, moral attitudes and conduct of individuals based on reiterating and reinforcing the duties and obligations they have to their communities and through emphasising the contractual and conditional nature of citizenship rights, including the right to access state-provided housing. Secondly, it leads to the identification of social capital as a key mechanism for neighbourhood renewal (Forrest and Kearns, 2001), based on Putnam's (2001) understanding of the contribution that civic engagement, cooperation and strong social relations and networks, conceived as operating at the neighbourhood level, may make to successful policy outcomes. Housing has a key role, both in framing conditional citizenship and contractual governance (see below) and also in contributing to the social capital of local neighbourhoods through 'Housing Plus' activities that broaden out the scope of housing management activities to include wider community development interventions relating to employment, education, health and tackling crime and ASB.

The neighbourhood governance of anti-social behaviour

The emerging neighbourhood governance of ASB identifies citizens as part of the wider policing family (Home Office, 2004; see also Garland, 2002) and attempts to empower residents and strengthen neighbourhood structures of governance:

> Local people, the residents, businesses and service users in a neighbourhood must be given real opportunity to have their say, and in some cases take responsibilities for, how their neighbourhoods are run. (ODPM, 2005a, p 14)

> Local people know best about the problems of anti-social behaviour. So we need to give more power to people to help them tackle it. (Tony Blair, Speech on Anti-social Behaviour, London, 28 October 2004)

> We see no problem with increasing community involvement in delivering safer communities, including ASBO functions, providing safeguards are in place and working effectively. (ODPM, 2005b, p 18)

These attempts to empower local people, through 'communities' in ASB policy, involve a spectrum of power transfer from the local state to neighbourhoods. Local communities are given an enhanced role in the development and delivery of ASB strategies (Home Office, 2003). Through mechanisms such as Neighbourhood Charters, local residents are empowered to set out their priorities and expectations on service providers and to hold local agencies to account (ODPM, 2005a). The government's *Building Communities, Beating Crime* document (Home Office, 2004) explicitly aims to both develop a neighbourhood-based policing model and to facilitate the greater involvement of communities and citizens in determining how their communities are policed. The Home Office proposes neighbourhood policing teams for England and Wales, while the Scottish Executive advocates the creation of 'dedicated community-based teams to tackle ASB and the supervision of anti-social families at the neighbourhood level' (Scottish Executive, 2003, p 12; Home Office, 2004). Communities are given enhanced scope to monitor and determine the activities of the police, with new powers to trigger action where a police force, local authority or other community safety agency are perceived by residents not to be delivering adequate or appropriate services (Home Office, 2004). The government also promotes community advocacy whereby local councillors or local authority community safety officers will be empowered, at the behest of residents, to request information from the police, and subsequently to demand the attendance of the police or other relevant agencies at a public meeting and to make requests for the police or others to undertake specific actions.

This shift from state to community governance of ASB is also extended to intervention and enforcement. The 2005 Clean Neighbourhoods and Environment Act provides powers to parish councils (conceptualised as a neighbourhood tier of local representative governance) to utilise powers through their authorised officers or employees to issue fixed penalty notices for a range of environmental offences including graffiti, littering and excessive noise. A further example of local state powers being devolved to community institutions are powers in the 2005 Serious Organised Crime and Police Act to enable the Secretary of State to extend the list of relevant agencies that may apply for ASBOs. To date, this power has been reserved to local authorities and registered social landlords in conjunction with the police, but may now be extended to include community bodies such as parish councils or neighbourhood watch schemes, and consideration is being given to enabling local communities to instigate ASBO applications through petitions, referendums and town hall meetings (ODPM, 2005a). In addition to increasing community involvement in applying for ASBOs, the promotion of publicity mechanisms (Home Office, 2005), more commonly referred to as 'naming and shaming', whereby the personal details of individuals subject to ASBOs and the conditions of their order are published, is aimed at increasing the role of local citizens in the enforcement of ASBOs through providing 24-hour surveillance regimes (Brown, 2004). In perhaps the most radical extension of community involvement in policing operations, a pilot scheme in Strathclyde enabled local residents to use police speed cameras to record speeding motorists in residential areas. These motorists are not prosecuted, but receive a warning letter from the police. This pilot is to be extended throughout the Strathclyde area, with any local community able to apply for permission to access and operate the speed cameras.

Local communities are also being given enhanced legislative powers with regard to ASB. Parish councils may now propose and implement local by-laws to regulate behaviour. The example given in the government's document is a resident-instigated law to prohibit skateboarding in order for a local community to indicate that 'skateboarding is not an acceptable form of behaviour in a local neighbourhood' (ODPM, 2005a, p 22). Finally, local residents are to be empowered in the judicial process, for example, through proposals within the government's Environmental Clean-Up campaign, to enable local communities to determine which particular programmes and schemes should be undertaken by offenders serving Community Reparation Orders (Home Office, 2004).

All of these processes represent the emergence of a community governance based at a neighbourhood level and founded on the empowerment of local communities to undertake functions of ASB governance that were previously the preserve of the state (local authorities or the police). They may also be identified as a range of mechanisms through which ASB is to be tackled by self-governing communities, with a reduced role for direct state intervention (see Hope, 2000; Garland, 2002). These developments in ASB policy are analogous to other developments in social housing, in which the long-standing emphasis on tenant participation has led to a reconfiguration of power and responsibility, based on the empowerment of tenants in all aspects of housing management (Flint, 2004b). Similarly the facilitation of self-governing and self-policing communities mirrors the promotion of community ownership in housing stock transfer rationales. Indeed this transfer of governance powers and responsibilities from the local state to 'community-based' housing organisations is explicitly applied to ASB through the government's proposal to enable local authorities to contract out their ASBO functions to organisations managing their housing stock, including ALMOs, Tenant Management Organisations (TMOs) and registered social landlords:

> Where a [local] authority delegates its housing management functions, it may also make sense to delegate responsibility for taking action to tackle Anti Social Behaviour as part of the management function. (ODPM, 2005b, p 7)

Making communities responsible for governing anti-social behaviour

As citizens become conceptualised as important governors of ASB, these new channels of empowerment are accompanied by a morally determined exhortation on citizens, individually and collectively as communities, to be more 'active' and to accept and act on the responsibilities that accompany this empowerment. The government's paper on ASB was explicit in this regard. It was entitled *Respect and Responsibility: Taking a Stand Against Anti-social Behaviour*, and stated that 'We [the government] believe it is time for the community to take a stand' (Home Office, 2003, p 13).

The implication here is that communities experiencing high levels of ASB (usually areas of social housing) are not presently taking such a stand. Local communities are conceived as the principal determinants of moral values and agents of social controls as 'the community sets clear standards of behaviour' (Home Office, 2003, p 7), and are to act as the primary governors of ASB, to be supported by public services rather than vice versa. The Prime Minister articulated this view:

> In return for the increased opportunities and help we have offered, society too, has a right to demand that everyone keep to their side of the bargain – to behave properly and to ensure effective action against those who refuse to do so. (Tony Blair, Speech on Anti-social Behaviour, London, 28 October 2004)

This statement broadens out the contract between citizen and government beyond the requirement of an individual to regulate their own conduct in order to avoid personally engaging in ASB, to incorporate an obligation on citizens to take action to regulate and govern the conduct of others (that is, those engaged in ASB), as the government makes explicit:

> As a community we have a responsibility to speak out against the minority which cause misery and distress. (Home Office, 2003, p 12)

In this conceptualisation, part of the problem of ASB is portrayed as the response of communities towards it, leading to the understanding within government rationales that to some extent communities end up with the levels of ASB that they deserve (O'Malley, 1992). Again there is an analogy with housing governance, where tenant participation structures have extended the empowerment of tenants into the strategic aspects of housing management, and therefore increased the role for tenants in the governance of others, and are increasingly accompanied by a moral exhortation for tenants to undertake these wider acts of citizenship and governance (Flint, 2004a). One change from the previous forms of social control in housing management and policing is this shift from the assessment of individualised behaviour to the collective conduct of tenants, and the increasing obligation on citizens to partake in the regulation of not only their own, but of others' conduct. Such elements are also apparent in the emergence of contractual governance.

Contractual governance

Crawford (2003) has identified the emergence of what he terms 'contractual governance' in diverse fields of social policy in the UK, including housing and criminal justice. These contractual modes of governance are used to foster conformity and social order, and, according to Crawford, differ significantly from traditional mechanisms for policing conduct. This form of governance may be linked to the Foucauldian concept of governance at a distance as direct command and control are replaced by 'regulated self-regulation' (Crawford, 2003, p 480). Crawford further identifies how these new forms of governance increase responsibilities on citizens as partners in crime control. Contracts are concerned with the distribution of responsibilities and obligations and confer active rather than passive responsibilities on subjects, involving both empowering and disciplinary elements (Crawford, 2003), and therefore link with the key features of the new governance of conduct described above. Housing is at the forefront of this emergence of contractual governance. As Diane Lister demonstrates in Chapter Six (this volume), access to social housing and the forms of behaviour required within it have always been governed by tenancy agreements, offering a model of rights and responsibilities that influences contemporary rhetoric about governance and ASB. Crawford (2003) identifies the use of ABCs and probationary tenancies by social landlords (see also Caroline Hunter, Chapter Seven, this volume) as further examples of an explicit contractual basis to the governance of conduct. Further techniques of social housing management, including good neighbour agreements and tenant reward schemes, provide a mixture of moral exhortation and financial incentive in order to promote desirable conduct. Both of these schemes and tenancy agreements are noteworthy for the extent to which they broaden the regulation of tenants' individual conduct in their own homes to include responsibility for the behaviour of others in the proximity of their dwellings and encourage and reward positive behaviours such as neighbourliness and volunteering (Flint, 2004b). A further element of contractual governance is its explicit link to notions of conditionality in welfare provision. For Field (2003), welfare, including affordable housing, needs to be reconfigured to fulfil its historic function of guiding what is acceptable and unacceptable conduct as well as meeting social need. Similarly Deacon (2004) sets out how notions of mutuality may be used to develop a legitimate linking of the right to social housing to desirable conduct, and such rationales are apparent in the debates about removing the entitlement to Housing Benefit for anti-social tenants.

Adam Crawford (2003) makes the important observation that contractual governance is not confined to social housing, but is an increasingly important element of the governance of behaviour in more affluent common interest developments, prevalent in the US and to a lesser extent in the UK, where residents are often subject to very detailed rules, regulations and covenants that prohibit a wide range of behaviours, many of which are not criminal (see Blandy, Chapter Twelve, this volume). Crawford describes how the contractual regulation of conduct often results in the emergence of parochial forms of control, often based on obligations to narrowly defined neighbourhoods and communities, and Hope (2000) argues that such processes of neighbourhood governance, occurring in both the social and private housing tenures, are creating secessionary spaces, preventing a more equitable distribution of risk and responsibilities in relation to ASB.

The 'mixed economy' governance of anti-social behaviour

This chapter has already indicated that neighbourhood governance comprises both empowerment and responsibilisation. It is also important to recognise that the quest for self-governing and self-policing communities in the UK sits ambiguously alongside a simultaneous enhancement of state visibility and control and surveillance mechanisms in local neighbourhoods (Brown, 2004). The UK now has a record number of police officers, to be supported by community support officers and often undertaking high visibility patrols as part of 'reassurance policing' strategies (see Adam Crawford, Chapter Eleven, this volume). These are accompanied by the widespread introduction of neighbourhood wardens with a range of prevention and enforcement functions (DETR, 2000). Housing also contributes to this visible authority through estate caretakers and the presence of housing officers, often acting as professional witnesses in ASB cases. In addition, a number of legal mechanisms increase the state policing 'at a distance' of local neighbourhoods, including ASBOs which prohibit individual and collective behaviours in public areas (see Chapter Eight, this volume) and Dispersal Orders which empower police officers to disperse groups of people in designated areas.

According to Brown (2004), social landlords have been the driving agencies behind ASBOs and as Hal Pawson and Carol McKenzie report in Chapter Eight (this volume), evidence from Scotland reveals that 85% of individuals subject to ASBOs are local authority or registered social landlord tenants.

The government has also introduced Curfew Orders enabling police officers to escort home any individual aged under 16 in the late evening (although this policy has been suspended after a successful legal challenge). These new mechanisms of visible authority and legal mechanisms of social control are combined with the use of environmental measures, often housing-based, to address ASB, including Secure by Design housing, alley gating and the use of CCTV. Within the context of 'self-governing' communities, social landlords also play a prominent role in managing neighbour relations and community disputes through the use of mediation services (see Chapter Eight, this volume) and allocation policies, and similar functions are undertaken by private management companies in common interest developments (see Chapter Twelve, this volume).

The contemporary governance of conduct also comprises a mixed economy of security providers and governors (see Chapter Eleven, this volume) including a variety of police officers, neighbourhood wardens, private security guards, housing managers and citizens. This plural policing reflects the ambiguous roles of the state, communities and citizens in the governance of ASB set out above (see also Garland, 2002). It also indicates a blurring of the boundaries in responsibilities and powers, not only between public agencies such as the police and social landlords (Brown, 2004), but also between public and community forms of governance, for example, the purchasing of additional policing patrols by social landlords for the benefit of their own tenants (Crawford et al, 2005), or the interaction between local authorities, the police and privatised governance regimes existing in some gated communities described by Sarah Blandy in Chapter Twelve (this volume).

Conclusion

This chapter has sought to place the role of housing in the governance of ASB within wider processes of governance that are increasingly dominated by a 'politics of conduct' (Rose, 1999; Field, 2003). The chapter has identified the key features of the contemporary governance of conduct as surveillance, classification, moralisation and an emphasis on self-discipline, obligation and responsibility, and has set out the prominent role of housing in these processes, while noting that these functions of housing management have a very long history. What does appear more recent is the emergence of community and neighbourhood governance, contractual governance and a mixed economy governance of ASB.

Much of the debate about ASB is linked to social housing, not least because in some aspects social housing organisations have become the lead agencies for tackling ASB and the governmental understanding of ASB is, to a degree, a product of social housing management (Brown, 2004). However, emerging forms of community and contractual governance undertaken by a range of state, private and community actors are occurring across all housing tenures.

This chapter has also sought to illustrate that the current governance of ASB demonstrates the limitations of the state as well as its authoritarian powers (Garland, 2002; Brown, 2004), and that contemporary modes of governance have potentially empowering as well as disciplinary effects (Deacon, 2004). Finally, the chapter has sought to confirm the importance of housing policy and practice to urban governance, and how this housing policy and practice are in turn influenced by a politics of behaviour that is required to be framed within more fundamental debates about the causes of ASB and the relative responsibilities of the state, deprived and more affluent citizens in seeking resolutions to this problem (Ravetz, 2001).

References

Bentham, J. (1995) *The Panoptican Writings*, London: Verso.

Bramley, G., Munro, M. and Pawson, H. (2004) *Key Issues in Housing: Policies and Markets in 21st Century Britain*, Basingstoke: Macmillan.

Brown, A. (2004) 'Anti-social Behaviour, Crime Control and Social Control', *Howard Journal of Criminal Justice*, vol 43, no 2, pp 203-11.

Card, P. (2001) 'Managing Anti-social Behaviour: Inclusion or Exclusion', in D. Cowan and A. Marsh (eds) *Two Steps Forward: Housing Policy into the New Millennium*, Bristol: The Policy Press, pp 201-19.

Chalmers, A.K. and Mann, J. (1933) 'Can the Undesirable Tenant be Trained in Citizenship?', Paper read before the Philosophical Society of Glasgow, November, Glasgow: Committee on Housing, Corporation of Glasgow.

Cowan, D. (1999) *Housing Law and Policy*, Basingstoke: Macmillan.

Crawford, A. (2003) '"Contractual Governance" of Deviant Behaviour', *Journal of Law and Society*, vol 30, no 4, pp 479-505.

Crawford, A., Lister, S., Blackburn, S. and Burnett, S. (2003) *Plural Policing: The Mixed Economy of Visible Security Patrols*, Bristol: The Policy Press.

Damer, S. (2000) '"Engineers of the Human Machine": The Social Practice of Council Housing Management in Glasgow, 1895-1939', *Urban Studies*, vol 37, no 11, pp 2007-26.

Deacon, A. (2004) 'Justifying Conditionality: The Case of Anti-social Tenants', *Housing Studies*, vol 19, no 6, pp 911-26.

Dean, M. (1999) *Governmentality: Power and Rule in Modern Society*, London: Sage Publications.

DETR (Department of the Environment, Transport and the Regions) (2000) *Report of the Policy Action Team on Neighbourhood Wardens*, London: DETR.

Etzioni, A. (1995) *The Spirit of Community*, London: Fontana.

Field, F. (2003) *Neighbours from Hell: The Politics of Behaviour*, London: Politico's.

Flint, J. (2004a) 'Reconfiguring Agency and Responsibility in the Governance of Social Housing in Scotland', *Urban Studies*, vol 41, no 1, pp 151-72.

Flint, J. (2004b) 'The Responsible Tenant: Housing Governance and the Politics of Behaviour', *Housing Studies*, vol 19, no 6, pp 893-910.

Forrest, R. and Kearns, A. (2001) 'Social Cohesion, Social Capital and the Neighbourhood', *Urban Studies*, vol 38, no 12, pp 2125-43.

Foucault, M. (1991) 'Governmentality', in G. Burchell (ed) *The Foucault Effect: Studies in Governmentality*, Hemel Hempstead: Harvester Wheatsheaf, pp 87-104.

Garland, D. (2002) *The Culture of Control: Crime and Social Order in Contemporary Society*, Oxford: Oxford University Press.

Giddens, A. (1998) *The Third Way: The Renewal of Social Democracy*, Cambridge: Polity Press.

Haworth, A. and Manzi, T. (1999) 'Managing the "Underclass": Interpreting the Moral Discourse of Housing Management', *Urban Studies*, vol 36, no 1, pp 153-66.

Home Office (2003) *Respect and Responsibility: Taking a Stand Against Anti-social Behaviour*, London: Home Office.

Home Office (2004) *Building Communities, Beating Crime: A Better Police Service in the 21st Century*, London: Home Office.

Home Office (2005) *Working Together: Guidance on Publicising Anti-social Behaviour Orders*, London: Home Office.

Hope, T. (2000) 'Inequality and the Clubbing of Private Security', in T. Hope and R. Sparks (eds) *Crime, Risk and Inequality*, London: Routledge, pp 83-106.

Jacobs, K., Kemeny, J. and Manzi, T. (2003) 'Power, Discourse and Institutional Practices in the Construction of Housing Problems', *Housing Studies*, vol 18, no 4, pp 429-46.

Levitas, R. (1998) *The Inclusive Society? Social Exclusion and New Labour*, Basingstoke: Macmillan.

Local Government Association (2004) *Towards Self-Governing Communities*, London: Local Government Association.

Malpass, P. (2004) 'Housing and the New Welfare State', Paper presented at the Housing Studies Association Spring Conference, Sheffield Hallam University, 15-16 April.

Millie, A., Jacobson, J., McDonald, E. and Hough, M. (2005) *Anti-social Behaviour Strategies: Finding a Balance*, York: Joseph Rowntree Foundation.

ODPM (Office of the Deputy Prime Minister) (2005a) *Citizen Engagement and Public Services: Why Neighbourhoods Matter*, London: ODPM.

ODPM (2005b) *Enabling Local Authorities to Contract their Anti-social Behaviour Order Functions to Organisations Managing their Housing Stock: A Consultation Paper*, London: ODPM.

O'Malley, P. (1992) 'Risk, Power and Crime Prevention', *Economy and Society*, vol 25, no 3, pp 252-75.

Power, A. and Bergin, E. (1999) *Neighbourhood Management*, London: Centre for the Analysis of Social Exclusion, London School of Economics and Political Science.

Putnam, R. (2001) *Bowling Alone: The Collapse and Revival of American Community*, Chicago, IL: Chicago University Press.

Ravetz, A. (2001) *Council Housing and Culture: The History of a Social Experiment*, London: Routledge.

Rose, N. (1999) *Powers of Freedom: Reframing Political Thought*, Cambridge: Cambridge University Press.

Rose, N. (2001) 'Community, Citizenship and the Third Way', in D. Merydyth and J. Minson (eds) *Citizenship and Cultural Policy*, London: Sage Publications, pp 1-17.

Scottish Executive (2003) *Putting Our Communities First: A Strategy for Tackling Anti-social Behaviour*, Edinburgh: Scottish Executive.

SEU (Social Exclusion Unit) (2001) *Bringing Britain Together: A National Strategy for Neighbourhood Renewal*, London: The Stationery Office.

TWO

Governing tenants: from dreadful enclosures to dangerous places

Pauline Card

Introduction

As several other chapters in this volume identify (see Chapters One, Three and Seven), the response of social landlords to anti-social behaviour (ASB) by their tenants became more legalistic and authoritarian during the 1990s. However, there is a long history of housing management as a control technique, beginning with Octavia Hill in the late 19th century and continuing through the growth of council housing in the 20th century. The way in which 'difficult' or 'problematic' tenants have been defined has changed over time, as have the techniques or approaches adopted to deal with their behaviour.

This chapter explores the different roles assigned to council housing since its introduction in the early 20th century, identifying the impact of changing 'political rationalities'. It then considers the dominant 'translation' discourses that have objectified council estates and individual council tenants making them the subject of differentiated treatment by governmental agencies. The problematic of ASB is used to explore the changing discourses around the control of tenant behaviour and the changing scope and nature of housing management practices that are applied to 'problematic tenants'.

Changing political rationalities

Rose and Miller (1992) argue that during the 20th century we have seen the emergence of two dominant political rationalities in Western nation states. By 'political rationality' Rose and Miller mean:

> ... the changing discursive fields within which the exercise
> of power is conceptualised, the moral justifications for
> particular ways of exercising power by diverse authorities,

> notions of the appropriate forms, objects and limits of politics, and conceptions of the proper distribution of such tasks among secular, spiritual, military and familial sectors. (Rose and Miller, 1992, p 175)

The first rationality or discourse informed the development of 'welfare' states during the late 19th and early 20th century. An array of technologies, programmes and projects arose from shared principles and values, for example, social insurance, healthcare provision, education system, public housing and so on. All such 'governmental' policies and programmes, it is argued, were devised from a 'social' point of view. A greater understanding of the collective experiences of certain societies gave rise to demands that the nation should be governed in the interests of social protection, social justice, social rights and social solidarity (Rose, 1996, p 329). The economic well-being of a country was, for the first time, seen as inextricably linked with the health and education of the working classes.

The 'welfarism' rationality which sought to '... encourage national growth and well-being through the promotion of social responsibility and the mutuality of social risk' (Rose and Miller, 1992, p 192), differed from the previous mode of 'social' rationality in that it attempted to link the previously disparate and piecemeal programmes and strategies for dealing with the many 'social' problems of society with the apparatus of the state. Although the specific problems addressed by the 'welfare' rationality were not new or novel, they were problematised by a growing number of official and unofficial experts and governed, innovatively, through attempts to link the fiscal, calculative and bureaucratic capacities of the apparatus of the state to the government of social life (Rose and Miller, 1992).

'Welfarism' was a 'responsibilising' mode of government (Rose and Miller, 1992, p 196) that introduced the notion of the responsible citizen in a new contractual relationship between citizen and society, a contract epitomised by the programme of 'social insurance' that was the centrepiece of Beveridge's postwar welfare state (Beveridge, 1942). Social insurance, it can be argued, introduced a new employment relationship between citizens and society, complementing the one between employee and employer, based on mutual obligation, rights and responsibilities. If citizens were insured by society against the risks of unemployment, they had a duty to act with thrift, industriousness and responsibility. They were bound into a '... system of solidarity and mutual interdependence' (Rose and Miller, 1992, p 196).

In Britain the emergence of a 'welfare' state was demonstrated by growing central and local government involvement in issues of social policy during the 40 or so years spanning the 19th and 20th centuries (see Fraser, 1984). The dominant political discourse during the initial period was 'National Efficiency', which sanctioned state intervention in previously private areas of life in the interests of society and the economy. Intervention began with public health legislation, introduced to improve the slum living conditions of the working classes, followed by reforms that introduced a level of social protection and basic education and eventually led to state-subsidised local authority housing for returning war heroes in 1918. Initially, small steps were made towards state provision of large-scale welfare policies during the interwar years as the new discourse of collective provision and state intervention vied for primacy with an earlier Benthamite utilitarian rationality that the state should at times intervene for the protection of the common good, that is, to ensure social stability (Fraser, 1984).

The final stage of transition or mutation, it could be argued, was the introduction of the welfare state and the political consensus reached on the postwar settlement in Britain post-1945. Following the Second World War there were strong feelings that political, economic and social relations could not revert to those of the prewar periods. Much of the debate, in Britain, centred on Marshall's 'social citizenship'[1] with its three elements of civil, political and social rights (Marshall, 1950). During the initial postwar period, the emphasis was firmly placed on the rights of citizenship, especially social rights. Marshall (1950) saw social rights as ensuring a positive freedom: the freedom not only to participate in society but also the right to the means with which to do so. Marshall's social citizenship can be seen as underpinning the development of the welfare state. The universalistic provision of state benefits enabled citizens to participate in society's activities, although the degree to which this could take place has always been constrained by benefit levels and access to services.

In the initial postwar period, it has been argued, housing policy was consistent with the general principles of the modern welfare state (Malpass, 1990), and '... seen in the same universalistic terms as the new National Health Service and state education system' (Saunders, 1990, p 27). Others disagree with this analysis:

> We would emphasise by contrast the limited horizons set for state intervention in the housing market, the acquiescence in the dominant role of the private sector and the inability to meet acute housing needs through

> public provision.... The role of public housing focused on issues of national production, rather than equity between tenures, the extent of housing need, or the local variations in housing markets....The Labour Government's approach to council housing appears as simply a more effective version of the post-1919 strategy rather than as an embodiment of the radical universalistic thinking behind health or education. (Cole and Furbey, 1994, pp 63-4)

While social citizenship can be seen to be influential in the provision of many welfare state services, council housing was never accepted as a social right to be provided on a collective, universalistic basis.

During the latter half of the 20th century we have seen a retrenchment of 'welfare' states or a mutation of the rationality of government to 'advanced liberal' democracies (Rose, 1993). The principles of social protection, social rights and collective provision have been replaced by the construct of the responsible individual in the marketplace who insures themselves and their family against the risks that they face in society. Such a mutation means that governments no longer govern from a 'social' point of view but through individuals as members of the many and various communities to which they belong, for example, family, faith community, neighbourhood, workplace, club or other affiliation.

As part of the mutation from 'social' government to 'community' government (see Chapter One, this volume) there has been a redefinition of the 'subject' of government. Rather than the inclusive notions of social citizenship and social solidarity there are now new dividing practices that differentiate between the affiliated and the marginalised. The affiliated are:

> ... those who are considered 'included': the individuals and families who have the financial, educational and moral means to 'pass' in their role of active citizens in responsible communities. (Rose, 1996, p 340)

The marginal are:

> ... those who cannot be considered affiliated to such sanctioned and civilised communities. Either they are not considered affiliated to any collectivity by virtue of their incapacity to manage themselves as subjects or they are considered affiliated to some kind of 'anti-community'

whose morality, lifestyle or comportment, is considered a
threat or reproach to public contentment and political order.
(Rose, 1996, p 340)

'Advanced liberal' government is concerned with the 'conduct of
conduct', not just the conduct of those considered to be outside, or
excluded from, society but also the conduct of the affiliated. Arising
from this concern are a whole array of programmes and technologies
that seek either to maintain order and obedience to law by binding
individuals into shared moral norms and values, or to rehabilitate, or
minimise the risk posed by, those who are marginalised. It can be
argued that during this period, when in housing terms the tenure of
owner-occupation has become the external demonstration of
'affiliation' and responsibility:

> Social housing has become, in political and popular
> discourse, a spatial segregation of the marginalised. As
> residualisation has gathered pace so the perception of social
> housing has become that of the tenure of last resort for
> those people who cannot or will not participate in
> mainstream society. (Card, 2001, p 207)

Programme translation

The process by which programmes of government devised at the centre
are linked to the activities in places that are far distant in time and
space, to the many spaces of government, and to the events in thousands
of locations, has been termed 'translation' (Rose and Miller, 1992;
Rose, 1999). Programmes are not 'realised' in these many locations,
and nor is it a matter of the execution of a centrally issued order:

> In the dynamics of translation alignments are forged
> between the objectives of authorities wishing to govern
> and the personal projects of these organisations, groups
> and individuals who are the subjects of government. It is
> through translation processes of various sorts that linkages
> are assembled between political agencies, public bodies,
> economic, legal, medical, social and technical authorities,
> and the aspirations, judgements and ambitions of formal
> autonomous entities, be these firms, factories, pressure
> groups, families or individuals. (Rose, 1999, p 48)

Translation mechanisms, of which there are many, are important in liberal forms of government because they seek to respect the autonomy of certain 'private' zones, for example the family and the home, and shape their conduct so it provides for the well-being of both the individual and the collective. Liberal rule is also bound to the activities of the many disparate forms of authority that have proliferated over time. It is dependent on legitimate non-state authorities for the influence or control they can bring to bear on the conduct of others, and the links they can provide between political aims and the strategies of experts. Rose and Miller (1992) describe this mode of government as 'government at a distance', whereby political forces use forms of authority other than 'the state' to govern. Government operates through opening lines of force, beyond the physical, across a territory through space and time. When operating in this mode, although processes of translation are rarely uninterrupted, autonomous subjects and targets of government are not seen as a threat as they can be aligned through translation discourses such as economic success, a healthy nation, the desirability of good education and training, and a decent home for all, for example. The actions and objectives of groups and individuals become aligned through the translation process when:

> ... actors have come to understand their situation according to a similar language and logic, to construe their goals and their fate as in some way inextricable, they are assembled into the mobile and loosely affiliated networks. Shared interests are constructed in and through political discourses, persuasions, negotiations and bargains. Common modes of perception are formed, in which certain events and entities come to be visualised according to particular rhetorics of image or speech. Relations are established between the nature, character and causes of problems facing various individuals and groups – producers and shopkeepers, doctors and patients – such that the problems of one and those of another seem intrinsically linked in their basis and their solution. (Rose and Miller, 1992, p 184)

Translation discourses develop, are applied or are aimed at different levels or spheres of government activity. The following section considers the development and changing role of council housing since its inception in the earlier 20th century and the translations that have shaped it over that time.

Translational discourses and council housing

During the period of 'welfare state' rationalities of government, the majority of welfare provision had been provided from 'a social point of view', but within that mode of government citizens were categorised as 'deserving' or 'undeserving' of welfare benefits, including access to council housing. Such categorisations were applied at different levels of government at different times, often at a 'distance', where local experts used the discretion and autonomy available to them to resist guidance and advice from the centre, thereby disrupting the translation process. From this situation developed both governmental technologies that are directed at the differential treatment of the 'deserving' and 'undeserving', for example the building of poorer standard dwellings for occupation by slum dwellers, and the subverting of the aims of technologies at the point of deployment, for example the use of discretion in the allocations process by elected councillors and housing officers, leading to discriminatory and exclusionary practices when selecting tenants. As the role of council housing has changed over time and the level of 'undeserving' council tenants has risen, so the management practices or technologies to control access to council housing and control or change the behaviour of council tenants have been modified and developed. Labelling applicants as 'undeserving' enabled political authorities and experts involved in the management of tenants to adopt practices that, in attempting to control tenant behaviour, reinforced the stigmatisation they already experienced.

Housing management has always had a social control element, as exemplified by the Octavia Hill method that aimed to control the behaviour of tenants and to rehabilitate them so that they met the social and moral standards demanded. Property managers in the private rented sector were less likely to seek to reform tenants but controlled behaviour through the liberal use of eviction and in restricting access to eliminate tenants perceived as problematic. Elements of both are found in council housing management that:

> ... has acted as a form of social control of the working class in the hope that 'order in the home' will generate social order and respect for the property in general, and the prompt payment of rent and respect for the council's property in particular. (Ginsburg, 1979, p 156)

The 'good' tenants who first obtained access to council housing were easily managed by the 'bureaucratic, impersonal, and functionally divided' housing management service provided by most local authorities (Clapham, 1987, p 108). During times of scarcity local authorities had been able to restrict access to 'respectable' tenants through the imposition of strict selection criteria. Even when advised and exhorted by housing experts to allocate property according to housing need, rather than subjective and discretionary local criteria, many members and officers continued to apply criteria based on their own standards of moral and acceptable behaviour. If applicants were seen as 'undesirable' or 'undeserving' they were unlikely to be allocated council housing no matter what their current housing situation. This not only made the management task easier by excluding potentially problematic tenants, but also acted as a warning to tenants that their landlord would not tolerate 'bad' behaviour.

When the object of council housing became the re-housing of the 'riff-raff' or slum dwellers, housing managers often adopted practices that treated such tenants as 'undeserving'. While households displaced by slum clearance could not be refused housing, they received different treatment to applicants categorised as 'deserving', that is, relatively affluent households with a record of good behaviour and housekeeping skills that were up to standard. 'Undeserving' tenants were housed in new or old substandard housing, often placed among other 'problematic' families, and subjected to the rehabilitative attentions of social workers and the constant surveillance of housing inspectors, who endeavoured:

> ... to persuade tenants to keep their houses, stairs and closets clean, their garden cultivated and the children cared for ... [in order to] help tenants and their children to become better citizens. (CDP, 1976, p 48)

Such constant surveillance was not, or maybe could not be, practised during the second period of mass slum clearance, but similar social control was:

> ... achieved by a process of amplifying the division amongst tenants, which stigmatises and punishes the less well-off and those labelled 'less respectable' by assigning them to the worst slum estates. (Ginsburg, 1979, p 162)

The degree to which practices of control and surveillance were adopted and deployed varied across the UK, as local authorities defined their role as landlords in very different ways. Some recognised the need to adopt forms of intensive housing management and techniques of rehabilitation and surveillance at an early stage, for example, Bristol City Council, which employed one of the first female housing officers to deal with the domestic problems arising from the re-housing of slum dwellers (Dresser, 1984). Others were overt in the linking of the provision of council housing with wider governmental objectives, for example, the adoption of a 'social hygienist' agenda by the Corporation of Glasgow when re-housing slum dwellers before it became a duty (Damer, 2000). While some of the more overt, intrusive and authoritarian elements of social control exercised by housing managers during the interwar period were discarded as outdated following the Second World War, many of the discretionary and discriminatory practices still remained at a local level, particularly in the area of allocations, with tenants still categorised as 'undeserving', based on occupation, or lack of it, moral and even racial prejudices. While not being refused council housing, they were often placed in the worst and most unpopular housing, creating areas of 'sink' estates and contributing to the labelling and stigmatisation of large areas of council housing. Landlords also retained the power to evict the most problematic tenants, whether 'bad' behaviour was the non-payment of rent, misuse or abuse of property or nuisance behaviour. While council housing remained in short supply and a council tenancy was still seen as desirable, the fear of eviction helped control tenant behaviour and its use gave rise to few concerns over the extent of rent loss.

Social exclusion

The discourse of social exclusion is considered important because, as Levitas (1998) argues:

> It represents the primary significant division in society as one between an included majority and an excluded minority. (Levitas, 1998, p 7)

Despite the term not having been in general political use in Britain much before 1997, Levitas (1998) identifies three discourses of social exclusion: a redistributional discourse, a moral underclass discourse and a social integrationist discourse. It is the latter two discourses that will be developed here as illuminating the way social housing has been made the subject of strategies of control.

The moral underclass discourse, which is concerned with the behavioural and cultural deviance of the excluded, gained prominence in Britain during the 1980s and early 1990s. Explanations of the underclass were both cultural and structural – it is either the pathology of the individual that makes them part of the underclass (Dahrendorf, 1987; Murray, 1990) or inequalities in the structure of society that have led to a growth in the underclass (Field, 1989). However, Levitas argues that both types of discourse present 'the underclass or the socially excluded as culturally distinct from the mainstream' (Levitas, 1998, p 21, and see Chapters Three and Four, this volume). Murray (1990) posited that an emerging underclass could be seen in Britain in the growing number of long-term unemployed young men, and the increasing numbers of never-married single mothers. In popular discourse these groups have come to be equated with social housing tenants, and in turn have been scapegoated for the many problems experienced in areas of social housing (see Campbell, 1993).

During this period there was a shift away from a concept of 'social' citizenship as envisaged by Marshall (1950) to one that came to be increasingly equated with civil rights (Dean, 1999). The provision of social rights by government was no longer seen as legitimate because it involved a call on the financial resources of the state. Those that had to make recourse to the safety-net welfare provision of the state, especially the non-universal provisions such as housing and income maintenance, were seen as excluded from full citizenship rights. During the 1980s the concept of 'active citizenship' was promoted, whereby:

> … such responsibilities as comfortable citizens might feel they owe to those who are less fortunate are a matter of choice and individual conscience and ought not to be collectively discharged through the payment of taxes. (Dean, 1999, p 219)

In the 1990s 'active' citizenship came to be associated with the citizen as consumer, with sovereignty vested not in social entitlements but the power to choose, complain or exit.

The identification of tenants of social housing as a morally deficient 'underclass' was exacerbated by the policies of the government. The drive for privatisation and the creation of a 'property owning democracy' underpinned the sale of council housing stock, through the introduction of the Right to Buy, throughout the 1980s and beyond. The mantras of choice, efficiency and economy and the battle against the 'dependency culture' fuelled the drive towards diversity of provision and the de-municipalisation that occurred during the final decade of the last Conservative government (1987-97). Home ownership was championed as the tenure that:

... ensures the wide spread of wealth through society,
encourages a personal desire to improve and modernise
one's home, enables people to accrue wealth for their
children and stimulates the attitudes of independence and
self-reliance that are a bedrock of a free society. (Michael
Heseltine, Secretary of State for the Environment, 1980,
cited in Monk and Kleinman, 1989, p 122)

Economic and social policies of the Thatcher and Major Conservative
governments accelerated, if not initiated, the process of residualisation
of social housing (Forrest and Murie, 1988). Social, and more
particularly council, housing became perceived as the safety-net tenure
for those who were dependent on welfare, and the only choice of
betterment available to tenants was through exit from the tenure. Those
who chose to, or had no other choice but to, remain were labelled as
an 'underclass' who, through their inability or unwillingness to enter
home ownership, were not contributing towards, and were therefore
outside, society.

During the late 1990s the social integrationist discourse gained
credence in the UK as a counter to the underclass debate. This discourse
emerged from French academic debate that defined social exclusion
as the breakdown of the structural, cultural and moral ties that bind
the individual to society, although it was later broadened to include
consideration of groups marginalised economically, socially, culturally
and spatially. However, in the hands of the European Union the concept
has been narrowed to a concern with the disadvantages experienced
by those excluded from paid work (Levitas, 1998), a definition adopted
by the Blair government:

> [Social exclusion is] ... a shorthand label for what can
> happen when individuals or areas suffer from a combination
> of linked problems such as unemployment, poor skills, low
> incomes, poor housing, high crime environments, bad
> health and family breakdown. (SEU, 2000a, p 1)

New Labour, Levitas (1998) suggests, has developed a discourse that is
an inconsistent combination of the moral underclass and social
integrationist ideal types outlined above. This is reflected in the emphasis
on getting people back into paid employment (for example, the New
Deal), and the emphasis placed not only on the rights of citizenship
but also the reciprocal responsibilities the individual has to the wider
community. Individuals have a responsibility to their communities as

well as themselves and their families. By building strong communities (a term itself as contested as citizenship) social cohesion, which was lost under individualistic Thatcherism, can once again be attained. Blairite communitarianism sees social cohesion in the community as being secured by a strong commitment to common moral values (Blair, 1997; Driver and Martell, 1997), and great importance is placed on family values and the duty to seek paid employment. If you are unwilling or unable to conform to these moral obligations then your claim to social rights, in particular the means with which to participate in society, is limited. Both the moral underclass and social integrationist discourses of social exclusion identify groups or locations that are outside or excluded from society. This may be because of their lack of morals and non-acceptance of society's norms, or their perceived inability or unwillingness to take up paid employment. Whatever the reason, such groups are seen as not qualifying for full citizenship rights either as consumers or through the fulfilment of the responsibilities and duties concomitant with the rights of citizenship.

Social exclusion and social housing

With the election of New Labour the rhetoric surrounding social housing changed. Social exclusion, and its eradication, and the building of 'balanced' or sustainable communities has become the major focus of policy documents and political speeches (for example, Blair, 1997; DETR, 1999). Despite evidence to the contrary (Lee and Murie, 1997), social exclusion has become synonymous with large council estates where there are high levels of disadvantage, high levels of crime and ASB and endemic low demand. Tenants are urged to become re-affiliated by improving, educating and training themselves, while being actively involved in the regeneration of their local communities. Social housing has become, in political and popular discourse, a spatial segregation of the marginalised. As residualisation has gathered pace, so the perception of social housing has become that of the tenure of last resort for those people who cannot or will not participate in mainstream society. Tenants of this tenure do not have the intellectual or financial resources to act responsibly and provide protection for themselves or their families against the risks encountered in life. The changing language of citizenship and labels such as 'underclass' and 'socially excluded' compound the negative image of social housing estates, reinforcing the perception of detachment and making them amenable to differential policy making.

As areas of social housing have become identified as socially excluded, inhabited by morally deviant individuals who do not work, are involved in crime and ASB and behave irresponsibly as parents, for example, they have become the legitimate target of governmental control strategies. They have become enmeshed in 'circuits of exclusion' that seek to rehabilitate them or mitigate the risk that they pose to the affiliated or included. Part of the process of rehabilitation has been the identification of behaviour that needs to be controlled, for example, truancy, teenage parenthood and ASB (SEU, 2000b), so that the individuals involved can become the subject of control strategies.

The above discourses interact and combine to enable governments to become more authoritarian in dealing with 'irresponsible' social housing tenants. To be a tenant of the social housing sector in the 1990s has a number of implications closely related to being seen as on the margins of society. Being a council tenant has become synonymous with membership of an 'underclass' who:

- do not share the morals and values of those in other tenures, especially owner-occupation;
- are socially excluded, many by choice it is thought, because they do not have and do not want paid employment; and
- have not taken on the responsibility of citizenship either in the terms of property ownership or in terms of paid employment. They therefore forfeit their social citizenship rights.

Further, if they reject the responsibility of being 'good' tenants through ASB they must forgo the right of a decent home provided by the state.

The problematic of anti-social behaviour

When significant levels of council housing were first built, from 1919, there was very little need for local authorities to consider strategies to deal with bad or difficult tenants. Demand for housing, the relatively high rents and strict selection criteria meant that the majority of council tenants were the 'respectable' working classes whose behaviour met with required standards. If it did not, eviction was relatively easy to obtain and a well-behaved replacement was waiting in a long queue.

The hands-off approach changed as large numbers of 'undeserving' slum dwellers were re-housed during the slum clearance programmes, and the perceived threat of bad behaviour grew. Not only were these tenants provided with poorer quality dwellings but they were also subjected to intrusive housing management practices that had not been used on earlier tenants (see Damer and Madigan, 1974; Damer, 2000). Their behaviour was put under constant surveillance as 'inspectors' attempted to rehabilitate or educate those tenants who did not meet strict hygiene and housekeeping standards. Conformity was rewarded by the promise of promotion to better housing in the future; non-conformity was punished by eviction or demotion to even poorer housing.

During the period that the problematic of the ASB of council tenants first became a governmental concern, the discourse was not of 'problem estates' but 'problem' or 'difficult tenants'. Explanations revolved around the pathology of the tenants involved and 'technologies' were aimed at the improvement of behaviour and conformity of the individual or household rather than wider social and structural explanations for their situation. For example, the hygienist and eugenic underpinnings of 'National Efficiency' discourses can be seen reflected in the emphasis placed on the housekeeping skills and deviant lifestyles of the ex-slum dwellers housed during the slum clearance programmes of the 1920s and 1930s (Barke and Turnbull, 1992; Damer, 2000). Such tenants were seen as 'undeserving' because their lifestyle did not meet the social and moral standards of 'good' society. The threat that their activities posed for society, including the production of large numbers of offspring that would continue the cycle of deviant behaviour, made them the target of disciplinary and controlling housing management techniques that had their origin in the practices of Octavia Hill (Power, 1987; Whelan, 1998). Of course, tenants were free to reject the draconian measures but such freedom was highly constrained by the circumstances in which they found themselves. If they did not conform they were evicted and left to find accommodation in the private sector from which they had only recently escaped.

During the period of burgeoning universalistic welfare provision, following the introduction of the welfare state post-1945, little attention was given, by central government, to the ways in which 'problematic' tenants should be dealt with by local authorities. Some guidance was provided by CHAC (1955) on dealing with 'unsatisfactory' tenants, which concentrated on the managerial aspects of bad behaviour, that is, non-payment of rent and poor housekeeping skills and the bad example set by 'unsatisfactory' tenants whose behaviour was not dealt with firmly. While it is difficult to assess how often eviction was used to deal with these problems there is evidence that local authorities tried to place all 'problem' families together so that their behaviour would not contaminate 'good' areas (Tucker, 1966). Dwellings in these areas were often in a poorer condition and easily identifiable as 'dreadful enclosures' (Damer, 1974) leading to stigmatisation. Once relegated to these 'ghettos', tenants could be more easily subjected to surveillance and rehabilitation. Promotion to better quality housing was earned through improvements in behaviour. Once again the 'undeserving' poor were the subject of differentiated and more authoritarian treatment than other tenants.

Until the mid- to late 1970s local authorities retained almost complete autonomy in the way that they organised the housing management function and the way in which they dealt with tenants. Steadily, from the early 1980s, this autonomy has been eroded. The role of local authorities as main providers of social housing has diminished and greater regulation on the form and scope of housing management has been introduced. This has occurred at a time when the social rented sector of the British housing system has become increasingly residual and the most vulnerable and disadvantaged groups have become over-represented within this sector. During this period the way in which problematic tenants and problematic areas have been described and defined has again changed, reverting, it could be argued, to the discourse of poverty, or social exclusion in more recent language, and the 'undeserving' that epitomised the objectification of certain council tenants during the slum clearance programmes of the interwar years.

Initial definitions during this period were area- or estate-based. Rather than individual families or households being labelled as 'unsatisfactory', there was growing recognition that some areas of council housing were becoming unpopular and therefore difficult-to-let (DoE, 1981). The causes of their unpopularity were seen as complex, with disadvantaged tenants, poor design, poor quality dwellings and poor management, among other things, contributing to the decline of some estates. Although high levels of vandalism and nuisance were identified as adding to the other problems experienced, the behaviour of individual households was not given any prominence in the suggested remedial action. The use of eviction in dealing with problem households had been curtailed by the 1980 Housing Act but objections raised to the new tenants' rights related to the inability of landlords to carry out their managerial function properly, particularly in relation to rent arrears and transfers for management reasons (Kay et al, 1986), rather than on an inability to deal with tenants who were causing a nuisance to neighbours. If legal action was required to curtail the behaviour of residents causing a nuisance, tenants were often advised to seek legal advice rather than seek support from their landlord.

In the late 1980s and early 1990s there was a shift in the level of coverage given to ASB among council tenants, especially in the media and to a lesser degree in housing literature. This shift occurred at a time when a number of other 'moral' panics were emerging: the identification of an 'underclass' in Britain (Murray, 1990, 1994), riots on a number of council estates across the country (see Campbell, 1993) and frequent film footage in the media of youths and young children 'joyriding' in stolen cars around the decaying streets of many council estates. There was a pervading atmosphere of impending disaster. The whole of society was seen as breaking down and at the centre of the catastrophe were council estates and the 'underclass' that inhabited them. Council estates had become perceived as 'dangerous places' (Campbell, 1993, see also Rowland Atkinson's discussion in Chapter Five, this volume). Such imagery made central and local government very aware of the need to address the issue of crime and ASB, further stigmatised council estates and council tenants and led 'good' tenants to exit the sector or demand that their landlords begin to act on their complaints.

It was in the early 1990s that local authorities began to take legal action against persistently anti-social tenants, many of whom were suspected of criminal activity (NACRO, 1996). As the police seemed unable to protect local communities from often violent and abusive residents because of a lack of resources, a lack of evidence or lack of witnesses, local authorities began to explore the use of civil action (for example, injunctions) rather than possession. Housing organisations also lobbied for greater powers to be given to social landlords to evict tenants on the grounds of nuisance, and these were provided in the 1996 Housing Act. For the first time ASB by a tenant could attract a criminal record: a breach of a housing injunction could result in a prison sentence. As council tenants were being labelled as an 'underclass', outside of society, so the treatment of them became more authoritarian and legalistic. Other, more inclusive and empowering ways to deal with ASB were being developed by individual local authorities but the solutions that received the greatest publicity and political and popular backing were those that were based in law and could result in loss of freedom or loss of home.

The strengthening of the grounds for possession in the 1996 Housing Act, it could be argued, returned the right to local authorities, lost when tenants were granted security of tenure in the 1980 Housing Act, to manage their housing stock; this was a swing in favour of public landlords that was further strengthened with the introduction of introductory tenancies (see Chapter Seven, this volume) and the accompanying notion that tenants have to earn the right to council housing by proving that they are 'good' tenants. Public landlords are no longer able to summarily inspect tenants' homes or allocate accommodation on the basis of subjective criteria such as housekeeping standards and quality and quantity of furniture but they are allowed to exclude on the basis of previous behaviour, especially non-payment of rent, reflecting the old definitions of 'unsatisfactory' tenants, and setting standards of behaviour to be met by tenants or prospective tenants.

Each changing definition of the type of tenant being housed in council housing, that is, the way in which they are objectified, has made the conduct of tenants the subject of new technologies of surveillance, control and rehabilitation. Housing management has always had disciplinary elements but the most authoritarian measures have been adopted at times when council tenants have been identified as 'deviant' and morally suspect. Recent emphasis on legal tools can be seen as a response to the 'moral panics' surrounding the behaviour of an 'underclass' during a period when tenants had gained greater rights.

Definitions of anti-social or problematic behaviour that have emerged over time have been informed not only by the managerial concerns of municipal landlords but also by the perceived characteristics of those being housed and the wider political discourses of the time. Such discourses have included 'National Efficiency', the 'deserving' and 'undeserving' poor and the continuing discourse of poverty or more recently social exclusion. These have been joined in more recent years by the 'residualisation' debate and the negative media coverage given to areas of problematic housing.

Conclusion

I would argue that the shifts in the way in which the 'problematic' behaviour of council tenants has been dealt with can be explained by an analysis of the definitions and descriptions of the poor and disadvantaged found in wider political and popular discourses. Council tenants have in turn been seen as returning war heroes, the respectable working classes, morally suspect ex-slum dwellers, citizens with a right to a decent home, and over recent times either members of an 'underclass' or the socially excluded. Each of these descriptions or constructions has enabled governments to govern the conduct of council tenants in particular ways. However, at times there have been other governmental aims and objectives, particularly at a local level, which have interrupted the translation of such programmes, leading to inconsistent treatment depending on geographical area and/or the political composition of local housing authorities.

As the role of council housing has changed and anti-welfare discourses have gained ascendancy over the rights of citizens so, as identified above, all council tenants have become perceived as irresponsible, work-shy and 'undeserving'. However, the disciplinary, control and surveillance technologies used previously are no longer available to housing managers because of improved tenants' rights and the clearer definition of the role of housing officers. This has meant that other technologies have been developed which aim to achieve the same outcomes without infringing on the rights of tenants. Hence the need for stronger legal remedies which enhance housing authorities' ability to obtain possession in cases of ASB or enable them to control the conduct of individuals in other ways, for example, housing injunctions and Antisocial Behaviour Orders (ASBOs). New tenancy agreements and improved grounds for possession now protect whole neighbourhoods or communities from ASB as the discourses around the importance of strong community have grown.

Note

[1] This is not an unproblematic or uncontested term. Critics have argued that at the very least it is gender neutral, anglocentric and blind to the complexity of difference (see, for example, Mann, 1987; Hall and Held, 1989; Turner, 1990; Lister, 1991).

References

Barke, M. and Turnbull, G. (1992) *Meadowell: The Biography of an 'Estate with Problems'*, Aldershot: Avebury.

Beveridge, W. (1942) *Social Insurance and Allied Services*, Cmd 6404, London: HMSO.

Blair, T. (1997) 'The Will to Win', Speech given on 2 June at the Aylesbury Estate, Southwark, London.

Campbell, B. (1993) *Goliath: Britain's dangerous places*, London: Methuen.

Card, P. (2001) 'Managing Anti-social Behaviour: Inclusion or Exclusion?', in D. Cowan and A. Marsh (eds) *Two Steps Forward: Housing Policy into the New Millennium*, Bristol: The Policy Press, pp 201-19.

CDP (Community Development Project) (1976) *Whatever Happened to Council Housing?*, London: CDP.

CHAC (Central Housing Advisory Committee) (1955) *Unsatisfactory Tenants: Sixth Report*, London: HMSO.

Clapham, D. (1987) 'Trends in Housing Management', in J. English, and D. Clapham (eds) *Public Housing: Current Trends and Future Developments*, London: Croom Helm, pp 107-25.

Cole, I. and Furbey, R. (1994) *The Eclipse of Council Housing*, London: Routledge and Kegan Paul.

Dahrendorf, R. (1987) 'The Erosion of Citizenship – Its Consequences For Us All', *New Society*, vol 113, no 2933, pp 12-15, 12 June.

Damer, S. (1974) 'Wine Alley: The Sociology of a Dreadful Enclosure', *Sociological Review*, vol 22, no 2, pp 221-48.

Damer, S. (2000) '"Engineers of the Human Machine": The Social Practice of Council Housing Management in Glasgow 1859-1939', *Urban Studies*, vol 37, no 11, pp 2007-26.

Damer, S. and Madigan, R. (1974) 'The Housing Investigator', *New Society*, vol 29, no 16, pp 226-7.

Dean, H. (1999) 'Citizenship', in M. Powell (ed) *New Labour, New Welfare State? The Third Way' in British Social Policy*, Bristol: The Policy Press, pp 213-34.

DETR (Department of the Environment, Transport and the Regions) (1999) *Code of Guidance for Local Authorities on Allocation of Accommodation and Homelessness: A Consultation Draft*, London: DETR.

DoE (Department of the Environment) (1981) *An Investigation of Difficult to let Housing*, vol 1, London: HMSO.

Dresser, M. (1984) 'Housing Policy in Bristol, 1919-30', in M.J. Daunton (ed) *Councillors and Tenants: Local Authority Housing in English Cities, 1919-1939*, Leicester: Leicester University Press, pp 155-216.

Driver, S. and Martell, L. (1997) 'New Labour's Communitarianisms', *Critical Social Policy*, vol 17, no 3, pp 27-44.

Field, F. (1989) *Losing Out: The Emergence of Britain's Underclass*, London: Basil Blackwell.

Forrest, R. and Murie, A. (1988) *Selling the Welfare State: The Privatisation of Public Housing*, London: Routledge.

Fraser, D. (1984) *The Evolution of the British Welfare State*, Basingstoke: Macmillan Education Ltd.

Ginsburg, N. (1979) *Class, Capital and Social Policy*, London: Macmillan.

Hall, S. and Held, D. (1989) 'Left and Right', *Marxism Today*, vol 33, no 6, pp 16-23.

Kay, A., Legg, C. and Foot, J. (1986) *The 1980 Tenants' Rights in Practice*, London: Housing Research Group, City University.

Lee, P. and Murie, A. (1997) *Poverty, Housing Tenure and Social Exclusion*, Bristol: The Policy Press.

Levitas, R. (1998) *The Inclusive Society: Social Exclusion and New Labour*, Basingstoke: Macmillan.

Lister, R. (1991) 'Citizenship Engendered', *Critical Social Policy*, vol 11, no 32, pp 65-71.

Malpass, P. (1990) *Reshaping Housing Policy: Subsidies, Rents and Residualisation*, London: Routledge.

Mann, M. (1987) 'Ruling Class Strategies and Citizenship', *Sociology*, vol 21, no 3, pp 339-54.

Marshall, T.H. (1950) *Citizenship and Social Class*, Cambridge: Cambridge University Press.

Monk, S. and Kleinman, M. (1989) 'Housing', in P. Brown and R. Sparks (eds) *Beyond Thatcherism: Social Policy, Politics and Society*, Milton Keynes: Open University Press, pp 121-36.

Murray, C. (1990) *The Emerging British Underclass*, London: Health and Welfare Unit, Institute of Economic Affairs.

Murray, C. (1994) *Underclass: The Crisis Deepens*, London: Health and Welfare Unit, Institute of Economic Affairs.

NACRO (National Association for the Care and Resettlement of Offenders) (1996) *Crime, Community and Change: Taking Action on the Kingsmead Estate in Hackney*, London: NACRO.

Power, A. (1987) *Property Before People: The Management of Twentieth-century Council Housing*, London: Allen & Unwin.

Rose, N. (1993) 'Government, Authority and Expertise in Advanced Liberalism', *Economy and Society*, vol 22, no 3, pp 282-99.

Rose, N. (1996) 'The Death of the Social? Re-figuring the Territory of Government', *Economy and Society*, vol 25, no 3, pp 327-56.

Rose, N. (1999) *Powers of Freedom: Reframing Political Thought*, Cambridge: Cambridge University Press.

Rose, N. and Miller, P. (1992) 'Political Power beyond the State: Problematics of Government', *British Journal of Sociology*, vol 43, no 2, pp 173-205.

Saunders, P. (1990) *A Nation of Homeowners*, London: Unwin Hyman.

SEU (Social Exclusion Unit) (2000a) *The Social Exclusion Unit Leaflet*, London: Cabinet Office.

SEU (2000b) *Anti-social Behaviour*, Report of Policy Action Team 8, London: SEU.

Tucker, J. (1966) *Honourable Estates*, London: Gollancz.

Turner, B. (1990) 'Outline of a Theory of Citizenship', *Sociology*, vol 24, no 2, pp 189-217.

Whelan, R. (ed) (1998) *Octavia Hill and the Social Housing Debate: Essays and Letters by Octavia Hill*, London: Institute of Economic Affairs.

THREE

Labelling: constructing definitions of anti-social behaviour?

Helen Carr and Dave Cowan[1]

Introduction

In this chapter we consider the epistemic underpinnings of anti-social behaviour (ASB). We identify its struggle to become simultaneously technical and vernacular as well as provide the conditions for a certain convergence in the roles of experts, legislators, interpreters and mediators (Osborne, 2004). We suggest that ASB is not just a concept but also a 'vehicular idea', rather like the 'third way', through which a diverse set of ideas about crime and society become melded together, and are driven on by both rationality and critique. Ultimately, such ideas may be 'utterly shallow and venal', but the essence of a vehicular idea is its ability to be 'open to the emergence of "radical" variants within it' (McLennan, 2004, p 497). The potency of ASB as a vehicular idea is its ability to be manipulated by different types of intellectual or expert. Like the third way, it has little in its core that is new but incorporates a multiplicity of diverse, low- and high-level deviant behaviours with a set of unconnected ideas about risk, crime and management underpinning it. It also has some powerful mediators who 'get things moving' (Osborne, 2004, p 440). Nevertheless, ASB also 'marks out a space in which people can argue, a space of diagnosis' (Osborne, 2004, p 440).

Although the concept of ASB may be utterly shallow, the space in which it exists is also one in which the circles of control have become much closer. This is, we suspect, partly because of the ragbag of ideologies, understandings and concepts that have invested power on the term, ASB. In particular, the space of ASB has been shaped by understandings about risk which, in turn, have related ASB to housing tenure, specifically social housing. That location of ASB has also been shaped, we suggest, by two further factors. Firstly, social housing is fundamentally *managed* housing and thus provides the conditions through which the control of the marginal becomes possible. Secondly and related to this point, ASB taps into a series of ethical values about poverty and pauperisation which have existed in this tenure since the heyday of private philanthropy and the development of the charitable instinct in housing, as described in Chapter One (this volume).

We suggest that a combination of rather diverse, unconnected disciplinary and governance techniques, combined with a synoptic focus on the management of the poor and marginalised, have provided the architecture for these strategies of control. Management implies a certain set of power–knowledge relations, more so when we now talk of the imported concept of 'zero tolerance' housing management (see, for example, the commentary on schemes in New York and Middlesbrough in Johnston and Shearing, 2003, ch 6). Although our attention is taken by the more coercive, disciplinary schemes prescribed by law, management implies a different set of techniques which operate at a different level, but which are also underpinned by reference to legal obligation (see Crawford, 2003, p 488).

Our analysis is divided into two broad sections. Firstly, we consider understandings, conceptualisations and definitions of ASB. We begin with the (common) assertion that ASB has been left undefined, but argue that this is precisely what invests the label with such power. Obscurity is a potent tool of governance (Cowan and McDermont, 2006). Secondly, we consider the ways in which the law has been used to play with understandings of ASB, and the way in which the courts have become the purveyors of a certain common knowledge. Our attention is diverted to the way in which management, entrepreneurialism and ASB, although strange co-conspirators, nevertheless work in tandem on the souls of the residents of social housing. By way of conclusion, we offer some thoughts on the place of law in Foucauldian analyses.

Defining anti-social behaviour

> The Government is placing increasingly high emphasis on the level of [ASB] and methods to tackle it through the formation of the Home Office Anti-Social Behaviour Unit, publication of the White Paper, *Respect and Responsibility – Taking a stand against Anti-Social Behaviour*, and the Anti-Social Behaviour Act (2003). The Home Office's Research, Development and Statistics Directorate (RDS) is now developing a programme of research on ASB to fill important knowledge gaps. (Home Office website,

www.homeoffice.gov.uk/rds/antisocial1.html, accessed
29 March 2004)

Despite all of the attention given over to it, there is no clear definition of ASB (Papps, 1998; Scott and Parkey, 1998). The government's Social Exclusion Unit argued that there could be no single definition as it covers such a 'wide range of behaviour from litter to serious harassment' (SEU, 2000, p 14). As Hunter (2001, p 223) points out, 'problems of definition clearly lead to problems of solution; if the nature of the problem has not been defined then defining a solution seems impossible'. At the heart of the discourse about ASB lies a paradox – we do not know what it is, although it is sometimes said in response that we all know what it is when we see or experience it. This paradox is about knowledge and measurement. As Whitehead et al (2003, p 6) have noted in a report to the Home Office, 'measurement of ASB is difficult because it is not clear what should be measured', and it is also problematic because the range of behaviours falling within any particular definition are covered by a wide range of agencies operating under different definitions.

This seems an important gap in our knowledge and, in one sense, a break in the relationship between power and (statistical) knowledge. There has been an assertion of sovereign power on the basis of apparently no evidence, beyond 'what everyone knows'. It is perhaps not surprising then that, using questionable statistical techniques[2], the Home Office produced an audit of ASB. It discovered 66,107 reports were made to participating agencies:

> This equates to more than one report every 2 seconds or around 16.5 million reports every year. Anti-social behaviour recorded on the day of the count cost agencies in England and Wales at least £13.5m; this equates to around £3.4b a year. (Home Office, 2003a)

This problem of knowledge provides an opportunity to observe a certain mentality of government, borrowing Valverde's discussion of 'knowledge formats' (2003a, 2003b). There are two objects of interest – the lengthy lists of what constitutes ASB, and the appeal to common sense.

First, the sometimes lengthy lists in various government, and government-funded, publications concerning ASB are important techniques in highlighting the core concerns about low-level deviance. What is remarkable is the range of behaviours regarded in these documents as 'anti-social', and placed in such lists. In Table 3.1 opposite we juxtapose three such lists from, respectively, the Social Exclusion Unit's report on ASB (2000, para 1.4), the Home Office White Paper on ASB (2003b, para 1.6) and the Home Office's own one-day count of ASB on 10 September 2003.

The range of behaviours placed together in each column seem random, with little replication at the margins. The Home Office and one-day count lists do not include behaviours that have been regarded as anti-social in some documents (such as racism, domestic violence, or homophobic attacks – see SEU, 2000, paras 1.11-1.19) but include low-level incidents (litter, unkempt gardens, rubbish, hoax calls). Nevertheless, the use of such lists is somehow persuasive. As Valverde (2003a, p 162) argues:

> ... it is a police powers, commonsense argument that persuades readers by listing a variety of objects that have a certain family resemblance to one another and that combine to form a general impression of disorder, without any quantitative or theoretical proof being given of these connections.

These lists also have an important quantification function. It is not for want of trying that the government was unable to quantify ASB until the one-day count. Attempts were made to do so (SEU, 2000, paras 1.8-1.10), but it was the translation of the list into hard cash that becomes the headline figure. We now know that ASB costs £3.4 billion per annum.

The technical knowledge produced in the list becomes more focused when it is made local and situated. This happens, for instance, in the poster which was strategically placed on the local council's notice board situated on the street corner in front of a block of local authority housing (see Photograph 3.1 on page 62).

Not only does the poster reproduce the information on the lists – containing the succinct 'bite' that every two seconds an incident of ASB occurs in Britain – but it also repeats examples of ASB as well as presenting photographs of ordinary events as self-evidently anti-social. The poster makes the vernacular of ASB technical despite being about daily occurrences that are reported in everyday language. The reader of the poster is educated by it into the technical language of ASB.

However, part of the power of the discourse of ASB is that coincidence of vernacular and technical language. Often professional language is used to defeat common sense, and local and particular

Table 3.1: Lists of ASB

Social Exclusion Unit	Home Office White Paper	Home Office's one-day count
Noise	Harassment and intimidating behaviour	Litter/rubbish
Conflicts, including harassment, domestic violence and racist incidents	Behaviour that creates alarm or fear	Criminal damage/vandalism
Litter and rubbish dumping	Noisy neighbours	Vehicle-related nuisance
Graffiti and vandalism	Drunken and abusive behaviour	Nuisance behaviour
Uncontrolled pets	Vandalism, graffiti and other deliberate damage to property	Intimidation/harassment
Using and selling drugs	Dumping rubbish or litter	Noise
Nuisance from vehicles, including parking and abandonment		Rowdy behaviour
Unkempt gardens		Abandoned vehicles
		Street drinking and begging
		Drug/substance misuses and drug dealing
		Animal-related problems
		Hoax calls
		Prostitution, kerb-crawling, sexual acts

Photograph 3.1: ASB poster

knowledge. In a vivid and direct manner, the poster fuses professional and common-sense understandings of a social 'problem'. The poster thus exemplifies the circularity of the discourse of ASB and the way in which that discourse both constructs the problem of the anti-social – and the solution. For the poster is, in Bakhtin's terms, dialogic (Bakhtin, 1981). It simultaneously constructs *us* – the social – and the *'other'* – the anti-social, in a process described more fully by Judy Nixon and Sadie Parr in the following chapter. Part of our social identity is to stop ASB and we are enjoined to do so – 'we can do it together'. There is, of course, a second dialogical force within the poster, that of victimhood: the 'victims R us' syndrome identified by Stanko which requires *us* to minimise danger from *them* 'by mustering our own individual resources for self-protection' (Stanko, 2000, p 13).

The second point, which highlights the tension between technical and vernacular knowledge, is about the creation of problem spaces; see, for example, Pauline Card's discussion of council housing estates in Chapter Two (this volume), and the importance of 'commonsense knowledge of specific, untheorized problem places and things...' (Valverde, 2003b, p 248):

> ... in a world in which there has been a huge explosion of technical knowledges that render risks 'calculable', there are still spaces ... in which other knowledges manage to govern without much contestation.

The link between common sense and space is both powerful and important in our analysis. What has been interesting is the ever-expanding circles of tenure which the state tells us is affected by ASB. In 1995, the Conservative government issued a rushed Consultation Paper entitled *Tackling Anti-social Behaviour on Council Estates*, which began with the assertion:

> Anti-social behaviour by a small minority of tenants and others is a growing problem on council estates. Every tenant has a right to quiet enjoyment of their home.... Whole estates can be stigmatised by the anti-social behaviour of a few. (DoE, 1995, para 1.1)

That stigmatisation, however, is clearly reflected in the then government's proposed solution – 'probationary tenancies': 'even the colloquial name itself, coined by the government, suggested that these tenancies were part of the system of crime control' (Cowan, 1999, p 490).

The debate was subsequently broadened to include housing associations (The Housing Corporation, 1999), and, more recently, broadened again to include parts of the private rented sector (DTLR, 2001) and owner-occupied sector (Home Office, 2003b). One reason for these circles may relate to the influence central government has on each particular tenure – it explicitly exercises oversight on local housing authority accommodation, implicitly over housing association accommodation, has certain levers over parts of the private rented sector, but little influence over the owner-occupied sector.

However, a more persuasive analysis is provided by Flint (2004), who argues that the normalisation of home ownership in the UK creates a presumption that the social sector is occupied by the other, the 'marginalised "flawed consumers"'. As Murie (1997a, p 27) suggests, there has been a 'clear sorting of the population into different tenures much more closely related to their affluence and employment'. Thus, hopes of social housing providing sites of social inclusion have given way to the realisation that the occupants of social housing are economically marginalised and that the stock has become residualised (see Forrest and Murie, 1990, pp 65-85). Broadly, social housing provides safety-net accommodation for those in the poorest income groups and has done so for some considerable time (Murie, 1997b). In particular, the role of social housing is partly as provider to those deinstitutionalised persons, single mothers, asylum seekers and others whom society considers to be dangerous either to morals, public funds or the body.

Social housing, in this sense, is also reproductive, as Murray (1990) argued in his essay on the UK underclass, describing such people as 'the new rabble' – there is no way out for such persons. It is this division from the norm which justifies a certain racism and a form of killing, in the sense in which Foucault used those terms. A focus on ASB in social housing is part of a process inherent in the normalisation of owner-occupation; social housing occupiers offer a threat to owners. And, 'the death of the other, the death of the bad race, of the inferior race (or the degenerate, or the abnormal) is something that will make life in general healthier: healthier and purer' (Foucault, 2003, p 255).

Controlling anti-social behaviour

Since the 1990s, there have been a number of quite dramatic responses to the problem of ASB at the level of sovereign state. A key force in this process was the formation of a local authority pressure group – the Social Landlords Crime and Nuisance Group (SLCNG) – which has had a similar impact on the centre of government as other (blue-coated) police pressure groups. There has been a '"democratisation" of ideas work; ideas no longer being the property of the few, such that it becomes almost everyone's responsibility to create ideas' (Osborne, 2004, p 436). The SLCNG is a group of experts who provide knowledge that is both autonomous from and ancillary to government. Experts are frequently instruments of reform, 'since the vast array of facts that he gathers come to serve, as if by slow, laborious accrual, in modifying the methods, needs and ends of government itself' (Osborne, 2004, p 440).

Legislative responses have provided further important structures for the devolution of crime control in two ways. First, they have sought to 'join up' local approaches, implying the 'collective deliver[y of] their services from coterminous locations developing common practices of information collection, collation, processing, management, and exchange in the process of so doing' (Johnston and Shearing, 2003, p 108). Section 5 of the 1998 Crime and Disorder Act required a multiagency 'crime and disorder plan' to be promoted and published.

Section 17 requires local authorities to exercise their powers and duties with reference to crime and disorder. Thus, local authorities and other agencies have become mediators of action against ASB. The role of mediators is:

> ... to get us from one place to another, to move things along; they are propellants – modest or immodest – associated with the very buzz of innovation and enterprise. The mediator is interested above all in ideas; not the 'big ideas' of the epoch of 'grand narratives' but ideas which are going to make a difference and especially ideas which are 'vehicular' rather than 'oracular'. (Osborne, 2004, p 441)

Mediators are particularly interested in information, as ideas in this context are essentially informational. It is for this reason that information sharing has become of paramount importance and explains the information sharing portals built into the 1998 Crime and Disorder Act.

The local focus of mediation is significant. The neoliberal attack on welfare was also an attack on local government. Thatcher capitalised on disenchantment with the inflexibility of local welfare bureaucracy and began to dismantle state welfare at its weakest point through her flagship housing policy of 'Right to Buy', which was followed by challenging the monopolistic supply of local social services through Compulsory Competitive Tendering. At the same time this promoted powerful ideologies of a property owning democracy and individual freedom conceptualised as empowered consumers. Inevitably therefore, New Labour had to, and continues to, articulate a renewed 'local' ideology that is distinct from its own discredited past as well as from neoliberalism. The contemporary grand narrative is one of fear and insecurity, and the elimination of risk becomes oracular in this context.

The notion of active citizenry provides the second feature of the approach. The law, as with the processes of governance described by Flint in Chapter One (this volume), also works through the regulatory and self-regulatory capacities of the individual. Although the recent history of legislative intervention has been to increase the powers of landlords, these presuppose and work on the role of the tenant. As with all these powers, it is not necessarily their use but their appearance and translation into everyday life that has power. Their form is both legislative and contractual – they are additions or alterations to the landlord–tenant contract. As Caroline Hunter describes in detail in Chapter Seven (this volume), social housing providers can now grant introductory (or probationary) tenancies, they can demote tenants from the secure tenancy, and they can take out injunctions against *anyone* (where two conditions are satisfied: see Section 13 of the 2003 Anti-social Behaviour Act).

The injunction provisions contained in the 2003 Act (designed to solve technical problems of existing powers in the 1996 Housing Act) mean that anyone can be the subject of such an injunction when their conduct *is capable of* causing nuisance or annoyance to any person as well as indirectly affecting housing management. The change was explained in Parliament as one that 'will enable social landlords to be more proactive in their management of anti-social behaviour and will avoid legal arguments about the exact severity or likelihood of anti-social behaviour causing nuisance and annoyance' (*Hansard*, 11 September 2003, col 497).

Then there are expanded grounds of evicting a household on the basis of ASB. The tenant may be evicted where they, or a person living with or visiting them, have 'been guilty of conduct causing or likely to cause a nuisance or annoyance to a person residing, visiting or otherwise engaging in a lawful activity in the locality', or have been convicted of an offence 'committed in, or in the locality of, the dwelling house' or 'using the dwelling-house or allowing it to be used for immoral or illegal purposes' (Section 144 of the 1996 Housing Act). In *Kensington and Chelsea RLBC v Simmonds* (1996) 29 HLR 507, it was made clear that the tenants themselves do not have to be personally responsible for the actions of the perpetrator. Merely allowing it to happen is sufficient. As Hunter and Nixon point out, these powers have been particularly used in dealing with non-conforming households, such as single parents: 'The language used by judges to describe single mothers reflects a view of single parents, which suggests that in the absence of a husband, they are "inadequate parents"' (2001, p 404).

Converging expertise and anti-social behaviour

Our argument now turns to epistemic understandings of ASB and its particular vehicular nature. Eviction is only possible where it would be 'reasonable' to evict. Concerns over the failure of judges to give effect to this newly expanded ground of eviction led to Parliament seeking to structure the court's discretion. So, in the 2003 Anti-social Behaviour Act, it is said that in any action under this ground for possession the court must consider the effect of the behaviour, and its potential repetition, on others.

In this way the Act limits the legislative role of the judiciary and gives them a new role requiring them to utilise a different sort of knowledge – an interpretive and predictive knowledge. Although the occupier must be a social housing tenant, it should be noted that the range of people covered here is, essentially, any person other than that tenant. Yet, in the *Simmonds* case, the courts had already reached this position:

> As to the justice of the position, it must be remembered that not only are the interests of the tenant and her family here at stake; so too are the interests of their neighbours. It would in my judgment be quite intolerable if they were to be held necessarily deprived of all possibility of relief in these cases, merely because some ineffectual tenant next door was incapable of controlling his or her household. ((1996) 29 HLR 507 at p 511).

Judicial ventriloquism

In interpreting these new powers, what is interesting is the epistemological basis of judicial knowledge. Judicial knowledge is in liberal traditions accomplished through conflict. So John Stuart Mill explains, 'On any other subject no one's opinions deserve the name of knowledge, except so far as he has either had *forced* upon him by others, or gone through of himself, the same mental process which would have been required of him in carrying on an active controversy with opponents' (Mill, 1859/1975, p 44; emphasis added). One might say that judicial knowledge is legislative, as an over-coding 'of opinions with the rationale of intellectual ordering as part of a more general aspiration to cultural and political order' (Osborne, 2004, p 438).

However, in considering ASB, judges also have recourse to a different source of knowledge. For example, in *Manchester City Council v Lee*

[2004] HLR 11 161, 170, Pill LJ observed that 'The court is conscious of the social problems which exist on many housing estates and that Parliament has intended in the 1996 Act and elsewhere to increase the power of local authorities to deal with them'. And in *Clingham v Kensington and Chelsea RLBC* [2003] HLR 17, in which the implementation of an Antisocial Behaviour Order (ASBO) was challenged as being contrary to the 1998 Human Rights Act, Lord Steyn described what he termed 'the social problem':

> It is well known that in some urban areas, notably urban housing estates and deprived inner city areas, young persons, and groups of young persons, cause fear, distress and misery to law-abiding and innocent people by outrageous anti-social behaviour.... In recent years this phenomenon became a serious social problem. There appeared to be a gap in the law. The criminal law offered insufficient protection to communities. Public confidence in the rule of law was undermined by a not unreasonable view in some communities that the law failed them. This was the social problem which section 1 was designed to address. (para 16)

Where this knowledge comes from is unknown, beyond what is common sense. There is a clear mapping of the spaces of deviance, and agents of deviance, as well as the security fears of other residents. To draw on Valverde again (2003a, p 47), the courts are 'ventriloquiz[ing] the "national" community'. What Lord Steyn is doing here is quite different from the normal legislative function of judges. This is interpretive – the epistemic purpose is to 'bring about understanding – or, being more contemporary, perhaps we should say mutual "recognition"'(Osborne, 2004, p 439). Lord Steyn tells us a story of the law failing. It fails not only law-abiding and innocent individuals; significantly it is also failing communities. However, the story is also one of progress; the law now has solved the problem, by enacting Section 1 of the 1998 Crime and Disorder Act. The implication is that the judges must not let communities or Parliament down by undermining this solution. So Lord Steyn continues:

> The view was taken that the proceedings for an anti-social behaviour order would be civil and would not attract the rigour of the inflexible and sometimes absurdly technical hearsay rule which applies in criminal cases. If this

supposition was wrong, in the sense that Parliament did not objectively achieve its aim, it would inevitably follow that the procedure for obtaining anti-social behaviour orders is completely or virtually unworkable and useless. If that is what the law decrees, so be it. My starting point is, however, an initial scepticism of an outcome which would deprive communities of *their* fundamental rights…. (para 18; original emphasis)

Lord Steyn's discursive strategy repays attention. While the logic of the law must be followed, Lord Steyn admits that it can be absurdly technical. He anticipates what he presents as a progressive outcome by distancing himself from an alternative and unwelcome outcome through his scepticism, as well as by his elevation of the importance of communities and their fundamental rights. Simultaneously through this narrative performance he achieves an alliance with Parliament in its problem-solving approach and with communities of innocent and law-abiding citizens. In effect he removes the judiciary from the moral opprobrium which has resulted from the presumed resistance of liberal lawyers to legislative responses to ASB while at the same time preserving their right to follow the logic of the law where circumstances demand it (even against the dictates of common sense).

Such discursive strategies also have a kind of negative encoding in which important elements are hidden away in what is left unsaid. Here, for instance, it is *unexamined* common sense that the police cannot protect witnesses against these out-of-control youths. The transformation of policing from protection to prevention and its consequences for the community is simply accepted. The dismantling of traditional restrictions on the use of anonymous evidence becomes inevitable and unchallenged. This operates to exclude the anti-social from the normal and oratorically universal protections of the law. Common sense therefore justifies the death of the social existence of the 'other' because of the need to enhance the protections of the 'innocent' and 'the law-abiding'.

Other stories in this case are also silenced. We hear nothing about the defendant's personal tragedy, of his mother dying of cancer when he was 13, of his father's subsequent suicide and his sister, barely an adult herself, succeeding to the secure tenancy, and her understandable inability to provide for the adolescent's needs. Thus there is no space for therapeutic or other responses to Clingham's circumstances. Nor do we hear of the dilemma the local housing trust faced in making a decision that reconciled the needs of other residents, the sister and the young man. In this version of events, seeking an ASBO becomes a complex balancing act that is justified managerially as preferable to evicting the sister. The story told by the House of Lords renders such complexity invisible and marginal, and means solutions can be achieved by the straightforward application of common sense.

Managing anti-social behaviour

Despite the discourses of marginalisation and deviance, intervention has been premised on regarding the occupier as a *consumer* of the service provided by the housing agency. It is this apparent contradiction between, on the one hand, the occupier as marginal, as socially excluded, and, on the other hand, as sovereign consumer, which is particularly distinctive in the debate. This reflects the reach of consumerism – even the marginalised have the right to act as consumers but, more so, have the obligation to act as responsible subjects. As Flint (2004, p 151) has argued, the specification of the subject of social housing as consumer is closely linked to 'the responsibilised agent of social control, acting within a dominant discourse of ethical conduct based upon prescribed aesthetics of consumption and moral codes of behaviour'.

However, ASB also works through the notion of consumerism in a different way. For, while the occupier has been recast as consumer, there has been increasing focus on the other, the anti-consumer. In the name of *social* housing, the *anti-social* have been excluded and segregated. Probably at no time since the foundation of social housing has more effort been put into dividing the anti-social from the social. These anti-consumers are too costly for housing management, in terms of supervisory and disciplinary interventions, and the households' negative impact on the communities management aspire to create for their estates.

The anti-social are, in some cases, divided off from the population in new therapeutic communities such as that pioneered in Dundee (see Chapters Nine and Ten, this volume). These therapeutic strategies for the anti-social contain the possibility of redemption held out for them on their moral reform; at the same time there is a show of sovereign force through the eviction process and intensive disciplinary techniques, such as demotion of tenancy status. New teams have been set up by housing providers to develop expertise in specifically dealing with the problem of ASB. Risk communications are now the stuff of everyday housing management, as housing officers engage in regular cross-disciplinary dialogues with other social agencies about individuals they perceive as risky (Cowan, 1999).

Brown (2004, p 210) makes a crucial point about locating ASB:

> Anti-social behaviour is 'found' largely in social housing areas because the physical presence of 'investigatory' people and technology ensure that it will be found. Anti-social behaviour is thus partly a *product* of social housing management.

Social housing is *managed* housing in ways beyond what is apparently possible in private housing. The pinpointing of social housing as dangerous and productive of ASB thus creates a self-fulfilling prophecy – if you go looking for it, you will usually find it (particularly when you are not sure what it is); and if you intensively go looking for it, you will find it in greater abundance.

These management techniques should be historically situated (see Chapter One, this volume). They provide an illustration of the link between the moral cleansing of the poor, their self-regulation and training. Octavia Hill explicitly linked the social and moral in describing her 'system' of improving the living conditions of the poor. This system sought to harness the capacities of the poor for self-government through the provision of better quality housing. In describing her system in relation to 'drunkards', she put the following position:

> I do not say that I will not have drunkards [in my properties], I have quantities of drunkards; but everything depends upon whether I think the drunkard will be better for being sent away or not. It is a tremendous despotism, but it is exercised with a view of bringing out the powers of the people, and treating them as responsible for themselves within certain limits ... you cannot get the individual action in any other way that I know of. (Royal Commission, 1885, p 297)

Octavia Hill's system was intensely moral, seeking the reform of the 'destructive classes'. The division was between poverty on the one hand, and pauperisation on the other, and the aim was to save the poor from pauperisation. As Procacci (1991, p 160, original emphasis) notes, pauperism 'consists in indicating a series of *different forms of conduct,* namely those which are not amenable to the project of socialisation which is being elaborated'.

Although Octavia Hill's housing management system was overtaken by other practices, this connection between the social and the moral was a key feature of housing management throughout the 20th century. Thus, it can be argued that housing management itself makes possible this focus on ASB in social housing. What is different now is the intensified gaze on the occupiers, through the use of modern technology and methods including CCTV, concierges and single-issue teams.

The occupier-manager as entrepreneur

One of the consequences of the outbreak of entrepreneurialism at the level of management is the way in which the targeting of ASB involves working on the self. Ultimately, the concern of managers is the creation of stable, or sustainable, communities as this will impact on the economics of managing estates and, at the same time, create positive living environments. Underlying many of these developments is a shift in rationality from rights towards responsibility and an explicit communitarian ethos (see Flint, 2003, 2004).

An outbreak of localised practices have been developed which reflect this ethos. There are informal mechanisms of social/moral regulation. So, for example, Saugeres (2000, p 595), in an interesting note on neatness and tidiness, suggests:

> The landlord is supposed to 'investigate' why tenants do not look after their gardens and either educate them to culturally acceptable standards or punish them through the enforcement of tenancy conditions or referral to other agencies of social control. Gardens can also be a way of rewarding well-behaved tenants. Indeed, in some organisations, it has become common practice to organise garden competitions for their tenants to enter, giving a prize to the tenant with the best garden.

Irwell Valley Housing Association has pioneered a form of 'good customer' scheme through which customers demonstrating required forms of behaviour are given a 'gold service' (Lupton et al, 2003). Members of the scheme obtain a variety of benefits, from quicker repairs to free flower seeds. The aims are not only to incentivise tenants but also to do likewise with housing management staff to 'go the extra mile' (Lupton et al, 2003). This scheme has been replicated by many other social landlords (Flint, 2004, p 164).

A central tool of the social landlord is the tenancy or occupation contract (see Diane Lister, Chapter Six, this volume, for a full discussion). This enables landlords to govern and responsibilise tenants, setting out norms of behaviour. This has always been so, although in the past local authorities were criticised for using tenancy agreements in this way (see, for example, Saunders, 1990). What is important is that these contracts have only become formalised since the 1980 Housing Act. This formalisation of the rights of occupiers of social landlords was something for which consumer groups and others campaigned (see Loveland, 1992). Setting out occupiers' rights is a positive development, but it has also created the conditions through which the behaviour of occupiers can be more closely controlled. Ultimately, in setting out rights, one also sets out obligations, including the threat of eviction in their breach.

Entrepreneurialism has been engaged in three ways. First, contracts are now extremely lengthy, up to 80 pages, in many areas, and are also often written in 'plain English'. They contain detailed rules on what behaviour is permissible and what is not. As Crawford (2003, p 481, original emphasis) suggests, 'these contracts have a decidedly behavioural characteristic in that they seek to govern *individual* conduct and secure a defined *sense of order*'. Yet, at the same time, 'the classical contract assumes a utilitarian understanding of human calculation and expresses virtues of freedom, autonomy and choice' (Crawford, 2003, p 488). It is this tension between freedom and constraint that makes the contract a potent technique. In defining what is acceptable, they leave open the occupier's freedom to act either in accordance with those norms or not. Failure to do so implies a tacit acceptance of eviction or therapeutic intervention.

Second, contracts in the entrepreneurial world have meaning in their own right. One way in which that meaning can be put over to the occupier is by making the signing of the contract an event. Contract signing ceremonies have become a recent invention in social housing. These seek to engender real respect for the contract and its terms, make the occupier appreciate the significance of the contract, and make them responsible for their conduct in relation to it.

Third, *enforcement* of the contract has become increasingly common, and there has been an incitement from all levels (centrally and locally) to enforce it specifically against the anti-social. The narrative of enforcement exercises a powerful control on the behaviour not only of the anti-consumers, but also the occupiers more generally. In other words, although enforcement is patchy – different landlords have different practices – it is the possibility of enforcement that is important in generating the will to self-governance. Those unable to work within this construct are liable either to retraining, injunctions, ASBOs or eviction. So, for example, parents with problematic children might be invited to multiagency meetings, the purpose of which is 'to identify new strategies for these parents to be able to regulate the behaviour of their children within expected norms of behaviour, without the need for future housing agency intervention' (Flint, 2002, p 630). But self-governance has a broader relation in that it is not only the occupier that is controlled, it is also their visitors, for their deviance can have negative consequences. Just like the pub landlord, the control of deviance is subcontracted by making the occupier responsible for the behaviour of their visitors.

The final point to make is that those who are made the subject of ASB sanctions are generally found to be those who are not able to act as entrepreneurs. They have extreme vulnerability arising from their marginal position (Hunter et al, 2000). This is not a particularly surprising finding of research studies, for these are the households who are perhaps less likely to be able to accept the freedom of contract, and are more likely to be highly controlled in the community. The 'new' label of ASB combined with the increasing resources given over to its control means that there has been a shift from reliance on social work as a rehabilitative tool in favour of mesh-thinning social control. This is the important point made by Brown (2004, p 209):

> In other words, the situations were generally not neighbour disputes, but problems in themselves, which the system (the penal-welfare complex) had failed to manage before and was now, in response to demands from neighbours, attempting to control by the anti-social behaviour route.

Conclusion

In this chapter we have argued that the idea of ASB is powerful because it is vehicular; it draws in combatants, and enables the idea to be refined, thereby giving it mobility. It is, therefore, no surprise that it is undefined, and that its principal mode of identification is through lists of unrelated, high- and low-level, deviant and subdeviant categories. Obscurity is a powerful tool of governance. We then looked at the way in which this power has become used to regulate occupiers through the law, specifically through processes of self-management, and the ways in which general themes about society are replicated by the judiciary.

The chapter then considered the way in which there was a

conjunction between the sites of housing management, occupier *qua* consumer, and the use of contract. We have argued that contract operates through the freedom of occupiers, setting out the constraints on that freedom (and, by implication, what is acceptable conduct), and the requirement to act in accordance with the norms of housing management.

ASB provides a testing ground not only for vehicular ideas, but also for the relationship between Foucault's triptych of sovereignty–discipline–government. ASB highlights the equilibrium in this relationship, the way in which each works together through freedom at the level of the occupier household. Foucault identified law with a certain repressive form of sovereign government and, thus, tended to ignore it. Although there have been some elegant attempts at retrieving it (Ewald, 1990; Hunt, 1992), an analysis of law in the context of ASB could similarly frame it as being repressive; an example of an almost hysterical form of sovereign attempts at crime control, doomed to failure (Garland, 1996). Yet, at the same time, ASB law can be analysed differently, as being constitutive of a certain subjectivity – indeed, of governing through the freedom of occupiers – as well as being reproductive of certain norms and forms of knowledge. Ewald (1990, p 141) makes the important point that:

> The norm is the principle that allows discipline to develop from a simple set of constraints into a mechanism; it serves as the matrix that transforms the negative restraint of the juridical into the more positive controls of normalizations and helps to produce the generalization of discipline.

Although one should not confuse the terms 'norm' and 'discipline', there is an important relation between them, one which law facilitates.

The gaze has been on social housing because that tenure historically provides the conditions under which the occupier can be subjected to control. Social housing is, and has always been, managed housing; and that housing management has always taken an interest in the ongoing moral reform of the occupiers. What has changed in recent times has been a more intensive gaze on the behaviour of those occupants that has tied in a constellation of diverse, unconnected developments and rationalities. The inculcation of a certain private sector ethos and values into social housing management has been a key instigator, but so has the shift away from regarding tenants as passive recipients of landlord bounty.

Notes

[1] The authors are grateful to Mariana Valverde for comments on an earlier draft of this chapter.

[2] The method was to undertake 'a snapshot count of reports that were made to agencies in England and Wales on one day [10 September 2003]' 'over 1500 organisations took part and information was received from every Crime and Disorder Reduction Partnership area in England and Wales' (Home Office, 2003a).

References

Bakhtin, M. (1981) *The Dialogic Imagination*, Austin, TX: University of Texas.

Brown, A. (2004) 'Anti-social Behaviour, Crime Control and Social Control', *Howard Journal of Criminal Justice*, vol 43, no 2, pp 203-11.

Cowan, D. (1999) *Housing Law and Policy*, Basingstoke: Macmillan.

Cowan, D. and McDermont, M. (2006) *Regulating Social Housing: Governing Decline*, London: Glasshouse.

Crawford, A. (2003) '"Contractual Governance" of Deviant Behaviour', *Journal of Law and Society*, vol 30, no 4, pp 479-505.

DoE (Department of the Environment) (1995) *Tackling Anti-Social Behaviour on Council Estates, A Consultation Paper*, London: DoE.

DTLR (Department of Transport, Local Government and the Regions) (2001) *Selective Licencing of Private Landlords, A Consultation Paper*, London: DTLR.

Ewald, F. (1990) 'Norms, Discipline and the Law', *Representations*, vol 30, no 1, pp 138-61.

Flint, J. (2002) 'Social Housing Agencies and the Governance of Anti-social Behaviour', *Housing Studies*, vol 17, no 4, pp 619-38.

Flint, J. (2003) 'Housing and Ethopolitics: Constructing Identities of Active Consumption and Responsible Community', *Economy and Society*, vol 32, no 4, pp 611-29.

Flint, J. (2004) 'Reconfiguring Agency and Responsibility in the Governance of Social Housing in Scotland', *Urban Studies*, vol 41, no 1, pp 151-72.

Forrest, R. and Murie, A. (1990) *Selling the Welfare State: The Privatisation of State Housing*, London: Routledge.

Foucault, M. (2003) *Society Must be Defended*, London: Penguin.

Garland, D. (1996) 'The Limits of the Sovereign State: Strategies of Crime Control in Contemporary Society', *British Journal of Criminology*, vol 36, no 3, pp 445-71.

Home Office (2003a) *TOGETHER: Tackling Anti-Social Behaviour: The One-Day Count of Anti-Social Behaviour*, London: Home Office.

Home Office (2003b) *Respect and Responsibility: Taking a Stand Against Anti-Social Behaviour*, London: Home Office.

Housing Corporation, The (1999) *Performance Standards, Addendum 4 to the Social Housing Standards for General and Supported Housing: Anti-social Behaviour*, London: The Housing Corporation.

Hunt, A. (1992) 'Foucault's Expulsion of Law: Towards a Retrieval', *Law and Social Inquiry*, vol 17, no 1, pp 1-38.

Hunter, C. (2001) 'Anti-social Behaviour: Can Law Be the Answer?', in D. Cowan and A Marsh (eds) *Two Steps Forward: Housing Policy into the New Millennium*, Bristol: The Policy Press, pp 221-37.

Hunter, C. and Nixon, J. (2001) 'Taking the Blame and Losing the Home: Women and Anti-social Behaviour', *Journal of Social Welfare and Family Law*, vol 23, no 4, pp 395-410.

Hunter, C., Nixon, J. and Shayer, S. (2000) *Neighbour Nuisance, Social Landlords and the Law*, Coventry: CIH.

Johnston, L. and Shearing, C. (2003) *Governing Security: Explorations in Policing and Justice*, London: Routledge.

Loveland, I. (1992) 'Square Pegs, Round Holes: The "Right" to Council Housing in the Post-war Era', *Journal of Law and Society*, vol 19, no 2, pp 339-61.

Lupton, M., Hale, J. and Sprigings, N. (2003) *Incentives and Beyond? The Transferability of the Irwell Valley Gold Service to Other Social Landlords*, London: ODPM/CIH.

McLennan, G. (2004) 'Travelling with Vehicular Ideas: The Case of the Third Way', *Economy and Society*, vol 33, no 4, pp 484-99.

Mill, J.S. (1859/1975) *On Liberty*, New York, NY: Norton and Company.

Murie, A. (1997a) 'Linking Housing Changes to Crime', *Social Policy and Administration*, vol 31, no 5, pp 22-36.

Murie, A. (1997b) 'The Social Rented Sector, Housing and the Welfare State in the UK', *Housing Studies*, vol 12, no 4, pp 437-61.

Murray, C. (1990) *The Emerging British Underclass*, London: Health and Welfare Unit, Institute of Economic Affairs.

Osborne, T. (2004) 'On Mediators: Intellectuals and the Ideas Trade in the Knowledge Society', *Economy and Society*, vol 33, no 4, pp 430-47.

Papps, P. (1998) 'Anti-social Behaviour Strategies – Individualistic or Holistic?', *Housing Studies*, vol 13, no 5, pp 639-56.

Procacci, G. (1991) 'Social Economy and the Government of Poverty', in G. Burchell, C. Gordon and P. Miller (eds) *The Foucault Effect: Studies in Governmentality*, Chicago, IL: University of Chicago Press, pp 151-68.

Royal Commission (1985) *Royal Commission on the Housing of the Working Classes*, London: HMSO.

Saugeres, L. (2000) 'Of Tidy Gardens and Clean Houses: Housing Officers as Agents of Social Control', *Geoforum*, vol 31, pp 587-99.

Saunders, P. (1990) *A Nation of Homeowners*, London: Unwin Hyman.

Scott, S. and Parkey, H. (1998) 'Myths and Reality: Anti-social Behaviour in Scotland', *Housing Studies*, vol 13, no 3, pp 325-45.

SEU (Social Exclusion Unit) (2000) *Anti-Social Behaviour*, Report of Policy Action Team 8, London: SEU.

Stanko, E. (2000) 'Victims R Us: The Life History of "Fear of Crime" and the Politicisation of Violence', in T. Hope and R. Sparks (eds) *Crime, Risk and Insecurity: Law and Order in Everyday Life and Political Discourse*, London: Routledge, pp 13-30.

Valverde, M. (2003a) *Law's Dream of a Common Knowledge*, Princeton, NJ: Princeton University Press.

Valverde, M. (2003b) 'Police Science, British Style: Pub Licensing and Knowledges of Urban Disorder', *Economy and Society*, vol 32, no 2, pp 234-52.

Whitehead, C., Stockdale, J. and Razzu, G. (2003) *The Economic and Social Costs of Anti-Social Behaviour: A Review*, London: London School of Economics and Political Science.

FOUR

Anti-social behaviour: voices from the front line

Judy Nixon and Sadie Parr

Introduction

Politicians and the media share a growing concern with anti-social behaviour (ASB), which is presented as a plaguing, degenerative and urgent problem that must be tackled if the government is to achieve its aim of tackling social exclusion and revitalising the most deprived neighbourhoods:

> Anti-social behaviour blights people's lives, destroys families and ruins communities. It holds back the regeneration of our disadvantaged areas and creates the environment in which crime can take hold. (Home Office, 2003, p 2)

As the above extract from the 2003 White Paper *Respect and Responsibility* (Home Office, 2003) illustrates, much of the policy literature emanating from government is typified by the use of a vocabulary of irresponsibility and stigmatisation. Anti-social acts are described in emotive terms as 'blighting lives', 'destroying families', 'shattering communities', and those responsible for such behaviour are constructed as a dangerous minority who ruin the lives of the decent law-abiding majority. The way in which the problem is portrayed in the popular press is also characterised by the use of assertion and a demonising polemic. Particular target populations, for example, young people who are described as 'feral', 'yobs' and 'louts', and lone-parent families who are deemed to be 'dysfunctional', are singled out as being responsible for 'terrorising' decent, hard-working citizens, and making life a misery for innocent people living in the same community.

The political and media rhetorical coverage of ASB shares an emotive narrative that persuasively suggests that punitive action is the only really effective way of controlling the behaviour of those who choose to behave in an anti-social manner. Such rhetoric has been described as populist and moralistic (Stephen and Squires, 2004), and there is a growing body of work critically exploring how the emerging governance of ASB has resulted in new forms of disciplinary social control which give rise to new forms of exclusion (Papps, 1998; Haworth and Manzi, 1999; Cowan et al, 2001; Hunter and Nixon, 2001; Flint, 2002; Jacobs et al, 2003; Brown, 2004; Stephen and Squires, 2004; Gillies, 2005).

In this chapter we explore the impact of political and media constructions of ASB on the private discourse of individuals living in hard-pressed areas where ASB is considered to be a big or fairly big problem (Wood, 2004). This chapter stems from our recent study (Hunter et al, 2004) examining the barriers that deter people affected by ASB from acting as witnesses in civil/criminal proceedings. Interviews with victims and/or witnesses were graphic and compelling. As participants told their stories, we were struck by the way in which their constructions of perpetrators echoed dominant political and media ASB discourses. It became clear that neighbour disputes often become a site where identities were established through a binary classification of 'them' and 'us', where the 'other' are the 'dysfunctional', 'irresponsible' and 'selfish' and 'we' are the 'normal', 'decent' and 'hard-working'. At no point was there an acknowledgement of the socially constructed nature of the problem (Hunter et al, 2003; Brown, 2004), or that people can simultaneously be both 'victims' and 'perpetrators' of anti-social acts (see Anwen Jones' discussion in Chapter Nine, this volume; also Jones et al, 2004; Stephen and Squires, 2004).

We start by briefly outlining the context within which behaviour is conceptualised and problematised in late modern times before undertaking an examination of New Labour official discourse, focusing on three extracts from statements made in 2003 by the then Home Secretary David Blunkett in which he outlined government policy proposals for tackling ASB (Blunkett, 2003a, 2003b, 2003c). This is followed by a detailed exploration of individual witnesses' and victims' subjective understandings of the way in which behaviour is constructed as a problem. By comparing private and public ASB discourses, we reflect on the extent to which individuals' constructions are commensurate with those employed by New Labour. In particular, we critically examine the way in which particular formulations of the problem contain either implicitly or explicitly a judgement on appropriate solutions. On initial reading of the two discourses, it appears that a consensus has been reached which ignores the complexity of the lived experience of ASB in favour of an emphasis on individual pathology. A discussion of the ways in which behaviour is constructed as a problem would, however, be incomplete without at least some reference to the views of those who have been labelled 'anti-social'. In the final section of the chapter the multilayered reality of ASB is revealed by consideration of the experiences of those who have been labelled the 'neighbours from hell'. The chapter concludes by suggesting that the current policy discourse, characterised by the use of emotive and demonising language, rather than promoting a 'culture of respect', is more likely to simply reinforce divisions between 'us' the normal, and 'them' the deviants, resulting in increased exclusions and engendering further divisions within fragile communities.

The control of conduct and conditions for demonisation

Scrutiny of private and public ASB discourses reveal striking similarities. As individuals told their stories about their relationship with their neighbours, construction of appropriate neighbourly behaviour emerged which enabled people to discern 'good' and 'bad' neighbours. Political constructions of ASB were also found to be based on a classification of alleged perpetrators in terms of normalised standards of behaviour. Foucault's work on governmentality (1991) informs an understanding of the way in which the 'normalising gaze' of governance works to regulate conduct in relation to a set of norms defined by a dominant discourse (Foucault, 1977; Flint, 2002; Flint and Rowlands, 2003). Flint (2002) illustrates how social housing agencies are seeking to direct the conduct of their tenants in two ways. Firstly, through the promotion of self-regulation, tenants are encouraged to take responsibility to ensure that their own and their children's behaviour conforms to normative standards of what constitutes good, appropriate and responsible behaviour. Secondly, if tenants do not conform to the constructed norms of self-conduct then a more explicit disciplinary power will be exerted through the use of punitive action including evictions, Dispersal Orders, injunctions, Acceptable Behaviour Contracts (ABCs), Antisocial Behaviour Orders (ASBOs) and Parenting Orders.

These strands of self-regulation and punishment in ASB policy are clearly reflected in the official and private discourses of ASB. Both discourses are inherently ideological and carry with them social and political consequences, many of which have been identified elsewhere in relation to criminal policy and youth justice discourse (Muncie,

1999; Stephen and Squires, 2004). Whether the behaviour in question is a criminal or non-criminal act, the problem is always individualised (although see John Flint's argument about the collectivisation of responsibility in Chapter One, this volume). Offenders are perceived to be essentially lacking in some way and are held individually responsible for their actions which are presented as plaguing and threatening communities. The anti-social have become the folk devils of our time, and similar processes are apparent in other countries, for example, see Chapter Thirteen (this volume) for a discussion of such developments in France.

In documenting the movement from an inclusive to exclusive society, Young (1999) identifies essentialism as the necessary prerequisite condition for the successful demonisation of individuals and groups. The appeal of essentialism, he elucidates, is that it '*allows us to blame the other*' (emphasis added), which in turn facilitates the inversion of causal reality:

> Instead of acknowledging we have problems in society because of basic contradictions in the social order it is claimed that all problems of society are because of the problems themselves. (Young, 1999, p 110)

The process of demonisation, Young explains, has three key components. First, it relies on *ascribing an essentialist other* – this is a process through which deviant acts are attributed to a fundamental essence inherent in the individual. It can also involve the use of dehumanisation in which deviants are cast as monsters, portrayed as lower forms of being who chose their deviance rather than being impelled by any structural or social circumstance – it is therefore their fault. The second component of demonisation comprises of a *reaffirmation of normality* that allows the boundaries of normal behaviour to be clearly identified by reference to essential core values promoted by powerful groups. Those who choose not to conform to these essential core values become 'othered' and excluded. Thirdly, *distancing* enables the dominant group to explain deviancy as an individual aberration rather than a reflection of a failure of structural factors.

The process of demonisation as it applies to those deemed responsible for anti-social acts is clearly apparent in public ASB discourses, leading the government's chief advisor on youth crime, Rod Morgan, to warn that 'Britain risks demonising a whole generation of young people' (Morgan, 2005). In the rest of this chapter we examine how private ASB discourses also reflect these processes at work. We do not presuppose there to be a simple causal relationship between the political rhetoric and individuals' construction of the problem. Rather, we argue that by foregrounding individual responsibility, the public ASB discourse has effectively set the limit for all subsequent discussion by framing what the problem is (Cowan, 1998).

The political discourse

We start with an examination of official government-articulated discourse, drawing on three extracts from texts on ASB by the previous Home Secretary, David Blunkett (2003a, 2003b, 2003c). The texts were analysed for narratives and concepts concerning the nature of ASB and the identity of its perpetrators.

Political constructions of anti-social behaviour

It is frequently asserted that there is no precise definition of ASB, and a lack of specificity and ambiguity is present in the texts considered. Reference is made to an assortment of incivilities, low-level disorder and environmental and social irritants under the catch-all phrase of 'anti-social behaviour':

> It might seem relatively small – spray painted graffiti, an abandoned car, a broken window. Or it can feel more threatening – a gang late at night, a beggar at the cashpoint, young kids using passers-by as target practice. (Blunkett, 2003a)

Notwithstanding the lack of specificity, a hierarchy of more and less threatening anti-social acts is constructed. Less threatening acts include 'spray painted graffiti', 'an abandoned car', 'a broken window', while more threatening behaviour includes 'a gang late at night' and 'a beggar at the cashpoint'. Although categorised as 'more threatening', the latter are not criminal and do not explicitly involve threatening behaviour. Furthermore, the 'threat' seems to lie within the conjunction of a particular type of person or people in a particular space or time which together amount to an anti-social act: 'a gang late at night' and 'a beggar at the cashpoint'. It is assumed that the reader or listener will draw on their own cultural knowledge to recognise that gangs meeting late at night are intimidating and mean trouble. The construction of the threat of ASB is made simply by reference to particular types of person or social group without recourse to any behaviour: 'frightening gangs', 'neighbours from hell' and 'tearaway children' (Blunkett, 2003a, 2003b). ASB starts to infer a disapproval of the person as opposed to disapproval of the behaviour.

This leads us to consider the terms used to describe the perpetrators of ASB. Typically emotive images are used to portray perpetrators who are described as a 'yobbish minority' and 'neighbours from hell'. These terms are stigmatising and demonising labels that infer notions of mindless aggression, disregard and incivility. These social groups are demarcated from the majority who are defined as 'the hard-working', 'the law-abiding' and 'the decent':

> I know that frightening gangs on street corners, neighbours from hell, tearaway children and drug pushers are the very things which make us feel uneasy and unsafe. They can ruin lives – they can certainly ruin the quality of our lives. Every town has problems with anti-social behaviour whether that is on a particular estate or in the town or city centre. A yobbish minority can still make the lives of hard working citizens a living hell. (Blunkett, 2003b)

They are the fearsome 'other', who frighten us and make us feel 'scared' and 'unsafe'. Criminal acts are rarely referred to in the extracts yet 'yobs' and their ASB are implicitly associated with criminality by pitting them against the 'law-abiding majority'. The 'law-abiding majority' are that which the anti-social are not:

> People cannot continue to expect something for nothing – they must realise rights in our communities can only come when they take responsibility for their actions and neighbourhood. That's why I am setting out how the government plans to reclaim communities for the decent, law-abiding majority. (Blunkett, 2003b)

The perpetrator is presented as a feckless, undisciplined individual unconcerned for others. The cause of the problem is clearly located with the individual:

> At the heart of antisocial behaviour is a lack of respect for others – the simple belief that one can get away with whatever one can get away with. (Blunkett, 2003a)

ASB is constructed as a personal problem, attributed directly to the failure of the individual to conform to normative values and requiring the individual to take responsibility for resolving. In turn, this serves as justification for individualistic solutions that are often punitive and intolerant such as eviction, ASBOs and Dispersal Orders, which involve expulsion, supervision, tracking and surveillance:

> We have an effective armoury of measures: fast-tracked, slimmed-down antisocial behaviour orders, acceptable behaviour contracts and parenting orders. Since August, almost 2,000 fixed penalty notices have been issued in the four pilot areas. We are clear that breaches of orders must be treated decisively. (Blunkett, 2003b)

Links are also made between the failure of the individual and the failure of families. This is emphasised in particular in the discourse around 'dysfunctional' families and bad parenting which deprives children of contact with civilised behaviour:

> We need to offer the chance for children who have been brought up in dysfunctional families for generations – a generational disadvantage and disengagement with civilized behaviour – to be able to pull round. (Blunkett, 2003c)

Children here become victims of their dysfunctional families who by implication are 'uncivilised'. It is the parents who have a 'duty' to their children:

> Parents have a duty to ensure that their children are in school and behaving. Persistent failure will result in parenting orders, fines or fast-track court action. We will support families in overcoming their problems, through parenting classes and new fast-track parenting orders. We will examine residential provision as a compulsory part of education and rehabilitation. (Blunkett, 2003c)

The political discourse is dominated by otherness and exclusion, a lack of specificity and a failure to reflect on the complex way in which the role of victim and perpetrator can be interchangeable. Simple pathological codes of 'other' are adopted as causal explanations of ASB. The reality that is complex and multilayered (see Chapters Three, Nine and Ten, this volume) is ignored in favour of a discourse that focuses on punishment, retribution, pathology and treatment. The political ASB discourse is based on an appeal to an apparent 'consensus' that individuals are responsible for their behaviour and if perpetrators 'choose' to transgress strict rules and norms of behaviour they must be punished. An advantage of this chosen approach is that it conveniently enables politicians to sidestep the more complex issue of social exclusion, which, Young (1999, p 78) argues, has its roots in: 'the material and moral reality in which individuals seek to live their lives'. We now turn to an examination of this lived reality of social exclusion.

Individuals' construction of anti-social behaviour

In exploring how private individuals' interpretation and representation fits with the broader official discourse, we present extracts from qualitative research with a sample of victims and witnesses. We examine the constructions of behaviour that made people feel 'uneasy' and 'frightened' and the way in which alleged perpetrators of these behaviours were classified. The analysis focuses on looking for related assumptions, logics, claims and categories that make up the discourse.

Witnesses' construction of anti-social behaviour

During interviews, witnesses were asked to describe the incident or series of incidents that had led them to report a neighbour. While different behaviours were cited ranging from environmental irritants to criminal offences, the picture that emerged was of a group of people who felt very frightened and vulnerable. In particular, fear of intimidation and reprisals combined with the failure of statutory agencies to respond to requests for help left people with acute feelings of powerlessness. Participants were united in their frustration at being unable to stop the problem behaviours and, in this context, discourses about behaviour were found to be saturated with notions of morality and the civil rights of ownership of private space.

Visual pollution including rubbish and littering of gardens, the immediate vicinity around their homes or even inside neighbours' own homes arose as examples of inappropriate and offensive neighbour activity. In the extract below, Mrs Brown (all names have been changed for anonymity) describes how she sees the estate where she lives as going 'down hill' and attributes this to the rubbish in her neighbour's back garden. In the quote, she mimics her neighbour's reasoning for leaving rubbish in the garden and in doing so invokes other examples of their disorderly behaviour: 'the door comes off in an argument', so it is thrown into the garden, 'somebody has thrown up on the settee', so it is slung outside. The rubbish is the illegitimate mess caused by disorderly behaviour:

> ... that's how the estate was going, litter everywhere, just down hill, tons of rubbish in the back garden, solvents in the back gardens, you getting the idea? The door comes off in an argument so let's sling it on the front garden – really out of their heads. So we've thrown up all over the settee so let's sling that out on the front garden and leave it there. (Mrs Brown)

This is an example of what Stokoe and Wallwork (2003) term 'neighbour spatial abuse', whereby visual pollution disrupts a person's sense of 'at-homeness' in their own private space. Participants' accounts therefore dismantle the common-sense notion that people are entitled to use private space as they wish; the status of private space is contingent on its appropriate use. Non-normative use of private space renders it open to public comment.

Similarly, smells and odours were also drawn on as interviewees described the problems they experienced with their neighbours. Illegitimate odour was defined in terms of that which impinged on participants' use of their own outdoor spaces. Appropriate and normative uses of outdoor space such as having barbecues, putting the washing out and children playing out were curtailed as a result of neighbours' anti-social action:

> They'd got a garden with mattresses in it, beds in it, dog muck all over it. It was horrendous and it stunk, it absolutely stunk, we couldn't have a barbecue or anything any more cause the whole of our garden reeked of it. (Mrs Brown)

Illegitimate and excessive noise was also cited by interviewees as ways in which their neighbours disordered their own private space. The illegitimacy of excessive noise was again often emphasised by reference to normative uses of private space:

> At the end of the day no one should have to live like that. All I want to do in the evenings is sit down, collect my thoughts, put my son to bed, so he can be up for school in the morning. Things like that. And sit and watch TV, not

> have blasting music out of the walls and punching the walls, and slamming the doors like they do. They have no respect at all; they shouldn't be there. (Emma)

Interviewees were keen to stress the suffering brought about by anti-social acts. There was a recognition that noise in particular might not be perceived as a 'real' problem but by reference to normative behaviour interviewees were anxious to explain the distress that noise nuisance can cause. In doing so, interference with routine activities associated with ordered households and disruption to family relationships was invoked:

> But it is not just noise. I am honestly on a verge of a nervous breakdown at times, lack of sleep and then you ring up. I have actually had tablets off the doctor to try to make me sleep. If they are not doing it you are anticipating them do it and you are wound up. People say it is only noise, but it is not only noise it affects the whole family, it affects my relationships with the children. One of my daughters has special needs, it affects the schoolwork, she needs her sleep. (Graham)

'Good' neighbours were perceived to have limited and unobtrusive contact, to respect household boundaries and normative uses of private space; creating an implicit moral order that regulates neighbourly activity and must be conformed to. Sarah described how only when her neighbour conforms to this moral order would she earn acceptance into a local communal space, reserved for 'decent' people:

> We have got a communal garden at the back of us. The gate comes to the back of our gardens with a padlock on it but it is by invitation this communal garden for people around it. The decent people get a key to use it. I said to her, if you pull yourself around and be neighbourly you are going to have a lovely place to sit in, and take the children in. (Sarah)

It was not just minor incivilities and noise disturbance that troubled some interviewees, but also more serious behaviours that involved acts of violence, harassment and intimidation. These acts of violence were often construed as irrational, unprovoked and motiveless actions against passive victims including the most vulnerable, for example, children or older people. In the following excerpt, Mrs Brown talks about the unreasonableness of the threats by emphasising how they were directed against children and by a woman, implying that a *woman* threatening *children* is particularly deplorable:

> My husband was attacked, my children were threatened to be burnt in their beds. My kids were intimidated if they were out. She would threaten them. A woman. Threaten both my children. When they went to play out on the corner, she had them. So it's very much constant provocation. (Mrs Brown)

A further example of unprovoked violence was provided by Joan, a pensioner, who recounted what had happened to her in the following terms:

> I finished up ... all night down at Accident and Emergency at the [name of hospital] from a head injury. All because I was taking a load of abuse from the [family name] family and I went and faced him about it and I was followed back to my property and knocked over. (Joan)

Alleged perpetrators' construction of anti-social behaviour

When we move from the activities associated with ASB to the characteristics of its perpetrators, interviewees' accounts were explicitly constructed using binary oppositions to distinguish between themselves and their neighbours. The language used is illustrative of the process of demonisation involving the use of ascribing an *essentialist other* and *reaffirmation of normality* (Young, 1999). Alleged anti-social neighbours were typically described as being 'abnormal' or 'uncivilised'. Perpetrators were labelled in a pejorative way as being a drug addict, an alcoholic, or an irresponsible mother or wife. The interviewees' construction of their neighbours was never hesitant but used language in a definitive ascribing of abnormality to people they lived in close proximity to.

Being an alcoholic or drug addict was attributed causal primacy in understanding the problem behaviour and served to explain why the neighbours did not care and were without limits. Mrs Brown illustrates this lack of control by reference to an attack her neighbour carried out on a vulnerable individual:

> You're not talking normal human beings here, you're talking of alcoholics and drug addicts that go out, steal cars and do anything, they don't care. The woman next door actually went in somebody else's house, an old chap's house and punched him in the face, this disabled guy, so you're not talking normal human beings. (Mrs Brown)

Direct reference to 'good' and 'bad' people was common, particularly in relation to calls for exclusionary housing policies to separate the bad from the good:

> How many times do adults need to be told? If it was a child then fair enough; you could say we had to tell him a couple of times before they learned. This is an adult, these are adults, everyone can live civilised. Obviously they are not civilised, put them somewhere else with other uncivilised people. They build beautiful homes, and then they push shit in them. They think we will put shit in them, and then we will shove a couple of good people in with them, because they think the good people can revert the shit. It doesn't work like that. (Emma)

Where such groups outnumber the 'decent', 'normal' neighbours, the outnumbering was considered to constitute a threat to the community:

> The trouble is when the council put in people who are young, with drink or drug problems, when the council have put them all together, it feels like there are more of them than there are normal decent neighbours on the street. We are outnumbered like two to one. (Graham)

In the above excerpts binaries of 'us' and 'them' were used to describe 'bad' neighbours. Concepts of 'civilised' and 'uncivilised' were used to distinguish the interviewee from their neighbours. Neighbours' unwillingness to conform to neighbourly rules of conduct resulted in them being considered abnormal and legitimised the use of dehumanising labels such as 'shit'. Perpetrators were regarded as bringing the problem on themselves and therefore victims' and witnesses' desired solutions were based on removing such neighbours through either a prison sentence or eviction.

Whether the alleged ASB was perpetrated by children or not, interviewees also constructed their neighbours as living in dysfunctional families, or being deficient mothers unable to partake in the normative activities associated with being a parent:

> She is not a normal person, she's not what you call a married woman with responsibilities. (Mr Fisher)

> They wouldn't put the bin out because they didn't know day from night. The kids didn't go to school, they didn't work, so it was day and night. The kids could be playing out at 1.00am. The young twins, playing out at 1.00am. (Sarah)

Such constructions and assumptions direct the gaze and the focus of attention onto the 'problem neighbours' and their conduct. The problem is individualised. The construction of the problem reflects a belief that people are anti-social due to personal choice; they have opted for a dysfunctional lifestyle and deficient moral framework. Being the 'other' is self-inflicted, rather than a result of social circumstances.

Across private and public discourses

There are clearly differences in the way private and public ASB discourses are articulated. Political statements and speeches are carefully constructed with particular audiences in mind and will follow a particular linguistic style, albeit framed in a language that appears rational and akin to common sense (Jacobs et al, 2003). Despite these important articulatory differences, there are common defining features:

- ASB and neighbour nuisance is often associated with low-level incivilities such as noise, litter and smells; non-criminal conduct is better described as infringements of common-sense moral order and values.
- The perpetrators of these incivilities are described in stigmatising, demonising and dehumanising language. They are clearly the 'other', culturally different and constructed as feckless individuals who live by a different moral framework to the rest of 'normal', 'civilised' and 'law-abiding' society.
- There is an emphasis on dysfunctional families and bad parenting. Expressed more explicitly within official discourse than by witnesses, morally deficient families are attributed causal primacy in explaining the behaviour of young people. Bad mothers and their poor parenting in particular are invoked.

- Whether the cause of the problem is laid at the door of parents or the individual, it is always associated with individual failure as opposed to wider social circumstances (Brownlee, 1998; Gillies, 2005).

By reference to normalised codes of conduct, the problem is framed in terms of 'other' which, in turn, is used as justification for individualistic solutions that are often punitive and intolerant. Such measures have been critiqued widely as being problematic (Pitts, 2003; Brown, 2004; Gillies, 2004; Stephen and Squires, 2004). They are exclusionary and divisive and may, particularly in terms of youth nuisance, serve to preserve the conditions under which a growing number of people turn to crime. Bringing young perpetrators into the orbit of a disciplining and criminalising discourse is not only disproportionate and encourages a view of young people as dangerous predators and a problem to be dealt with (Hill and Wright, 2003), but as critics point out is also fundamentally criminogenic in nature (Muncie, 1999; Hoyle and Rose, 2001; Stephen and Squires, 2004).

Similarly, we would question whether low-level problems of environmental pollution and public order should be subsumed within a criminalising and demonising discourse and addressed through repressive, punitive legislation. As well as the problems identified above, zero tolerance approaches that prioritise an aggressive approach to low- and middle-order offending can serve to stimulate a taste in the public for punishment. And, once provoked, meeting the expectation that ever more offenders will be punished for minor infractions means putting at risk other forms of social spending of a kind more likely to impact on the structural correlates of crime as well as undercutting the viability of less punitive approaches (Brownlee, 1998).

Alongside punitive interventions there are now a raft of further measures designed to resocialise the dysfunctional family manifest in Parenting Orders, parenting classes and rehabilitative programmes (Gillies, 2005). As Pitts argues in relation to youth crime, such programmes may present themselves as new forms of rehabilitation but are essentially correctional in both intent and content:

> Whereas the rehabilitative techniques of the 1960s had aimed to ameliorate emotional and social deprivation, these newly disinterred rehabilitations aimed to restructure the modes of thought, the values, the attitudes and the behaviour of young offenders, the control strategies of their parents,

and the classroom regime presided over by their teachers.
(Pitts, 2003, p 181)

Laying the blame on parents is a populist approach that fails to take account of wider social circumstances, such as poverty, that make parenting far harder (Hill and Wright, 2003; Gillies, 2005). It is incisive that a majority of families defined as anti-social are headed by single mothers (Hunter and Nixon, 2001; Jones et al, 2004). By identifying causal primacy with the family the government is absolved of any further responsibility. The problem is never put in a social context or conceptualised as a manifestation of outcomes generated by wider economic, social and political forces (Gillies, 2005).

In both the official discourse of politicians and the private discourse of victims and witnesses, attention is focused exclusively on the 'problem neighbour'. The emerging consensus reinforces a viewpoint that the most effective responses are those aimed at the level of the individual. We now turn to the voices of those who have been labelled 'the neighbours from hell'.

The dissenting voices of the 'neighbours from hell'

Alongside authoritarian intervention, there is also an acknowledgement among community safety agencies of the need to mediate between individuals and to engage in holistic community development and empowerment strategies (Flint, 2002). Indeed, there has been a growing awareness among practitioners that many legal 'remedies' can have the perverse effect of simply displacing the problem behaviour from one locality to another (Hunter et al, 2003). More recently, drawing on the model of intensive intervention developed by the pioneering Dundee Families Project (Dillane et al, 2001), a small number of authorities have set up rehabilitation projects to work intensively with people at risk of losing their home as a result of ASB (the subject of Chapters Nine and Ten, this volume).

Our recent research with a sample of families supported by these projects (Nixon et al, 2005) found that rather than being 'feckless' 'undisciplined' individuals, families referred to the projects were characterised as a particularly vulnerable group, having high support needs particularly in relation to mental health problems and domestic violence. For most people, being labelled 'anti-social' simply served to reinforce a sense of unfairness, marginalisation and exclusion.

The reasons why families had been referred to the projects varied significantly and it is impossible to depict a 'typical' case. Reflecting witnesses' and political constructions of the nature of the problem, the type of complaints that had been made about family members varied widely from playing football in the street, hanging around shops, noise nuisance arising from shouting, music and arguments, through to disruptive visitors or tensions with neighbours and other local residents. The vast majority of complaints appeared to involve repetitive, 'low-level' nuisance behaviour although in a minority of cases behaviour complained about was serious and criminal in nature.

In some respects, alleged perpetrators' constructions of ASB were not so very different from those of witnesses and victims. Without exception, they found the experience of being labelled 'anti-social' to be 'humiliating', 'upsetting' and 'embarrassing'. The term was perceived to carry with it a host of negative connotations including being a bad parent, having out-of-control children and a disregard for neighbours. For these reasons people distanced themselves from the charge of being 'anti-social' and made clear distinctions between their own behaviour and their constructions of behaviour which could legitimately be described as anti-social:

> What I say's anti-social is like, say if like, a neighbour, neighbours have got disputes, so that your going onto their property shouting, screaming, banging doors, causing trouble and things like that…. If you are playing music really loud and things like that, fair enough, that is anti-social behaviour. But I know for a fact I don't do that. I won't expect someone to do it to me, so I don't do it to them. I expect to be treated the way I treat people. I always have, I were brought up like that. (Mary)

Many of the individuals disputed the legitimacy of either all or at least some of the claims being made against them. They reported that the behaviour being complained about either did not happen, was exaggerated or was simply behaviour that is common to many families. These perceptions engendered a strong sense of unfairness and it was common for people to describe feelings of being victimised and confused as to why they had been singled out as the target of complaints, as Teresa, a mother of three teenage children, explained:

> They're good kids. They've never been in trouble with the police ever. They do know right from wrong but I think when they are out with their friends they try and show off a bit, but they are just normal kids and they're not, they're

not really bad. I know they are not angels, no kids are but they're not as bad as half of them round here and I can't understand why it's us. I really can't. (Teresa)

I know they are no angels, I know that for a fact but like there's kids round here, really really, naughty kids that have got ASBOs against them. I know they have and then when we went to that meeting and they threatened them with an ASBO, I thought God you're putting my kids in the same category as that. They are nowhere near as bad as that, nowhere near. (Linda)

Stephen and Squires' work on contemporary constructs of marginalised youth illustrates the way in which judgements about appropriate behaviour are commonly made by reference to perceived norms of behaviour in a neighbourhood (Stephen and Squires, 2004). We also found that adults referred to support projects assessed the severity of behaviour, particularly the behaviour of their children, by reference to relative norms. They were aware of binary oppositions that are employed to distinguish the 'anti-social' from the 'responsible' neighbour and were anxious to affirm that they and their children conformed to norms of conduct.

The interviewees understood that when children were accused of being anti-social there was an implicit criticism of the adequacy of their parenting skills. While some individuals acknowledged that due to their own ill health, or their children's special needs, they found it difficult to manage their children's behaviour, they were rarely indifferent or disinterested and most expressed a desire to enhance their ability to cope. Some resisted such criticism, commonly reflecting on the failure of statutory agencies to address their children's special educational needs, while others stressed the impact of peer group pressure and referred to the importance of individual agency:

I used to blame myself and I thought 'Well no, why?'. You know, me other two children are fine, you know, it's just a shame he's got in with a bad crowd. But I am not blaming myself for it. (Nathalie)

In talking to families who had been labelled as 'anti-social' we became increasingly aware of the complex reality of ASB. Although government rhetoric makes clear distinctions between 'victims' and 'perpetrators', in practice these roles can be experienced interchangeably and no such objective categories actually exist (see Stephens and Squires, 2004). Rather than the dangerous 'other', some families told us how they too had been victims of other people's aggressive behaviour but too often when they tried to seek help from statutory agencies they reported that either they were not believed or no action was taken. The experience of not being heard was directly related to being labelled as anti-social and it was strongly felt by many families that once labelled no one would be prepared to hear their side of the story. These experiences left many families feeling further marginalised and powerless to defend themselves against the damaging consequences of the demonisation process.

Conclusion

What we have tried to illustrate in this chapter is the hegemonic nature of ASB discourses articulated, albeit in different ways, by different social groups. In Chapter One (this volume), John Flint describes how a coalition of central government, local authorities, community safety agencies and community representative organisations has been created to tackle ASB. Within this coalition the voices of 'victims' and politicians reinforce each other and at no point are the dissenting voices of alleged perpetrators considered.

Given the pervasive influence of the news media on political discourse and public opinion, it is not surprising perhaps that witnesses' and victims' portrayal of perpetrators shares a vocabulary of irresponsibility and stigmatisation. It does, however, highlight an interesting paradox inherent in New Labour's approach to ASB. The use of demonising images may serve to justify punitive action against offenders but when such images are internalised by victims, witnesses and perpetrators themselves, the result is a sense of powerlessness. In this context the government ASB polemic is likely to result in an increased unwillingness on the part of individuals to intervene. Rather than stimulate individuals to become active citizens contributing to the governance of communities in which they live, the political discourse may in practice engender further exclusions and divisions within already fragile communities.

References

Blunkett, D. (2003a) 'Tackling the Scourge of Anti-social Behaviour', Statement to the House of Commons, London.

Blunkett, D. (2003b) 'Blunkett's Yob Culture Purge', BBC News, 12 March.

Blunkett, D. (2003c) Speech to the National Neighbourhood Watch Association Conference, Nottingham, 22 March.

Brown, A. (2004) 'Anti-social Behaviour, Crime Control and Social Control', *Howard Journal of Criminal Justice*, vol 43, no 2, pp 203-11.

Brownlee, I. (1998) 'New Labour – New Penology? Punitive Rhetoric and the Limits of Managerialism in Criminal Justice Policy', *Journal of Law and Society*, vol 25, no 3, pp 313-35.

Cowan, D. (1998) 'Reforming the Homelessness Legislation', *Critical Social Policy*, vol 18, no 4, pp 435-64.

Cowan, D., Pantazis, C. and Gilroy, R. (2001) 'Social Housing as Crime Control: An Examination of the Role of Housing Management in Policing Sex Offenders', *Social and Legal Studies*, vol 10, no 4, pp 435-57.

Dillane, J., Hill, M., Bannister, J. and Scott, S. (2001) *Evaluation of the Dundee Families Project*, Edinburgh: Scottish Executive, Dundee City Council and NCH Action for Children.

Flint, J. (2002) 'Social Housing Agencies and the Governance of Anti-social Behaviour', *Housing Studies*, vol 17, no 4, pp 619-38.

Flint, J. and Rowlands, R. (2003) 'Commodification, Normalisation and Intervention: Cultural, Social and Symbolic Capital in Housing Consumption and Governance', *Journal of Housing and the Built Environment*, vol 18, no 3, pp 213-32.

Foucault, M. (1977) *Discipline and Punishment: The Birth of the Prison*, Harmondsworth: Penguin.

Foucault, M. (1991) 'Governmentality', in G. Burchell (ed) *The Foucault Effect: Studies in Governmentality*, Hemel Hempstead: Harvester Wheatsheaf, pp 87-104.

Gillies, V. (2005) 'Meeting Parents' Needs? Discourses of "Support" and "Inclusion" in Family Policy', *Critical Social Policy*, vol 25, no 1, pp 70-90.

Haworth, A. and Manzi, T. (1999) 'Managing the "Underclass": Interpreting the Moral Discourse of Housing Management', *Urban Studies*, vol 36, no 1, pp 153-66.

Hill, J. and Wright, G. (2003) 'Youth, Community Safety and the Paradox of Inclusion', *The Howard Journal of Criminal Justice*, vol 42, no 3, p 282.

Home Office (2003) *Respect and Responsibility: Taking a Stand Against Anti-social Behaviour*, London: Home Office.

Hoyle, C. and Rose, D. (2001) 'Labour, Law and Order', *Political Quarterly*, vol 72, no 1, pp 76-85.

Hunter, C. and Nixon, J. (2001) 'Taking the Blame and Losing the Home: Women and Anti-social Behaviour', *Journal of Social Welfare and Family Law*, vol 23, no 4, pp 395-410.

Hunter, C., Nixon, J. and Parr, S. (2004) *What Works for Victims and Witnesses of Anti-social Behaviour*, London: Home Office Antisocial Behaviour Unit.

Hunter, C., Nixon, J., Reeves, K. and Jones, A. (2003) *Tackling Anti-social Behaviour in Mixed Tenure Areas*, London: ODPM.

Jacobs, K., Kemeny, J. and Manzi, T. (2003) 'Power, Discursive Space and Institutional Practices in the Construction of Housing Problems', *Housing Studies*, vol 18, no 4, pp 429-46.

Jones, A., Pleace, N. and Quilgars, D. (2004) *Shelter Inclusion Project: Interim Evaluation of Findings*, London: The Housing Corporation and Shelter.

Morgan, R. (2005) 'Crime Czar: Stop Calling Children "Yobs"', *The Observer*, 22 May.

Muncie, J. (1999) *Youth and Crime: A Critical Introduction*, London: Sage Publications.

Nixon, J., Hunter, C., Myers, S., Parr, S., Sanderson, D. and Whittle, S. (2005) *An Interim Evaluation of 6 Intensive Support Projects*, London: ODPM.

Papps, P. (1998) 'Anti-social Behaviour Strategies – Individualistic or Holistic?', *Housing Studies*, vol 13, no 5, pp 639-56.

Pitts, J. (2003) *The New Politics of Youth Crime: Discipline or Solidarity?*, Luton: House Publishing.

Stephen, D. and Squires, P. (2004) 'They Are Still Children and Entitled To Be Children: Problematising the Institutionalised Mistrust of the Marginalised Youth in Britain', *Journal of Youth Studies*, vol 17, no 3, pp 351-69.

Stokoe, E. and Wallwork, J. (2003) 'Space Invaders: The Moral Spatial Order in Neighbourhood Dispute Discourses', *British Journal of Social Psychology*, vol 42, pp 551-69.

Wood, M. (2004) *Perceptions and Experiences of Anti-social Behaviour*, Home Office Findings 252, London: Home Office.

Young, J. (1999) *The Exclusive Society: Social Exclusion, Crime and Difference in Late Modernity*, London: Sage Publications.

FIVE

Spaces of discipline and control: the compounded citizenship of social renting

Rowland Atkinson

Introduction

Safety is now top of both the domestic and international political agendas. A recent edition of *The Economist* (5 February 2005) gave front-cover prominence to the issue of anti-social behaviour (ASB) in the UK and drew parallels between it and international terrorism. One result of the high profile given to the crime and ASB agendas has been an attempt to locate and tackle those spaces most strongly associated with these problems via increasingly punitive measures. The aim of this chapter is to consider the way that an unwinding of this agenda has focused on areas of social rented housing through the co-opting of residents of these areas as a means of tackling disorder. This connection, between poverty and ASB, can be seen in the key documents that set out the government's agenda:

> [ASB] includes a range of problems – noisy neighbours, abandoned cars, aggressive begging, vandalism, graffiti, litter and youth nuisance. It can hold back the *regeneration* of our most *disadvantaged areas*, creating the environment in which crime can take hold. (See www.homeoffice.gov.uk/anti-social-behaviour/ for the Home Office ASB web pages.)

This agenda is focused on areas in which social housing predominates where it has become a key space within which a wider social politics of conduct is being played out (Flint, 2002). In this latter sense housing is a site of disciplinary action wherein certain behaviours have been increasingly delimited within wider normative frameworks (Ellison and Burrows, 2004). The current agenda of enforcement, punitive sanctions and being tough on the symptoms of social problems and ASB have made residential areas the primary spaces of control under a mantle of community empowerment. This chapter seeks to examine these issues in the context of spatial aspects of control implied by current policy developments while trying to consider the social forces that have given rise to the social geography of ASB.

Constituting the geography of anti-social behaviour

How then is the geography of ASB constituted and represented? A piece in a recent edition of the *Daily Telegraph* offered an unusual, but illuminating, commentary on ASB. It described the summer gathering of the University of Oxford's Bullingdon Club at which heavy drinking had led to fighting in a pub cellar which was 'redecorated with clots of blood' (Mount, 2004). The club, comprising businessmen, lawyers, art historians and journalists, has been banned from within a 15-mile radius of Oxford ever since all 500 windows of a college there were smashed by club members in 1955. The behaviour at the pub was described as 'extreme playful joshing' with the violence taking on a 'polite skittish guise'. This highlights a focus in this chapter on the way that representation, context and social class have provided filters through which the agenda on ASB has been shaped.

In common with the 'downward-looking' gaze of much social policy research the focus of treatments of ASB has been with the poor, with social renting and the spaces where such groups and housing tenure are seen to conjoin. However, it is a largely affluent political body with a populist punitive mandate that is setting the tone of responses to what is called ASB. While the fights of the Bullingdon Club apparently represent the high jinks of respectable citizens-to-be, those which might be found in the pubs of 'sink estates' have become the prototypical behaviours of an underclass that is seen as having detached itself from the normative frames of reference that better-off neighbourhoods apparently choose to observe. I want to suggest here that the single-minded way in which this double-standard is enforced serves to stigmatise areas and groups of people whose problems continue to be found rooted in deeper socio-structural conditions which are not being addressed by the agenda created to deal with ASB.

Nevertheless, I want to make it clear that ASB is undoubtedly a more significant and entrenched problem in many areas and that this is often but by no means exclusively socially rented estates. While areas of private renting, student villages, shopping streets and night-time entertainment districts are often linked to problematic and 'anti-social' behaviour, as Pauline Card identifies in Chapter Two (this volume), it has been housing tenure that has dominated our understanding of the location of social problems (Lee and Murie, 1997; Lee, 1999) and its role in shaping responses to such problems. This is linked to an equivalence drawn between the dangers of crime, disorder and ASB and areas of social renting due to the tenure's social residualisation. The tenure has now become the primary political battleground on which attempts at the modification of behaviour and control of the unruly have become inextricably linked:

> Social housing has become a site of crime control because it has become a residual tenure for marginalised groups. Although crime is ubiquitous, anti-social behaviour is deemed to occur principally in social housing areas. This is partly for instrumental reasons – an attempt to solve the problem of low demand social housing by excluding undesirable applicants. But it is also part of the broader social control of marginalised populations who can be 'managed' in social housing. (Brown, 2004, p 204)

Social housing has, in other words, become both a site (estates and schemes) and process (socio-legal contracts of tenure) through which an urban poor are first concentrated, then managed and subsequently disciplined in line with the normative expectations of wider society given voice by a hostile, hysterical and sensationalist media. The concentration of poverty has served to contain problematic populations and helped to keep unacceptable behaviours spatially contained away from respectable and higher-income neighbourhoods (Ellison and Burrows, 2004). A stigmatised tenure and perceptions of the growth of problematic behaviour have fed off one another, exacerbated by sensationalist media coverage. In particular, our tenure profoundly affects the degree to which we may be subject to discipline by a range of institutions now charged with the management of those dwellings and the neighbourhoods they are located in. In areas of social housing there has been an increase in the burden of duties on residents required by landlords and central government in their attempts to reduce problems of disorder. The tentative development of this idea of compounded citizenship is explored later on in this chapter.

Old and new spaces of disciplinary control

Much analysis of the current state of social housing has been concerned with its social residualisation (Cole and Furbey, 1994; Malpass, 2003). That is to say, as the 'Right to Buy' has allowed more affluent tenants to purchase their properties a wider series of social changes, which have included the stigmatisation of social renting, have altered the relative social diversity of the tenure. The growing spatial concentration of social renting, increased proportions of the tenant base in conditions of benefit dependency and low environmental quality have been seen themselves as symptomatic of social problems, problem people and problematic areas which should be avoided where possible.

The loss of social diversity in areas of public rented housing has also increased challenges to local service providers where this loss has increased management costs (Cole and Goodchild, 2001). In particular these 'concentration effects' of poverty have also challenged the ability of the local state to provide an equitable and acceptable geographical distribution of basic services, some even arguing that key actors in deprived areas ration services, talk down to and otherwise actively manage residents (Lipsky, 1980).

These various factors have created pronounced differences in resident experiences of services and have created self-fulfilling prophecies attached to poor areas where low educational achievement, prevalent social problems and what some have seen as a deviant and disengaged community, operate outside the normative framework of 'ordinary' society (Murray, 1996), and which appear as both the result and cause of poverty. Without recourse to these particular arguments it should be acknowledged that areas of concentrated deprivation and the 'area effects' generated by them may hold back and negatively impact on the life-chances of their residents (Atkinson and Kintrea, 2004). However, a lazy logic often underpinning policy dealing with deprived areas has resulted in a punitive and flawed approach to the treatment of symptoms of deprivation and a continuation of blaming victims for their plight rather than dealing with the structural foundation of such problems.

While it is important not to stress the novelty of problems in areas of social renting or concentrated deprivation, a retrenchment of these relationships has ratcheted the chain connecting problematic behaviour and distinctive geography. The 'old' spaces of disciplinary control then were those areas of social housing which were linked to control by the state through the profession of housing management used to:

... gain intelligence upon, moralise and discipline the emergent working class. The purpose of these efforts was to secure the social reproduction of its labour power in ways compatible with both local and national capitalist power relations. (Damer, 2000, p 2010)

In such materialist analyses a key role of social housing was not only to provide shelter and welfare but also to systematise the surveillance, control and disciplining of the working class. Damer's vision of an older carceral, or disciplinary, tenure has now spread beyond the confines of social housing management and the earlier role of that tenure to a wider range of agents and an invigorated agenda of control which seeks to secure iconic non-residential city centres (Atkinson, 2003) as much as estates of social housing. However, even while these territories have been expanded (including to some extent other housing tenures; see Chapter Three, this volume) there has been a renewed vigour to policy interventions directed at deprived areas of social renting.

Consider first the increasing range of agents involved in policing ASB. Far from being the preserve of official agencies of law enforcement, we now see a proliferation of actors involved in dealing with ASB. These now include neighbourhood, street and city centre wardens, housing officers, private security personnel and professional witnesses. These actors also have at their disposal a greater range of sanctions which have both spatial and socio-legal underpinnings including Antisocial Behaviour Orders (ASBOs), curfews and eviction with which to curtail, 'educate' and punish the actions of those in areas of predominantly social housing. The range of institutions involved in what are now multi-actor and coordinated responses to ASB has also grown, with housing associations (increasingly taking on the role previously undertaken by local authorities), community groups and individual residents now called on to get involved in order to improve the quality of local neighbourhood life.

The second aspect of this extension of disciplinary activities is linked to the spatial territories on which a perceived battle is being enacted against ASB. While the focus of activity has been on areas of social housing, action is also linked to iconic city centre spaces, with the application of sanctions to beggars and prostitutes as well as aggressive binge drinkers, to say nothing of traveller communities in rural areas. Examples of this can be found in the use of local by-laws to eliminate behaviour which the street homeless find necessary (begging) as well as curfews directed at certain neighbourhoods and social groups, namely young people (Mitchell, 1997). These attempts at behavioural management and an extension of surveillance activities have increased the responsibilities of institutions and key actors as well as the residents of such apparently disorderly spaces. This expansion of scales of intervention can be linked to neoliberal discourses of city competitiveness and improvement where it has been seen as essential to remove the poor and minimise visible disorder to attract footloose capital (Wyly and Hammel, 2005). Much of this has come about in order to boost city fortunes, but has also been linked to the vengeful actions of local states employing law enforcement agencies, planning actions and housing programmes in ways which support the re-emergence of middle-class dominance of the daily affairs of the city (Smith, 1996).

All of this suggests a reframing of those spaces and social groups that are considered to be problematic. A widened and extended attempt to deal with ASB has appeared in which housing officers and other co-opted intermediaries (such as teachers and social workers) may be seen as agents of local control as well as the potentially vengeful and watchful emissaries of a local capitalist state. However, it is also essential to recognise that this rise in punitive actions is popular among the poor as well as middle-class and policy-making elites. Even within Damer's analysis of the control functions of housing factors (private property agents) one of his participants remarks: 'Oh he was quite a good chap, quite a good fellow. Especially he wouldn't allow anything happening in the scheme' (Damer, 2000, p 2021). Any answers may not therefore be as simple as some left-leaning commentators might suggest.

Social housing = trouble?

Current media treatment has become focused on areas of social housing as a spatial synonym for ASB. So closely linked are they that we seldom lack images of high-rise or badly maintained social housing as the backdrop to media reports on crime, ASB, child and domestic abuse and drug addiction among other social problems even when no specific location to these problems is given in reporting. The socialisation of policy makers is equally prone to such associations, evidenced in policy documents that have set out the government's agenda with regard to disorder in which a focus on deprivation is evident:

> ASB blights people's lives, destroys families and ruins communities. It holds back the regeneration of our

> *disadvantaged areas* and creates the environment in which crime can take hold. (Home Office, 2003, p 3, emphasis added)

and:

> Tackling anti-social behaviour is critical to our success in empowering deprived neighbourhoods and communities. (Home Office, 2003, p 64)

These areas and their communities have been cast as normatively different, even deficient, in their judgement of acceptable behaviour, thereby reinforcing the apparent normality of communities outside these regulated spaces. The kinds of connections between place, tenure, community and disorder set out above can be illustrated by the visual syntax of British policy documents on ASB which have set the tone, and legitimated the punitive character, of the interventions which have followed (see Figure 5.1 overleaf).

Neighbours from hell: containment and surveillance in poor neighbourhoods

So far I have argued that the increasing social residualisation of public housing has led to the concentration of problems that has led to a significant response to ASB and that this has also spilled over into central city spaces. The equivalence drawn by the wider mass media, the public and policy makers between social housing and such behaviour has led to a geographically targeted system of sanctions which ignores the more widespread foundation of such problems. An ecology of ASB is linked in recent policy documents to environmental triggers contained within deprived localities. The government's White Paper, *Respect and Responsibility* (Home Office, 2003) discusses spirals of ASB, linked to the broken windows thesis (Wilson and Kelling, 1982; see Matthews, 1992, for a critical discussion), and a wider loss of social control. Other cited causes are given, which include dysfunctional family behaviour, education (truancy), alcohol and drugs – all seen to cluster in areas of deprivation and social housing.

A clear example of the way that the government has theorised the connections between community and disorder can be seen in the deployment of neighbourhood wardens (see Adam Crawford's discussion in Chapter Eleven, this volume). Their role was conceived in terms of aiding crime prevention, improving local environments

Figure 5.1: The politicisation of fear. Cover of *Putting Our Communities First* (Scottish Executive, 2003)

and aiding the process of housing management. A fourth key aim was to facilitate community development. In other words, neighbourhood wardens would help build social cohesion which itself could provide the bonds needed to impose local sanctions, and create a climate of intolerance towards local problem behaviours. Within such actions the residents of deprived areas are seen as embattled locals struggling to deal with a disruptive minority and yet the subtext is that it is partially the fault of such local communities that such behaviour is allowed to occur in the first place. From these common-sense theories emerges one of the central aspects of community empowerment and control:

> This White Paper is about asking *communities* to enforce the *standards of behaviour* they want to see locally. (Home Office, 2003, p 16; emphasis added)

The underpinning logic appears to be that were communities to exhibit greater social cohesiveness and informal social controls, a wider climate of intolerance might be facilitated:

> ASB is a problem experienced at the local level and therefore requires effective action locally. This includes individuals, families, residents associations, community groups and also the public services. It is vital that the right people have the power, the authority and the support to tackle ASB. (Home Office, 2003, p 51)

However, as sociologists increasingly recognise, local social networks which might support such interventions are increasingly rare as social and geographical mobility has increased. Social networks are more often extra-local with both kin and friendship networks dispersed (Wellman, 1999; Delanty, 2003). These factors have commonly been used to understand crime and disorder but have been underutilised in the analysis of ASB.

Workplace insecurities, restructuring and a relative democratisation of personal autonomy through increased material wealth have led to a diminution in local social ties (Sennett, 1998). Middle-class communities are now in fact at the vanguard of significant qualitative changes to the way in which communities function and which are now having a significant impact on urban society. In fact, while effective local sanctions are seen by policy makers as key mechanisms for dealing with disorder they are undermined by the absence of strong local social networks. This applies to the majority of localities rather than just deprived areas, again suggesting a misdirection in policy focus. In a society that many commentators have suggested increasingly lacks social cohesion how can policies manufacture the unity required to deal with disorder and ASB?

Regardless of whether such social changes are good or bad, analysts have long argued that a decline in local social ties has been associated with disorder and the breakdown of local sanctions. As primary local social ties have declined, the possibility of implementing local informal sanctions has been curtailed. The 'Take a Stand' prizes, issued by the Home Office in recent years to citizens who have intervened or made a difference to local problems, apply this logic of communitarian sanctions as the basis for a reduction of disorder in many communities. However, this initiative is targeted at places in which even the mild reprimand of 'locals' or young people generates such profound fear (Atkinson and Flint, 2004) that it seems unlikely to be effective as part of a wider strategy of reducing ASB. It would seem to be the case that mechanisms of informal control have been severely challenged at the same time that policy makers see them as virtues to be upheld.

If policy diagnoses of 'the solution' appear problematic it is also evident that liberal treatments of ASB that have searched for its social roots contain deficiencies. These debates have often failed to acknowledge the profound effects arising from the links between the social residualisation and clustering of social housing and intergenerational poverty. These effects have been felt in areas where there have been qualitative shifts in attitudes to authority, fatalistic beliefs surrounding personal life-chances and problematic behaviour. These issues have often been under-examined in the European context where such analytical departure points are seen as blaming the victims of poverty. However, the ritual call-out and physical assault of firefighters in deprived areas, interneighbour aggression and territorial and intimidating youth behaviour suggest conduct connected to the ways in which we have simultaneously housed and contained poorer households. The recognition of such changes and the policy interventions required to challenge these problems are where consensus has broken down.

Neighbours from heaven? The disaffiliation of affluent neighbourhoods

It is not possible to discuss the problems of deprived areas without considering the wider impacts of residential choice and location by more affluent groups. A withdrawal of middle-income households from social housing has been part of the process of its residualisation. Equally, the provision of pockets of private new-build housing away from social housing reinforces existing patterns of segregation that emphasise the social distinction between areas. Implicated in the patterns of isolation and stigmatisation of social housing has been the increasing ghettoisation of the affluent.

Aspirations to secure housing and the control conferred by privacy and spatial isolation may be viewed as part of a wider strategy seen in its most extreme form in the growth of gated communities in the UK, as outlined by Sarah Blandy in Chapter Twelve (this volume). The banding together of homeowners and higher-income groups may also be interpreted as part of a wider tactic to exert control over disorder by maintaining a maximum social and physical distance from areas viewed as problematic. Affluence not only confers a thinning of the risk factors and social problems concentrated in deprived areas, but also layers additional risks onto less wealthy neighbourhoods (see Hope, 2000).

All of this forms part of what we may consider to be a socio-spatial contract between residential areas of differing social status (Atkinson and Blandy, 2005). Responsibility for security is mediated by the local state to provide protection from ASB and crime, but this often breaks down in practice in relation to the social geography and increasingly different expectations placed on areas of differing social status. In countries like South Africa the breakdown of this spatial contract can be seen where gated communities create bubbles of safety for their residents while displacing crime to adjacent poor areas. The links between deprived and affluent areas can also be seen through the fears identified by writers such as Low (2003), who have shown that the apparent security conferred by gated communities is counter-intuitively associated with anxieties linked to personal safety. Maher (2003) has also suggested that residents of affluent gated communities in the US are fearful of the poorer service personnel employed in their estates and their social connections to more deprived areas nearby.

As more affluent groups attempt to find security we seem to find a shunting of problems onto more deprived areas. This suggests that affluent residential areas are not unproblematic spaces. They are connected to other areas in a number of ways – through the local state and its mediated distribution of access to security, environmental services and housing, through the displacement of risk to other neighbourhoods and through a voice amplified by the media which calls for the civilising of spaces deemed to be a threat.

The compounded citizenship of social renting

A policy focus on the most deprived areas connects with much of the geography of social housing in the UK. Just as public housing has been seen as a social good to which access and continued enjoyment were predicated on acceptable behaviours, these principles have been extended. Being poor increasingly means residence in an area in which surveillance is high, sanctions extended, curfews perhaps enforced, participation in partnerships to improve the area expected, and behaviour thereby regulated. This only serves to extend the negative imagery of social renting which is regularly broadcast back to a wider society that responds by stigmatising the residents of deprived areas even further (Hastings and Dean, 2000).

As has been argued here, living in a deprived area brings with it a greater range of risks of intrusion from unwanted social problems. However, with the increasing range of actors and policies involved in bringing order, the process of co-opting local residents within deprived areas that Flint describes in the opening chapter to this volume is leading to an increase in the range of responsibilities and efforts required to achieve lifestyles deemed ordinary or acceptable by a wider citizenry. In this sense we can identify a *compounded form of citizenship* in which the duties of the state have declined (Rose, 1996), but where the residents of deprived areas have to work much harder to attain a sense of normality or reduction in local social problems supported and stage-managed by current policy action on disorder and ASB. This has set about:

> ... improving the quality of life of residents by fostering community spirit...and raising confidence and self-esteem....We want to encourage *their* efforts. (SEU, 2002, p 9; emphasis added)

Areas of concentrated deprivation potentially overload agencies of formal social control, leading to requirements by the central state for their residents to become more active in attempting to achieve crime-free neighbourhoods. In contrast, those on moderate incomes remain free to exercise locational choices whereby they are not required to join community partnerships to ensure good policing and services, are not expected to use community facilities to encourage community spirit nor are they even expected to face down direct challenges to social order in their own neighbourhood. In this sense rights are diminished and responsibilities accentuated in those neighbourhoods where we tend to find greater levels of ASB.

In the context of current policy on ASB the terms 'local' and 'community' are, in effect, references to deprived households in deprived areas, now written in as their own saviours and empowered by new structures of governance created to enable residents to take charge and make their own lives better. I have argued that wider changes in social mobility, affiliation and group identity are in fundamental conflict with this communitarian policy drive and the authoritarian response of the UK government in its attempt to tackle disorder. Aspirations to generate modes of informal social control that rely on high levels of social cohesion are unlikely to be found either in areas of high poverty (often with high population turnover and paralysing fears of intervening) or affluent areas (where social ties are primarily non-local and problems are low). Nevertheless, the residents of both aspire towards lives of relative safety from intrusion by neighbours, anti-social or otherwise.

As public service budgets have diminished the local presence of public officials in most neighbourhoods (such as park attendants, beat police officers, firefighters and doctors), the relative coherence of daily social life has been transformed, expressing a loss of belief in deprived areas. Cities like Chicago in the US have tried to challenge these changes by compelling police officers at least to live within the city boundary, and Kathy Arthurson and Keith Jacobs describe an interesting variation of this in Australia in Chapter Thirteen (this volume). In the UK local housing officers provide often poorly maintained bridges into deprived areas by public service providers. We also find that housing professionals sometimes choose to minimise contact with anti-social or problematic tenants, or teachers avoid pupils, by locating home away from workspaces of relative risk. For many public service professionals then, a separation of residential and work activities is important but the effect is also a perception of a loss of faith in such localities.

We might also take the example of postal workers who now work in the UK for an organisation whose public esteem has dropped significantly. Postal workers are often casually employed while growing rates of staff turnover have impacted on previously stable connections between themselves and residents. In no small way the presence of such uniformed personnel helped to create absent ties (Granovetter, 1972) which played roles of minor authority as eyes on the street monitoring the presence of older people, the vulnerable and so on. An increasing institutional 'thinness' in deprived areas and an absence of regular and legitimate authority remains unaddressed in current strategies on ASB.

What is needed is a demonstrable conviction in more deprived neighbourhoods by policy makers and public service professionals to bridge the legitimacy gap created by public policy mantras which demand that 'communities' take a stand, just as their public services and servants leave them. Activist academics like Holman (1998) have consistently argued the need for greater confidence in deprived areas, while others have seen that some form of caretaking is an essential part of delivering self-esteem through environmental amenity and maintenance (Mumford and Power, 2003). Arguments have also been made that the police need to remodel local stations often seen as user-unfriendly by many communities (Rogers and Houston, 2004). One might even suggest that these policy responses betray a deep-seated feeling that these are spaces of last resort and emergency social management beyond hope of reclamation.

What does this do for our understanding of policy linked to disorder and ASB? ASB has been seen primarily as a public housing and community issue. However, if the issue is linked to the spatial distribution of inequalities it is possible to see wider urban, housing and planning policies as important tools in dealing with ASB. A commitment to social diversity as an element of sustainability but also as a platform for reducing the kind of concentration effects discussed here is surely essential as a means of reducing the socio-environmental preconditions for behaviours now widely seen as problematic. Critically, continuing socio-spatial segregation dilutes social diversity and creates additional pressures on both local social institutions and those residents seen as 'part of the solution'. The means by which social and private housing development is provided and integrated is therefore an essential component of wider policies aiming to deliver sustainable neighbourhood units in which social diversity is vital to achieving relative immunity from local and concentrated patterns of disorder. Policy responses built on understandings of the cultures of neighbourhoods remain deficient in their understanding of the causes of many problems of ASB that are now seen as being part of impaired connections and lax local normative frameworks. This has resulted in a punitive and incrementally criminalising approach to ASB that is unlikely to be effective, except in its demonisation of ever-younger groups.

In particular we can examine the discretionary use of ASBOs (see Chapter Six, this volume). Between 1 April 1999 to 30 June 2004, 2,955 ASBOs were served (only 42 were refused), but this belies a wide range in the distribution of their usage, from 11 in Lincolnshire and Wiltshire to 509 in Greater Manchester. Explanations that this might be linked to relative levels of urbanisation or deprivation are unable to account for the extremity of this skewed distribution given that Greater London issued approximately half the number of ASBOs

(268) issued in Greater Manchester over the same period, similar also to the number for West Yorkshire (247). More importantly the civil injunction itself provides grounds for imprisonment if breached so that the National Association of Prison Officers has become alarmed at increasing rates of incarceration, particularly of young people, through the use of ASBOs in what it sees as a 'geographical lottery'. This serves to reiterate the point that where we live and our housing tenure critically affects how we are told how to behave, how we are monitored and also our relative experience of disorder and ASB to which current policies seem ill equipped to deliver anything more than short-term gains.

Conclusion

Public housing management is only one strand of public services, institutions, social controls and a wider normative fabric that may provide a community with resources to deal with disorder and ASB. Moral panic surrounding disorder has traditionally been located in areas of social housing and dealt with formally by the police and more subtly by the actions of housing managers who, it has been argued, were also there to discipline as well as house the urban poor. However, in the course of a residualisation of social housing and in the transformation of its management there has been a growing geographical concentration of the worst-off living in the poorest environmental conditions and in a housing tenure which has itself become stigmatised. As media treatments of deprived areas have increasingly created an equation between danger, poverty and social renting these sites have become places of profound public anxiety, not least for the bulk of their residents who have been portrayed contradictorily as both the means by which problem behaviours are created and challenged. It is in these places that there has been a retrenchment of action against ASB by a proliferation of institutional actors.

The widely observed and perhaps indisputable growth in impunity appears to be linked to wider sociological changes in a society characterised by geographical hyper-mobility which has broken down local connectivity and cohesion that previously created a fabric of mutual support, codes of conduct and responsibility – even if these were not the panacea that some might now claim. Aspirations towards the control of disorder have increasingly stressed the need for communities to become involved even while residents in these areas express their deep unease at exerting the kinds of informal social control and moral co-opting that the government now seeks to promote. More importantly public solutions to disorder have attacked symptomatic disaffiliation with punitive sanctions rather than looking for the social forces that have seen these problems grow.

Public policy has seen social housing as a site incapable of dealing with behavioural and environmental problems that have led to subsequent impunity and a breakdown in social cohesion. In this chapter it has been suggested that this has led to action directed at socially rented estates as well as the involvement of a significantly extended family of key actors involved in disciplining spaces of deprivation and, by association, social renting. This has also led to an increasing burden of responsibilities falling on the residents of deprived areas in order to live a 'normal' life, termed here 'compounded citizenship'. Where we live may determine not only our experience of social problems but also the degree to which public policy exhortations are made urging us towards action, participation, intervention and partnership within new informal and formal agencies of control. Whether or not such policy diagnoses will ultimately resolve these problems, rather than displacing or deferring them, remains to be seen.

References

Atkinson, R. (2003) 'Domestication by Cappuccino or a Revenge on Urban Space? Control and Empowerment in the Management of Public Spaces', *Urban Studies*, vol 40, no 9, pp 1211-45.

Atkinson, R. and Blandy, S. (2005) 'The New Enclavism and the Contractual Neighbourhood: The Search for Security and the Rise of Gated communities', *Housing Studies*, vol 20, no 2, pp 177-86.

Atkinson, R. and Flint, J. (2004) 'Order Born of Chaos? The Capacity for Informal Social Control in Disempowered and "Disorganised" neighbourhoods', *Policy & Politics*, vol 32, no 3, pp 333-50.

Atkinson, R. and Kintrea, K. (2004) '"Opportunities and Despair, It's All In There": Practitioner Experiences and Explanations of Area Effects and Life Chances', *Sociology*, vol 38, no 3, pp 437-55.

Brown, A.P. (2004) 'Anti-social Behaviour, Crime Control and Social Control', *Howard Journal of Criminal Justice*, vol 43, no 2, pp 203-11.

Cole, I. and Furbey, R. (1994) *The Eclipse of Council Housing*, London: Routledge and Kegan Paul.

Cole, I. and Goodchild, B. (2001) 'Social Mix and the "Balanced Community" in British Housing Policy – A Tale of Two Epochs', *GeoJournal*, vol 51, pp 351-60.

Damer, S. (2000) '"Engineers of the Human Machine": The Social Practice of Council Housing Management in Glasgow, 1895-1939', *Urban Studies*, vol 37, no 11, pp 2007-26.

Delanty, G. (2003) *Community*, London: Routledge.

Ellison, N. and Burrows, R. (2004) 'Citizenship, Exclusion and the Politics of Fear', Unpublished working paper.

Flint, J. (2002) 'Social Housing Agencies and the Governance of Anti-Social Behaviour', *Housing Studies*, vol 17, no 4, pp 619-38.

Granovetter, M. (1972) 'The Strength of Weak Ties', *American Journal of Sociology*, vol 78, no 6, pp 1360-80.

Hastings, A. and Dean, J. (2000) *Challenging Images: Housing Estates, Stigma and Regeneration*, Bristol/York: The Policy Press/Joseph Rowntree Foundation.

Holman, B. (1998) *Faith in the Poor*, Oxford: Lion Publishing.

Home Office (2003) *Respect and Responsibility: Taking a Stand Against Anti-Social Behaviour*, London: Home Office.

Hope, T. (2000) 'Inequality and the Clubbing of Private Security', in T. Hope and R. Sparks (eds) *Crime, Risk and Inequality*, London: Routledge, pp 83-106.

Lee, P. (1999) 'Where Are the Socially Excluded? Continuing Debates in the Identification of Poor Neighbourhoods', *Regional Studies*, vol 33, no 5, pp 483-6.

Lee, P. and Murie, A. (1997) *Poverty, Housing Tenure and Social Exclusion*, Bristol: The Policy Press.

Lipsky, M. (1980) *Street-level Bureaucracy: Dilemmas of the Individual in Public Services*, New York, NY: Russell Sage Foundation.

Low, S. (2003) *Behind the Gates: Life, Security, and the Pursuit of Happiness in Fortress America*, London: Routledge.

Maher, K.H. (2003) 'Workers and Strangers: The Household Service Economy and the Landscape of Suburban Fear', *Urban Affairs Review*, vol 38, no 6, pp 751-86.

Malpass, P. (2003) 'The Wobbly Pillar? Housing and the British Postwar Welfare State', *Journal of Social Policy*, vol 32, no 4, pp 589-606.

Matthews, R. (1992) 'Replacing Broken Windows: Crime, Incivilities and Urban Change', in R. Matthews and J. Young (eds) *Issues in Realist Criminology*, London: Sage Publications, pp 19-50.

Mitchell, D. (1997) 'The Annihilation of Space by Law: The Roots and Implications of Anti-Homeless Laws in the United States', *Antipode*, vol 29, no 3, pp 303-35.

Mount, H. (2004) 'A Smashing Time Was Had By All When We Earned "Blue" for Drinking', *The Daily Telegraph*, 4 December.

Mumford, K. and Power, A. (2003) *East Enders: Family and Community in East London*, Bristol: The Policy Press.

Murray, C. (1996) 'The Emerging British Underclass', in R. Lister (ed) *Charles Murray and the Underclass: The Developing Debate*, London: Institute for Economic Affairs, pp 23-52.

Rogers, B. and Houston, T. (2004) *Re-Inventing the Police Station: Police–Public Relations, Reassurance and the Future of the Police Estate*, London: Institute for Public Policy Research.

Rose, N. (1996) 'The Death of the Social? Refiguring the Territory of Government', *Economy and Society*, vol 25, no 3, pp 327-56.

Sennett, R. (1998) *The Corrosion of Character: The Personal Consequences of Work in the New Capitalism*, London: W.W. Norton.

SEU (Social Exclusion Unit) (2002) *Neighbourhood Wardens*, Policy Action Team 6, London: SEU.

Smith, N. (1996) *The New Urban Frontier: Gentrification and the Revanchist City*, London: Routledge.

Wellman, B. (1999) *Networks in the Global Village*, Boulder, CO: Westview Press.

Wilson, J.Q. and Kelling, G.L. (1982) 'Broken Windows', *Atlantic Monthly*, vol 249, no 3, March, pp 29-38.

Wyly, E. and Hammel, D. (2005) 'Mapping Neo-liberal American Urbanism', in R. Atkinson and G. Bridge (eds) *Gentrification in a Global Context: The New Urban Colonialism*, London: Routledge, pp 18-38.

Part 2
Legal techniques and measures utilised by social landlords to address anti-social behaviour

SIX

Tenancy agreements: a mechanism for governing anti-social behaviour?

Diane Lister

Introduction

> It must be said that law's ideals must always appear attainable, yet law must always appear an idealised form of social relations, not a replication of actually existing ones. (Cotterrell, 1992, p 172)

This chapter focuses on 'the oldest, most common ... of contractual relations' (Englander, 1983, p 4), the relationship between landlord and tenant, and explores whether there is scope for tenancy agreements, as an embodiment of the legal relationship between contracting parties, to be used more effectively as a management tool to contribute towards preventing and controlling anti-social behaviour (ASB).

The above quote by Cotterrell, highlighting the prominent distinctions between ideals of legal behaviour and actual social relations, seems highly appropriate to introduce a discussion about the role of the law as embodied in tenancy agreements shaping behaviour. This theme is explored throughout this chapter and links to Helen Carr and Dave Cowan's discussion in Chapter Three (this volume) of how interpretations of legislation and legal rhetoric shape the conceptualisation of ASB. This chapter revisits the landlord–tenant relationship where traditionally breaches of covenants in tenancy agreements were dealt with through the mechanisms of contract and property law, and explores the role and use of tenancy agreements as a device to control behaviour. Theoretical perspectives about the limitations of the law in influencing individual behaviour are acknowledged and discussed. Evidence from empirical research about the ways in which landlords and tenants use tenancy agreements is drawn on, and in the light of the findings, the chapter discusses the extent to which the process of setting up the tenancy can be used actively and constructively to ensure that chosen lifestyles do not infringe the covenants that have been signed up to. In this sense, control and prevention of ASB in a civil law context are explored rather than disciplinary procedures and sanctions.

Legal mechanisms and individual behaviour

This chapter highlights the difficulties in assuming that individuals are aware of the role of the legal framework in influencing their behaviour, and argues that a more proactive approach on the part of landlords at the initial stages of the tenancy, and if appropriate, throughout, may have a more positive impact on tenant behaviour than legislation and the threat of sanctions as embodied in tenancy agreements. It is argued here that the increased contractualisation of landlord–tenant and tenant–neighbour relationships via, for example, 'good neighbour agreements' and Antisocial Behaviour Orders (ASBOs) may have a limited impact on behavioural outcomes given the limitations of the law. Furthermore, in discussions about ASB, the role of the landlord and the law in regulating the conduct of tenants often only seems to be significant once tenants behave in an anti-social manner and enforcement action is required to remedy the breach. The contemporary agenda of zero tolerance and enforcement appears to overlook the relevance and often unacknowledged success of preventative measures and more focused management techniques, such as mediation and tenancy support to control and/or avoid the incidence of ASB (see, for example, Papps, 1998; Atkinson et al, 2001; Hunter and Nixon, 2001), notwithstanding that, as Rowland Atkinson points out in Chapter Five (this volume), the impacts of ASB are significant and no one should have to tolerate ASB, low-level criminality or live in fear.

Although 'risk' theorists have argued that through the process of 'reflexivity' (Giddens, 1991; Beck, 1992) individuals in late modernity have become adept at dealing with uncertainty in everyday life by adopting rational behaviour and making informed decisions based on perfect knowledge, many people do not behave, or are unable to behave, in an instrumental fashion or according to legal prescriptions as they lack the cultural, social, psychological and material resources to compile knowledge and make informed choices (Portes, 1998; Lupton, 1999). As Anwen Jones et al's study of the Shelter Inclusion Project in Rochdale in Chapter Nine (this volume) vividly illustrates, recognition of the often complex care and support needs of individuals is increasingly important given the youthfulness and vulnerability of many tenants embarking on independent living in the private and social rented sectors, who may be leaving foster care, children's homes and Young Offenders Institutions or prison, and may be ill equipped to deal with their housing and personal circumstances (see also Rhodes and Bevan, 1997; Broad, 1998; Quilgars and Pleace, 1999).

Following on from this, concerns have recently been expressed about the increased use of ASBOs. As Caroline Hunter (Chapter Seven, this volume) demonstrates, since ASBOs were introduced in the 1998 Crime and Disorder Act their use has significantly escalated. A recent report by the probation union (The Trade Union and Professional Association for Family Court and Probation Staff) found that during the first eight months after their introduction in 1999 only 104 Orders were made but since November 2003 more than 2,600 Orders have been made (www.napo.org.uk). However, their escalation in use is only one dimension of the picture. There is also evidence to suggest that ASBOs are being used inappropriately in some circumstances and that individuals are receiving a custodial sentence where the original offence was not punishable by prison. In addition, evidence is emerging that most people subjected to ASBOs are either mentally ill, have problems with drugs or alcohol or have a learning difficulty (*Howard League Magazine*, 2005, p 2). In these circumstances, treatment and support to address the underlying causes of ASB would be a useful response. However, solutions of this type of practical nature are either unavailable, complex to deliver, often involving a number of agencies, or simply not provided, frequently resulting in deteriorating behaviour, breach of the ASBO and eviction or custodial sentences. This situation is aptly described by Rod Morgan, chair of the Youth Justice Board:

> Rather than being regarded as a victory for neighbours or communities blighted by nuisance behaviour, ASBOs should be seen as a failure by agencies to stop anti-social behaviour escalating to such intolerable levels. (*Howard League Magazine*, 2005, p 14)

ASBOs are issued after a breach of terms of a tenancy agreement and follow a similar, if more stringent, line to tenancy agreements in a contractual sense (see below for a more detailed discussion). An ASBO, as its name suggests, is a written Order from the court for an individual to behave, or refrain from behaving, in a particular manner, rather than an agreement between parties based on trust. The Order can also contain explicit instructions that restrict an individual from being in a particular area or neighbourhood. This is usually the case where the incidence of ASB has been in a distinct public area, for example, around local shops. A breach of the Order results in the implementation of sanctions to remedy the breach and can include imprisonment depending on the nature of the original offences. Although ASBOs were introduced as a response to distressing behaviour and to preserve community safety and the quality of life of those affected by ASB, there seem to be few effective routine measures or initiatives available at the outset of a standard tenancy (with the exception of Supporting People, where social sector tenants may benefit), to identify whether tenants have any particular needs which, if not addressed, would result in them being at risk of behaving in an anti-social manner.

The contractual relationship between landlord and tenant

Traditionally, the contractual relationship between landlord and tenant is enshrined in the use of a tenancy agreement or lease that embodies legal principles and each party's rights and obligations. The tenancy agreement is a legally binding reciprocal agreement based on classical liberal assumptions that contracting parties enter into relationships as equals and freely negotiate the terms of arrangements to their mutual satisfaction. In broad legal terms, tenancy agreements are used to manage uncertainty and risk while also enhancing the predictability of each party's behaviour in their social and economic exchanges. In a basic sense 'contracts are at one extreme of trust' (Baier, 1986, p 248), and their purpose is to foster agreement between the parties where they have no previous knowledge of each other. They are designed to make life less uncertain by engendering rational expectations about acceptable behaviour and invoking confidence in the parties that obligations will be fulfilled as part of a limited commitment, and, if not, explicit terms and sanctions for non-compliance can be invoked.

In current relationships between landlords and tenants, the tenancy agreement has a dual function. Firstly, and of practical importance, relevant legislation is reduced to the contractual form of the tenancy agreement. In this way complex issues are simplified and routinised, often into standardised forms, expressly embodying some of the legal rights and obligations pertaining to the relationship. The agreement is often regarded by both parties as the main or only legal aspect of the relationship, with the parties often assuming that all of the legal provisions relevant to their conduct are embodied within the document

(Lister, 2002). This may be the closest the parties come to engaging with the legal framework which they rely on to uphold their rights.

Secondly, the tenancy agreement is a written source of information for both parties about their rights and responsibilities pertaining to the relationship. In terms of managing uncertainty and risk, tenancy agreements imply different levels of trust and mistrust depending on the wording used, how onerous the terms are, whether the agreement is standardised or negotiated and individualised, and the vagueness or comprehensiveness of the contents. In the social rented sector a variety of agreements exist across local authorities and in the private rented sector a range of 'off the shelf' agreements are widely available from stationers as well as those negotiated and individually drafted. The main distinctions hinge on whether they are 'complete' – covering, as far as possible, a wide range of contingencies – or 'incomplete' and vague, and whether they are 'explicit' or 'implicit' with unspecified obligations emerging as a feature of relationships over the course of time (Mackintosh, 2000, p 3; Collins, 2002, p 140). Although the tenancy agreement may provide a common central basis for relationships between contracting parties, even if negotiated, it does not often provide the basis of a common or shared understanding of the relationship as a whole. It cannot be presupposed that an agreement provides a blueprint for the effective regulation of the behaviour of the parties.

In practice, the terms of tenancy agreements are 'interpreted and used' (Mason, 1991, p 103) in social contexts by the individuals whose behaviour they are designed to regulate. The effectiveness of tenancy agreements in controlling individual behaviour is dependent on the extent to which individuals engage with them, their perceptions and (mis)understandings of them and whether or not they assign the law a significant role. As a result there is considerable scope for a 'gap' to develop between the intentions of the law to promote legal ideals in behaviour and actual behaviour depending on the ways in which tenancy agreements are 'interpreted and used', if at all:

> ... there is a considerable gap between the law and actual practice.... This does not mean that the law has no relevance.... But the law is only one factor ... and it may not be the most important one. (Harloe, 1985, p 380)

In this sense the law provides an atmosphere, rather than a regime, in which to influence behaviour and has a limited impact (see below). In addition, individuals do not always perceive or interpret the issues they are confronted with as legal issues given that for most people their experience of the law is remote, acting only as a backdrop to social relations (see, for example, Conley and O'Barr, 1990, p 58).

Anti-social behaviour and contractual relationships

The tenancy agreement has traditionally been the focus of the landlord–tenant relationship from which remedies and sanctions for breaches of covenant emanate. For example, the traditional standard clauses relating to 'un-tenant like' behaviour or what is now defined as ASB are by causing 'noise or nuisance' or using 'the premises for immoral or illegal purposes', and the onus is on the landlord to take action and serve a Notice of Seeking Possession (NSP) on the tenant and take any further action through the courts if the breach continues. This attaches the breach of covenant or ASB within the contractual context of the landlord–tenant relationship even if the perpetrator is not a party to the tenancy agreement, is a visitor to the property, or is a child. In addition, such behaviour is placed within the distinct locale of a domestic setting, notwithstanding that misconduct may be in the surrounding area and not in the home and may adversely affect only third parties, that is, neighbours and those in the locality, and not the landlords themselves. This focus on the home renders ASB the concern of both landlords and neighbours. Moreover, the licensing of private landlords also places stringent duties on them to deal with the ASB of their tenants. These issues of balancing the interests of occupiers and third parties with those of the landlord are important in relation to ASB and also highlight the distinct 'hybrid nature' (Bright and Gilbert, 1995, p 69) of a contract in a property relationship, where conceptual difficulties arise between the interpretation of a tenancy agreement as a contract for property and services which the landlord must provide over the duration of the tenancy, and the proprietary nature of the agreement where the ongoing relationship between landlord and tenant is often considered to be largely unimportant. In terms of the remedies and enforcement measures available for ASB, agreements have generally been interpreted from a contractual perspective with the stress on intervention and the ongoing nature of the relationship, with the ultimate sanction, and physical and emotional costs, of loss of home or being compelled to stay away from it.

In recent years there has been a concentrated move towards the intense contractualisation of social relations (as explored in Chapters One and Three, this volume), particularly with regard to neighbourliness. This 'commodification' of social life where neighbourly relations are subject to contract is not confined to leasehold property but also to freehold where it is prominent in affluent developments. As Sarah Blandy describes in Chapter Twelve (this volume), these include gated residential developments, where residents sign up to a stringent code of conduct as a safeguard against the behaviour of fellow residents and to regulate their own behaviour (see also Blandy and Lister, 2005). Similarly, many local authorities in response to ASB have recently introduced a 'good neighbour agreement', with stringent conditions about noise, nuisance, the behaviour of children, visitors and pets, conditions of gardens and communal areas and untaxed or unroadworthy vehicles and their repair. These agreements exist alongside the tenancy agreement forming a separate and discrete contract *solely* relating to the prevention and management of ASB. These agreements also transcend the boundaries of the landlord–tenant relationship by extending the spatial context of the right to 'quiet enjoyment' of the home to include the wider neighbourhood and community as well as having the underlying aim of enhancing community safety and maintaining community stability.

'Good neighbour agreements' compel tenants to form a contract with landlords and also to form a promise with neighbours and the community to respect the terms of the agreement. They provide a way of enmeshing landlord and tenant in a legal relationship but also enmeshing neighbours into a formalised cohesive social arrangement, where previously the ability of the parties to trust each other to continually fulfil unspecified obligations would have formed a fundamental feature of community life and social exchange (see, for example, Young and Wilmott, 1957; Hoggart, 1958; Blau, 1964; Molm, 1997). Such interventions into community life by local authorities via the contractualisation of traditional relationships highlights a fundamental shift towards social control in the absence of trust and legitimate expectations among neighbours, in addition to the breakdown of cohesive associative interactions in communities, which Rowland Atkinson outlines in Chapter Five (this volume). Fragmentation, risk and weak ties in neighbourhood and social groups have become the norm (see, for example, Albrow, 1997; Beck, 1997; Crow et al, 2002), and individuals now form part of a 'community of strangers' where relationships, rather than based on status, are now based on voluntary, specific and limited contracts (Cotterrell, 1992, p 119). Third-party promises to bind individuals together who live in close proximity to each other resist claims for social solidarity and emphasise social relations as a network of contractual opportunities that each individual has the capacity to accept or reject.

Limitations of the law in influencing behaviour

In attempting to influence and regulate behaviour, as illustrated in the quote by Cotterrell at the beginning of this chapter, the law sets high ideals, prescribing objective conditions and standards of conduct which are universal in their application to individuals. Legislation is designed to curb instinctual and excessive behaviour by providing sanctions and a right to redress if either party crosses a legally unacceptable boundary. Legislation therefore prescribes the 'condition of civil association' (Rousseau, 1968, p xxiv) where individuals are forced to override their 'natural liberty' in order to gain their 'civil liberty':

> The passage from the state of nature to the civil state produces a very remarkable change in man, by substituting justice for instinct in his conduct and giving his actions the morality they had formerly lacked. (Rousseau, 1968, p 15)

In applying the role of legislation to landlord–tenant relationships and the prevention and control of ASB, its purposes are twofold. Firstly, legislation defines the limits or sets boundaries within which relationships should function and, secondly, it provides each party, in theory, with a set of rights and responsibilities that operate within the context of the relationship. The imposition of behavioural boundaries and restrictions is part of the civilising effect of legislation as described above. However, the progression 'from the state of nature to the civil state' is reliant on an individual's access to, and requisite knowledge of, the legal framework and the limits of legal boundaries that apply to their circumstances. If individuals do not possess requisite knowledge, then instinctual behaviour is likely to prevail over the civil state. Moreover, even if individuals possess the requisite knowledge, there is no guarantee that they will behave according to the law. Dissemination of information about sanctions and modes of redress for unlawful behaviour, particularly criminal behaviour, is common; however, relatively little information is available or easily accessible about rights and responsibilities and guidelines in relation to appropriate civil behaviour. This highlights that the law does not perform an informative role and as a result no account is taken of individuals' (lack of) knowledge of the law or its acquisition in relation to this civilising process. Nor is the role or responsibility of the legal system in disseminating information to the parties that it seeks to regulate questioned, notwithstanding that legal knowledge plays a key role for individuals in acquiring and asserting rights.

In order to legitimise the civilising effect of the law on behaviour, the law operates according to an implicit, often unacknowledged, assumption that individuals have perfect knowledge and understanding of the legal framework which affects them and so are capable of adjusting their behaviour accordingly. Hence, ignorance of the law cannot be used as a legitimate reason for non-compliance. This assumption is mistaken, yet serves to dismiss other factors as having a significant influence on individuals' behaviour (see Helen Carr and Dave Cowan's discussion of the Clingham case in Chapter Three, this volume), and helps sustain the illusion that the law produces the desired effect on social action. In spite of this assumption, legislation often fails to fulfil its purposes as a result of its remoteness from real life situations. In its application, legislation does not fully address the nature of the social relationships it attempts to regulate, nor does it specify the conditions required for the practical attainment of ideal forms of behaviour. These issues are discussed in further detail below.

Interpreting and using tenancy agreements

The previous discussion suggests that the role of the law in influencing behaviour is limited. Tenancy agreements, as an embodiment of the law, therefore appear to be sanction-oriented and an insurance against difficulties, as opposed to the product of shared understanding between the parties from the outset that has a positive impact on behaviour. This sanctions-oriented approach appears to be reflected in the increased use of ASBOs. Although there has been a shift towards the intense contractualisation of all types of relationships, there is very little research or empirical evidence that explores how tenancy agreements, and other associated documentation, such as freehold documents, and 'good neighbour agreements', are understood and used in practice. Although previous research has touched on some of these issues in passing and indicated that often landlords, tenants and purchasers do not have an understanding of their rights and responsibilities or the contents of the legal documents they sign (Thomas et al, 1995; Crook and Kemp, 1996; Lister, 2002; Blandy and Lister, 2005), there has been little attention paid to the ways in which agreements are used between the parties from the outset and whether they constitute a useful way of promoting positive behavioural outcomes or not.

Drawing on my own empirical research, what follows is a discussion of the ways in which tenancy agreements are interpreted and used in relationships between landlords and tenants in the private rented sector. My study focused on the setting-up phase of the tenancy and explored both the role of the tenancy agreement and the landlord during this initial stage. The research, although small-scale (15 landlords and 15 tenants), was detailed and respondents were asked about their attitudes towards tenancy agreements, whether they read and understood them, the extent to which they were engaged in the letting process and if they understood their rights and responsibilities. In addition, the tenants interviewed were all young people, some of whom were experiencing independent living for the first time and/or were vulnerable and who were often in need of information and advice. The material presented here exemplifies some typical experiences and is used to highlight some of the ways in which tenancy agreements can be used as informative documents (but often are not), and instances where the setting up of the tenancy is an educative phase where information is exchanged, providing some common points of understanding.

The private rented sector accommodates a large number of young people and vulnerable households who are often experiencing independent living for the first time. There are considerable differences in security of tenure for tenants in this sector in comparison to those in the social sector. Given the limited security of tenure in the private rented sector, typically six-month tenancies with two months' notice to quit without a Court Order, landlords are likely to dispense with tenants quickly if they so wish. In addition, private landlords can exercise their discretion and may reject prospective tenants from the outset if they regard them as potentially troublesome (Lister, 2002), and so minimise the risks of ASB in that way. Given the differences in tenants' security of tenure between the two sectors, the practices and procedures between social and private landlords will inevitably vary. However, a number of issues at the outset of the tenancy are likely to be broadly similar for tenants in both rented sectors. These points of similarity relate to the extent to which tenants are engaged in the legal process of reading and signing their agreement, the extent to which they understand what they have signed up to, the ways in which landlords explain and discuss practical issues with tenants at this stage and the extent to which needs (support or practical) are appropriately identified at this stage in order to minimise the risk of ASB.

The precontractual or setting-up phase of the tenancy is arguably the most important part of the relationship for both parties. During this formative phase the parties engage to varying degrees with legal, social and financial arrangements. Initial impressions and expectations are also formed during this phase. Interactions and exchanges at this point can set the general tone of the relationship and affect its relative success with the outcomes of discussions providing the basis for the evolving relationship between the parties. In addition, this stage is, in some instances, the only time where landlords and tenants meet together face-to-face to discuss issues relating to the property and the terms of the tenancy. However, the views of the landlords and tenants interviewed suggested that, in practice, levels of participation in this process were limited and subsequent behaviour was not based on the product of fruitful discussions and understandings about the terms of tenancy agreements.

Tenancy agreements are a social construction of legal phenomena and the ways in which they are used provides an insight into the level of importance attached to the legal framework by the parties involved. A lack of industry standards makes it procedurally easy for landlords in the private rented sector to access and use 'off the shelf' tenancy agreements without obtaining knowledge of the legal framework. Empirical evidence from the landlords interviewed revealed that they regarded the presence of a tenancy agreement in the relationship as important. However, the contents were rarely regarded as significant as they were hardly engaged with in detail. The extent to which agreements were used to minimise risks, clarify rights and responsibilities and to provide tenants with adequate information, was minimised by the actions of landlords who rarely engaged with agreements or explained their contents. The extent to which agreements constitute informative documents, clarifying rights and responsibilities and providing tenants with relevant and adequate information to aid the smooth running of their tenancy, was therefore minimal. Information from the landlords interviewed and from the experiences of tenants indicated that landlords very rarely explained the contents of agreements to tenants in order to clarify expectations and obligations. Only one landlord recognised a feature that may be common to vulnerable and young people, in that even if they read the agreement, they may not necessarily understand it, making it essential that he explained the contents to them:

> I normally sit down here and I say, 'This is what I'm going to do and this is what you've got to do'. Otherwise they wouldn't read it and they wouldn't understand it. Most of them would just sign anything you gave them, they just want to move in and they don't really care what they sign. (landlord 8, male)

This landlord was familiar with the legal framework and so was *able* to explain the contents of the agreement. However, landlords were often unable to explain agreements to tenants as they did not possess a thorough understanding of the contents or the legal framework, as they used agreements simply to formalise the relationship. For the majority of landlords interviewed, the legal framework was regarded as external to the landlord–tenant relationship, rather than as a basis for it. However, explanations can constitute an important stage in the formation of relationships as landlords can reassert the positions of the parties, clarify expectations so that disappointment is minimised when the tenancy begins, and attempt to safeguard against the risk of ASB by reiterating and making explicit rights and responsibilities. The potential for utilising this stage was evidently eroded by lack of knowledge. Instead, exchange of information between the parties was limited rather than maximised. The prevailing attitude among landlords was that once tenants had been given a copy of their agreement and other associated documentation, further explanations were unnecessary:

> Well I mean, all the things that they expect to ask me about are laid out, [in the agreement], you know like what they'll have to pay for and what the rent includes, what they can and can't do, all those sort of things. So really it's all explained to them.... (landlord 14, female)

The information, or lack of information, exchanged during these face-to-face interactions creates an image in the tenant's mind that is likely to be more prominent than the image gained from documentation, given that agreements may not be read or understood properly. One tenant highlighted the tension between the written and the spoken word, attributing what he is (not) told to be of greater significance than the provisions in his letting agreement:

> I mean there's no rules, like you know, some houses, kind of like they don't like smokers or something like that. There's nothing like that. Nothing was ever specified about it. We were never told. (tenant 8, male, 21 years old)

The responsibility for reading and understanding agreements was placed on tenants as they entered into the relationship, in theory, as a legal equal with the landlord. A further reason cited by some landlords for not explaining agreements to tenants was that they would not appreciate it as it would appear patronising and as if they were being treated like 'kids'.

The tenants interviewed did engage to some extent with the contents of agreements; however, the extent of this engagement is generally superficial. Fourteen of the 15 tenants stated that they had read their agreements. This figure may be misleading as tenants may be reluctant to admit that they had entered into a legal arrangement without reading the contents of the document they signed. In addition, illiterate individuals and those for whom English is a second or foreign language may have trouble reading. The circumstances in which the tenant received the agreement inevitably had an impact on whether the agreement was read, how it was read, how well it was understood and whether information and/or advice was sought about its contents. All of these 14 tenants were given the opportunity to read through the agreement prior to signing. However, the time available to read and digest the contents varied from a number of weeks to circumstances where 'he [the landlord] wandered off for a while and we read through it and yeah, we signed it in his presence'. The experience of one tenant highlights some of the difficulties encountered by the presence of landlords:

> I wasn't really given the opportunity to read it. They were sitting there kind of 'Oh you know if you just kind of like initial' and when I started to read through it then he'd start talking to me so I couldn't actually read it. (tenant 9, female, 21 years old)

The overall impression from the research is that tenants read 'some of it, not all of it' and these 'bits' are 'skimmed over briefly' with little attention given to details or 'the small print'. Some tenants expressed a confident and trusting attitude stating that 'you don't imagine that there will be anything in there but you always want to check', and therefore superficial readings were satisfactory because 'it's a standard form so there's not going to be anything in there which is going to catch you out'. However, more cautious approaches were evident from some tenants because 'you should read what you're signing otherwise you don't know what rights you have', and also to check for 'anything out of the ordinary, just anything completely unreasonable' to safeguard against 'attempts to sort of trip us up or ram us in some horrible contract'. However, although some tenants exercised at least a degree of caution by reading through agreements, this level of engagement with legal documentation does not necessarily translate into understanding the contents. Although the legal terminology used is described by tenants as being 'a bit weird', the responses indicated that the 14 tenants who said they had read their agreements at least 'got the gist' of the main points. Levels of understanding inevitably vary depending on the contents and the knowledge and experience each individual brings to the document. In addition, lack of understanding is likely to be under-reported for similar reasons to failing to read the agreement. Two tenants admitted that they 'didn't understand everything'; however, they did not approach their respective landlords to clarify these particular terms. It was also evident from the data that tenants accepted the terms of agreements in good faith as being a true and accurate reflection of the law and did not question the legal validity of the document.

It is evident from the research that although tenants do not negotiate the terms of agreements, they rely on the contents as an accurate reflection of the law. The onus is placed on the tenant to interpret and understand agreements as landlords rarely explain them, and the interviews suggest that tenants' readings are often superficial and that they rarely have a clear understanding of their position in relation to the legal framework. In the light of these practices, entering into a legal arrangement is fraught with risk, as tenants have little opportunity to engage with, or attempt to understand, the contents effectively, and remain unaware of what is expected of them in terms of conduct. This is tantamount to entering into a legal arrangement without knowledge of the key terms and is legitimised by the commonplace and routine nature of tenancy arrangements. Only in a few instances did the tenancy agreement and information imparted by the landlord serve to clarify expectations. Therefore, the process of setting up the tenancy and exchange of information emanating from the tenancy agreement appears to be rather limited in the extent to which they can shape subsequent behaviour and act as a safeguard against the risk of ASB.

Conclusion

This chapter has revisited the landlord–tenant relationship to assess how tenancy agreements are 'interpreted and used', and to explore whether there is scope for the setting-up phase of the tenancy to be used more actively and productively to influence subsequent behaviour and prevent the incidence of ASB. The research presented here has revealed that there are difficulties and shortcomings in assuming that tenancy agreements can be used as a mechanism to ensure compliant behaviour as both landlords and tenants often use agreements passively and are not active in their interpretation, exchange of information or in reaching a shared understanding about their contents. A gap between idealised versions of social relations as laid down in contractual documents and real life situations exists, as the quote by Cotterrell indicated at the beginning of this chapter. The current ways in which agreements are administered can be improved to make the signing up process more educative; however, this is reliant on social and not legal processes.

The social process of entering into a legally binding arrangement can be used to impart knowledge and information. Therefore, the personality of the landlord, the amount of time spent, and the ways in which information is communicated are crucial. However, if agreements have limited significance from the outset in fostering the social relations they aspire to promote, this inevitably leads to a rethink of their role and use in a preventative capacity.

Although intense contractualisation and commodification is apparent across all forms of social relations in an attempt to prevent ASB, there is little point in signing tenants up to extensive tenancy and neighbourhood agreements if there is little attention paid to the causes of ASB. It is important that measures are adopted to resist an increase in the use of ASBOs and to respond to the support and care needs of tenants in both the social and private rented sectors. Attempts across local authorities have been made to provide intensive management programmes, such as Supporting People, and the provision of more routine tenancy support services for those with support needs and/or at risk of behaving in an anti-social manner. However, these services are often inadequate, particularly if support needs are acute and behaviour is extreme and disruptive to both neighbours and the wider community. In the private rented sector, the provision of services is difficult to generalise and much more reliant on the individual and their skills and abilities in accessing services. In some instances where behaviour is extreme, independent living is obviously no longer an option. However, it seems futile to regard a prison sentence for a breach of an ASBO as an adequate response in these situations, where support and control rather than punishment would seem a more reasonable response, notwithstanding that the impacts of ASB on neighbours and communities are profound. The use of a range of tenancy and neighbourhood agreements in themselves is not an ideal solution; however, used in conjunction with more proactive preventative measures, where needs are identified and intensive support services are adopted, they may serve to formalise tenancy arrangements in a more responsive way.

Acknowledgements

The research from which this chapter is drawn was funded by the Economic and Social Research Council. Thanks to the landlords and tenants who gave up their time to be interviewed.

References

Albrow, M. (1997) 'Travelling Beyond Local Cultures', in J. Eade (ed) *Living the Global City*, London: Routledge, pp 37-55.

Atkinson, R., Mullen, T. and Scott, S. (2001) *The Use of Civil Legal Remedies for Neighbour Nuisance in Scotland*, Legal Studies Research Findings No 28, Edinburgh: Scottish Executive Central Research Unit.

Baier, A. (1986) 'Trust and Antitrust', *Ethics*, vol 96, pp 231-60.

Beck, U. (1992) *Risk Society: Towards a New Modernity*, London: Sage Publications.

Beck, U. (1997) *The Reinvention of Politics*, Cambridge: Polity Press.

Blandy, S. and Lister, D. (2005) 'Gated Communities: (Ne)Gating Community Development?', *Housing Studies*, vol 20, no 2, pp 287-301.

Blau, P.M. (1964) *Exchange and Power in Social Life*, London: John Wiley & Sons, Inc.

Bright, S. and Gilbert, G. (1995) *Landlord and Tenant Law: The Nature of Tenancies*, Oxford: Clarendon Press.

Broad, B. (1998) *Young People Leaving Care*, London: Jessica Kingsley.

Collins, H. (2002) *Regulating Contracts*, Oxford: Oxford University Press.

Conley, J.M. and O'Barr, W.M. (1990) *Rules Versus Relationships: The Ethnography of Legal Discourse*, Chicago, IL: University of Chicago Press.

Cotterrell, R. (1992) *The Sociology of Law: An Introduction*, London: Butterworths.

Crook, A.D.H. and Kemp, P.A. (1996) *Private Landlords in England*, London: The Stationery Office.

Crow, G., Allan, G. and Summers, M. (2002) 'Neither Busybodies nor Nobodies: Managing Proximity and Distance in Neighbourly Relations', *Sociology*, vol 36, no 1, pp 127-45.

Englander, D. (1983) *Landlord and Tenant in Urban Britain 1838-1918*, Oxford: Clarendon Press.

Giddens, A. (1991) *Modernity and Self-Identity: Self and Society in the Late Modern Age*, Cambridge: Polity Press.

Harloe, M. (1985) 'Landlord/Tenant Relations in Europe and America – The Limits and Functions of the Legal Framework', *Urban Law and Policy*, vol 7, pp 359-83.

Hoggart, R. (1958) *The Uses of Literacy*, Harmondsworth: Penguin.

Howard League Magazine (2005) 'Anti-social Behaviour', vol 23, no 1, February.

Hunter, C. and Nixon, J. (2001) 'Social Landlords' Responses to Neighbour Nuisance and Anti-Social Behaviour: From the Negligible to the Holistic?', *Local Government Studies*, vol 27, no 4, pp 89-104.

Lister, D. (2002) 'The Nature of Tenancy Relationships – Landlords and Young People in the Private Rented Sector', in S. Lowe and D. Hughes (eds) *The Privately Rented Sector in a New Century*, Bristol: The Policy Press, pp 95-108.

Lupton, D. (1999) *Risk*, London: Routledge.

Mackintosh, M. (2000) 'Flexible Contracting? Economic Cultures and Implicit Contracts in Social Care', *Journal of Social Policy*, vol 29, no 1, pp 1-19.

Mason, T. (1991) 'Tenant and Landlord Relations', in D. Donnison and D. Maclennan (eds) *The Housing Service of the Future*, London: Longman Group Ltd.

Molm, L.D. (1997) *Coercive Power in Social Exchange*, Cambridge: Cambridge University Press.

Papps, P. (1998) 'Anti-social Behaviour Strategies – Individualistic or Holistic?', *Housing Studies*, vol 13, no 5, pp 639-56.

Portes, A. (1998) 'Social Capital: Its Origins and Applications in Modern Sociology', *Annual Review of Sociology*, vol 24, pp 1-24.

Quilgars, D. and Pleace, N. (1999) 'Housing and Support Services for Young People', in J. Rugg (ed) *Young People, Housing Policy and Social Policy*, London: Routledge.

Rhodes, D. and Bevan, M. (1997) *Can the Private Rented Sector House the Homeless?*, York: Centre for Housing Policy, University of York.

Rousseau, J.J. (1968) *The Social Contract and Discourses*, London: JM Dent and Sons Ltd.

Rugg, J. (ed) *Young People, Housing Policy and Social Policy*, London: Routledge, pp 93-108.

Thomas, A. and Snape, D. with Duldig, W., Keegan, J. and Ward, K. (1995) *In From the Cold – Working with the Private Landlord*, London: HMSO.

Young, M. and Wilmott, P. (1957) *Family and Kinship in East London*, Harmondsworth: Penguin.

SEVEN

The changing legal framework: from landlords to agents of social control

Caroline Hunter

Introduction

In this chapter I examine how the legal framework in which social landlords operate in England and Wales has changed since 1996[1]. This period has seen an enormous amount of legal change, offering social landlords one legal tool after another. It seems that social landlords are expected to implement a series of new measures with little time being available to assess the impact of previously introduced measures.

As the chapters in this volume by Helen Carr and Dave Cowan (Chapter Three) and John Flint (Chapter One) illustrate, those providing social housing have historically always had some interest in the control of the behaviour of their tenants (Clapham, 1997; Burney, 1999). This has shown itself both in the control of access to social housing and the control of conduct, exemplified through the old housing visitors, who would come and inspect how tenants kept their home (Damer, 2000). Notwithstanding this history, however, Haworth and Manzi (1999) have noted how the control of tenants' conduct has emerged more forcefully in recent years and is strongly influenced by the specific policy discourse of 'residualisation', 'social exclusion' and 'underclass' theories (see Pauline Card, Chapter Two, this volume, for a further discussion). In this context the ever-increasing legal tools can be seen as part of the technologies of government, seeking to shape the conduct of social tenants.

Rather than provide a chronological account of the changes, I have sought to identify various thematic changes that emerge from the legislation. The first part of this chapter considers two specific legislative changes: the introductory tenancy and the statutory injunction. The second part of the chapter considers how changes to legal powers have broadened the scope and focus of housing interventions. I also consider what evidence there is about how these changes have been implemented by social landlords and assess the nature of these tools in order to question whether they are more symbolic than real.

It is helpful to identify at the outset the different legislative changes that will be discussed in the remainder of the chapter. These changes should be understood in the context that the vast majority of local authority and housing association tenants are either secure or assured tenants, who can only be evicted from their homes if the landlord can prove that one of the grounds for possession has been met and (generally) that it is reasonable for possession to be granted. Those rights were established in 1980 and had existed in their current form from the 1985 Housing Act.

The first changes to this well-established legal framework were made by the 1996 Housing Act, which contained a number of measures that directly addressed the issue of anti-social behaviour (ASB). The grounds for possession were widened, a new form of tenancy, 'the introductory tenancy', with less security, was introduced, and local authorities were given freestanding injunction powers.

The 1998 Crime and Disorder Act first introduced the Antisocial Behaviour Order (ASBO) that at that time could be applied for by either the police or local authorities. The 2002 Police Reform Act strengthened ASBO provisions, through the introduction of an interim ASBO, and also permitted registered social landlords to apply for them. In 2003 further legislation in the form of the Anti-social Behaviour Act introduced a raft of measures designed to tackle a range of ASB. This chapter focuses on housing-related measures including the demoted tenancy, extended injunction powers and the requirement for every social landlord to have an ASB policy and procedure.

Legislative changes

Reductions in security

One of the battles of the 1970s concerned the granting of security of tenure to tenants of social landlords, a classic rights-based approach to welfare. Those rights were granted by the 1980 Housing Act, and consolidated into the 1985 Housing Act. Notwithstanding the move of tenants of housing associations to the assured tenancy regime of the 1988 Housing Act, both types of tenants had extensive rights which limited the power of the landlord simply to evict because the landlord thought that the tenant's behaviour was unsuitable, inappropriate or whatever standard was cared to be applied. Evictions of secure and assured tenants require evidence, and decisions about the outcome were in the hands of the county court judge, not the landlord.

The 1996 Housing Act saw the first step in reducing the security of tenure, through the permission given to local authorities to use introductory tenancies. This reduction in security was suggested by Smith and George (1997, p 315) to 'represent the beginning of the end of the security of tenure of local housing authority tenants'. Where a local authority chooses to adopt an introductory tenancy scheme, for the first 12 months of all new tenancies the tenant is not secure but introductory. An introductory tenant does not have the same protection as a secure tenant; in essence control over the eviction process is put in the hands of the landlord. The landlord must give notice of intention to end the tenancy, but rather than this being followed by a court hearing at which evidence must be brought before the court, any challenge is made through an internal review procedure. Provided that the landlord has followed the procedure, the court has no choice but to grant possession on the landlord's application.

For housing associations the legal framework is rather different. Since 1989 the 1988 Housing Act has governed housing association tenants. In general housing associations grant fully assured tenancies and are encouraged to do so by The Housing Corporation (2002, para 3.5.2). During the 1990s any move away from the use of fully assured tenancies (apart from some specified uses) required the permission of The Housing Corporation. In 1995 permission was given to two housing associations working in North Manchester to use assured shorthold tenancies as a means of controlling ASB on estates that were being regenerated (Ruggieri and Levison, 1998). In this context the tenancies are generally referred to as 'starter tenancies'. An assured shorthold tenant only has security for a fixed term period (a minimum of six months) and at the end of the time may be evicted simply by the landlord serving a two-month notice.

The operation of 'starter tenancies' has been described thus:

> Starter tenancies were seen as a means of allowing those new tenants whose behaviour was found to be anti-social to be evicted quickly and without protracted legal procedures. It was hoped, however, that rather than eviction, the 'probationary' nature of the tenancy would influence the behaviour of tenants. It was designed to bring home to the tenants the seriousness with which the tenancy

agreements was regarded by the landlord and to emphasize that action could and would be taken if breaches occurred. (Ruggieri and Levison, 1998, para 2.32)

There are differences between introductory and starter tenancies. Once an introductory tenancy scheme has been introduced all new tenants throughout the local authority's stock will fall within it. On the other hand, starter tenancies may be targeted on particular areas, or even particular types of tenants, although this is not something that is encouraged by The Housing Corporation. The current guidance from The Housing Corporation states that:

Associations that use assured shorthold tenancies as starter tenancies should do so as part of a managed strategy for dealing with ASB either: across their whole stock; across their stock in a local authority area; or in defined street areas or estates. (The Housing Corporation, 2004a, para 3.3.3)

The 1996 Housing Act introductory tenancy scheme also provides greater legal safeguards, in that local authorities must offer an internal review, and ultimately if they adopt unfair practices or act in a completely unreasonable manner they may be challenged through judicial review (see *Manchester CC v Cochrane* [1999] 1 WLR 809). No such protection exists for tenants of housing associations.

The take-up of the use of introductory and starter tenancies was initially relatively slow. By 1998, 30% of local authorities had adopted a scheme, with a further 7% indicating that they were intending to do so in the next 12 months (Nixon et al, 1999). More recent figures on the uptake of the use of introductory tenancies can be found by analysis of the Office of the Deputy Prime Minister's (ODPM's) 2004 'Housing Strategy Statistical Appendix' (ODPM, 2004a), which indicates that in fact growth has been slower than might have been predicted from the earlier study. By 2001/02 the percentage of authorities allocating introductory tenancies was still at 30% with a small growth to 35% by 2003/04. The take-up in Wales has been greater with 14 authorities (67%) using introductory tenancies (Rowan Associates, 2004).

Nixon et al (1999) showed that there was enormous variation in take-up between regions. By 1999 three quarters of local authorities in the North East region of England had adopted an introductory tenancy scheme, compared to only 12% in the eastern region. That variation is still apparent in the ODPM (2004a) figures. A total of 83%

of local authorities in the North East now operate an introductory tenancy scheme, while only 23% of local authorities in the eastern region do so.

What evidence there is indicates that for housing associations, take-up has always been patchier. Nixon et al (1999) found that 13% of associations were using starter tenancies, with a further 14% indicating that they intended to adopt them in the next 12 months. There are no more recent figures available in England, but in Wales as at August 2003, 18 housing associations (62%) reported they were using them (Rowan Associates, 2004).

Two questions emerge from the take-up of introductory and starter tenancies. First, are they effective in tackling ASB? Although very much promoted as a tool for tackling ASB, the evidence suggests that in fact the majority of evictions from such tenancies are for rent arrears. Concern about their use in this way emerged in Ruggieri and Levison's study (1998, para 5.12), where they noted that:

> ... particular concern was also expressed by some housing professionals that introductory tenancies may be used as an easy route to evict tenants who have built up rent arrears.

Nixon et al (1999) found that 68% of evictions from introductory tenancies were for rent arrears rather than neighbour nuisance. In Wales significant differences were found in the way landlords used introductory/starter tenancies for rent arrears (Rowan Associates, 2004). In a study of eight landlords, three out of four housing associations would not end a starter tenancy for rent arrears. In contrast, all four local authorities used starter tenancies to deal with rent arrears. The majority of evictions of introductory/starter tenants by Welsh social landlords were for rent arrears.

Leaving aside the question of whether in fact introductory/starter tenancies are being used to tackle a different housing management issue, what evidence is there as to their effectiveness in tackling ASB? The two studies which have sought to answer this question (see Ruggieri and Levison, 1998; Rowan Associates, 2004) both concluded that there was evidence that introductory/starter tenancies were effective as part of a package of tools. They were not able to isolate the particular effect of such tenancies, as they were generally adopted as part of a package of measures to tackle ASB. In the Welsh study (Rowan Associates, 2004), a majority of tenants stated that the introductory/ starter tenancy had had an effect on how they acted in their home and that they were more anxious not to cause a nuisance to neighbours, indicating that there may be some direct effect on behaviour, although the staff of social landlords were not generally of this view.

The second question on introductory/starter tenancies relates to the unevenness of their take-up. Why have some landlords chosen to adopt them while others have not? Rowan Associates (2004) indicated that those landlords in Wales who had not adopted them felt they were not necessary due to the rural nature of the area they operated in, low levels of ASB and/or the design and size of estates. The take-up found by Nixon et al (1999) indicates that introductory tenancies were adopted least frequently in England in non-metropolitan areas, also supporting the view that the nature of the social landlords' stock and the areas in which they operate may play a part in the decision as to whether they are felt necessary.

The 2003 Anti-social Behaviour Act introduced another form of lessening of security. This enables social landlords to apply to the court for a 'Demotion' Order. Demotion reduces the security of the tenant for a period of 12 months; thus local authority tenants are reduced to the same position as introductory tenancies, and tenants of housing associations become assured shorthold tenants. Some may see demotion as a lesser form of disciplining than possession, and it is too early to comment on how it is used by landlords and the courts. If it is used in place of possession it might be argued that it at least keeps the tenant in their home with the possibility of returning to full security. On the other hand, landlords may use it in cases where they are not confident that they would be able to obtain possession. Further it could be argued that for a landlord the demoted tenancy gives them more control, certainly more than a suspended Possession Order, where the tenant is entitled, in the case of a warrant for eviction being issued for breach of the terms of the suspension, to return to the court and seek a further suspension.

What we see in both the introductory/starter tenancy and the demoted tenancy are legal measures to reduce the rights of the tenants of social landlords. Control over possession is moved away from an independent arbitrator (the court) to the landlord. However, not all social landlords have chosen to take advantage of this increased control.

From possession to injunction

While possession has been seen as the traditional landlord response to tenant misbehaviour (see Hal Pawson and Carol McKenzie, Chapter Eight, this volume), policy developments since 1996 have encouraged other forms of action, which may not require possession to be obtained.

In legal terms, landlords have always been able to obtain a court injunction requiring compliance with the tenancy agreement; such an order is a common law remedy based on the contractual relationship between the landlord and the tenant. In practice, prior to the early 1990s it was virtually unheard of for landlords to use this remedy.

It is almost impossible to identify why this position changed, but the injunction has become part of the range of remedies used by social landlords to control ASB. They were not mentioned in the White Paper that preceded the 1996 Housing Act (DoE, 1995). Nonetheless the 1996 Housing Act gave local authorities (but not housing associations) a freestanding power to seek injunctions in cases involving violence or threats of violence. This was intended primarily for use against non-tenants (see below). The 1996 Act also sought to enhance the efficacy of responses to a breach of tenancy injunction by permitting a power of arrest to be attached in certain circumstances. These measures thus provided part of the impetus for the increased use of the injunction, so that by 2002 the government wrote extolling their virtues:

> Injunctions are a swift, inexpensive and effective means of stopping anti-social behaviour.... They have the additional advantage of stopping this behaviour without necessarily excluding the perpetrator from their home – although, in appropriate circumstances, they can specifically do so. (DETR, 2002, p 19)

The 2003 Anti-social Behaviour Act further broadened injunction powers, through a series of amendments to the 1996 Housing Act. A general freestanding power to issue an injunction was given to all social landlords in relation to behaviour which 'is capable of causing nuisance or annoyance to any person and which directly or indirectly relates to or affects the housing management functions of a [social] landlord' (Section 153A, 1996 Housing Act). Further amendments gave a power to seek injunctions against the unlawful use of premises, strengthened the power of arrest, and also permitted the courts to add an exclusion order to an injunction.

The use of injunctions by social landlords has been very variable. Perhaps the most well known proponent of their use has been Manchester City Council. In 1995 their newly formed ASB team obtained 28 injunctions or undertakings[2] during the year and by 2003 the annual figure was 521 (Pitt, 2004). Evidence from other social landlords, however, indicates a much less frequent use of injunctions.

In England, Nixon et al's study (1999) showed that local authorities were more likely to use injunctions than housing associations. A total of 61% of local authorities, as compared with only 45% of housing associations, stated that they sometimes or always used injunctions. Surveys of the Social Landlords Crime and Nuisance Group (SLCNG) also indicated differences in use between housing associations and local authorities (Hunter and Nixon, 2003). Thus, in 2000/01, 62% of local authorities as compared with 39% of housing associations had taken out one or more injunctions for breach of tenancy during the year. However, in subsequent years the gap between local authorities and housing associations has reduced, indicating a greater take-up in their use by housing associations (at least by those who are members of SLCNG, who might be presumed to be those with a particularly active interest in ASB issues). In 2002/03, 53% of local authorities had obtained at least one injunction compared with 41% of housing associations. A study in Wales (Thomas, 2001) also indicated a low use of injunctions. While 18 social landlords indicated that they were committed to using the approach in principle, only five landlords had actually used the remedy. This compared with 30 landlords who stated they were committed to the use of notices of seeking possession (the first step to eviction), and 13 who stated that they had actually issued notices.

For those landlords using injunctions there seems to be a high rate of success in obtaining the order. Figures provided by landlords for 1997/98 showed that 95% of all injunction applications were granted, and this does not compare unfavourably with possession action where, although dismissal of the case is very rare, over 10% of cases are adjourned (Nixon et al, 1999).

Given this likely success, why do landlords not use injunctions more frequently? A study by Hunter et al (2000) found differing views among housing professionals as to the appropriateness of using injunctions – some felt they were inappropriate for minor cases and should only be used in combination with possession, while others saw them as particularly effective for minor cases where possession was not appropriate. Other reasons identified for landlords not utilising injunctions included a lack of training, concerns as to what steps should be taken on breach of an injunction and a belief that injunction proceedings were extremely expensive. In evidence to the Home Affairs Committee (2005, p 86), The Housing Corporation stated that 'associations have in the past found it difficult to make full use of their injunctive powers', and welcomed the changes made in the 2003 Act. Whether these changes increase landlords' use of injunctions remains to be seen.

What is clear from the Home Affairs Committee report is that there is very little evidence available as to how the injunction powers are being used by social landlords and what their effect is. The Committee concluded:

> The Government does not collect data relating to the use of housing injunctions or possession orders. There is thus no objective means of assessing the extent to which powers have been used, the level of variation around the country, [or] whether there is a tendency for particular powers to be used in combination with other powers.... (Home Affairs Committee, 2005, p 89)

In the light of this, it cannot be authoritatively determined whether there is a move from possession to injunction. It may be the case that, in place of possession, some landlords are genuinely using injunctions. It may also be the case that they are being used to control behaviour that previously would not have been subject to legal action at all. What does seem to be clear is that although all social landlords have the power to seek injunctions, many have not used this power.

These statutory changes were explicitly aimed at giving landlords new powers to control ASB. They cannot be thought of alone, however, and together with various other changes to existing powers (for example, eviction) and the introduction of non-housing specific measures such as ASBOs, they have strengthened the powers of social landlords to tackle ASB in a much broader way. The next part of this chapter considers these changes.

The growth of housing as social control

Liability for and control of non-tenants

A number of changes made since 1996 have moved social landlords from simply being concerned with the behaviour of their tenants to a wider concern for that of non-tenants. This can be seen in two particular changes.

First, the wording of the main ground for possession available against tenants (Ground 2, 1985 Housing Act; Ground 14, 1988 Housing Act) was amended by the 1996 Housing Act to include a liability not just for those residing in the tenant's home but also to visitors to the home. There is no evidence to indicate how often social landlords take action based on the behaviour of visitors rather than household members. There is some anecdotal evidence to suggest that landlords have acted to evict women tenants for the behaviour of their ex-partners, even when that behaviour consists of harassing the woman (see, for example, Home Affairs Committee, 2005, p 88).

The second change has already been indicated above. Injunction powers were given to local authorities in 1996 in relation to non-tenants. These were extended by the 2003 Anti-social Behaviour Act to give all social landlords the power to give an injunction to anyone for nuisance and annoyance behaviour, provided that the behaviour in some way affected the landlord's 'housing management functions'. It is too early for any evidence as to how the 2003 Act powers are being used, but there is some evidence as to the use of its predecessor, the 1996 Housing Act (Section 152).

A total of 60% of local authority respondents to the SLCNG surveys (Hunter and Nixon, 2003) indicated that they had used the Section 152 power in 2001/02, although this fell to 45% in 2002/03. It is not clear from this data whether the use is against non-tenants as the remedy is available against both tenants and non-tenants, although it seems likely that a good proportion will be against non-tenants, given in most instances a breach of tenancy injunction would also be available against a tenant.

What we see in the changing nature of the legislation is a move away from the social landlord taking legal action based on the tenant's behaviour, as one would expect in litigation based on the landlord–tenant relationship. Rather the landlord's powers have been extended to evict the tenant for the behaviour of non-tenants, and to take direct action against those non-tenants through an injunction.

From neighbours to neighbourhood

A further change in the legislation is the protection not just of 'neighbours', but rather to control behaviour in a 'locality' or 'neighbourhood'. Thus, when the grounds for possession were changed in 1996 the liability was extended from 'nuisance or annoyance to neighbours' to nuisance and annoyance to 'a person residing, visiting or otherwise engaging in a lawful activity in the locality'. Similarly eviction could be sought for convictions not just relating to use of the dwelling house but for offences committed in the locality of the dwelling house. At the same time the freestanding injunction power (Section 152, 1996 Housing Act, see above) was to afford protection to any person residing in, visiting, or otherwise engaging in a lawful activity in, the local authority's residential premises or in 'the locality of such premises'.

The courts showed some resistance to interpreting this in an expansive manner. Thus, in *Manchester CC v Lee* [2004] EWCA Civ 1256; [2004] HLR 11, an injunction was refused under Section 152 of the 1996 Housing Act to protect a neighbouring owner-occupier. These limitations have been addressed through the extension to the injunction powers in the 2003 Anti-social Behaviour Act. Under the new Section 153A, an injunction can be sought to prevent conduct which is a nuisance and annoyance to any person and which directly or indirectly affects the housing management functions of a relevant authority, provided the nuisance or annoyance is to one of the specified people, that is, residents of the landlord's properties, other residents of housing accommodation 'in the neighbourhood', those engaged in lawful activity 'in the neighbourhood', or staff.

It is not clear whether there is any significance in the change in the wording from 'locality' in the 1996 Act to 'neighbourhood' in the 2003 Act. In *Manchester City Council v Lawler* [1998] 31 HLR 119, the Court of Appeal held that 'locality' can encompass the whole or part of an estate. In every case, it is a question of fact for the judge whether the place in which the conduct occurred is or is not within the locality. The change in the wording from locality to neighbourhood in the 2003 Act was made at a late stage of the passage of the Bill through Parliament. Lord Bassam of Brighton explained it thus:

> Landlords have a responsibility for the protection of the communities who live in and around their housing stock. As I argued earlier, that responsibility does not stop at a particular distance from a particular unit of housing. Nor is the responsibility to non-residents in the area limited to protecting certain people carrying out certain activities in relation to individual premises. Landlords have a wider responsibility to the community and the neighbourhood. (*Hansard*, 2003, col 1796)

This encapsulates quite clearly the move away from social landlords being concerned with disputes between neighbours who are its own tenants to a broader requirement to use their powers to provide forms of 'policing' or 'social control' in areas where they have some stock.

Non-housing powers

Alongside these changes to the powers of landlords, there has been a different set of developments that have not been linked directly to the management of social housing. These have come through the 1998 Crime and Disorder Act, in particular the development of ASBOs. These initially gave power to the police or local authorities to seek Orders, which are defined without any reference to the nature of the residence of the perpetrator. One significant feature of the ASBO power is its availability against anyone aged 10 or over, whereas injunctions are not generally available against minors (see *G v Harrow LBC* [2004] EWHC 17 [Admin]).

But even here we see the difficulty in viewing enforcement powers outside the prism of social housing. Thus the 1992 Police Reform Act extended the power to apply for ASBOs to housing associations against people residing in or who are in the vicinity of 'premises provided or managed by the' association (Section 1(1B)(d) 1998 Crime and Disorder Act). Further, an ASBO could be sought in the county court proceedings as an adjunct to civil proceedings such as a possession action. Those most likely to do this are social landlords, although there is as yet no data on the use of this power.

The management of ASB in local authorities has generally emanated from housing departments. Thus in a study which looked at how ASB was being tackled in mixed tenure areas (Hunter et al, 2003), even where local authorities stated that they implemented ASBOs on a cross-tenure basis, in fact they often obtained all their ASBOs in relation to behaviour on their own housing estates.

Again there has been very differential take-up of the use of ASBOs, although generally their use has grown significantly since 2003 (Table 7.1), and Hal Pawson and Carol McKenzie's chapter in this volume (Chapter Eight) provides similar findings in Scotland.

Table 7.1: Number of ASBOs taken out from April 1999 to September 2004

Period	Number of ASBOs taken out
April 1999-March 2001	317
April 2001-March 2002	321
April 2002-March 2003	492
April 2003-March 2004	1,323
April 2004-September 2004	1,813

Source: Home Affairs Committee (2005, p 65)

On a general scale the Home Affairs Committee reported:

> There has been a very large variation in the use of ASBOs across the country. For instance, a person is 12 times more likely to receive an ASBO in Greater Manchester than in Lincolnshire. There is a similar variation in terms of the number of ASBOs made in relation to particular age groups. It is estimated that 56 percent of ASBOs made in Magistrates Courts between April 1999 and September 2003 related to under 18s: however, the local figures ranged from 33 percent in Bedfordshire and Derbyshire to 100 percent in Dorset. (Home Affairs Committee, 2005, p 66)

Turning specifically to applications by local authorities, the Local Government Association (2001) found that by mid-2001 district councils and unitary Welsh authorities were least likely to have applied for an ASBO, while metropolitan authorities were most likely to have applied for more than five. Exactly half of local authority respondents to the 2002/03 SLCNG survey (Hunter and Nixon, 2003) had used an ASBO, while only 24% of housing association respondents had. There was clearly a preference among associations responding to the survey to work through the police and local authority, rather than make a direct application to the court for an ASBO. Housing associations also expressed an unwillingness to take action directly because of the difficulty, cost and their own lack of experience (very similar responses as were given for not taking injunction action). Some also expressed the view that at the time of the survey they had not had any suitable cases, but they were not ruling it out in the future. For some this was allied to a fourth reason of seeking to use other measures such as Acceptable Behaviour Contracts (ABCs), where they were more effective in dealing with the problems.

In the ASBO we see a measure which was not initially intended to be housing specific, but which in both practice and through subsequent legal changes has been targeted at those living in areas of social housing. As with other measures, take-up among social landlords had been extremely differentiated.

Policies and strategies

The techniques of control that have been considered so far can all be said to be directed at the individual. The individual tenant (or other person) may be disciplined through the law. Techniques of government are not, however, limited to such individualised approaches. A regulatory approach that seeks to ensure that all social landlords prioritise dealing with ASB can be seen in the requirement of the 2003 Anti-social Behaviour Act for all social landlords to produce an ASB policy and procedure by 31 December 2004. It is, as yet, too early to comment on their impact on the way that social landlords tackle ASB.

In producing their policies and procedures, local authorities in England must have regard to the guidance issued by the Secretary of State, and housing associations must have regard to that issued by The Housing Corporation (Section 218A(7), 1996 Housing Act). It may be noted that the current guidance (The Housing Corporation, 2004b; ODPM, 2004b) does not lay a great emphasis on enforcement action in terms of the policy statement, although it is clear that the use of such action must be part of the procedure (see para 4.10 of both sets of guidance). Rather, more emphasis is given to prevention and rehabilitation through working in multiagency partnerships. The requirement for this type of action is much more difficult to prescribe through statutory form compared to giving landlords powers to take enforcement action against individual perpetrators.

The guidance, while much less enforcement-led in tone than many other government documents (cf DETR, 2002), does echo the changes in the legislation outlined above in setting out the wider role of social landlords. The ODPM guidance states:

> Your powers and responsibilities to tackle ASB extend beyond your own sector and housing stock. You may act to protect owner-occupiers or those in other tenures from the actions of tenants, and equally, you may take action against people in other tenures to protect your tenants. (ODPM, 2004b, para 3.40; see also The Housing Corporation, 2004b, para 3.34)

This section has illustrated how the powers given to landlords have been widened. Not only have their explicit housing powers enabled them to take action relating to the behaviour of non-tenants and in relation to a broader area, they have been given other powers with no explicit reference to their role as landlords. This has been placed in a regulatory framework that at least requires social landlords to be explicit in how they will use those powers in this broader context.

Conclusion

Since 1996 there has been an enormous change in the legal powers given to social landlords to control ASB. Two themes emerge from this survey of the changing legal landscape of powers.

Firstly, the new powers have given social landlords much greater tools of social control. This has been achieved first by lessening the security of their tenants, primarily through the use of introductory and starter tenancies. Second, the law has been changed to widen the role from one that is concerned primarily with the relationship between the landlord and tenant, to one where the landlord is concerned with the behaviour of those who are not tenants, and encompasses behaviour not just towards immediate neighbours, but also all those in the 'locality' or 'neighbourhood'.

Secondly, although there is to date only partial evidence as to how these powers have been used by social landlords, it is clear that it takes time for landlords to overcome the barriers to take-up and become familiar and confident with the use of particular remedies. This is illustrated most clearly in relation to ASBOs where we can examine centrally collected statistics. It would also seem to be the case with injunctions, although the evidence is less compelling. The evidence also indicates a patchy and differential take-up. There are some reasons for these differences suggested, and most seem to be in terms of the barriers perceived by some social landlords, in particular, housing associations.

For those landlords who have actively sought to use the powers given to them, a view is emerging that there is no need for further change. This was expressed to the Home Affairs Committee:

> Mr Winter, Chief Executive of the Social Landlords Crime and Nuisance Group, told us the view of officials at the London Borough of Camden: They said, 'The legislation is great. There are no excuses now. We cannot see the need for new remedies'. (Home Affairs Committee, 2005, p 86)

So perhaps we will see an end to the constant change in the legal landscape and the clamour for ever-greater powers of control over the behaviour of those living in social housing. Given the existing powers, it can be said that for those landlords who wish to exercise them, the tools of social control are extensive and powerful.

Notes

[1] There have also been changes in Scotland, but these have not been identical and space precludes a detailed discussion of them. For further details see Atkinson et al (2000).

[2] Where a defendant to an injunction case is willing to give an undertaking to the court about his/her future behaviour, the court will often accept this in place of making a formal injunction. An undertaking can be enforced in the same way as an injunction, but no power of arrest can be added to it.

References

Atkinson, R., Mullen, T. and Scott, S. (2000) *The Use of Civil Legal Remedies for Neighbour Nuisance in Scotland*, Edinburgh: Scottish Executive Central Research Unit.

Burney, E. (1999) *Crime and Banishment: Nuisance and Exclusion in Social Housing*, Winchester: Waterside Press.

Clapham, D. (1997) 'The Social Construction of Housing Management Research', *Urban Studies*, vol 34, no 5, pp 761-74.

Damer, S. (2000) '"Engineers of the Human Machine": The Social Practice of Council Housing Management in Glasgow, 1895-1939', *Urban Studies*, vol 37, no 11, pp 2007-26.

DETR (Department of the Environment, Transport and the Regions) (2002) *Tackling Anti-social Tenants: A Consultation Paper*, London: DETR.

DoE (Department of the Environment) (1995) *Our Future Homes: Opportunity, Choice, Responsibility*, Cm 2901, London: HMSO.

Hansard (2003) House of Lords, 23 October, vol 653, part 156.

Haworth, A. and Manzi, T. (1999) 'Managing the "Underclass": Interpreting the Moral Discourse of Housing Management', *Urban Studies*, vol 36, no 1, pp 153-66.

Home Affairs Committee (2005) *Anti-Social Behaviour*, 5th Report of 2004-05, HC 80-1, London: The Stationery Office.

Housing Corporation, The (2002) *The Regulatory Code and Guidance*, London: The Housing Corporation.

Housing Corporation, The (2004a) *Tenancy Management: Eligibility and Evictions*, Housing Corporation Regulatory Circular 07/04, London: The Housing Corporation.

Housing Corporation, The (2004b) *Anti-social Behaviour: Policy and Procedure: Guidance for Housing Associations*, London: The Housing Corporation.

Hunter, C. and Nixon, J. (2003) *Initiatives by Social Landlords to tackle Anti-social Behaviour*, Coventry: SLCNG.

Hunter, C., Nixon, J. and Shayer, S. (2000) *Neighbour Nuisance, Social Landlords and the Law*, Coventry: CIH.

Hunter, C., Nixon, J., Reeves, K. and Jones, A. (2003) *Tackling Anti-social Behaviour in Mixed Tenure Areas*, London: ODPM.

Local Government Association (2001) *Partners Against Crime: A Survey of Local Authority Approaches to Community Safety*, Research Report 24, London: Local Government Association.

Nixon J., Hunter, C. and Shayer, S. (1999) *The Use of Legal Remedies by Social Landlords to Deal with Neighbour Nuisance*, CRESR Paper H8, Sheffield: Sheffield Hallam University.

ODPM (Office of the Deputy Prime Minister) (2004a) 'Housing Strategy Statistical Appendix' (www.odpm.gov.uk).

ODPM (2004b) *Anti-social Behaviour: Policy and Procedure: Code of Guidance for Local Housing Authorities and Housing Action Trusts*, London: ODPM.

Pitt, B. (2004) 'Anti-social Behaviour – Experience and Expectations From a Local Authority Perspective', Paper presented at the New Housing and Anti-Social Behaviour Legislation Conference, CLT, London, March.

Rowan Associates (2004) *Evaluating the Use of Introductory and Starter Tenancies*, Cardiff: Welsh Assembly Government.

Ruggieri, S. and Levison, D. (1998) *Starter Tenancies and Introductory Tenancies: An Evaluation*, London: The Housing Corporation.

Smith, N. and George, C. (1997) 'Introductory Tenancies: A Nuisance Too Far?', *Journal of Social Welfare and Family Law*, vol 19, no 3, pp 307-20.

Thomas, R. (2001) *The Law: An Adequate Response to Anti-social Behaviour?*, Cardiff: CIH.

EIGHT

Social landlords, anti-social behaviour and countermeasures

Hal Pawson and Carol McKenzie

Introduction

The rising tide of counter-anti-social behaviour (ASB) legislation and the continuing salience of the issue in political and media debates in part reflect how unruly and yobbish behaviour blights some local communities. However, the prominence of ASB as a 'national problem' is also symptomatic of the government's emphasis on communitarian approaches to social policy more generally (Driver and Martell, 2002; Martell et al, 2004) and an associated inclination to 'talk up' the issue as one demanding firm official countermeasures.

The increasing prominence of countering ASB as a social landlord activity raises issues about the role of the housing manager as a key agent of crime and social control. As demonstrated in Chapter Seven (this volume), social landlords have acquired a growing range of legal powers to help tackle ASB. The main purpose of this chapter is to review the research evidence on how social landlords make use of legal measures, including repossession and Antisocial Behaviour Orders (ASBOs), and non-legal measures, including mediation and Acceptable Behaviour Contracts (ABCs); and organise their approaches, for example, establishing specialist teams, in order to tackle ASB.

The material presented here provides empirical evidence drawn mainly from the authors' recent work for the Office of the Deputy Prime Minister (ODPM), the 'ODPM study' (Pawson et al, 2005) and for the Scottish Executive (DTZ Pieda Consulting and Heriot-Watt University, 2005), although we also refer to research evidence from other studies.

The chapter begins by reviewing debates about the connection between social housing and ASB and about the specific relevance of ASB to social landlords (see also Chapters Two, Three and Five, this volume). We then examine the definitions of ASB and assess the evidence about the extent to which ASB is a growing phenomenon. The chapter continues by examining social landlords' practices in countering ASB, looking in turn at changing approaches to the organisation of counter-ASB action and how legal and non-legal measures are used in practice. We conclude by offering observations about the themes emerging from the evidence and identify arising questions posed for policy makers and for social landlords.

Defining anti-social behaviour: a social landlord perspective

As Chapters Three and Seven in this volume discuss, the concept of ASB has no commonly agreed definition and therefore comprises a very wide range of phenomena. The increasing official emphasis on legal devices for countering ASB has necessitated the development of legislative phraseology specifying what the problem involves. In Scotland, Section 143 of the 2004 Antisocial Behaviour etc (Scotland) Act defines anti-social manner and anti-social conduct (which includes speech) as: 'that which caused or was likely to cause alarm or distress to one or more persons not of the same household'.

Individual local authorities and other bodies have their own lists of activities defined as 'anti-social' for the purposes of their policies to counter such actions. Scott and Parkey (1998) suggest a threefold classification of ASB:

- *neighbour:* a dispute arising from nuisance, for example, noise
- *neighbourhood:* incivilities within public space, for example, litter
- *crime:* all forms of criminal activity, for example, housebreaking.

Thus, the ASB concept spans both criminal and non-criminal activity and has been criticised for blurring the 'fundamental boundary' between the civil and criminal law (Burney, 2002). Scott and Parkey (1998) also draw attention to the distinction drawn by some social landlords between:

- minor disputes of a personal nature between tenants
- breach of tenancy conditions, and
- criminal activity.

Essentially, the difference between the first and second behaviours might be one of degree (partly depending on the precise wording of the tenancy agreement concerned). An earlier survey of social landlords found that the most common tenant complaints regarding neighbour behaviour related to noise, noisy parties and problems with gardens and common areas (Jones, 1997, cited in Scott and Parkey, 1998).

As the chapters by Pauline Card (Chapter Two), Helen Carr and Dave Cowan (Chapter Three) and Rowland Atkinson (Chapter Five) in this volume outline, there has been a long-standing tendency among policy makers to see ASB as being an issue largely associated with social housing and hence primarily a social housing management issue (Scott and Parkey, 1998). However, evidence suggests that although lifestyle clashes between tenants on council estates are a common manifestation of ASB, ASB is not confined to such areas (Scott and Parkey, 1998). Furthermore, the increase in housing ownership resulting from the Right to Buy makes it increasingly inaccurate to speak of ASB occurring in 'public housing estates'.

Evidence appears to confirm that, while the incidence of ASB experienced by social renters is above average, private sector residents are far from immune. The Scottish Household Survey 2001/02 (www.scotland.gov.uk/Topics/Statistics/16002/shs-search, accessed 8 November 2005) found that 13% of council tenant respondents reported some personal experience of 'neighbour disputes', as compared with 9% of households across all tenures and 5% of those living in dwellings owned outright. Similarly, the Survey of English Housing 2003/04 (www.odpm.gov.uk/index.asp?id=1155177, accessed 8 November 2005) found that 18% of council tenant respondents considered vandalism to be a 'serious problem' in their locality as compared with 9% of homeowners.

Brown (2004) argues that the growing official concern with ASB in recent times places an increasing emphasis on social landlords rather than the police as the main agency of social control. This tendency is seen as having been particularly evident in Scotland, where the local authority, rather than the police, is the lead agency in relation to ASBO applications.

These arguments link with the devolution of powers and responsibilities for countering disorder to local state and other agencies, including housing associations (see the discussions in Chapter One by John Flint and Chapter Eleven by Adam Crawford, this volume). Cowan et al (2001) argue that through this process a crime control function has become explicitly part of the role and processes of housing management, although they also argue that housing management has always been used to achieve social conformity.

Brown (2004, p 207) contends that ASB is a social construction that has created a new domain of power and knowledge among social landlords arising from the appropriation by the housing management profession of an area of expertise and authority that has to be demarcated as a separate disciplinary territory from that of the police. For Brown, 'a new profession is forming around ASB, with its own purposes and methods for gathering knowledge' (Brown, 2004, p 207). Central to the ethos of this new profession, in the view of Burney (2002), is the blurring of the fundamental distinction between the civil and the criminal law based on measures to control ASB that are, according to Brown (2004), disinterested in causes or mitigating factors. This chapter assesses these arguments in relation to the practices of social landlords.

Nature and incidence of anti-social behaviour

Nature of anti-social behaviour experienced by social landlords

Our recent research for the ODPM (Pawson et al, 2005) confirmed the findings of previous studies (Scott and Parkey, 1998) that social landlords regarded the term 'anti-social behaviour' as encompassing a wide range of criminal and non-criminal phenomena, from poor garden maintenance through to assaults on staff or neighbours and drug dealing. Common complaints related to noise and environmental incivilities and many complaints stemmed from lifestyle clashes and other minor frictions between neighbours.

Our study found that social landlords commonly classified reported ASB in relation to (a) its perceived seriousness, and (b) its persistence, and these judgements were of key importance in guiding appropriate landlord responses. Incidents involving violence, harassment (including racial harassment), intimidation and drug abuse were viewed as inherently 'serious' and, hence, potentially justifying robust intervention such as immediate ASBO application or possession action. However, the imprecise nature of definitions and the frequent absence of detailed guidelines meant that applying distinctions such as 'minor' versus 'serious' was often inexact.

The 'growing problem' of anti-social behaviour

The ODPM study found that social landlords in England tended to subscribe to the view presented by politicians and the media that ASB is a growing problem. Housing practitioners related this growth in particular to drug and alcohol abuse and disruptive activity by mental ill health sufferers and the residualised nature of social housing, including the polarisation in the ages of the tenant population (see Bramley et al, 2004). However, social landlords perceived that increases in incidences of ASB were also related to a growing tendency to report incidents on the part of victims. This was attributed both to 'media hype' and more broadly was interpreted as illustrating a declining capability of communities to negotiate relations and resolve problems informally, for example lifestyle difference between older and young tenants and between families and single-person households (see Rowland Atkinson's discussion of this issue in Chapter Five, this volume).

A number of landlords in the study believed that their own organisation's strengthened focus on responding to ASB had, in itself, helped to stimulate the flow of complaints. In part, this was seen as something to be encouraged, and one local authority has sought to achieve a cultural change so that reporting nuisance or harassment ceased to be seen as 'grassing'. Other interviewees were more ambivalent about what were seen as tenants' growing expectations of their landlord, although it was recognised that tenants' reluctance to address ASB issues themselves was often based on a genuine, even if unfounded, fear of retaliation and recrimination. It is not possible to identify therefore to what extent the perceived growth in ASB results largely from increased sensitivity to the issue or an actual rise in misconduct. More broadly, given that ASB represents a somewhat nebulous and socially constructed concept it is not easy to evaluate this belief against objective data.

Recorded crime statistics relating to ASB offences appear to indicate a 'rising tide' of such misconduct (see Figure 8.1). Reported offences involving criminal damage to a dwelling appeared to rise well ahead of 'all crimes' in the six years to 2003/04. However, all these statistics have to some extent been inflated in recent years due to important changes in police recording practices such as the new National Crime Reporting Standard (NCRS) introduced in 2002/03 that pushed up reported figures by 10%. Hence, the apparent increase of 7% in total crimes reported in 2002/03 as compared with the previous year in fact masked a real *reduction* of 3% (National Statistics, 2005). Such procedural changes may well have been compounded by an increased tendency to report perceived offences.

However, survey data based on public perceptions of the incidence of crime and neighbourhood problems provide little evidence of a 'rising tide' of ASB (see Figure 8.2). This is not to deny that ASB problems have intensified in certain neighbourhoods, but casts doubt on the generalised picture conveyed by politicians and the media.

Figure 8.1: Trends in recorded crime (raw figures) (England and Wales) (1998/99-2003/04)

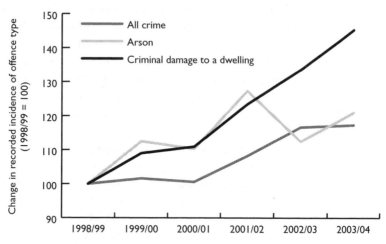

Source: National Statistics (2005)

Figure 8.2: Trends in perceived 'serious problems in the neighbourhood' (England) (1994-2004)

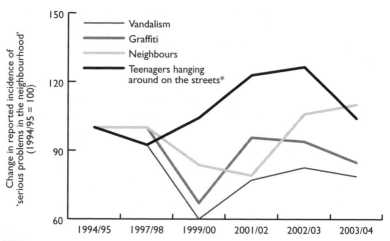

*GB figure
Source: Survey of English Housing and British Crime Survey

Perpetrators of anti-social behaviour

,There is little quantitative evidence about the types of household responsible for perceived ASB. Scott and Parkey (1998) found that couples with children, single parents and single people were most likely to have been complained about. Other studies (Atkinson et al, 2000; Dillane et al, 2001) found strong links between alleged perpetrators of ASB and vulnerability, including physical and mental health problems, single-parent households, alcohol and drug dependency and issues relating to parenting and the behaviour of children (see Chapters Four, Nine and Ten, this volume).

Our study for the ODPM confirmed the findings of other studies (Hunter and Nixon, 2001) that tenants with support needs are most likely to be the subject of ASB complaints to social landlords. ASB complaints were frequently directed at mental ill health sufferers and substance abusers, and housing staff also cited the overlapping categories of 'out of control' children and youth gangs as increasingly generating complaints (Pawson et al, 2005).

How social landlords counter anti-social behaviour

Anti-social behaviour policy development themes

The period since the late 1990s has seen very considerable policy development activity in relation to social landlord action in tackling ASB. In part, this reflects 'top-down' pressures imposed by central government through new legislation, guidance and monitoring obligations. Other trigger factors for policy evolution in specific case studies included the need to implement recommendations arising from internal auditors, regulatory inspections and Best Value reviews.

Much of the thrust of recent policy development in this area has been reflected in the organisational and staffing changes described below. In policy and practice terms, the strongest theme has been the adoption of a growing range of techniques to run alongside the long-established recourse to possession action as the 'nuclear option' in addressing ASB. Part of this follows directly from legislative activity including the creation of new instruments such as ASBOs. It is also apparent that many landlords have recently rediscovered the potential utility of long-established legal remedies such as injunctions, as well as non-legal approaches such as mediation.

Good practice guidance has re-emphasised the importance attached to preventative rather than strictly reactive stances, such as eviction, on the part of social landlords. Recognition of the necessity for a strong foundation for tackling ASB has also been reflected in the widespread adoption of new clauses within tenancy agreements in recent years, more explicitly defining activities considered to represent breach of tenancy, as well as the sanctions to be deployed by the landlord in response.

Another policy development theme has been the perceived efficacy of publicising landlord action in response to ASB in order to boost tenant confidence in the likelihood of firm ASB countermeasures with the expectation that this will encourage cooperation and vigilance. For certain social landlords this has involved more explicit 'naming and shaming' of individuals (for example, those convicted of criminal offences associated with ASB or subject to ASBOs) (Pawson et al, 2005).

Changing approaches to the organisation of counter-anti-social behaviour action

Our research (Pawson et al, 2005) indicated that most social landlords in England continue to manage their response to ASB as a 'primarily generic' function carried out by housing officers handling a variety of other tasks. Among local authorities, however, this was true of only a minority (46%). Rather, most local authority landlords, particularly those managing over 10,000 homes, had moved away from a primarily generic structure, suggesting a significant shift towards a more specialist approach to tackling ASB (see Figure 8.3). Only a small proportion of landlords reported that their approach to the management of ASB had remained 'unchanged' since 2000.

The findings described above are consistent with previous research evidence of moves towards specialist officers and specialist teams to deal with ASB. Both Atkinson et al (2000) and Hunter et al (2000) found that landlords who employed specialist staff appeared to have a better understanding of the legal issues and were more likely to take, and win, legal action in response to ASB.

Our study identified a common organisational model for ASB response as involving generic housing officers (whether or not tasked with rent arrears collection) initially responding to complaints and carrying out investigations. Serious cases were subsequently referred on to specialist staff who would usually initiate and pursue legal action. Such systems were operated by a majority of the 15 landlords in the case study. A variant on this approach involves a degree of specialisation within area-based housing management teams, where designated

Figure 8.3: Changes in social landlords' organisation of counter-ASB functions (2000-03)

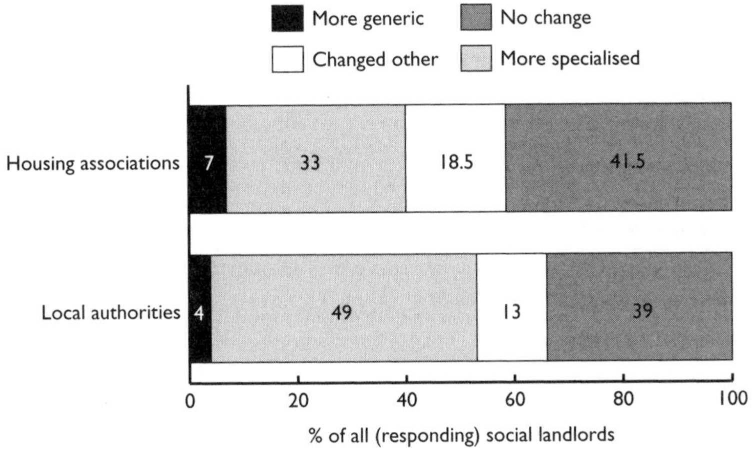

Source: Pawson et al (2005)

housing officers specialise in ASB response within local housing offices, with complex and/or serious cases being referred on to a centrally located ASB team. Models of this kind appear to be replacing the more traditional approach where multi-role housing officers are supported in tackling serious ASB mainly by their line managers and by generalist legal departments and external solicitors.

The use of legal measures in tackling anti-social behaviour

Overview

Table 8.1 indicates the relative use of the main forms of ASB legal countermeasures by local authorities. These are estimates based on a postal survey of local authority landlords in England conducted in 2003, which generated a response rate of 50%. The figure for ASBOs will not correspond with published Home Office statistics on the issue because it relates only to Orders obtained against local authority tenants. It is also important to stress that the use of ASBOs has been on a very steep upward trajectory in recent years (DTZ Pieda Consulting and Heriot-Watt University, 2005), hence, the numbers of ASBOs granted against social renters in years subsequent to 2002/03 are likely to be substantially higher than those shown here.

Table 8.1 indicates that almost half of local authority landlords in

Table 8.1: Use of ASB legal countermeasures by local authority landlords (England) (2002/03)

	Eviction actions	ASBOs	Injunctions
Estimated no of cases entered in court	2,700*	–	–
Estimated no of ASBOs/injunctions obtained against LA tenants	–	500	1,200
Estimated no of evictions undertaken	1,600*	–	–
Estimated % of LAs obtaining ASBOs/ injunctions/ undertaking ASB evictions	49	42	49

Notes: LA = local authority; * includes cases brought by housing associations
Source: Authors' postal survey (2003)

England made some use of evictions, or obtained an ASBO or injunction to counter tenant misconduct in 2002/03. At the same time, the actual number of cases involved is relatively modest. For example, the estimated 1,600 tenants evicted for ASB during the year equates to around one for every 2,000 tenants in local authority housing at that time. To put this in perspective, around one in every 200 council tenants was evicted for rent arrears in 2002/03 (Pawson et al, 2005).

Eviction action

Where it is seen as sufficiently serious as to constitute breach of tenancy conditions, ASB committed by a tenant (private or social) can be tackled by the landlord taking legal action to repossess the property. Contracts may, for example, specifically prohibit the use of the tenant's house for illegal or immoral purposes, enabling repossession action to be taken in response to evidence of drug dealing or prostitution. Similarly, proceedings could be triggered by neglect leading to deterioration of the property, or to counter nuisance to neighbours. Repossession can take place only if endorsed by the county court (or sheriff court in Scotland). Hence, the court needs to be convinced that the acts concerned constitute a genuine breach of tenancy and that it is consequently reasonable to grant possession to the landlord (Scott and Parkey, 1998). Ultimately, such actions can lead to the tenant's eviction.

The incidence of social landlord evictions has greatly increased in recent years. In the period from 1994/95 to 2002/03 the numbers of tenants evicted by English local authorities annually rose more than threefold, from 0.2% to 0.6% of all tenants (Pawson et al, 2005). However, the vast majority of social landlord evictions are for rent arrears not ASB and the extent to which the numbers of ASB evictions have paralleled the overall eviction trend over the past few years is unknown.

Our study found that ASB-related eviction actions by social landlords were generally invoked in response to two types of misconduct: (a) 'serious' ASB – for example, involving violence, harassment or drug dealing – where there was a definite intention to secure possession, and (b) as a 'last resort' reaction to persistent though less severe 'offences' where all other attempts to secure a change in the offender's behaviour had failed (but where there was little or no genuine expectation that the action could be carried through). Some landlords were also motivated by the view that the 'shock value' of a Notice of Seeking Possession (NSP) could help alter a tenant's conduct where all other means of doing so had failed – although this view was strongly disputed within the sector.

The first step in an eviction action is to issue an NSP. In contrast with the way NSPs are sometimes used in rent arrears cases, evidence from the study suggests that issuing an NSP on ASB grounds is usually preceded by lengthy preparatory work and consultation with legally qualified personnel. It is widely appreciated by landlords that the courts will not normally entertain possession actions to remove 'anti-social' tenants except where there is clear evidence of substantial prior efforts to resolve the problem by non-legal means. Increasingly, practice here involves consideration of whether the problem could be most appropriately addressed through mediation. As one case study landlord's procedure manual states:

> The decision about whether or not to take legal action can be made at any stage but only after full consideration (of) non-legal remedies. [Legal action might involve an injunction, ASBO or repossession but] only in very extreme circumstances should possession be considered as an outcome – eg illegal trafficking of drugs with solid evidence or continuing damage to property in breach of a suspended order. Not only is possession difficult to secure, it also displaces the problem and creates social exclusion. (Notting Hill Housing Trust ASB Procedure Manual, 2001, p 9, cited in Pawson et al, 2005, p 80)

A landlord's decision as to whether a case of ASB should be pursued via possession action is not simply a matter of assessing its nature and persistence. It also depends on a landlord's confidence that the complainant (and/or others) will agree to provide a witness testimony in court, as housing officers are well aware that judges will not accept hearsay evidence.

While social landlords increasingly emphasise their receptiveness to ASB complaints, such allegations are usually investigated in detail before an eviction action is initiated. Our study found it was standard practice to interview both the complainant and the alleged perpetrator so that both sides of the story could be assessed. Other than in exceptional cases, for example, instances of violence or threats against staff, it was common for landlord personnel to have repeated personal contact with the alleged offender before the initiation of any court action.

Another issue reportedly considered routinely by social landlords in determining the appropriateness of legal action is whether the alleged perpetrator is subject to any form of vulnerability such as mental ill health that could affect their behaviour. In such circumstances it might be more appropriate to refer the tenant to a specialist support agency rather than to proceed with legal action. In part, such actions are dictated by the expectation of the courts that the landlord's conduct has been 'appropriate'. While such initiatives remain rare, there is growing social landlord interest in emulating the intensive family support approach to tackling ASB provided by initiatives such as the Shelter Inclusion Project in Rochdale (the subject of Chapter Nine, this volume) and the Dundee Families Project (Dillane et al, 2001; see Chapter Ten, this volume). Some authorities have sought to establish schemes embodying these principles but implemented entirely through outreach work, rather than involving a residential facility (Jones et al, 2004). Such a scheme, run by one of the ODPM case study local authorities, was described as a 'last chance saloon' for problem families, and was utilised post-eviction or prior to eviction, after ABCs and/or ASBOs had failed to work.

Shelter contends that there continue to be cases where vulnerable people are subject to ASB-triggered possession actions (Neuburger, 2003). ODPM case study interviewees acknowledged that this did, sometimes, occur. However, they contested Shelter's view that such actions are sometimes taken forward without the landlord having previously exhausted other potentially appropriate measures. While this may not always be so, the ODPM evidence does appear to call into question the assertion that landlord actions to counter ASB ignore perpetrator vulnerability (Brown, 2004).

Antisocial Behaviour Orders

As explained in the introductory chapter, ASBOs are Orders granted by a civil court against named individuals and which impose conditions on the subject's future conduct. Breaches of such conditions are a criminal offence that can result in imprisonment. Key arguments underpinning the creation of ASBOs included reducing the reliance on eviction as the 'nuclear option' for tackling ASB in the social rented sector and providing a legal tool that could address ASB in other tenures. However, most ASBO subjects are individuals living in social rented housing. For example, 85% of ASBOs granted in Scotland in 2003/04 involved local authority or housing association tenants (or members of their households) and 88% of incidents prompting ASBO action in 2003/04 were in residential areas near perpetrators' homes (DTZ Pieda Consulting and Heriot-Watt University, 2005). Despite the fact that ASBOs have been utilised to tackle alleged ASB in city centres, for example begging and prostitution, and that in most local authorities consideration of possible ASBO applications is a corporate responsibility not confined to the remit of the housing department, the research evidence suggests that the use of ASBOs typically remains closely integrated with social housing estate management.

Our study confirmed previous research evidence (Campbell, 2002) that ASBO subjects are usually young people, as housing officers often saw ASBOs mainly as a means of responding to ASB committed by children of tenants. Some housing officer interviewees saw them simply as a 'young person's injunction' – a comment on the fact that civil law injunctions can be obtained only for persons aged 18 and over (Pawson et al, 2005). The use of ASBOs for under-16s has sparked particular concerns stemming from the resulting detention of young people in breach of Orders. Holmes (2004) reported that, at current rates, more than 500 young people a year are being held in custody for breaching ASBOs in England and Wales.

While Scottish legislation allowing the granting of ASBOs in relation to 12- to 15-year-olds came into force in 2004, major differences with the situation in England and Wales are likely to remain, due to (a) the 'more demanding' Scottish procedures needing to be navigated prior to an ASBO application for a young person, and (b) the Scottish commitment not to incarcerate children in breach of Orders.

Housing officers interviewed in our study generally welcomed ASBOs as a means of targeting action on disruptive young people rather than initiating eviction action against the whole household. A counterview was that an ASBO is a weaker deterrent to ASB than an eviction action, as well as being much more expensive in legal costs. This connects with the argument that ASBOs are more appropriate than eviction actions to deal with problems caused by a tenant's children over whom the parents have little influence. The counterview here is that the threat of eviction could be valuable in emphasising that parents must accept responsibility for controlling young people's behaviour.

In practice, eviction actions and ASBO applications are not mutually exclusive options. In a case of serious ASB both measures might be adopted – either in parallel or in sequence. In response to an alleged assault on a neighbour, for example, an interim ASBO might be sought alongside an eviction action being entered in court. The conditions imposed on an alleged perpetrator by an ASBO may be duplicated in a Suspended Possession Order granted in response to an eviction action. Such a scenario is implied by Brown (2004, p 209) who asserts that where ASBO breaches are concerned: 'Eviction is a more likely sanction than imprisonment ... in practice ... local authorities may use ASBOs and techniques of surveillance and investigation primarily as a way of guaranteeing a swifter and surer eviction ... an accepted way to demonstrate that eviction is justified'.

Evidence suggests that monitoring a subject's adherence to ASBO conditions can be problematic. Since the breach of such conditions constitutes a criminal offence, this whole area is often regarded as the exclusive province of the police. Some landlords in our study saw 'breach monitoring' as at least partly their responsibility. In certain areas newly created neighbourhood warden officers were reported as playing a potentially useful role here. One case study local authority circulated information about ASBOs throughout the local area surrounding a subject's home. This included information about the terms of the Order, contact details of the agencies to whom breaches could be reported, and the identity of the offender – increasingly known as 'naming and shaming'. For adults, it had become routine to include the offender's photograph with this material, although this was not normal practice in relation to minors (Pawson et al, 2005).

Injunctions

Injunctions are a legal device available in England and Wales that can prohibit a named individual from carrying out specified acts (see Chapter Seven, this volume, for further discussion). A county court judge will hear applications for injunctions from social landlords and will make a decision on the basis of the strength of the evidence submitted. As with ASBOs, breaching the terms of an injunction is a criminal offence and can result in criminal prosecution. Unlike ASBOs, however, injunctions cannot be obtained to restrain the actions of people aged under 18.

As shown in Table 8.1 the proportion of local authorities making use of injunctions to tackle ASB in 2002/03 was similar to that using ASBOs. Subsequently, however, it may well be that the relative use of the two devices has changed. This is because of the 2003 change to the ASBO regime enabling the granting of interim ASBOs. A local authority's newly found ability to obtain an ASBO at short notice may well have eliminated what was previously seen as a key advantage of the injunction device.

Social landlords make much less use of the apparently analogous interdict device available in Scotland to tackle ASB (DTZ Pieda Consulting and Heriot-Watt University, 2005). Interdicts are seen as of very limited value because of the lack of sanctions in the event of breach, and the lack of power of arrest, unlike in England and Wales where limited powers of arrest have existed since the 1996 Housing Act.

Facilitating witness testimony

Successful legal action against anti-social tenants depends crucially on whether a landlord's case (for example, for an ASBO or Possession Order) is backed by witness evidence against the alleged perpetrator. The reluctance of witnesses to testify against their neighbours in court – sometimes due to genuine fears of retribution – is widely seen as one of the most significant barriers to tackling ASB; indeed, Burney (2002) argues that the concept of ASB came into being partly in response to witness intimidation as a crucial factor hampering the collection of evidence capable of supporting criminal convictions.

In the ODPM study, 41% of landlords reported that they operated some kind of victim support/witness protection scheme. In one example, provision of CCTV, lifeline alarms and mobile phones and a specialist repairs team to install spyholes and door chains were used to support witnesses. The aims here were to reassure vulnerable witnesses and to demonstrate the landlord's seriousness about tackling ASB. Another landlord had created a witness support officer post to work with witnesses in court (Pawson et al, 2005).

Another approach tried out by substantial numbers of social landlords has been the employment of 'professional witnesses' – often specialist organisations subcontracted to provide such services. The opinions on the merits of such an approach differ. In most of our research case studies it was said that professional witnesses were relatively expensive and not always effective in presenting evidence in court. A number of case study landlords reported making use of their own staff as in-house professional witnesses. Several were enthusiastic about the contribution of warden or patrol officers, seeing this as providing much better value for money than commissioning professional witness services externally. Posts of this kind seemed to be increasing in number, with some landlords expanding the establishment of this service in this way (Pawson et al, 2005).

Use of mediation and other non-legal remedies

Mediation

Mediation is described as offering a non-adversarial, non-judgemental, confidential, relatively inexpensive and speedy way of tackling disputes (Mackay and Brown, 1998; Gray et al, 2002). Partly because of its perceived role as an alternative to potentially costly and largely punitive measures, mediation is strongly recommended in good practice guidance on ASB (Richards et al, 1998; Housing Corporation, 2004; ODPM, 2004). Most social landlords in our study claimed to make some use of mediation in tackling ASB, mainly through referral of cases to external organisations, although just over a fifth of landlords reported providing mediation as an in-house service (Pawson et al, 2005).

In practice, mediation tends to be found useful by social landlords in dealing with mild ASB or serious personality or lifestyle clashes – including those where there are counter-allegations (Brown et al, 2003; Pawson et al, 2005). In most of these cases the main victim complaint was noise of one kind or another, although they also encompassed pets, rubbish, parking disputes, shared boundary disputes and the behaviour of children. Landlords viewed cases involving threats, fear of or actual physical violence, verbal abuse and racial harassment as being unsuitable for mediation. It can be argued that mediation – as a form of early intervention in an escalating dispute between neighbours – might help to defuse a situation that could otherwise become serious enough to warrant eventual legal action (for example, eviction proceedings). However, given the relatively 'low-level' issues seen as appropriately tackled through mediation, this form of intervention is likely to offer a very limited form of alternative to legal measures such as ASBOs.

Research evidence (Brown et al, 2003) suggests that appropriately targeted mediation can have a relatively high success rate in resolving or partially resolving a majority of suitably referred neighbour disputes. Further, mediation was found to be a highly cost-effective approach, with the cost of handling cases averaging just £121. This compared with the cost of legal action to tackle ASB that averaged £3,546 (although, as acknowledged by the authors, the dramatic difference between these two figures reflected the typically different seriousness of the incidents involved, as well as the nature of the responses invoked).

Nevertheless, agreements between disputants achieved through mediation cannot be legally enforced. The appropriate use of mediation also requires tenants to be willing to participate and our research revealed that this condition was frequently unfulfilled, partly because complainants often prefer to hand the problem to the landlord, seeing it as a matter for enforcement rather than negotiation (Pawson et al, 2005).

Acceptable Behaviour Contracts

ABCs were pioneered by Islington London Borough Council to reduce ASB by young people. An ABC is defined as 'a written agreement between a person who has been involved in anti-social behaviour and one or more local agencies whose role it is to prevent such behaviour' (Home Office, 2003, p 52). The agreements are drawn up by the police and housing officers, along with the young people and their families, and specify a range of behaviours that the young people agree to avoid. Home Office research (Bullock and Jones, 2004) suggests that ABCs have enjoyed some success in heading off the need for legal action.

Our study found that the use of ABCs had spread very quickly in the years to 2003, with nearly three quarters of responding social landlords having made some use of this device by this date. Landlords reported having found ABCs generally effective as an initial response to certain types of ASB including vandalism and graffiti, loud music and misuse of communal areas, particularly on the part of young people. ABCs are normally used in less severe anti-social problems than those for which ASBOs are applied (Campbell, 2002). Opting – at least initially – to negotiate an ABC rather than to seek an ASBO gives a chance of avoiding the high cost and court delay associated with ASBO applications. Evidence of ABC breach can also be used as evidence in an ASBO application. While it might appear logical for negotiation of an ABC to be a standard precursor to a possible ASBO application (or eviction action) this is not borne out by current practice. In Scotland, for example, only four of 13 local authorities that had experience of using ABCs reported having adopted such a policy (DTZ Pieda and Heriot-Watt University, 2005).

There is, in any case, a debate as to whether the term ABC is a misnomer, since such understandings 'have an uncertain legal status, not enforceable as a contract but not without consequences for the future of one's tenancy' (Brown, 2004, p 205). For the sake of technical accuracy, Brown argues, the term Acceptable Behaviour Agreement (ABA) should be used.

Social landlords and anti-social behaviour: scope for improved practice

Our research suggests some scope for social landlords to improve their counter-ASB practices. Mediation is one such area. While most landlords reported reliance on referral to external mediation, such arrangements were often of a purely ad hoc nature. Here, landlord action was limited to facilitating contact between the disputing parties and a local agency offering mediation services. This is quite different from the type of arrangement found in other areas where the landlord had a formal contract with a specialist mediation provider, with cases formally referred being either set against an annual quota, or charged to the landlord on a per case basis. Both of these latter types of arrangement deserve promotion. Landlords also need to ensure that referrals are made at an early stage in any neighbour dispute. While social landlord staff in our study generally acknowledged this, some third party mediators strongly disputed that early referral was normal practice.

Contrary to the assertions of some critics, it does not appear to be the case that, in seeking to tackle ASB, social landlords ignore the possibility of ASB perpetrator vulnerability. However, it seems likely that there is scope for improved practice in terms of developing systematic procedures for making such assessments and for considering possible action to provide appropriate medical, social or other support.

In terms of supporting dysfunctional families at risk of eviction and its potentially devastating consequences, it is encouraging that the pioneering work of the Dundee Families Project has been attracting growing attention (see Chapter Ten, this volume, and also Chapter Nine). As yet, however, this is probably confined mainly to highly rated local authorities. Further encouragement to learn from this approach should be provided by central government. Housing association inspection findings (see Camp, 2003) have also stressed the need for housing authorities to:

- develop more systematic recording practices to facilitate analysis of trends in ASB incidents and in landlord performance in this area;
- bridge the gap between landlord and tenant perceptions of how ASB is handled – for example, to keep complainants more closely in touch with action being taken to tackle reported neighbour problems; and
- improve staff training on tackling ASB with the aim of boosting officers' confidence in their ability to deal with such issues.

Conclusion

New Labour's communitarian ethic has placed social landlords at the centre of community safety initiatives. While measures such as ASBOs have been presented as empowering communities to act against troublesome individuals outside the social rented sector, the reality has been that such devices have been used mainly as part of the social landlord's armoury of measures to achieve social conformity within the tenant population.

There is little evidence that ASB is the growing menace sometimes portrayed by politicians and the media. Social landlords nevertheless face rising expectations on the part of both tenants and central government. Intensifying pressures also follow from the ongoing residualisation of social housing, accommodating a growing concentration of vulnerable people. For many social landlords, this has meant reconfiguring structures in favour of a more functionally specialist approach to ASB, potentially leading to what Brown (2004) describes as 'a new profession' with its own ethos and methods.

The past few years have seen social landlords reducing their sole reliance on powers to repossess the homes of disruptive tenants. Many local authorities and larger housing associations have enthusiastically embraced recently established remedies such as ABCs and ASBOs. However, while the potential contribution of mediation is increasingly widely appreciated, there remains substantial further scope for service development here.

While there is a growing volume of research activity focusing on social landlords' actions in tackling ASB, many important practice issues remain to be examined. How, for example, do social landlords combine the use of different counter-ASB devices? How do increasingly functionally specialised housing organisational structures impact on the management of ASB? How are breaches of ASBOs managed? More broadly, there is as yet little systematic knowledge on policy intervention outcomes – to what extent does the deployment of devices such as

ASBOs actually result in an improvement in the subject's behaviour and in what circumstances is this most likely? It is clear that much work remains to be undertaken in this field.

References

Atkinson, R., Mullen, T. and Scott, S. (2000) *The Use of Civil Legal Remedies for Neighbour Nuisance in Scotland*, Edinburgh: Central Research Unit, Scottish Executive.

Bramley, G., Munro, M. and Pawson, H. (2004) *Key Issues in Housing: Policies and Markets in 21st Century Britain*, Basingstoke: Palgrave.

Brown, A.P. (2004) 'Anti-social Behaviour, Crime Control and Social Control', *Howard Journal of Criminal Justice*, vol 43, no 2, pp 203-11.

Brown, A.P., Barclay, A., Eley, S. and Simmons, R. (2003) *The Role of Mediation in Tacking Neighbour Disputes and Anti-Social Behaviour*, Edinburgh: Scottish Executive Social Research Unit.

Bullock, K. and Jones, B. (2004) *Acceptable Behaviour Contracts: Addressing Anti-social Behaviour in the London Borough of Islington*, London: Home Office.

Burney, E. (2002) 'Talking Tough, Acting Coy: Whatever Happened to Anti-social Behaviour Orders?', *The Howard Journal*, vol 41, no 5, pp 469-84.

Camp, S. (2003) *Inspection Uncovered: Anti-social Behaviour*, London: The Housing Corporation.

Campbell, S. (2002) *A Review of Anti-Social Behaviour Orders*, Research Study 236, London: Home Office.

Cowan, D.S., Pantazis, C. and Gilroy, R. (2001) 'Social Housing as Crime Control: An Examination of the Role of Housing Management in Policing Sex Offenders', *Social and Legal Studies*, vol 10, no 4, pp 435-59.

Dillane, J., Hill, M., Bannister, J. and Scott, S. (2001) *Evaluation of the Dundee Families Project*, Edinburgh: Scottish Executive, Dundee County Council and NCH Action for Children.

Driver, S. and Martell, L. (2002) 'New Labour, Work and the Family', *Social Policy and Administration*, vol 36, no 1, pp 46-61.

DTZ Pieda Consulting and Heriot-Watt University (2005) *Use of Anti-social Behaviour Orders in Scotland*, Edinburgh: Scottish Executive.

Gray, J. with Halliday, M. and Woodgate, A. (2002) *Responding to Community Conflict: A Review of Neighbourhood Mediation*, York: Joseph Rowntree Foundation.

Holmes, C. (2004) 'What's With the Attitude?', *Housing Today*, 10 December, p 21.

Home Office (2003) *A Guide to Anti-Social Behaviour Orders and Acceptable Behaviour Contracts*, London: The Stationery Office.

Housing Corporation, The (2004) *Anti-social Behaviour: Policy and Procedure: Guidance for Housing Associations*, London: The Housing Corporation.

Hunter, C. and Nixon, J. (2001) 'Social Landlords' Responses to Neighbour Nuisance and Anti-social Behaviour: From the Negligible to the Holistic?', *Local Government Studies*, vol 27, no 4, pp 89-104.

Hunter, C., Nixon, J. and Shayer, S. (2000) *Neighbour Nuisance, Social Landlords and the Law*, Coventry: CIH.

Jones, R. (1997) 'Neighbour Nuisance and Anti-social Behaviour: Policy and Practice in Legal Remedies by Local Authorities', Dissertation submitted for MPhil in Housing Studies, Glasgow: University of Glasgow.

Jones, A., Pleace, N. and Quilgars, D. (2004) *Shelter Inclusion Project: Interim Evaluation of Findings*, London: The Housing Corporation and Shelter.

Mackay, R.E. and Brown, A.J. (1998) *Community Mediation in Scotland: A Study of Implementation*, Edinburgh: Scottish Office Central Research Unit.

Martell, L., Hale, S. and Leggett, W. (2004) *The Third Way and Beyond: Criticisms, Futures and Alternatives*, Manchester: Manchester University Press.

National Statistics (2005) 'Long Term Trends: National Recorded Crime' (www.crimestatistics.org.uk/output/Page108.asp, accessed 5 June 2005).

Neuburger, J. (2003) *House Keeping: Preventing Homelessness Through Tackling Rent Arrears in Social Housing*, London: Shelter.

ODPM (Office of the Deputy Prime Minister) (2004) *Anti-social Behaviour: Policy and Procedure: Code of Guidance for Local Housing Authorities and Housing Action Trusts*, London: ODPM.

Pawson, H., Flint, J., Scott, S., Atkinson, R., Bannister, J., McKenzie, C. and Mills, C. (2005) *The Use of Possession Actions and Evictions by Social Landlords*, London: ODPM.

Richards, J., Forbes, D. and O'Carroll, D. (1998) *Neighbour Nuisance: New Initiatives*, Good Practice Briefing, No 14, Coventry: CIH.

Scott, S. and Parkey, H. (1998) 'Myths and Reality: Anti-social Behaviour in Scotland', *Housing Studies*, vol 13, no 3, pp 325-45.

Part 3
The emerging mechanisms of addressing anti-social behaviour in housing governance

Evaluating the Shelter Inclusion Project: a floating support service for households accused of anti-social behaviour

Anwen Jones, Nicholas Pleace and Deborah Quilgars

Introduction

Social landlords in the UK have become more rigorous in responding to anti-social behaviour (ASB), partly reflecting increasing public expectations and central government priorities. There are no figures to indicate whether social landlords' use of possession actions for ASB has risen in recent years but research has shown that the use of possession action and eviction is widespread (see Chapter Eight, this volume). More than two thirds of social landlords initiated possession actions in response to ASB in 2002/03, with more than a third implementing evictions on these grounds (ODPM, 2005). It has been suggested that figures may understate the real impact of ASB on evictions as social landlords may prefer to cite rent arrears as the main reason for eviction (Communities Scotland, 2005). While enforcement is clearly an important aspect of any policy it is widely recognised that in order to be effective the problem of ASB has to be addressed holistically.

Research suggests that perpetrators of ASB are often vulnerable and usually poor, that they often have mental health problems and community care needs and may themselves be victims of ASB (see Chapter Four, this volume, and also Nixon et al, 2000; Campbell, 2002). Although ASB is not tenure-specific it tends to be associated with wider social exclusion problems such as poverty, family stress, community disorganisation, drug dependency, and truancy and school exclusion (SEU, 2000). The impact of eviction and exclusion from social housing may exacerbate these problems leading to a cycle of eviction and homelessness. As the Social Exclusion Unit has noted:

> Evicting anti-social people does not mean that the problem
> will go away. Some people will be deterred from future
> anti-social behaviour by the experience of eviction … some
> will not. If their problems are not addressed, the pattern of
> behaviour will repeat itself. (SEU, 2000, p 58)

Although the need for a 'three-pronged' approach to ASB, embracing
prevention, enforcement and rehabilitation, has been recognised by
the government (SEU, 2000; DTLR, 2002), research suggests that
most of the initiatives and measures developed to deal with ASB tend
to focus on enforcement and, to a lesser degree, the prevention of
ASB. Social landlords have deployed a range of remedies other than
eviction such as Noise Abatement Notices, Antisocial Behaviour
Orders (ASBOs) and injunctions, as well as non-legal measures such
as Acceptable Behaviour Contracts (ABCs) and, to a limited extent,
mediation (see Chapter Eight, this volume, and also Pawson et al,
2005). However, despite the reported successes of the Dundee Families
Project (see Chapter Ten, this volume, and Dillane et al, 2001) very
few initiatives have been developed which focus on the resettlement
of perpetrators (Nixon et al, 2003)[1]. Many services, including local
authorities, social landlords and voluntary agencies, work with
vulnerable households providing broad packages of support to help
people maintain their tenancies or to resettle following homelessness.
Such low-intensity support is a central plank of the Supporting People
programme and the research on such services is considerable, indicating
that such interventions are effective in helping people maintain
tenancies (Jones et al, 2002; Jones and Quilgars, 2004), but it has been
suggested that some households would benefit from interventions
specifically designed to address the underlying support needs which
may lead to ASB, to help people to change their behaviour and to
minimise the perverse outcomes of exclusion such as homelessness
(SEU, 2000; Dillane et al, 2001; ODPM, 2003).

This chapter aims to examine the role of support measures for
perpetrators of ASB within ASB strategies by presenting the interim
findings of an ongoing evaluation of the Shelter Inclusion Project, a
pilot resettlement and rehabilitation service for households at risk of
homelessness because of ASB. The Project was established by Shelter[2]
in partnership with Rochdale[3] Metropolitan Borough Council and
was developed to test a new approach to addressing ASB and social
exclusion. The Project builds on Shelter's recent experience of
delivering Homeless to Home, a low-intensity floating resettlement
service for homeless families (Jones et al, 2002).

Evaluation of the Shelter Inclusion Project

The Shelter Inclusion Project aims to reduce ASB; to promote social inclusion and community stability; to prevent eviction; and to provide a route back into settled housing. The Project, uniquely, works with families with children, single people and couples living in the social rented or private sector. The main criteria for referral are that households must be homeless or at risk of homelessness, have a history of ASB and be willing to engage with the Project. Preference is given to households with a history of homelessness and households consisting of people with complex needs.

The Project employs a manager, four support staff (two full-time and two part-time), two children and young persons' workers (job share), a young persons' team leader and administrative support. The Project can work with upwards of 31 households at a time; the staff user ratio is approximately 1:10-11 and, at the time of writing (2005), the children's workers can work with up to 26 children or young people. The Project has an annual budget of approximately £300,000, with key funding sources including Supporting People, the Neighbourhood Renewal Fund, the Children's Fund and Shelter.

The Centre for Housing Policy at the University of York was commissioned by Shelter to conduct an independent evaluation of the service, funded by The Housing Corporation. The overall aim of the study was to evaluate whether the Project met its stated aims and objectives and would assess the extent to which the Project:

- helped households address ASB;
- assisted households to maintain tenancies and avoid homelessness;
- resettled households that experienced homelessness due to their ASB; and
- impacted positively on service users, agencies and the wider community.

The evaluation tracked the service's progress over two-and-a-half years (April 2003-September 2005) and involved detailed monitoring of all referrals, interviewing users (including adults and children) and key stakeholders, tracking closed cases and assessing cost-effectiveness. The evaluation approach is presented in this chapter in four sections:

- identifying the personal and housing circumstances of service users and the nature of their ASB;
- evaluating the Shelter Inclusion Project referral process;

- describing and evaluating the assessment and delivery of support needs;
- conclusions and discussion about the potential contribution of support initiatives to reducing and managing ASB.

The personal and housing circumstances of Project users and the nature of reported anti-social behaviour

Assessment information had been collected on 47 households containing 159 people (68 adults and 91 children). This demonstrated a very particular service user profile in terms of gender, ethnicity and economic status. The majority of referrals were from the local arm's-length management organisation (ALMO) – Rochdale Borough-wide Housing – while most of the remainder came from registered social landlords. The referral routes had become more diverse since the start of the pilot with referrals being made by community-based workers, school nurses, health visitors, drug and alcohol workers and social services. A few service users contacted the Project directly. At the time of writing (early 2005) the Project had received one referral from the private rented sector.

These households were overwhelmingly made up of people of White European origin (99%). Almost two thirds of adult service users were women (68%). The largest single group of key service users[4] were women aged between 22-39, who collectively represented over two thirds of the female key service users and almost two thirds of all key service users.

Table 9.1 shows the broad type of each household. Households containing children predominated, representing nearly three quarters (71%) of all the households with which the Shelter Inclusion Project

Table 9.1: All households in Shelter Inclusion Project, by type and by gender of key service user (current and former cases)

Household type	Male	Female	All
Lone adult	4	5	9 (19%)
Adult couple	1	0	1 (2%)
Lone parent with one child	0	6	6 (13%)
Lone parent with two or more children	1	17	18 (39%)
Couple with one child	1	1	2 (4%)
Couple with two or more children	1	4	5 (11%)
Extended family	0	2	2 (4%)
Other arrangements	0	4	4 (9%)
All	7	39	47 (100%)

Note: Percentages are rounded.

Source: Project monitoring

worked. The largest group within these households were lone-parent households headed by a woman (50% of all households). Lone adults made up under a fifth (17%) of all households.

Thirteen of the households had five or more members and within this group, six households had six or more members. The most common reason for this was the presence of an older adult or adults, who had one or more adult children with their own offspring living in the same household. Two thirds (66%) of key service users had been living in Rochdale for more than five years and only three key service users were relatively recent arrivals in the area. A few key service users had spent all of their lives within the Rochdale area and three quarters (75%) of key service users reported having friends and family living in Rochdale.

The households contained few adults who were economically active at the point of their initial assessment and none of the key service users was in employment at the point of their assessment. Half of this group were full-time carers for dependent children, a small number were unemployed, unable to work for health reasons or in some other situation in which they were not economically active.

Housing situation at assessment

At the time of their assessment, five households had been found homeless or were about to become homeless. Another nine households had received or were about to be issued with a Notice of Seeking Possession (NSP) by their landlord, representing just under one fifth of the households. Collectively, those households under imminent threat of eviction, or who were homeless, represented one third (33%) of the households. The remaining two thirds (66%) of households had received warnings about ASB, 20 households had received a written warning from their landlord, and 10 households had received a verbal warning. The majority of households (65%) were tenants of Rochdale Borough-wide Housing, while three local registered social landlords housed the remainder. Households housed by the local authority were more likely to have been issued with an NSP. Most of the small number of households who were, or were imminently going to be, homeless, were currently living in registered social landlord stock when assessed. Seventeen households had a previous experience of homelessness (including three of the five households who were homeless at the point of assessment). Those households with prior experience of homelessness tended to have been homeless just once before (75% of those with prior experience), although a handful of households reported having been homeless several times.

Reported anti-social behaviour at assessment

The greatest proportion of households (one half) were involved in noise nuisance, while a third were involved in youth nuisance[5] or neighbour disputes. Ten households were experiencing ASB by people visiting the key service user or other household members. Twenty per cent of households had one or more members involved in more serious criminal activity, including theft, arson and criminal damage. Fewer households were involved in more minor crimes, such as vandalism. The nine lone-person households using the service were most likely to be reported to be involved in noise nuisance or arguments with their neighbours (five out of the nine in both cases).

The 68 adults were collectively subject to 78 forms of action as a result of ASB at the point of their assessment. Most of these actions were in the form of written and verbal warnings (32 of the former and 33 of the latter), although a few adults were also subject to ASBOs, injunctions and NSPs because of ASB. A small number of adults had been excluded from the housing register as a result of ASB. Only one adult was subject to an Acceptable Behaviour Contract (ABC) at the time of their assessment. The 91 children and young people in the households were unlikely to be directly subject to actions related to ASB. However, the fieldwork for the research suggested that actions against adults for ASB were sometimes linked, in whole or in part, to ASB by one or more of their children. Two thirds of the households reported being subject to ASB; households most frequently complained of neighbour disputes followed by youth nuisance or criminal activity and ASB from visitors.

Evaluating the referral process

Service users were asked why they thought they had been referred to the service and how they felt about this at the time of referral. Many respondents said they were referred to the Project following neighbours' complaints to their landlord. Others reported that a member of the household had an ASBO or was the subject of an ABC. However, service users rarely said that they had been responsible for any ASB, although a number said that their children or a third party had been responsible. Not all service users mentioned ASB at all; some said that they had been referred to the Project for general support, for example, help with children. A small number of respondents were unsure why they had been referred and a number asserted that they seemed to be taking the blame for the ASB of others. Many respondents explained that they had mixed reactions to the idea of working with the Project, with a number feeling that they had little choice but to accept the service if they were to keep their homes:

> [The housing officer] said basically if I didn't take up the help off Shelter then I could face losing the tenancy ... it just put me off them totally, I didn't really want them to come round.... I get on with me workers now, but when I first met them I didn't know what to think of them, you know what I mean?

> The council said something about help with the children – it was either that or get evicted – I was a bit nervous at first ... it was like all my children were naughty and out of control and I was a bad mother but then I realised that they were just trying to help.

Overall Project staff felt that the referral procedure was satisfactory but they were concerned that some agencies were making inappropriate referrals or not making referrals until a very late stage when households were almost at crisis point. This was despite the efforts of the Project to promote the service and its aims and objectives in the local area. Project workers reported that the service tended to work with households with low-level ASB issues. Although these households often had quite complex support needs and required the support of the Project in order to maintain their tenancies, workers were concerned that other households with more serious ASB problems were not being referred to the Project. As one worker explained:

> Maybe it is the housing officers who think that there are people who are easier to engage with and have lower level problems so they are the ones who get referred. There are others who think 'I'm not going near him, we'll get him evicted'.

Although Project staff felt that the work of the Project was valued by many agencies and individuals, they thought that some remained sceptical about their work and/or that some individuals/agencies preferred to adopt a more hard-line, enforcement approach to ASB.

Risk assessments were carried out for all new cases and the Project tried to involve service users in risk assessment wherever possible. In a few cases, households had been described, following assessment, as presenting potential risks to Project workers. The perceived risks were usually derived from a history of violent and abusive behaviour patterns from one or more individuals within a household, including a history of domestic violence. Where a particular risk existed, workers would not make lone visits to a household and in a very small number of cases they would not provide a service at their tenancy, but would instead meet the individual or household in a neutral area, such as a day-centre. A small number of households included individuals who had used or attempted to use weapons as part of a wider pattern of criminal activity. In one instance, one member of a household had a history of firearm offences and in another an individual with mental health problems had attempted to use explosives within their tenancy. Households with these characteristics were unusual within the Shelter Inclusion Project caseload. No households had been turned down for having too high a risk profile.

Assessment and delivery of support needs

Households tended to be characterised by high support needs. Nearly two thirds (60%) of the adults reported that they had depression or other mental health problems, while one quarter reported a drug or alcohol dependency. Just under a quarter described themselves as having a limiting illness or disability. Smaller numbers of children were reported as having a limiting illness or disability, while just over one tenth of children were reported as having behavioural or mental health problems. Eight of the nine lone-person households using the Shelter Inclusion Project were reported as being alcohol dependent at the time of their referral. Most of this group were reported as having depression and more than half were also reported as having mental health problems. Debt was widespread among the households, with three quarters reporting that they had one or more debts at the time of their assessment.

Just under half of the group of school-age children were attending school with no reported problems. One quarter of the children and young people were described as 'regularly attending school with some problems'. A small number of children were reported as being in special education, that is, they had a statement of special educational needs or were in a special school or attending a pupil referral unit. Just over 80% of the children and young people who should have been in full-time education were in some form of full-time education. A minority of children were permanently or temporarily excluded from school or were routinely truanting. A few were also awaiting a school place. Contact between children and young people in the households and services for their age group was very low at the point of assessment. Despite the socioeconomic profile of the households and their situation of housing insecurity, only three children were reported as in contact with either Sure Start or Connexions services at the point of assessment. Rather more children and young people were in contact with local youth services or projects for young people but few children were in contact with educational welfare services and only a small number had a social worker at the point of referral. Seven children (just under 10%) were on the Child Protection Register. Most of the children were not receiving support from any service.

Adult contact with support services was also quite low, with most adults not receiving support services. Contact with social services was most common, with 12 adults out of 67 reporting having a social worker or receiving other forms of social services support. Only seven adults reported contact with mental health services despite almost 60% reporting depression or other mental health problems. Contact with drug and alcohol services was similarly low (10%) despite a quarter reporting drug or alcohol dependency as a support need. Most of the adults were not receiving support services.

Households were asked at assessment what types of support they required. They most frequently wanted support around management of their ASB, with quite high numbers of households wanting support related to depression and stress. Smaller numbers of households reported a need for help with a range of emotional and social support issues, including help with building self-confidence, developing social skills and anger management. Households also wanted assistance with accessing other services, support with re-housing and setting up a new home, and help in accessing community groups and other local community support services. Households reported needs for a diverse range of low-intensity housing-related support, including help with managing money, claiming benefits and accessing other services. Several households also wanted low-level practical help with decorating and managing the garden, and a small number requested assistance with securing furniture and white goods. One quarter of households wanted access to Shelter Inclusion Project children's and young people's workers at the point of their assessment. Smaller numbers wanted help with adapting their home for children (modifications such as stair gates) or help with their children's school attendance. A small number of households also wanted advice and support with parenting.

Just under one fifth of the adults in households reported a need for help with accessing education and training services for themselves.

The Shelter Inclusion Project provided a wide range of practical, emotional and social support and interventions to households including:

- housing advocacy
- help with re-housing and setting up a new home
- help with benefits and money management
- support with addressing ASB issues
- practical assistance (such as decorating, gardening and repairs, providing goods)
- limited financial assistance (for example, providing decorating vouchers)
- liaising with, and referring to, other agencies
- general emotional support
- developing self-confidence, social skills and social activities
- support with health issues, particularly depression
- assistance with accessing education and training
- parenting advice and support
- fun days for households
- working with children (for example, addressing school attendance and behavioural issues and activities for children).

Evaluating the delivery of support needs

Service users found all types of support useful and many reported that the Project had been able to help with everything they needed. Some types of assistance appeared to be particularly highly valued, including: liaison with their landlord with respect to ASB issues and eviction proceedings, liaison with other agencies, practical support, assistance with managing money and setting up repayment schemes and helping with parenting advice and support on better ways of managing their life, as well as the behaviour of children. Project workers explained that the service offered a general resettlement support but they felt that their work was becoming more focused on ASB as the pilot project developed. Although they found it difficult to describe any method or strategy for dealing with ASB, they believed that much of the support had an indirect effect on people's behaviour:

> We'll provide or do anything where we can see some sustainable outcomes in terms of anti-social behaviour. For

example, the project will provide beds for children where they do not have one – outcomes are considerable in terms of self-esteem, behaviour, meeting curfews and emotional well-being.

Project staff also explained that it was often necessary to address a range of pressing issues, such as debt or urgent property repairs (for example, replacing windows) before being able to address behaviour directly, and that it took some time to build up trust so that the user felt confident in discussing ASB issues.

Work with children was seen as an integral and crucial area of the Project's role and one appreciated by service users. However, staff shortages meant that not all families that might have benefited from the support of a children's or young person's worker had been assigned a worker. Some service users commented in earlier interviews that activities were not suitable for older children and the Project had since employed a children's and young persons' team leader to coordinate provision for all age groups. Where households had the support of a children's worker this support was highly valued. Support included liaison with schools over attendance problems, behavioural difficulties and bullying as well as referral to specialist services, for example, child psychologists. Parents also appreciated support and advice in helping them control their children's behaviour:

> I had problems controlling the children – I couldn't and they controlled me but since working with Shelter things have improved, the swearing has stopped. Now instead of shouting at them I do things that [worker] suggested like making them sit on the naughty step or stopping them from watching telly.

The Project also organised fun days and leisure activities for households and children. Some of these activities, such as 'pamper days' for parents, aimed to provide some relaxation and a break from routine for households. Over the period of the evaluation many activities, especially those for children, had become more focused on challenging or rewarding behaviour rather than simply providing a diversion for children and young people. Activities such as outdoor pursuits and sports were also seen as a way of helping children and young people develop confidence and self-esteem and, ultimately, to address ASB. By involving parents or other adult household members in affordable activities locally, it was hoped to encourage adults to spend quality time with their children.

Closing cases

The Project aimed to work with households for up to 12 months although support could be provided for shorter and longer periods as required. Most service users were aware that the Project could only support them for a limited time and most understood that the service would gradually taper off as they became more able to cope. They also knew that they could contact the Project if they experienced problems in the future. However, a number suggested that they would like to have the support for an indefinite period. Where cases had closed most people felt that this was appropriate and understood that they had 'had their time'. Project staff explained that they tried to be clear with service users about how long support would last and the process of ending support; they used regular reviews to discuss ongoing support needs and to raise the issue of ending support. Nevertheless, Project staff reported that some service users raised issues and problems only when their time with the Project was coming to an end:

> A number of people, when we have gone to sign them off, it's suddenly ... everything has come out. Massive child protection issues have been raised, real issues of vulnerability have come up. Whether it is only when people realise that we are really going – that it is voluntary and that it is going to end, that they suddenly start telling us loads of stuff, or suddenly things start coming to the fore....

A second issue was that some service users were very reluctant to be referred on to mainstream agencies. It appeared that trust and positive working relations had developed between Shelter workers and service users but that the households, many of whom reported negative experiences of statutory agencies in the past, were still not ready to engage with mainstream agencies. Project workers were concerned that these households would find it difficult to cope and to sustain their tenancies without ongoing support.

Impacts of the service

While it is not possible to assess the longer-term full impacts of the Project, monitoring data, reports by service users, local stakeholders and Project staff indicate that the Project had enjoyed some success, most significantly in helping people maintain their tenancies and reduce ASB. All the households were referred to the Project on the basis that their tenancy was at some degree of risk due to ASB and all 47 of the households were variously subject to NSPs, written warnings and verbal warnings, while a minority were actually homeless at the time they began working with the service. Tenancy sustainment data provided by the Project indicate that most households that the service was working, or had worked, with were still in the same tenancy or had made planned moves.

Some service users explained that they would probably have been evicted from their tenancy if they had not received the support of the service. In some cases service users explained that their willingness to accept the support of the Project appeared to make housing and enforcement agencies treat them more fairly and more willing to give them a second chance. For others, the support they received meant that ASB warnings did not proceed to the point of eviction. Some households were still struggling with ASB issues, and also felt that they were victims of ASB. Most service users, however, including those who had stopped receiving support, had managed to address these issues, or were in the process of addressing them. In some cases problems had been caused by visitors, ex-partners or older children and these problems ceased once they had left the property. In one case, for example, complaints of ASB stopped when a service user's son was sent to prison. However, for most service users, the process was much longer and involved learning how to communicate more effectively with others in their life and wider community. A number of service users described how the Project's support, including emotional and practical, had helped them to manage their lives better:

> At one time it was just a free for all in here every morning … they'd all be scrapping so I'd just go back to my bedroom and shut the door…. Now if they are creating and they are up before me I'll get up and sort them out … they are not as bad as they were and I feel better in myself because now when I get up in the morning I've got windows and a front door I can use … it was horrible. The front garden was the same but my son has been doing [the garden]. [Children's worker] took him to the garden centre and bought a load of flowers that he planted…. I don't know whether she talked to the children about their behaviour

and they haven't advised me how to cope – I just feel better and can manage better.

They did help a lot. I started sorting myself out once I met them. She [the support worker] noticed the difference in the house. She sort of bucked me up and got my life back. I had got to the point where I didn't give a monkeys, I'd get up in the morning and go and have a drink and not worry. Same routine every day. I was always worrying about money but then I'd think 'sod that' and go for a drink. But drinking isn't the answer because the debts are there the next day plus a crappy head....

Closed cases

Of the 17 households that had ceased to use the Shelter Inclusion Project, all but six were in contact with the Project for 40 weeks or more, while eight households had been in contact for a year or more. Two thirds of the 17 households had stopped using the Shelter Inclusion Project because they no longer required assistance; two stopped using the service because they had made a planned move out of the Rochdale area. Only one household had moved from its last known address without notifying the Project. This suggests that exits from the Shelter Inclusion Project were generally planned and managed by the households and the Project.

At the time the 17 cases closed, none of the households were assessed as at risk of homelessness. Information on the housing status of these households at the time they started working with the Project was available for 11 households. Seven of these households had a written warning, two had a verbal warning, one was homeless and another had been issued with an NSP. None of the key service users who had been subject to actions for ASB were still subject to action at the point the service ceased. There were no current written or verbal warnings, or ABCs or higher-level actions such as ASBOs, injunctions or evictions linked to ASB against any of the key service users. In 12 of 14 cases, involvement in ASB by the key service user was reported to have ceased altogether. In five of the six cases where children and young people were reported as having been involved in ASB at the time of assessment, this involvement in ASB was reported to have ceased. However, in one case, the only instance of any individual in any household continuing to be involved in ASB, one young person had been made the subject of an ABC which was still current when contact with the Project ceased.

The 17 households were most likely to have received support with managing money followed by support directly related to addressing involvement with ASB, practical assistance with decoration and claiming benefits. Assistance was also given to 13 households in accessing other services such as health services, social services, youth projects, Connexions and Sure Start. A majority of households received help around self-confidence and managing depression and stress and a third of households received assistance with parenting and support from a children's worker. Practical assistance with housing was also widely provided, including assistance with improving the state of gardens, which in some instances was one of the reasons why the household had been the subject of action from their landlord. Six households were given assistance with setting up new homes and eight had either been re-housed following support from the Project or had been assisted in seeking re-housing. Most of the households (13 out of 17) reported that there were no areas in which they would have liked more help from Shelter. In the other cases one household would have liked ongoing emotional support while two households would have liked more help with gardening and moving home.

Information was available on 27 of the children and young people within the 17 households; of these children 23 were of school age. Three quarters of these children were reported as regularly attending school with no problems, one young person had left school and had entered training and the remainder were in special education. Two children were reported as truanting at the time that contact with the Project ceased. This compares positively with the typical situation of children at the start of their contact with the Project. Although full data were not available for every child this early evidence suggests that some improvements in children's educational situations were associated with contact with the service.

Achievements with individual households were sometimes impressive. In one instance a household containing three children who had been out of full-time education for three years was supported in getting all the children back into school. In addition, a few adults had secured paid work during the time they worked with the Project, three had full-time work and a fourth had secured part-time work. The remaining adults were mainly carers for dependent children.

Conclusion

These findings suggest that the Shelter Inclusion Project is making a positive impact on the lives of its service users. Although information was only available on 17 closed cases it has been seen that leaving the Project was almost always a planned process and occurred only at the point where people's housing situations had been stabilised. In addition, service users had made good or some progress in addressing ASB and none of the key service users who had been subject to actions for ASB were still subject to these actions at the point of leaving the service.

Tenancy sustainment figures suggest that most households still working with the Project were also successfully managing their tenancies. Service users interviewed for the research spoke of the considerable benefits of the Project and many felt that it had made a significant positive impact on their lives, preventing debt accumulating, eviction and, importantly, helping them feel better able to cope. The extent to which these improvements can be sustained will be examined through further research that aims to track the progress of households over time.

While the Project had been successful in meeting two of its main aims (addressing ASB and preventing homelessness), and appeared to be impacting positively on service users, it is more difficult to assess the impact of the Project on agencies and the wider community. The next stage of the research will address this issue, but it is anticipated that, while the Project may have a positive impact on individual households, and possibly their neighbours, it would be difficult for a small project working with only approximately 31 households to have a significant impact on the community as a whole. Similarly, while the Project has certainly appeared to have helped households to avoid the most extreme form of exclusion – homelessness – and had helped a small number of people into employment and training and children back into school, the client group as a whole is a poor and marginalised one, characterised by complex and often quite high support needs. The Shelter Inclusion Project aimed to support people for a limited amount of time, thereafter referring those with ongoing needs to mainstream agencies for support. It was clear that some service users were not willing to be referred on to statutory agencies and this has implications for the sustainability of the progress they had made.

To date little is known about the effectiveness of rehabilitation projects for perpetrators of ASB. The only completed study is of the Dundee Families Project (Dillane et al, 2001; see also Chapter Ten, this volume), which was found to be successful in helping families address and change their behaviour and to avoid eviction. Forthcoming studies, including a two-year evaluation of six projects in the North West of England funded by the government, will add to our extremely limited knowledge of such interventions. Emerging evidence from the study of the Shelter Inclusion Project suggests that the combination of enforcement (from verbal and written warnings to NSPs) and rehabilitation may be effective as perpetrators who are forced to recognise the serious consequences of their behaviour may be more willing to accept support and change their behaviour. However, little is known about the reasons why some perpetrators refuse support despite the seriousness of their housing situation. Further, very little is known about the attitudes of referral agencies and how individual housing officers and other key workers decide who is suitable for or deserving of help.

There remains a tension between enforcement and rehabilitation and, despite government rhetoric promoting a three-pronged approach to the problem of ASB, there is still a strong emphasis on punitive approaches. Even less is known about public attitudes towards perpetrators of ASB (although see Chapter Four, this volume). Media reports and government policy documents suggest that people are increasingly intolerant of ASB and their expectation is that the problem should be removed rather than 'treated'. If rehabilitation is to succeed in helping households to maintain their tenancies and contribute to sustainable communities then projects will require the support of all those involved including neighbours, community groups, statutory services and housing providers. Research findings to date demonstrate that rehabilitation can be effective and can benefit both service users (in terms of housing stability and improved quality of life) as well as service providers (saved costs of eviction proceedings and so on). There is, however, a need for more longitudinal research to examine the sustainability of interventions.

Notes

[1] Research currently being conducted by the Centre for Research in Social Exclusion at Sheffield Hallam University and the University of Salford and the Building Research Establishment for the Office of the Deputy Prime Minister has identified only eight projects developed specifically to work with perpetrators of ASB in England, all based in the North West.

[2] Shelter is a national homelessness organisation working on behalf of homeless people in England, Scotland and Wales.

[3] Rochdale is a metropolitan district in Greater Manchester and serves a population of just over 200,000 people. Rochdale is one of the 88 most deprived areas in England and Wales.

[4] The Shelter Inclusion Project often worked with several individuals in a household but the Project also identified a main applicant for the service who was both the point of referral and what the Shelter Inclusion Project termed the 'key service user'.

[5] For the purposes of the evaluation, 'youth nuisance' refers to low-level disturbances. Criminal offences committed by young people are recorded under 'serious crime'.

References

Campbell, S. (2002) *A Review of Anti-Social Behaviour Orders*, Home Office Research Study 236, London: Home Office.

Communities Scotland (2005) 'Thematic Study: Evictions in Practice' (www.communitiesscotland.gov.uk/stellent/groups/public/documents/webpages/cs_008343.pdf).

Dillane, J., Hill, M., Bannister, J. and Scott, S. (2001) *Evaluation of the Dundee Families Project*, Edinburgh: Scottish Executive, Dundee City Council and NCH Action for Children.

DTLR (Department of Transport, Local Government and the Regions) (2002) *Tackling Anti-Social Tenants*, London: DTLR.

Jones, A. and Quilgars, D. (2004), *Advice Note on the Prevention of Homelessness*, Cardiff: National Assembly for Wales.

Jones, A., Pleace, N. and Quilgars, D. (2002) *Firm Foundations: An Evaluation of the Shelter Homeless to Home Service*, London: Shelter.

Nixon, J., Hunter, C. and Shayer, S. (2000) *Neighbour Nuisance, Social Landlords and the Law*, Coventry: CIH.

Nixon, J., Blandy, S., Hunter, C., Jones, A. and Reeves, K. (2003) *Tackling Anti-Social Behaviour in Mixed Tenure Areas*, London: ODPM.

ODPM (Office of the Deputy Prime Minister) (2003) *Tackling Anti-Social Behaviour in Mixed Tenure Areas*, Housing Research Summary No 178, London: ODPM.

ODPM (2005) *Possession Actions and Evictions by Social Landlords*, Housing Research Summary No 219, London: ODPM.

Pawson, H., Flint, J., Scott, S., Atkinson, R., Bannister, J., McKenzie, C. and Mills, C. (2005) *The Use of Possession Actions and Evictions by Social Landlords*, London: ODPM.

SEU (Social Exclusion Unit) (2000) *Anti-social Behaviour*, Report of Policy Action Team 8, London: SEU.

TEN

Tackling anti-social behaviour: an evaluation of the Dundee Families Project

Suzie Scott

Introduction

Although many social landlords have begun to take a preventative approach to anti-social behaviour (ASB), few landlords have developed intensive support services for families as a means of dealing with ASB (Scott et al, 2001; see Chapter Nine, this volume). This chapter provides an evaluation of an innovative approach to tackling ASB, based on a longitudinal study of the Dundee Families Project (Dillane et al, 2001). The Scottish Executive, Dundee City Council and NCH Action for Children Scotland jointly funded the research.

The Dundee Families Project was established with government Urban Programme funding to assist families who are homeless or at severe risk of homelessness as a result of 'anti-social behaviour'. The Project was run by a charitable voluntary agency, NCH Action for Children Scotland, in partnership with Dundee City Council housing and social work departments. The Project worked with families deemed to have exhibited a range of ASB, with the aim of enabling them to avoid eviction or be restored to satisfactory tenancy arrangements. The Project provided an all-year 24-hours-a-day service and was intensively staffed, with a total of 15 staff in May 2001. The service was offered in three main ways:

- admission to the *core block*, which comprised accommodation for up to four families where residents received intensive support;
- support to a small number of *dispersed* flats run by the Project, for families needing accommodation but less intensive support;
- an *outreach service* provided to selected families in their existing accommodation, where they were at risk of eviction due to ASB.

The Project followed a systemic approach to family difficulties and offered a range of services through individual and couple counselling, family support and group work. These included:

- after-school groups
- young persons group
- cookery group
- parenting group
- parenting skills group
- craft group
- anger management group
- residents support group
- tenancy workshops.

Decisions on entry to the Project were made by an admissions panel, which assessed referrals and reviewed cases. The membership included representatives from the Project, NCH and Dundee City Council housing and social work departments. A project advisory group was also set up to provide guidance and feedback from service users and local residents.

The research

The research was intended to evaluate the processes, outcomes and costs of the Project, using primarily qualitative methods. The objectives of the study were to:

- examine the work carried out by the Project;
- obtain the perspectives of service users and other key stakeholders;
- ascertain the opinions of local residents about the Project;
- assess the progress and outcomes for families served by the Project;
- gather information about the costs associated with the Project.

The multiple objectives of the study required gathering data from a range of sources. The main methods of gathering information were:

- initial and final interviews with 19 Project staff, NCH managers and external stakeholders;
- a 10% sample survey of 23 local residents;
- initial interviews with 53 individuals in 20 families;
- follow-up interviews with 24 individuals in 10 of the families;

- interviews with three families referred to the Project who did not engage;
- detailed analysis of 126 case records;
- questionnaires to housing and social work staff on 70 closed cases;
- discussion of vignettes (brief case scenarios) with housing and social work staff;
- examination of Project reports and financial figures;
- observation of the work of the Project over a two-year period.

The origins of the Dundee Families Project

Dundee City Council had a large public sector housing stock of around 23,000 properties. Like any significant public sector landlord, Dundee had problems with the behaviour of a small minority of its tenants: in 1996/97 the council received around 800 complaints about neighbour nuisance (around 3.5% of all tenancies). A number of families were causing serious problems to their neighbours.

During the early 1990s, the housing department responded to pressure from tenants and councillors to take stronger action against people who were causing a nuisance to neighbours. By the mid-1990s, the council had a very high rate of court action for eviction and had also pioneered the use of interdicts (the Scottish equivalent of injunctions) to stop behaviour that caused concern. In 1993, 20 families were evicted for ASB (Dundee City Council, 1999).

However, although the council maintained its firm policy, the initial enthusiasm for legal action began to decline: in 1996/97, 13 tenants were taken to court and seven were evicted for ASB. Council interviewees said it became clear that eviction was not solving the problem. In part, this was because the legal process was perceived to be slow and the outcome uncertain. Sometimes neighbours were afraid to act as witnesses due to fears of reprisals and in a number of cases it was not possible to take legal action due to lack of evidence. Where problems continued, there was an impact on neighbouring properties, leading to requests for transfers and subsequent high void levels. There was agreement that the costs of ASB were high, as a councillor explained:

> You've got a ripple effect of these families ... that are causing anti-social behaviour and time involvement.... As we've found out, it only takes one bad family to clear a block ... and that's all costing, you know.

The interviewees also felt that arrangements for families who were facing eviction for ASB were problematic. Up to 1996, public sector housing was a district council responsibility and social work was a regional council responsibility. The housing department had a very firm policy on ASB, which aimed to pursue legal action to evict the perpetrators. The social work department, meanwhile, would not provide accommodation where a family had been made homeless from council accommodation. The families who were facing eviction fell through the gap created by these opposing policies.

As a result, interviewees said that many families ended up in the private rented sector, bed and breakfast accommodation or temporary housing. In some cases evicted families would move in with friends or relatives in the same area or rent a flat in an ex-council property. The problems were therefore simply displaced. In some cases, the housing department would reconsider families who had previously been evicted, using the provisions of the Homeless Persons legislation. However, even where a decision was made to re-house a family, staff in area housing offices had to be persuaded to accept them. This had time and resource implications for the Homeless Persons Service as officers tried to negotiate a solution with housing and social work departments, as a housing officer explained:

> It is difficult to actually say 'X' amount of staff time was spent on issues around anti-social families. But what used to take up an awful lot of time was when we had a family who were homeless, who we had assessed as statutory homeless, and whom we were fairly clear that we had a duty to re-house; but we knew that we could likely encounter opposition and an awful lot of time was spent in negotiation with our colleagues in area offices.

The policy of taking legal action therefore proved cumbersome, did not solve the underlying problems and did not necessarily diminish the demands made on housing and other services.

The catalyst that sparked the idea for the Families Project was a family with a long history of severe ASB in council tenancies. The family was evicted for ASB and presented as homeless to the housing department's Homeless Unit. The Unit's staff deemed the family to be intentionally homeless, offered temporary accommodation, and gave them 28 days to find their own accommodation. Social workers involved with the family intervened on their behalf but the housing department were reluctant to re-house the family. Eventually a compromise position was reached, and a voluntary agency was asked to take a tenancy and support the family, as a housing officer described:

> Various supports were put in from Barnardo's and from Social Work and some of the housing issues were addressed in terms of the anti-social behaviour ... plus debt issues with the Housing Department. After something like about six months there had been a remarkable change in this family and everything was going well. The kids were at school and things were progressing and she had made payments towards the debt and it was then agreed ... to re-house the family.... So the long and the short of it was that this was seen to work.

Following that successful precedent, the housing department developed a proposal to set up a larger and more permanent model. An application for funding was submitted to the Scottish Office for Urban Programme funding in 1993. The Project was formally established in 1995 and officially opened in November 1996.

Overview of cases dealt with by the Project

Around 126 cases were referred to the Families Project between November 1996 and October 2000. Nearly all the referrals came from housing or social work services. During the four-year period the Project accepted 69 cases (55% of those referred). Around a third of the referrals (43) were refused on the grounds that they were 'inappropriate' because the family did not fit the Project criteria, most commonly because, although the families had problems, there was no evidence of ASB. Around one tenth (14) of families did not engage with the Project, either expressing unwillingness to take up the offer of assistance or, more commonly, failing persistently to keep appointments with Project staff. These figures indicate that the Project spent quite a lot of time on families who were not ultimately offered a service. While this might be seen as wasteful, workers and other agencies indicated that it was important to have a careful system for ensuring the work was well targeted on appropriate and motivated families.

The majority of families received support from the project on an outreach basis, while they were living in the family tenancy. Of the 69 cases accepted and worked with, 11 received intensive support in the core block, 16 were supported in dispersed accommodation and 42 received outreach services in their own home, to prevent eviction action.

Family characteristics and needs

Previous studies (Atkinson et al, 2000; Hunter et al, 2000) found that many of the perpetrators of ASB could be classified as vulnerable. However, neither study was able to consider the characteristics of families accused of ASB in depth. The Dundee Families Project research provided a unique opportunity to do so. This was achieved by examining the Project's detailed records of 34 families and interviews with a further 20 families.

Around two thirds of the households were headed by a lone parent and one third were two-parent households. In a number of the lone-mother households, there was contact with a male partner. In some cases, the partners had separated but there was contact with the children. In four cases, the male partner was in prison. The number of children ranged from one to 13. The average family size was 3.4 children, considerably higher than the national average. Virtually all the families were poor and reliant on state benefits.

The most common forms of 'anti-social behaviour' that families had engaged in were neighbour disputes and poor upkeep of property. Many of the families had a long history of serious ASB and, in some cases, criminal activity. The main types of ASB exhibited by the families accepted by the Project were noise, violence, damage to property, drug dealing, arson and running a protection racket. These problems were equally likely to be caused by the adults or the children in the family. The other main factors prompting referral were related to family relationships and control of children. In most instances, professionals also had concerns about parenting and care of children. Overall, 70% of the adults had drug or alcohol problems and over half had criminal convictions for offences including: assault, theft, shoplifting, housebreaking and car- and drug-related offences. There was also evidence of abuse or neglect affecting almost half the children interviewed and over half the women had suffered domestic abuse.

Most of the families had a complex and mobile housing history. The common experience for most was of several involuntary moves (a number had been evicted previously). The number of previous tenancies per family ranged from two to 11 with an average number of five. The unstable housing history of the families was evidenced by the fact that, on average, each child had attended four schools. One child had attended nine separate schools. As a consequence of family instability, many of the children had significant school-related difficulties including behavioural problems, leading to exclusion and chronic non-attendance. Seven of the 11 young people interviewed had attended some kind of special school or educational unit.

A number of the families were found to have serious health problems: eight of the 20 case study families had physical health problems including heart problems, kidney problems, cancer and epilepsy. Several of the children had attention deficit/hyperactivity disorder (ADHD) which required constant supervision and regular medication. Half the mothers in the case studies were receiving treatment for depression. There was evidence of post-natal depression, sleep disorders, agoraphobia and mental health problems (see Chapter Nine, this volume, for similar findings).

Outcomes for families actively worked with

The Project recorded an assessment of work achieved and perceptions of the degree of success for each case. These were used to assess outcomes of all 56 closed cases actively worked with. Cases were treated as 'successful' when the record indicated that the main goals were achieved. On this basis, just under two thirds of the total cases (59%) had 'successful' outcomes. Just under one fifth of the cases (18%) were 'unsuccessful' in that major goals had not been met. The rest of the cases had either moved away (6) or their circumstances had changed (7).

In order to assess the views of other agencies about the impact of the Project, questionnaires were distributed to both the social work and housing teams that had contact with 70 families who had been referred to the project. The 70 cases included a range of project involvement from brief contact to residence in the core block. Five families had been supported in the core block, five in dispersed tenancies and 32 were supported as outreach cases. In the remaining families, the cases were closed after the initial assessment. Responses were received for every family, with responses from both housing and social work received for 44 cases.

In some cases, a family had moved away from Dundee or was no longer in contact with council staff. There were 48 cases where there was still some contact and Dundee Council staff were asked to give an evaluation of the current functioning of the families. Social work respondents judged the situation satisfactory in 19 out of 25 cases and housing officers felt that the situation was satisfactory in 26 out of 30 cases. Where both housing and social work staff expressed an opinion, there was some divergence of views, reflecting the different issues on which the respective professionals were making their judgements. It seemed that some families were maintaining their tenancies successfully and causing fewer problems to neighbours but had not resolved parenting or family-related difficulties. In summary, information from housing and social work staff about the progress of closed cases indicated that a considerable number of the families that the Project had worked with were still doing well. However, some still had serious difficulties and in two instances the children had been taken into care.

The research team followed up 10 families who had received support from the Project to assess their views. All of the families were very positive regarding the amount of contact that they had with the Project and the services they had received. A few examples of families' views are given below:

> I think that they do a pretty good job. You get to express your views. (father)

> Nobody else is doing anything; they are the only ones, the last hope. (mother)

> Staff are quite friendly, understanding and they actually listen to you and take on board your views. (mother)

> Very good team, they do their best to help you. (mother)

Family members did not express any overly negative comments regarding the operation of the Project, but they did give several suggestions where they felt improvements could be made:

> They could get more staff and deal with the families that they have taken on. (father)

> Staff could be more consistent. (father)

> They don't speed things up getting us moved and get us out of this poor house, it gets worse by the minute. (11-year-old boy)

Parents and children were asked for their views on whether their housing and family situations had changed, improved, stayed the same or got worse. Seven families said that their housing and family situation had improved. One family stated that life had been quieter and that there had not been any problems with the neighbours. Another mother felt that 'things might be starting to improve, slowly but surely'. Her eight-year-old daughter summed up her housing and family situation:

> ... we used to have two dogs and now we only have one ... my room is tidier and my brother's, my mum is tidying up more, she never used to.... Things are starting to go back to normal, mum's getting on better, she is putting on weight ... dad's not staying here anymore.

Two families deemed their housing situation to be unchanged. One was still suffering from overcrowding, while another was living in the core block, waiting to be re-housed to suitable accommodation. One parent receiving an outreach service felt life had got worse: 'things have got so bad that we are like prisoners; afraid to go out'. However, her son felt that there had been some improvement and that neighbours were not so hostile. Family members were also asked what they thought their housing and family situation would be like if they had not become involved with the Project. Eight of the 10 families felt that their housing situation would have been considerably worse had the Project not become involved with them and made comments, including:

> We would not have had a house and the kids would probably be in care. (mother)

> It would have been hell.... Probably the same; the kids would have still been terrified if the neighbour situation had not died down. (mother)

While one family indicated that it was too early to identify benefits from their involvement and engagement with the Project, the remaining nine families listed several benefits including: 'They made me admit to the problem and face up to it'; 'The Project helped me realise the extent of my relationship problems'; 'They provided practical suggestions as to how to deal with neighbours'; 'Before I was just making basic meals, and now I am getting on better with my children and we have developed a better relationship'. Other benefits mentioned for families included:

- evictions stopped
- re-housed/improved housing

- a gain in confidence
- able to express personal views better
- taking and getting control of one's own life
- help with alcohol misuse
- controlling anger
- dealing with stress more effectively
- kids' groups
- help and support with children's behaviour
- better parenting skills
- awareness of basic care for children
- increase in children's sense of security
- better quality of life.

The research team also interviewed 22 children in families who had received support from the Project. Nearly all those interviewed recognised changes in themselves and/or in their parents. Thus, a young man said that the Project helped his parents to talk about their problems. He added 'My dad listened and so did mum'. A young boy, aged eight, said that his family had been re-housed in dispersed accommodation and that everything was stable and normal again, and everyone was happy. His older brother, aged nine, described living in the Project as 'brilliant'. He felt that he had received lots of attention and learned to develop better relationships. Other changes mentioned by the children included:

- improved behaviour
- having more of a say
- attending school regularly
- new friends
- parents stopped arguing
- father gets angry less often
- getting more attention
- more opportunities to play
- everyone happier.

Some young people did register disappointments. For example, a girl was generally pleased with developments in the family, but expressed regret that her sister was still away from home. Another young girl felt that her own behaviour and school attendance had improved, but her mother was still unhappy and still had a serious drug dependency problem.

In summary, both parents and children were nearly all positive about the Project. They valued the helpfulness and availability of staff. All families but one identified significant improvements in their situation. They believed that they benefited from improved access to housing, facilities for children and staff input, which resulted in personal development and changes in family relationships and behaviour.

Interagency relationships

The core partners in the Dundee Families Project were the housing and social work departments of Dundee City Council and NCH Action for Children Scotland. These agencies collaborated strategically at senior management level. However, the Project worked with a wide variety of other agencies (see Figure 10.1). The number of agencies involved in each case depended on the needs of the family. Typically, there might be two or three agencies working with a family alongside the Project staff. However, in some more difficult cases many more agencies might be involved. One member of the Project noted the involvement of 12-15 agencies in families with complex needs and suggested that this was not uncommon.

The most frequent contact was with housing and social work, but drugs and specialist counselling agencies were also very important. This reflects the needs of families. An NCH respondent suggested that the result of good cooperation is that 'families get a comprehensive service based on commitment to a tailored plan'. The same person also indicated that 'collaboration with other agencies is highly significant' and estimated that Project social care staff would spend up to 40% of their time on liaison and collaboration.

Overall, the relationship between housing practitioners and the Project was perceived, by both sets of staff, to be working well. Senior social work personnel expressed strong commitment to the Project, but greater tensions were evident in the relationships between Project and social work staff, particularly at a local level. This was thought to be due to the greater input to families expected from social workers by the Project. Relationships with other agencies were weaker, in most cases because contact was intermittent and occasional. For most of these agencies, the Project was involved with a very small proportion of their caseload. There was evidence of clashes of culture between the Project and certain agencies they were dealing with as a result of their differing roles, responsibilities and values. Some of the stakeholder interviewees did hold negative views, but they often had very limited contact with the Project and their perceptions sometimes resulted from a single incident.

Figure 10.1: Map of partnership relationships

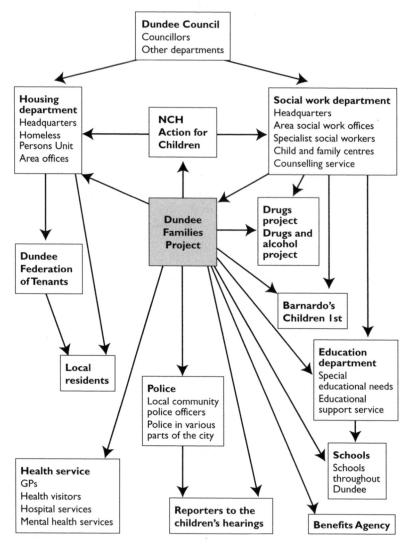

Both the key partners, Dundee City Council housing and social work departments, were making changes to their service, but both saw a key role for the Families Project in future. None of the stakeholder interviewees thought that the Project should be abandoned, and there was strong support from other core stakeholders, including the local councillor. There were differences in emphasis about the way that the Project should develop, with some interviewees favouring earlier intervention with a wider range of families and others favouring more intensive work with the most problematic cases.

Strengths and weaknesses

Overall, the majority of the stakeholder interviewees considered the Project to be successful. They identified a number of strengths and weaknesses of the Project, but no one factor was seen to be pre-eminent.

Independence: on the positive side, the independence of the Project, because it was run by a voluntary agency, was seen to be important. All the stakeholders agreed that the Project was more effective than a project run directly by the housing or social work departments.

Multiagency working: the Project succeeded in bringing together a wide range of agencies to deal with the problems of individual families and obtained their commitment to support the family. However, a few stakeholders commented on the gaps in the agencies who supported the Project and mental health services were identified as a particular area of weakness.

Intensive, integrated and flexible intervention: the Project staff themselves did not feel that there was any 'magic formula' to their approach, but rather indicated that the basis of their success was to bring together in a holistic manner a repertoire of working methods that had been used elsewhere. Nevertheless a number of the external stakeholders commented that the Project did bring new ideas. Several suggested that this was due to a combination of the multidisciplinary backgrounds of the staff, and their skills, which made it possible for 'thinking out of the box'. Others thought that the fact that the work was time-focused and targeted prompted more flexible and creative thinking. Only two of the stakeholder interviewees made negative comments about the Project's approach and both acknowledged that they had limited contact with a small number of families.

Commitment: research suggests that successful partnerships depend on trust and cooperation and become stronger when positive results from partnership working can be demonstrated (Flint et al, 2001). Most of the stakeholder interviewees felt that the Project had demonstrated positive results and that there was a high degree of trust and cooperation. However, a few of the agencies, or individuals within those agencies, were not as committed. Clearly, the Project had won the support of core partners but perhaps had not been able to devote sufficient time to agencies where there is less frequent contact.

Selection of families: the stakeholders felt that the referral and assessment process was important in ensuring that the Project was targeted at the right families. There were two aspects to this: first, that the families should meet the criteria and, second, that the families would likely benefit from the support offered. However, several interviewees stressed that the Project would only be effective if the family had a commitment to change and a need to change. The stakeholders generally felt that substance abuse and addiction problems were the most difficult to overcome and that this was a major factor where the Project had been less successful, as a Project worker described: 'Alcohol and drugs, I think, have been things that have got in the way'. However, stakeholders accepted that the Project would not succeed in every case and some suggested that the Project probably had a higher success rate with these types of cases than other family support services.

Funding: several interviewees acknowledged funding difficulties, most notably the uncertainty of long-term funding. Some interviewees also noted that this had a potentially serious impact on staff morale in the Project and suggested that the staff could be tempted to seek more secure employment elsewhere.

Costs and savings

The Project dealt with relatively small numbers of families per year: there were an average of 32 referrals a year, of which just over half were accepted for longer-term work. At any one time the Project was dealing with about three cases per worker, allowing it to offer a very intensive service. The operating costs of the Project were around £345,000 per annum. However, this means that the expense per family was high, so it is right to consider whether the expenditure was justifiable. Although the research team had access to the financial records of the Project, it was more difficult to assess the cost of the alternatives. In general, respondents were not able to quantify the precise costs incurred in managing ASB nor the savings accrued by their own agency as a result of the Families Project. The analysis of costs and benefits was therefore derived from a number of sources. First, stakeholders were asked about their perceptions of the cost, effectiveness and financial savings that could be attributed to the Dundee Families Project. Second, a number of staff were asked how they would assess and manage a series of hypothetical cases (vignettes). Third, cost data derived from the Project and other agencies was used to assess the cost–effectiveness of the Project.

Bannister and Scott (2000) suggest that cost-effectiveness analysis can be used to assess the costs and savings associated with measures to deal with ASB. Costs can be identified from a number of perspectives. These can be divided into operational costs and societal costs. The operational cost perspective examines the costs of the service provider(s). The societal cost perspective aims to measure more 'holistically' the costs of delivering a service. At an organisational level, and from the perspective of a housing landlord, for example, the costs of managing ASB can be classified as direct costs, indirect costs and societal costs.

Cost savings

Stakeholders said that the benefits accrued by housing services were a reduction in the costs associated with managing ASB, a reduction in legal expenses, and a reduction in the costs associated with homeless presentations. The benefits accrued by social work services relate to the intensity of interventions and the costs of taking children into care. A range of other agencies identified a reduction in their day-to-day case management costs as a result of a successful intervention by the Dundee Families Project, such as reducing the number of complaints reported to the police. The main savings associated with the Project were taken to be the cost of evictions, the cost of homeless person presentations and the cost of taking children into care. The savings were:

- Utilising data collated by Atkinson et al (2000), the cost of an eviction for ASB was assessed as £10,700.
- The average cost, incurred by the Dundee Homeless Persons Unit, of processing a homeless application was £942. However, the costs for more complex cases, such as those typically referred to the Dundee Families Project, was higher than this due to more extensive investigations and greater negotiations required to find the family suitable support and accommodation. This was estimated to be £1,900 per case.
- The average cost of placing a child in foster care was estimated to be around £200 per week. The average cost of placing a child in a residential school or a children's unit was estimated to be at least £1,000 per week.

The data from the Project indicated that, over a three-year period, there were 33 successful outcomes. The calculations were therefore based on 11 successful cases per year. The research aimed to assess the cost of the likely outcomes if the Project were not there. The following assumptions were made. If the 11 cases, involving 34 children, had not had support from the Dundee Families Project, seven families would have been evicted and would have presented as homeless, five children would have been placed in residential care and 11 children would have been placed in foster care. The costs associated with these assumptions can be expressed as follows:

Eviction process:	£74,900
Homeless presentations:	£13,300
Residential school:	£260,000
Foster care:	£114,400
Total illustrative cost:	£462,600

The total estimated annual expenditure for these 11 cases is therefore £462,600, which compares with the average operating cost of the Dundee Families Project of £345,000. This represents an immediate financial saving of around £117,600 per annum. These calculations do not take into account the long-term costs incurred by such families, such as the extended costs of residential or foster care over a number of years. Nor do they take into account long-term improvements in families' quality of life or savings from reduced expenditure on problems such as offending behaviour, to which the Project might contribute. At worst, therefore, the Project costs no more than the conventional way of dealing with these families. However, it is more likely that the Project actually generated real cost savings, particularly when long-term costs are taken into account. In addition, it had the potential to deal with families in a more effective way.

Conclusion

The Dundee Families Project developed in response to a number of factors. The local authorities in Dundee faced pressures to take action against people who caused problems to neighbours. Their initial response was traditional and reactive: using legal remedies to evict such families. However, having implemented a very firm policy, they found that eviction often only displaced the problem. Following a successful attempt at rehabilitation with one family, they decided to establish a specialist intensive project.

The Project received 126 referrals in its first four years of operation. About half the referrals led to active work by the Project. The referred families were all poor and many households were headed by a lone parent. The nature of the 'anti-social behaviour' was varied but was usually serious and prolonged. In addition to such housing and neighbour-related difficulties, families often had one or more serious problems with respect to parenting and care or control of children.

Achievements of the Project

Overall, the research data showed that the Project was very successful in terms of its image, collaborative relationships and production of change in families. The key achievements were:

- *Inter-agency cooperation:* the Project had established good working relationships with most of the key agencies. Senior staff were involved with and supportive of the Project. Relationships with housing services were reported to be especially close and positive.
- *Staffing and management:* outsiders universally saw the Project as being very well managed. The involvement of a voluntary agency was regarded as making it more acceptable to families who were suspicious of the council due to its 'coercive' statutory powers.
- *Referrals and assessment:* the referral criteria were tight and appropriate. This meant that the Project concentrated its work on families with severe difficulties. Most families using the Project had long histories of problems and professional attention. The assessment process was lengthy but was valued by Project staff and some other agencies for its comprehensiveness.
- *Family progress, outcomes and views:* the research found that the great majority of families who engaged with the Project made progress. The decline in their circumstances and prospects was halted. There were indications that closed cases were generally doing well, especially with regard to housing, although some were doing poorly with regard to family issues.
- *Eviction rates:* since the Project was established, the number of evictions in Dundee had dropped markedly. While this change was influenced by changes in housing department policy and the introduction of Antisocial Behaviour Orders (ASBOs), housing staff felt that the Project contributed to the downward trend.

Weaknesses and issues requiring attention

The following weaknessess ere identified:

- *Referral processes:* some staff in collaborative agencies had an unclear or misleading idea of referral criteria. The Project had spent a considerable amount of time and expertise in dealing with cases that turned out to be inappropriate. The Project has subsequently sought to clarify its referral criteria and further communication with other agencies would help reduce unsuitable referrals.

- *Families' disengagement from the Project:* it was not clear that the transition for families as they moved towards ceasing contact with the Project was handled in an optimum way. There were indications that a few families deteriorated after the service ended and that not all received adequate support or monitoring. The preparedness of other agencies to continue with support was crucial.
- *Collaboration with other agencies:* although interagency relationships were generally good, there were exceptions. While the Project had striven to establish good relationships with housing, social work and police services, the links with health services appeared to be given less priority.

Cost-effectiveness

On the whole, the study evidence indicated that the Project offered good value for money, although it must be emphasised that a complex and long-term study would be required to demonstrate this conclusively.

Nearly all stakeholders were agreed that the Project gave long-term benefits to families in three main ways:

- avoiding high-cost options (like children becoming looked after or supported accommodation for the family);
- reducing behaviours (including crime) with potential long-term cost implications for society;
- promoting the quality of life of family members.

Overall, the research demonstrated the value to families and other agencies of the model adopted by the Dundee Families Project.

References

Atkinson, R., Mullen, T. and Scott, S. (2000) *The Use of Civil Legal Remedies for Neighbour Nuisance in Scotland*, Edinburgh: Scottish Executive Central Research Unit.

Bannister, J. and Scott, S. (2000) *Assessing the Cost-effectiveness of Measures to Deal with Anti-Social Behaviour*, Glasgow: Housing and Social Policy Research Group, University of Glasgow.

Dillane, J., Hill, M., Bannister, J. and Scott, S. (2001) *Evaluation of the Dundee Families Project*, Edinburgh: Scottish Executive, Dundee City Council and NCH Action for Children.

Dundee City Council (1999) 'Dundee Families Project Evaluation Report', unpublished.

Flint, J., Mullen, T. and Scott, S. (2001) *Multi-agency Working in Barmulloch and West Drumoyne*, Edinburgh: Scottish Executive.

Hunter, C., Nixon, J. and Shayer, S. (2000) *Neighbour Nuisance, Social Landlords and the Law*, Coventry: CIH.

Scott, S., Currie, H., Dean, J. and Kintrea, K. (2001) *Good Practice in Housing Management in Scotland: Case Studies, Conclusions and Recommendations*, Edinburgh: Scottish Executive Central Research Unit.

ELEVEN

Policing and community safety in residential areas: the mixed economy of visible patrols

Adam Crawford

Introduction

A recurring theme of this book is that the control of tenants' conduct and the policing of social behaviour have been ever-present features of social landlordism from the late Victorian era onwards. Since the 1990s, however, there has been a renewed preoccupation in social housing management with responding to tenants' anxieties about crime and victimisation and with governing anti-social behaviour (ASB). In England and Wales, social landlords have been drawn into local partnerships focused around crime prevention and community safety and have been encouraged to assume greater responsibility for ensuring safe and secure environments for their tenants. In support of this enhanced role, social landlords now have recourse to a greater variety of legal instruments of control (see Chapters Six, Seven and Eight, this volume). Social landlords have also been enlisted into participating in an array of initiatives concerned variously with improving the quality of the built environment, joining up local services, neighbourhood liveability and sustainability, civic renewal and community governance, all of which are linked, either implicitly or explicitly, with issues of crime and disorder.

There is a growing connection made in urban and housing policy between community safety and urban renewal, with security forming the bedrock on which community life flourishes and without which communities will tip into spirals of decline and decay (ODPM, 2005). The provision of reassurance and security are regarded as prerequisites for attracting people and capital to move to, invest in, or remain in, certain urban locations. This is particularly salient with regard to unpopular social housing estates where crime and disadvantage have become concentrated.

Governing through crime has become a major component of modern social housing, with an intensification of the reach and depth of social landlords' role in policing ASB. One manifestation of this has been social landlords' involvement in the provision of forms of contracted additional patrol services dedicated to specific residential areas. It has become acceptable, and to some degree expected, for social landlords to take control of their own policing and security needs, to select the providers of security and provide or access funding to pay for it. This represents an erosion of the ideal that the police constitute the monopolistic guardians of public safety and order, providing a universal service to all regardless of their capacity to pay, and a pluralisation of policing 'beyond the police'. As a result, a more complex division of labour in the provision of security has emerged, with the police now part of a varied assortment of organisations with diverse policing functions and security practices.

In this chapter I locate the current concern for providing 'reassurance' through visible patrol personnel and the growing market for security within the context of urban regeneration. The chapter considers the role of, and division of labour between, the police, private security and neighbourhood wardens in providing reassurance in residential areas. It explores the increasing role of social landlords in procuring additional policing resources for their tenants. Drawing on recent research, the chapter identifies key issues that emerge for the local governance of crime and ASB, the role of housing providers and the provision of security within local communities.

In search of security

A number of social transformations have occurred in recent years that have impacted on the nature of, and demand for, security personnel within urban housing. The polarisation of rich and poor has been a marked feature of socioeconomic change over the past 20 years or so, alongside the spatial concentration of poverty and the flight of people and capital out of certain localities (Hills, 1995; Goodman and Oldfield, 2004). Social polarisation has been fuelled by the residualisation of the public housing stock, exacerbated by the 'Right to Buy' legislation of the 1980s (Minton, 2004). At the same time, the distribution of victimisation in England and Wales has become more spatially concentrated since the 1970s (Trickett et al, 1995).

Despite various attempts to promote 'community policing' since the 1980s, the reactive demands on, and crime-fighting focus of, the police have served to undermine the capacity of the police to deliver public reassurance through locally tied patrol officers, exacerbated by managerial pressures to measure and monitor performance prioritising the easily quantifiable aspects of police work. In this, public reassurance through locally responsive patrols has lost out. Cajoled by successive governments since the 1990s, the police have increasingly concentrated on target setting and performance measurement against quantifiable impacts or outputs, resulting in a reduction in the public's sense of investment in professional policing, and reducing levels of public confidence and trust in the police (Mirrlees-Black, 2001). Home Office survey research conducted in 2003 found that 'an increased police presence' was the measure most likely to convince people that crime was being dealt with more effectively (Page et al, 2004). The numbers of intermediaries such as caretakers, park-keepers, train guards and bus conductors have been reduced, as has the presence of secondary social control occupations and occupations providing 'natural surveillance' and other low-level controls as a part of their primary functions (see Chapter Five, this volume, and also Jones and Newburn, 2002). We have also witnessed a loss of deference to authority, a decline of trust in professionals and public bodies, juxtaposed against increased public expectations over what public services can and should deliver.

Recent years have also witnessed the blossoming commercialisation of security. It is estimated that some 600,000 people are now employed across the private security industry. Not all of these personnel are visible security guards. As well as contracted security guards there are many 'in-house' employees with primary or secondary security functions. According to the British Security Industry Association (BSIA, 2005) there are an estimated 2,000 manned security guarding companies and over 125,000 dedicated security officers. The estimated turnover of the BSIA security guarding sector in 2004 was £1.57 billion, nearly a threefold increase on the figure 10 years earlier[1].

We face a contemporary 'reassurance paradox', arising from general crime risks declining but perceptions of victimisation risk rising. Since 1995, both the BCS and recorded police figures have shown a significant decline in crime. According to the BCS the overall crime rate fell by 35.8% between 1995 and 2003. While victimisation remains highly concentrated by area and falls largely on a minority of the population, the aggregate risk of crime is now estimated to be lower than at any point since 1981. Despite this reduction, according to the BCS 2003/04, some 48% of the public still thought that crime in their area had increased (Dodd et al, 2004). The BCS shows that, apart from a dip in 2003/04, concerns over low-level incivilities and ASB have continued to increase despite real falls in crime, suggesting no significant reassurance dividend from reduced crime risks. Paradoxically, with police officer numbers at an all-time high and more civilian staff than ever before, as well as declining aggregate crime rates, public insecurity and fear of crime remain stubbornly high. Latest figures show there were 142,972 police officers in England and Wales at the end of September 2005. This takes the total number of the immediate police family to over 220,000, including 73,357 police staff (Kirwan and Bibi, 2006)[2]. This represents more than an 11% increase in the number of police officers and a 43% increase in civilian staff in the past decade (Christophersen and Cotton, 2004). Despite this, public demands for more 'bobbies on the beat' and visible figures of authority in public places remain apparently insatiable.

Recent policy initiatives

Against this background, a number of government policy initiatives since the 1990s have served to shape the current mixed economy of patrol and raise the profile of additional security provision, among which the following are the most significant:

The *1994 Police and Magistrates' Courts Act* allows police forces to charge more widely for goods/services, including subcontracting police officer time.

The *1998 Crime and Disorder Act* places a statutory duty on local authorities and the police together to develop, coordinate and promote Crime and Disorder Reduction Partnerships (CDRPs)[3]. Section 17 of the 1998 Act requires local authorities, police authorities and national parks authorities to consider the crime and disorder implications of all their activities and decisions[4]. The Act has done much to encourage local authorities, housing departments and registered social landlords to place increased emphasis on issues of safety and security within their estates.

The *Neighbourhood Wardens Programme* launched by the government in 2000, aims to offer a semi-official presence in residential areas to improve quality of life and the local environment. Warden schemes have been closely tied to an agenda of neighbourhood renewal and the revival of public spaces (SEU, 2001; ODPM, 2002).

The *2001 Private Security Industry Act* established the Security Industry Authority (SIA) to license and regulate all 'contract' private security providers, creating the first national regulatory regime of the private security industry in England and Wales, which now covers door supervisors, vehicle immobilisers and security guards, requiring them to be adequately trained and subject to criminal record checks[5].

The *2002 Police Reform Act* introduced community support officers, without the full powers or training of a sworn police constable, intended to provide public reassurance by being dedicated to patrol. The government committed itself to expand the number of community support officers to 4,000 by 2005. The Act also enables chief police officers to establish and maintain community safety schemes that accredit suitably skilled and trained non-police employees able to undertake specified support functions, and they are authorised to issue penalty notices for disorder. Accredited community safety officers may be local authority, housing association or private security employees. The Act also extended the power to apply for an Antisocial Behaviour Order (ASBO) to registered social landlords.

The *2003 Anti-Social Behaviour Act* extends powers to issue fixed penalty notices for ASB to community support officers, local authority officers and accredited persons. The Act creates new powers for police officers and community support officers to disperse groups (see Chapter One, this volume). The Act also extends the power to apply for an ASBO to county councils (in England) and Housing Action Trusts.

The *Reassurance Policing Programme*, launched in March 2004, aims to strengthen community involvement in policing to identify and tackle crimes which fuel fear in local neighbourhoods. The programme's intention is to deliver dedicated high visibility police, to target the 'things that matter most' to local people and to address subjective public fears and falling confidence.

The *Building Communities, Beating Crime* White Paper (Home Office, 2004) plans inter alia to support dedicated neighbourhood policing teams across the country, and put in place by the end of 2006 standards of customer service to the public, creating a policing 'contract'. The power of detention for community support officers is to be extended nationwide. The government reiterated its intention to increase the number of community support officers to 24,000 by March 2008 (to a total of 24,000), funded through a new Neighbourhood Policing Fund.

The *2005 Serious Organised Crime and Police Act* gives community support officers additional powers to direct traffic, deter begging, search detained persons for dangerous articles and to enforce certain licensing offences. The Act also extends the remit of the SIA to cover Scotland.

The mixed economy of patrol

These developments have produced a mixed economy of patrol incorporating a range of contracted sworn police officers or community support officers, neighbourhood wardens, private security guards and citizen volunteers. As housing providers, businesses and the public have increasingly lost confidence in the capacity of the police to deliver community-based patrol officers as part of routine police provision, they have begun to experiment with diverse forms of additional security. Consequently, dedicated visible patrols have increasingly become *additional*, provided by plural auspices and often distinct from residual public policing. Whereas the latter remains largely driven by reactive demands on it, additional policing and security provision has the capacity to be more proactive, focusing on crime prevention and community engagement.

Recent research identified public frustrations with traditional levels of 'public' policing and apparent inadequacies of police responses to calls, notably in residential areas, as the primary driving force in creating a market for additional security and policing services (Crawford et al, 2005a). The Home Office has considered plans to formalise this market by encouraging community groups to purchase their own policing. Under the proposals, an organisation such as a residents' association would be able to hire a community support officer or neighbourhood warden to patrol their area. As proposed, the scheme would require residents to pay about £10,000 per year for an officer, estimated to be half the cost, with the Home Office matching the additional funding. A Home Office spokesperson said that the intention would be: 'to make it easier for people in a particular street, community or estate to raise a levy if they want to pay for a community support officer' (Sparrow, 2003). The implication here would be to pass the responsibility for providing such patrols directly to social landlords in areas where communities themselves would be unable to pay directly, raising the question as to whether social landlords should fund such arrangements through levies to rents.

A survey of social housing providers in the Yorkshire and Humberside region found that the majority (57%) said they had become significantly or a lot more concerned with crime and disorder issues in recent years (Crawford and Lister, 2004, pp 12-13), due principally to residents' demands and increased fear of crime (identified by 47% and 45% respectively). Nearly a third of respondents also identified a limited police presence as an influential factor and over half indicated that responding to residents' demands for some form of visible policing or patrol presence was an important issue. These findings suggest that a variety of external forces are encouraging social landlords to assume a new responsibility for tackling disorder, increasingly through the procurement of additional security patrols.

Competition and poor coordination

The mixed economy of patrol in England and Wales has become highly competitive as different providers, including public police forces, seek to access finite public and private resources (Crawford et al, 2005a). The introduction of community support officers has significantly increased the competitive edge of the police, by reducing the cost of contracted police patrol personnel. Moreover, the funding of community support officers will become increasingly linked to income generation through subcontracting and matched funding arrangements, as the government's initial funding declines. At the same time, the advent of national licensing and regulation by the SIA will both increase the price and (it is hoped) the quality of private security.

The current state of the mixed economy has developed in an uneven and largely ad hoc manner. The main factors influencing this uneven development include:

- variations in the approach and cultural attitudes of senior police managers;
- differences in the manner in which local authorities and registered social landlords have responded to public anxieties about crime and the requirements of partnership working;
- divergences in local responses towards central government funding regimes;
- variations in the capacity of local communities, housing providers and businesses to organise themselves effectively into 'clubs' for the purpose of purchasing additional patrol schemes (Crawford, 2005);
- differential access to sufficient financial resources to purchase additional security; and

- disparities in the availability of private sector provision.

Our research found that relations between providers vary considerably from effective co-production through partnerships to mutual indifference and sometimes outright rivalry (Crawford et al, 2005a). All too often, relations are poorly organised, suffer duplication of effort and are marked by competition and mistrust. The market itself often fosters fragmentation, producing significant coordination deficits. Historically, there has been weak governance and segmented regulation of plural policing, resulting in an absence of any rigorous oversight and a lack of public accountability for the burgeoning private and parochial initiatives. Oversight and accountability within policing networks are rendered particularly difficult by 'the problem of many hands' (Rhodes, 1996, p 663) where many contribute but no single contribution can be identified. As authority is shared it becomes difficult to disentangle and apportion responsibility.

The short-term nature of many security contracts and government funding initiatives has engendered a piecemeal approach to the mixed economy, generating significant turnover and flux in the delivery of community safety. This often renders it difficult for patrol personnel and providers to develop strong bonds with those they police, in large part undermining the very appeal of dedicated local personnel developing important trust relations and in-depth local knowledge.

Our research highlights the following key functions of visible security personnel in residential areas:

- patrol and visibility;
- crime prevention and problem solving;
- environmental management and improvement;
- community engagement;
- linking and referral;
- information and intelligence gathering; and
- law enforcement.

In practice there are tensions in the appropriate balance to be struck between these potentially competing functions. Government funding initiatives have tended to emphasise different elements of these functions[6] and local authorities and registered social landlords have often been required to adapt local initiatives to fit shifting funding streams. There are considerable concerns that the government's current proclivity for providing patrol personnel with additional powers to issue fixed penalty notices, as with community support officers or through accreditation schemes (Home Office, 2004), may transform the nature of officers' roles and public interactions, as well as undermine perceptions of independence, local trust relations and crucial non-law enforcement tasks. It is difficult for patrol personnel to be issuing fixed penalty notices to tenants one minute and expecting them to engage in community development initiatives the next. Enhancing enforcement powers will often draw patrol officers into more adversarial relations, potentially placing them in more dangerous situations. The exercise of legal powers also requires robust procedures for ensuring that powers are appropriately used and that complaints are administered fairly. The following sections consider the different roles of the key plural policing personnel involved in patrolling social housing.

Community support officers

Community support officers represent a major new initiative in neighbourhood policing. As dedicated patrol officers with limited powers, community support officers are freed from most of the pressures that serve to abstract constables from policing dedicated local areas and contractual arrangements. Across the country, local authorities and registered social landlords have match-funded (with the local police authority) community support officers in order to ensure a visible police presence in particular neighbourhoods and estates, sometimes by diverting funds from neighbourhood warden schemes (Crawford et al, 2005b).

Our research found that community support officers in Bradford and Leeds spent on average between 77% and 80% of their time out of the station on patrol-based activities (Crawford et al, 2004, p 19). Importantly, the proportion of their time spent on visible patrol did not decrease during implementation, but rather increased slightly, to an average of between 82% and 83% in the last six months. This 'visibility dividend' associated with community support officers contrasts starkly with the estimated 17% average police officer time spent on reassurance patrols (PA Consulting Group, 2001, p 9). Furthermore, as specialist patrol personnel, community support officers are less subject to the 'tyranny of the radio' as interviewees described the reactive pressures affecting police constables, and are more able to dedicate themselves to the policing of given localities on foot rather than in vehicles.

Our research exposed considerable public confusion over the roles, responsibilities, powers and limitations of different plural policing personnel, notably community support officers. This may engender uncertainties and false expectations over what legitimately can be expected of officers. The research highlights that patrol is not an end in itself, but rather a means to an end. It is not just the presence of uniformed patrol officers alone that influences public confidence and fosters reassurance, but also the nature of public interactions (Crawford et al, 2004, p 75). The research encountered some concerns that officers were uncertain what to do beyond walking their beat as a 'reassurance beacon' or 'mobile scarecrow'. A central challenge is to ensure 'patrolling with a purpose', supplementing the visible presence of community support officers with other activities including proactive crime prevention, intelligence gathering and community engagement.

Neighbourhood wardens

Research shows that wardens can build sustained relationships within communities afflicted by high levels of crime and disorder (ODPM, 2004; Crawford et al, 2005b) and may help improve the physical environment, advance regeneration and civil renewal efforts and act as important street-level links in the chains that bind together local service provision. Wardens can engage with different community groups in matters relating to crime and ASB in ways that police officers often find difficult given levels of distrust between some communities and the police. Given the relative absence of time pressures and the discretionary nature of their role, wardens are well placed to work with vulnerable individuals within communities and help ensure that people do not 'fall between the gaps' by referring them on to relevant local services. However, the discretionary nature of the warden's role renders it important that wardens are appropriately managed and sufficiently accountable. As communities comprise diverse groups with different interests and priorities, notably with regard to security, it is critical that wardens do not become too closely associated with particular sections within a community.

There is a dilemma for wardens, in that by 'filling the void' vacated by other local service providers and community inactivity, other services and residents themselves can come to rely too heavily on wardens and hence withdraw from their own responsibilities. The challenge for wardens therefore is both to fill service gaps and to encourage communities and partner organisations to enhance their own efforts. Wardens represent a new channel through which communities can communicate with partner agencies, and potentially identify novel ways in which service providers may operate or react to new challenges. The work of wardens in the collection of intelligence in support of applications for ASBOs and their enforcement is more controversial.

It can constitute a relatively quick way to demonstrate to communities that wardens can make a difference with regard to persistent offenders who adversely impact on community life and help build trust relations. However, it can draw wardens into an explicit law enforcement role that may actually undermine trust and community-building endeavours. This reminds us that policing is ultimately bound up with the use of coercive force against some citizens in the name of good order or in the protection of others. It entails normative conceptions of appropriate behaviour. Hence, certain people are more likely, due to their age, lifestyle and habits, to find themselves the subjects of policing endeavours.

Neighbourhood wardens work particularly well in communities in which there are high levels of distrust between residents and the police or those that lack collective efficacy, defined as 'the linkage of mutual trust and the willingness to intervene for the common good' (Sampson et al, 1997, p 919). Unlike other patrol personnel, wardens tend to be dedicated to tight geographic boundaries, and remain working in the same area over a period of time, allowing them to build relationships with the communities they serve. As visible figures of authority wardens can act as intermediate institutions between the formal structures of police and local housing authorities and the informal institutions of civil society, such as families, schools, peer groups, businesses and community associations. As such, they may foster different forms of social capital. Wardens are particularly good at encouraging bonding social capital (among similar groups) and can play an important role in linking social capital, notably where communities are reasonably cohesive and have developed informal networks. For example, wardens in different parts of Leeds have helped generate new resources for the areas in which they work and linked residents into appropriate local services (Crawford et al, 2005b). Enhancing bridging social capital (between different social groups and across communities) constitutes a particularly important yet challenging aspect of wardens' work (Crawford, 2006).

Wardens afford social landlords a frontline means of furthering their role in the field of community development, offering the capacity to foster approaches to local problems of order beyond policing and security solutions and thereby opportunities to tackle more fundamental social issues that often lie behind such problems. There are dangers that constructing the warden's role primarily in policing or security terms will draw wardens increasingly into law-enforcement activities which place them in situations of conflict, possibly undermining their capacity to perform other non-policing functions.

The more that a community's problems are seen through a security lens, the more that policing, exclusion and law and order solutions dominate.

Private security patrols

The establishment of the SIA reflects the growing role of the private security industry within the mixed economy of policing and, by legitimising it, is likely to contribute to its continued expansion[7]. Traditionally, private security patrols have employed low-skilled and poorly paid labour, with little investment in career development or training and high staff turnover, leading to poor industry reputation and a lack of trust between the police and large sections of the private security industry. The provision of private security has been dominated by cost overriding service quality, with estimates that some 60% of contracts are determined by price alone (BSIA, 2005).

Increasingly registered social landlords, local authority housing departments and community groups (often using devolved council budgets) are turning to the private sector to police local neighbourhoods. In York, the introduction of a private patrol scheme in one council ward led within three years to all but three of the remaining 19 wards using their local improvement budget to procure mobile patrols. Such private security patrols are often vehicle-based with on-board CCTV cameras and are focused around evening times and weekends (when wardens, if they operate, are not usually on duty). They tend to adopt a non-interventionist approach, recording and passing incidents on to relevant authorities. A chief constable (from a different force) noted that the growth of private security patrols in residential areas had significant implications for the police:

> It was proved conclusively that all that having private guarding services in residential suburbs did was divert the police resources out of the areas of greatest need in the inner city to answer peripheral and largely meaningless 999 calls from security guards wandering around in leafy suburbs, jumping at the sight of their own shadows. (quoted in Crawford et al, 2005a, p 25)

A 2003 national survey of manned security companies (Crawford et al, 2005a, pp 15-19) found:

- over one third provided mobile patrols in residential areas;
- 21% identified residential areas as holding the greatest growth potential across the sector;
- 94% welcomed the introduction of national licensing;
- the majority of respondents agreed that licensing will improve public perceptions of the industry, the general standards of service delivery and industry relations with the police;
- the majority of respondents believed that licensing will increase costs to the industry and concentrate market activity across fewer companies, while just over half of respondents (52%) believed that licensing will increase pressures to purchase in-house security;
- 61% indicated that the level of cooperation with local police was good, while 39% said it was not very good or poor. Cooperation varied significantly between different police forces according to 59%;
- 39% agreed and only 14% disagreed that the police reform agenda will intensify competition within the 'extended policing family'.

Clearly, the capacity of the SIA to set appropriate standards and enforce them effectively will determine the level of confidence in regulation and trust in the efficacy of private security. The perceived quality of regulation will undoubtedly colour future police willingness to engage with the private sector, as it will influence public acceptance. Given the current legislative exemption there remain considerable concerns about the potential movement of disreputable providers to the 'in-house' security sector.

An empirical vignette: New Earswick

The experience of the New Earswick 'community policing' initiative is a salutary reminder of some of the pitfalls and unintended consequences involved in the purchase of additional security by social landlords (see Crawford et al, 2003). In response to local concerns expressed by vocal residents, in 2000 the Joseph Rowntree Housing Trust entered into a formal agreement with North Yorkshire Police to purchase an additional level of policing cover for the village of New Earswick, which was not an area experiencing high crime or social disorder. The initiative was also the product of increasingly close relations between the Housing Trust and the local police. Benefits of the initiative were anticipated to include closer partnership collaboration and enhanced trust relations for both parties, re-engaging the police with the local community and resurrecting police–community relations.

At a cost of £25,000 per year, the police time of a designated officer equivalent to 24 hours per week was purchased as part of an initial three-year experiment. This contracted police 'time' was to be additional to the level of policing provision already available to the village, namely the reactive round-the-clock cover and a limited amount of community policing.

Due to a number of implementation difficulties, including the designated officer being drawn away from the village to cover for other colleagues or wider emergencies and the turnover of police personnel, the initiative failed to meet its stated aims and was terminated early. During the period of implementation both crime and the fear of crime increased while residents' satisfaction with the local police service declined.

More broadly, the following lessons were evident. First, the provision of additional policing, qua commodity, can raise false expectations regarding reassurance outcomes associated with their provision. The launch of the New Earswick scheme stimulated a variety of expectations among residents about policing and its impacts on social order. These expectations resonated with the belief that the scheme would result in significant increases in resident reassurance through greater levels of police visibility, accessibility and familiarity. The scheme also fuelled 'unrealistic' expectations articulated by residents that extended far beyond the narrow stated aims of the project, including resolving deep-rooted structural problems, such as drugs and cultural antagonisms between young people and adults. It also served to evoke a powerful memory of the local community police officer as a stable and familiar presence, living in the village and remaining in the role for almost 20 years, in comparison to which the community policing initiative inevitably lost out. Second, the scheme raised perceptions of local 'ownership' and demands for greater accountability in relation to the policing service provided. The public police were not well attuned to meeting these commercial demands, acknowledged by the police as a weakness nationally (ACPO, 2004).

In New Earswick, the purchase of additional policing *as a commodity* seemed unwittingly to transform residents into *consumers*, thereby arousing heightened expectations over the provision of commercial forms of accountability and responsiveness to consumer demands in order to demonstrate 'value for money'. Residents often expected greater responsiveness to incidents, reports on activities and results and greater levels of access to the officer. When contacting the police, they expected immediate response from the officer because, in the words of one resident, 'he's *our* community policeman'. In addition, some residents felt that with 'ownership' would come greater control over the purchased resource, notably in relation to steering the officer's duty time and activities. However, the officer remained under the operational control of the chief constable at all times and was subject to organisational pressures that served (too often) to abstract the officer from duties in the village. More positively, the initiative allowed for a potential re-engagement on the part of residents with locally based policing, precisely by investing some notion of ownership, through purchase, over the policing resource, and facilitating more active resident engagement with issues of crime prevention and community well-being.

Third, seeking solutions to problems of local order through a policing and security lens alone may serve to exacerbate residents' fears and solidify lines of difference within and between local communities (see Chapter Twelve, this volume, for an account of similar processes in gated communities). In New Earswick, the focus on policing solutions to local problems served to increase insecurity thresholds. Consequently, the failure of the contracted policing initiative left local people searching for alternative security solutions. This resulted in the installation of CCTV cameras in perceived 'hot spots' around the village where youths congregated and the employment of a private security firm to provide vehicle-based patrols of the area funded by the local authority. These initiatives also failed to meet residents' expectations and by the summer of 2004, applications for a Dispersal Order were mooted as the latest in an increasingly long line of 'security solutions'.

Fourth, the quest for policing or security solutions to local problems of order may fail to tackle more fundamental and structural social issues that may lie behind these problems and prevent local dialogue. The problem of order in New Earswick was partly rooted in intergenerational conflicts and misunderstandings between youths and a significant elderly population. Latterly, the principal social landlords in New Earswick (Joseph Rowntree Housing Trust) came to acknowledge this, by establishing, in 2004, an innovative scheme, HOTEY (Helping Others to Enjoy Yourself), with the joint aims of 'rewarding young people who make a positive contribution to the community while at the same time encouraging greater tolerance of young people's visible presence'.

Finally, this case study illustrates that the provision of additional policing raises normative questions about the equitable distribution of security. Parochial initiatives may have adverse implications for surrounding areas where additional security is absent. As public policing is largely demand-led, the creation of the existence of additional policing schemes often skews scarce police resources by creating new demands: to respond to calls; to process information and community intelligence generated; and to coordinate the services provided. Organised communities are better able to respond to police-led community crime prevention initiatives and hence may draw on police resources (Hope, 2000).

Conclusion

We stand at a crossroads in the way in which residential areas are policed, with significant implications for styles of policing, community engagement, social inclusion and citizenship. Simultaneously, as current housing policy promotes the devolution of decision making over services and forms of neighbourhood management, security concerns have come to the fore. The more active role envisioned by policy for residents and neighbourhood groups in determining services include the provision of additional security. Hence, social landlords are presented with both demands from tenants to provide additional security and an array of choices regarding how and by whom this should be provided.

One future uncertainty relates to funding and, thereby, access to the market for additional security. Should an element of tenants' rental income be used to provide additional policing? Or, as the York experience implies, should local authorities provide ringfenced devolved security budgets so that local communities can purchase the form of policing they see fit? This may further bolster the commodification of policing and raise awkward political questions about the allocation of such resources between areas of starkly contrasting crime-related needs. If security is a universal good, how do we ensure its even distribution? To date, the funding for many new initiatives has been short term. If additional policing becomes 'normalised', in the sense that residents and tenants come to expect it, then they are likely to be disenchanted by its withdrawal. This is likely to be particularly evident in neighbourhoods where residents are unable, themselves, to purchase additional policing but are reliant on governmental sources of funding. If additional policing is not sustainable, raising residents' expectations and then disappointing them may leave a legacy of frustration and disillusionment.

This raises the prospect of a highly differentiated and patchwork distribution of additional security in which parochial solutions arise in response to local perceptions. Unlike some areas of public policy, the segregated and uneven distribution of crime and victimisation has significant neighbourhood effects, namely the social consequences of neighbourhood disparities, which are both persistent and not reducible to the effects on the individuals who inhabit given locales (Gibbons et al, 2005). In the apparent shift from the social to the communal as the site of governance (Crawford, 1997; Rose, 1999), the capacity to access the market or government resources, or to come together to provide additional policing as a club good, may become a defining attribute of neighbourhood security with spillover effects for adjacent areas. It also has implications for people's expectations over the role of public policing as its parameters are redefined and redrawn. The emerging fragmented mixed economy of visible security patrols raises fundamental questions concerning the challenges of coordination, relations between plural policing personnel and those they serve, as well as accountability, governance and regulation.

The uneven coordination, weak accountability and segmented regulation of plural policing demands appropriate forms of governance, not presently in place, that address coordination deficits and contain the social consequences of parochial initiatives, safeguarding the public interest. There is a need to consolidate and clarify relations between members of the 'extended policing family' and secure suitably robust forms of governance to ensure policing is delivered in accordance with democratic values of justice, equity, accountability and effectiveness. Local CDRPs offer an important vehicle to assist coordination and provide a degree of local oversight, which should be supported by regional level policing boards (Crawford et al, 2005a, pp 86-7).

This chapter raises deep-rooted questions about the current predilection for policing solutions to problems of social order. Can there be too much security? How does community safety impact on individual freedoms? To what extent should policing be driven by consumerist notions of giving the public what they want? If so, whose interests should be prioritised? How can plural policing endeavours be harnessed in the furtherance of public safety? To what extent do parochial security initiatives contribute to social justice? Due process and individual rights often stand in tension with the demands of community safety. The function of policing as a public good is not necessarily to resolve this tension in favour of prevailing consumer demands or perceived public sentiment but to manage it in accordance with wider normative values that recognise the experiences and claims of diverse social groups and safeguard human rights.

Additional security and policing, while unifying some around a common fear of others or 'otherness', may prove introspective. By creating strong in-group loyalties, such cultural capital constructed around insecurities and ASB may also create strong out–group antagonisms. It may do less to construct 'bridging social capital', which is outward-looking and seeks to bind together people from across different social groups, in ways that foster reciprocity and mobilise solidarity. A preoccupation with policing and security solutions to local problems may not be a prerequisite for bridging social capital, but an impediment to it given the fears and anxieties crime can generate. In the process it may blind local housing authorities and residents to the structural and social problems that underlie much ASB and disorder.

Notes

[1] The BSIA estimates that at the end of 2004 its members' share of the manned security market was 84% and the total industry turnover (including non-members) stood at £1.87 billion.

[2] In addition, there were just under 12,000 special constables, 6,324 community support officers, 1,151 traffic wardens and 2,319 British transport police across England and Wales.

[3] Under the 2002 Police Reform Act, from April 2003 Police Authorities and Fire Authorities became legally 'responsible authorities' for the purpose of formulating and implementing crime and disorder reduction strategies, as did Primary Care Trusts in April 2004.

[4] The 2002 Police Reform Act added fire authorities to the list of organisations covered by Section 17.

[5] Importantly, the Act does not extend to 'in-house' security provision.

[6] For example, the Office of the Deputy Prime Minister and the Home Office have different understandings of the core functions of neighbourhood and street wardens.

[7] Accreditation, where this is available, is likely to serve as a Kitemarking exercise with commercial benefits.

References

ACPO (Association of Chief Police Officers) (2004) *A Guide to Income Generation for the Police Service in England and Wales*, London: ACPO.
BSIA (British Security Industry Association) (2005) 'Interesting facts and figures in the UK security industry' (www.bsia.co.uk/industry.html).

Christophersen, O. and Cotton, J. (2004) *Police Service Strength, England and Wales, 31 March 2004*, London: Home Office.

Crawford, A. (1997) *The Local Governance of Crime: Appeals to Community and Partnership*, Oxford: Clarendon Press.

Crawford, A. (2005) 'Policing and Security as "Club Goods": The New Enclosures?', in J. Wood and B. Dupont (eds) *Democracy, Society and the Governance of Security*, Cambridge: Cambridge University Press, pp 111-38.

Crawford, A. (2006) 'Fixing Broken Promises?: Neighbourhood Wardens and Social Capital', *Urban Studies*, vol 43.

Crawford, A. and Lister, S. (2004) *The Extended Policing Family*, York: Joseph Rowntree Foundation.

Crawford, A., Blackburn, S. and Shepherd, P. (2005b) *Filling the Void, Connecting the Pieces: An Evaluation of Neighbourhood and Street Wardens in Leeds*, Leeds: CCJS Press.

Crawford, A., Lister, S. and Wall, D. (2003) *Great Expectations: Contracted Community Policing in New Earswick*, York: Joseph Rowntree Foundation.

Crawford, A., Blackburn, S., Lister, S. and Shepherd, P. (2004) *Patrolling with a Purpose: An Evaluation of Police Community Support Officers in Leeds and Bradford City Centres*, Leeds: CCJS Press.

Crawford, A., Lister, S., Blackburn, S. and Burnett, J. (2005a) *Plural Policing: The Mixed Economy of Visible Patrols in England and Wales*, Bristol: The Policy Press.

Dodd, T., Nicholas, S., Povey, D. and Walker, A. (2004) *Crime in England and Wales 2003/2004*, London: Home Office.

Gibbons, S., Green, A., Gregg, P. and Machin, S. (2005) 'Is Britain Pulling Apart? Area Disparities in Employment, Education and Crime', in N. Pearce and W. Paxton (eds) *Social Justice: Building a Fairer Britain*, London: Institute for Public Policy Research, pp 301-32.

Goodman, A. and Oldfield, Z. (2004) *Permanent Differences? Income and Expenditure Inequality in the 1990s and 2000s*, London: Institute of Fiscal Studies.

Hills, J. (1995) *Joseph Rowntree Foundation Inquiry into Income and Wealth, Volume 2*, York: Joseph Rowntree Foundation.

Home Office (2004) *Building Communities, Beating Crime: A Better Police Service in the 21st Century*, London: Home Office.

Hope, T. (2000) 'Inequality and the Clubbing of Private Security', in T. Hope and R. Sparks (eds) *Crime, Risk and Insecurity*, London: Routledge, pp 83-106.

Jones, T. and Newburn, T. (2002) 'The Transformation of Policing? Understanding Current Trends in Policing Systems', *British Journal of Criminology*, vol 42, no 1, pp 129-46.

Kirwan, S. and Bibi, N. (2006) *Police Service Strength England and Wales, 30 September 2005*, Statistical Bulletin 01/06, (www.homeoffice.gov.uk/rds/pdfs06/hosb0106.pdf).

Minton, A. (2004) *Mind the Gap: Tackling Social Polarisation Through Balanced Communities*, London: Royal Institute of Chartered Surveyors.

Mirrlees-Black, C. (2001) *Confidence in the Criminal Justice System: Findings from the 2000 British Crime Survey*, London: Home Office.

ODPM (Office of the Deputy Prime Minister) (2002) *Living Places: Cleaner, Safer, Greener*, London: ODPM.

ODPM (2004) *Neighbourhood Wardens Scheme Evaluation*, Research Report 8, London: ODPM.

ODPM (2005) *Sustainable Communities: People, Places and Prosperity*, London: ODPM.

PA Consulting Group (2001) *Diary of a Police Officer*, London: Home Office.

Page, B., Wake, R. and Ames, A. (2004) *Public Confidence in the Criminal Justice System*, Findings 221, London: Home Office.

Rhodes, R.A.W. (1996) 'The New Governance: Governing Without Government', *Political Studies*, vol 44, pp 652-67.

Rose, N. (1999) *Powers of Freedom: Reframing Political Thought*, Cambridge: Cambridge University Press.

Sampson, R.J., Raudenbush, S.W. and Earls, F. (1997) 'Neighborhoods and Violent Crime: A Multi-Level Study of Collective Efficacy', *Science*, vol 277, pp 918-23.

SEU (Social Exclusion Unit) (2001) *National Strategy for Neighbourhood Renewal*, London: Cabinet Office.

Sparrow, A. (2003) 'Blunkett Will Let Residents' Groups Buy Own Policing', *The Daily Telegraph*, 17 November.

Trickett, A., Ellingworth, D., Farrell, G. and Pease, K. (1995) 'Crime Victimisation in the Eighties: Changes in Area and Regional Inequality', *British Journal of Criminology*, vol 35, no 3, pp 343-59.

TWELVE

Gated communities: a response to, or remedy for, anti-social behaviour?

Sarah Blandy

Introduction

Gated communities[1] hold out the promise of a sanitised residential cocoon, from which anti-social behaviour (ASB) can be excluded if perpetrated by outsiders, or controlled through internal regulation if residents are involved. This chapter examines the validity of this promise and how gated communities, which are increasingly seen in areas of social rented housing as well as in affluent private housing neighbourhoods, fit within the current government policy agenda, which positions housing in general as central to neighbourhood renewal. The privatised and collectively managed space of gated communities seems to foreshadow the devolved neighbourhood governance and community ownership of housing described by John Flint in Chapter One (this volume), which are currently being promoted through the stock transfer programme and other initiatives.

This chapter examines whether the physical and sociolegal features of gated developments can contribute to community capacity, and explores the implications of the legal framework that sets clear rules for residents and gives them responsibility for managing their own development. It considers whether such features might beneficially be used in deprived neighbourhoods. Further, it considers whether gated communities might contribute to the aim of mixed communities by encouraging the 'colonisation' of primarily social rented areas by owner-occupiers. The chapter concludes by linking the focus on ASB with the wider implications of gated communities for fostering a socially inclusive society.

Gated communities

Gated community developments combine a particular sociolegal framework with a built form that denies or restricts public access to space such as driveways, internal roads and grounds around buildings, which non-residents would usually expect to be able to walk or drive through. Buildings such as a block of flats, where public access is restricted only at the front door, for example, by means of a concierge or entryphone system, therefore do not fall within this definition of gated community. It is also important to distinguish between two kinds of gated community. One type is an existing neighbourhood which is subsequently gated by, or at the request of, its residents. Barriers are erected across the public access roads and a boundary is built around the neighbourhood. This type of gated community is common in South Africa, for instance, where some neighbourhood enclosures are blatantly unlawful while the local authority sanctions others.

The English planning system makes it extremely difficult to close off a formerly public road (see Gooblar, 2002) so this chapter deals only with the other type of gated community: the enclosed housing estate with private internal roads[2]. In England, most gated communities are designed from the outset to prevent non-residents from entering the development. However, some have been formed from existing developments whose internal roads had never been adopted by the local authority; planning constraints do allow the erection of barriers to restrict access in such cases. This retro-gating has been mainly applied to private housing developments, but there is anecdotal and visual evidence that a small number of housing estates owned by social landlords in England have been gated at some time after original construction[3]. Thus gated communities in England can be private, social, or mixed tenure housing developments. The key features, whether purpose-built or retro-fitted with gates, is that their internal grounds and roads are privately owned and maintained, and that the residents are involved in the management of the developments.

Gated communities have been the subject of intense academic interest in recent years (see, for example, McKenzie, 1994; Blakely and Snyder, 1997; Caldeira, 2000; Low, 2003; Glasze et al, 2005; and special issues of *Environment and Planning B*, 2002, vol 29, no 3; *Geographica Helvetica*, 2002, vol 57, no 4 and 2003, vol 58, no 4; *Housing Studies*, 2005, vol 20, no 2; and *GeoJournal*, 2006: forthcoming).

International comparisons initially focused on how their global growth could be explained. Three responses were commonly put forward: that gated communities were a response to increasing crime and disorder; that they reflect a growing disillusionment with the ability of government to provide services and security; or that their spread has resulted from the globalisation of North American taste and aspirations. This type of development can be found in countries with very serious socioeconomic inequalities and high rates of violent crime, for example, certain South American countries. They are also a common built form in countries undergoing economic and political transition, such as China and some Eastern European countries. However, enclosed and guarded housing developments have also been emerging in some Western European countries, although it is notable that in those countries where a low percentage of the population has household incomes below 60% of the median (see Forster, 2000), there are fewer gated communities.

With more published research available from a wider geographical base, it now seems accepted that gated communities are a product of the specific political, economic, social and design history and culture of each country in which they have appeared. Nevertheless, some common themes deserve further consideration before outlining what is known about gated communities in England. The rise in gated communities can be seen as illustrative of the movement from informal to formal, privatised, systems of social control, and further examples of this trend are outlined by Diane Lister and Adam Crawford in Chapters Six and Eleven (this volume) respectively (see also Soja, 2000). In gated developments, social control is provided both by the defensive walls that restrict public access, and by legally enforceable rules of conduct within the walls. This picture may be contrasted with – possibly rose-tinted – depictions of the first half of the 20th century when residential occupiers looked outwards from their homes, reassured by kinship networks and established social patterns. In such neighbourhoods, 'eyes on the street' provided surveillance, and civilised behaviour was enforced through good neighbourliness and a communal sense of responsibility (see, for example, Jacobs, 1961).

The change to more formal social control over the last half-century has been explained both by the breakdown in relationships of trust within communities, and by the appearance of what Garland (2002) terms the 'crime complex'. This is characterised by a number of attitudes and assumptions: a fascination with crime, institutionalised in the media and dominating public policy, alongside a lack of confidence in the criminal justice system and a corresponding growth in private defensive routines and privatised security (Garland, 2002, p 163). Taken together, these factors turn a high crime rate into a 'fact of life', although, of course, fear of crime has long exceeded actual crime rates in most

Western countries. Nevertheless, the awareness of crime has become 'continuous with normal social interaction ... a routine risk to be calculated' (Garland, 2002, p 128). The crime complex affects decisions about where and how to live, for those able to choose, whether actual victims or not. Thus 'protection against risk of crime through an investment in measures of security becomes part of the responsibilities of each active individual ... if they are not to feel guilt at failing to protect themselves [and] their loved ones ... against future misfortunes' (Rose, 2000, p 327).

The private defensive routines and privatised security that the crime complex demands of responsibilised residents have taken an increasingly physical form. The idea of 'designing out crime' originated with Oscar Newman (1972). His concept of defensible space was combined with Jacobs' earlier (1961) theories to suggest ways of improving residential areas and reducing fear of crime. Newman's design principles call for the reduction of public areas, the creation of physically private space around individual dwellings, and intensive monitoring and control by residents themselves. He stressed the importance of boundaries to differentiate between public areas and the private space over which individual residents should be encouraged to feel ownership. The primary purpose of the community thus became the surveillance of public space, characterised by Newman as a potentially dangerous no-man's-land. These propositions have been criticised for their emphasis on 'territoriality, proprietal interest and felt responsibility' (Cohen, 1985, p 215), but have been widely put into practice. Gated communities, with their pragmatic prevention of risk through target-hardening and simple prevention of access by non-residents, exemplify situational crime prevention. Within their walls, residents have collective responsibility for managing the communal facilities, grounds and internal roads.

Only limited empirical research has so far been undertaken into gated communities in England. In 2003 the Office of the Deputy Prime Minister (ODPM) funded a national study into gated communities, the main element of which was a survey sent to all English local planning authorities that produced a 93% response rate (Atkinson et al, 2003). This indicated at least 1,000 gated communities distributed throughout all regions of England, although concentrated in London and the South East. However, nearly two thirds of local authority areas had no gated communities in their area, and those that did had very few, certainly in comparison with many North American states. In addition, English gated communities are small, the vast majority having fewer than 50 dwellings. Only eight local authorities said they had any such developments in their area that contained more than 150 dwellings. It also seems that, in England, gated communities are a recent trend, with the majority developed since 1995, and overwhelmingly built by private developers. Only 1% of local authorities reported that gated communities in their area were built by a social landlord. Although this may be an undercount, most of these developments are certainly built for affluent owner-occupiers.

There is less information available about why people might want to live in a gated community. A small-scale study of new purchasers in one gated community found that maintenance of property values was more important than any other motivation, including security (Blandy and Lister, 2005). Certainly, publicity material for English gated communities tends to emphasise the prestige and exclusivity of the developments, rather than fear of crime or ASB. For residents interviewed for the ODPM study, security was an issue, but it was not the only or even the most pressing motivation cited by any resident of a gated community. One developer explained that, 'our customers value it just as much for their property being secure while they're absent, as they do for their own security'. However, a London estate agent reported that 'over the past five years we have become aware of clients with really nasty stories to tell. More than 80 percent of them say they want to live in a gated community because they have experienced some ongoing security problem – burglary, cars damaged or stolen, muggings – in an ungated development' (Atkinson et al, 2003, p 26).

In a telephone survey of 1,000 people who were not residents of gated communities, which was carried out for the Royal Institute of Chartered Surveyors, half of all the respondents said they approved of gated communities. While only one third agreed with the statement that 'living in a gated community appeals to me personally', for them, greater security was the most attractive feature. Younger people, renters and those on lower incomes were more likely to find the idea of living in a gated community attractive, compared to older age groups, owner-occupiers and those on higher incomes (for further details of this survey, see Blandy et al, 2003).

Anti-social behaviour

It is not surprising that renters and those on lower incomes would find the security promised by gated communities to be attractive. In terms of which groups are the most likely to fear and experience crime and disorder, the above telephone survey findings mirror the analysis of responses to a new set of questions in the 2003/04 British Crime Survey (BCS), which has enabled analysis of respondents' perceptions and experiences of the problems of ASB, together with the impact on them and their communities (Wood, 2004). The results showed that residents of 'hard-pressed areas' (as defined by ACORN: low-income families, areas of council housing, high-rise and inner-city estates) are four times more likely to perceive and experience ASB than are residents of 'wealthy achiever' areas.

ASB is defined in Section 1 of the 1998 Crime and Disorder Act as acting 'in a manner that caused or was likely to cause harassment, alarm or distress to one or more persons who are not members of the perpetrator's own household'. As Carr and Cowan (Chapter Three, this volume) and Nixon and Parr (Chapter Four, this volume) suggest, this legal definition defines ASB by its effects on others, making it hard to classify exactly *what* constitutes ASB, and leaving open the possibility that the same actions could fall within the legal definition in one set of circumstances or location, but might not cause harassment, alarm or distress in another place or at a different time. Sixteen types of conduct amounting to ASB were included in the BCS. Those most commonly experienced by respondents were speeding traffic and inconveniently or illegally parked cars, with abandoned cars coming in tenth on the list (Dodd et al, 2004).

The BCS's other categories of ASB included inconsiderate conduct such as vandalism, graffiti and leaving litter and dog mess, and potentially intimidating actions such as letting off fireworks, drug dealing and drunkenness. Conduct directly affecting another person, such as 'pestering', noisy neighbours, racial attacks and neighbour disputes, was included in the list of ASB, although overlapping with clearly criminal behaviour. The sixth most commonly experienced form of ASB was teenagers 'hanging around', coming higher than drunkenness, noise or neighbour disputes; these groups of young people were usually strangers to the 'victim' although from the same local area (Wood, 2004). A qualitative study of ASB found that although the majority of people in Britain are not affected by such conduct, it has an acute impact on the lives of a minority. All groups considered ASB to be primarily perpetrated by young people (Millie et al, 2005).

Transferability of key characteristics of gated communities to deprived neighbourhoods

This section explores whether gating might prove beneficial for residents of 'hard-pressed' areas. In a speech to the New Local

Government Network, the then Home Secretary David Blunkett suggested that, if gated communities were to be established in deprived areas, this would 'make available to the many what is currently available to the few' (Blunkett, 2004). He went on to elaborate his view that residents who pay for the upkeep and security of their immediate surroundings would be encouraged to feel a greater sense of ownership and involvement in their neighbourhood. Many aspects of gated communities that attracted David Blunkett resonate strongly with the current government agenda for tackling ASB. Indeed, analogous features are already being introduced into deprived areas. In terms of physical security, measures such as target hardening, neighbourhood wardens, concierge schemes and CCTV are now standard on many social rented housing estates. Whether this provides surveillance of the residents themselves, rather than outsiders, remains a moot point. In some rundown areas of private housing, 'alley gating' has gated off access to back alleys behind terraced housing, enclosing them to create collective space. Alley gating does not have the same exclusionary effect as gated communities, because the main access roads are not closed to non-residents (Landman, 2003). The government-sponsored Operation GateIT was set up in 2004, and there are now over 70 alley-gating projects nationally. Evidence suggests that these initiatives have been successful in reducing ASB and encouraging a sense of collective identity. However, residents were found to be reluctant to participate in the subsequent governance of the 'community space' created by alley gating (Blandy et al, 2004).

In relation to sociolegal measures, tenants' management organisations are engaged in the management of social rented housing, just as gated community residents are in their development. Tenancy agreements (see Chapter Six, this volume) are used by social landlords as the basis for defining acceptable behaviour. As other contributors to this book identify (for example, see Chapters Six and Seven) contractual governance is being extended beyond the landlord–tenant relationship. The Hollingdean Estate in Brighton provides an example of a mixed tenure area where a Neighbourhood Agreement has been introduced, covering 'the kind of unspoken code that most people would live by anyway' (local resident, quoted in *The Guardian*, 5 April 2005). The code is voluntary and unenforceable, but all residents aged over 10 are being encouraged to sign up. It includes promises to keep properties and their immediate environment in a clean and presentable state, to ensure that children do not play ball games in undesignated areas; and it forbids swearing, dumping rubbish, trespass, graffiti, noise and unruly behaviour. Unlike the agreements governing most gated communities, which it closely resembles, the Hollingdean agreement was proposed by residents, who were also involved in drawing it up.

Current government proposals for a Neighbourhoods Charter would put such agreements on a more formal footing. If implemented, neighbourhood bodies (so far ill defined) could contract with service providers, own and manage community assets and take on devolved responsibilities for delivering services, levying fixed penalty notices and applying for Antisocial Behaviour Orders (ASBOs) (see Chapter One, this volume, for a further discussion). The possibility is also envisaged that:

> Where national legal remedies are proving insufficient ... a model set of bylaws might be an effective way of indicating to a community expected standards of behaviour ... it could be established that parking on verges or skateboarding on the street were not acceptable types of behaviour in a particular neighbourhood. (ODPM and the Home Office, 2005, p 22)

The idea that gated communities provide a model for engaging 'people in making decisions, and to reinforce the message that they are part of the solution' (Blunkett, 2004) exemplifies the 'appeals to community', so characteristic of government strategies for dealing with ASB (Crawford, 1998, p 262). As we have seen, a range of tools of formal social control for tackling ASB is already available and more may be introduced, particularly in 'hard-pressed areas'. Even though these techniques do not quite add up to the creation of gated communities as defined at the beginning of this chapter, the similarities are undeniable. Thus research into the impacts of gated communities has wider relevance because of the analogies with measures now being used in deprived neighbourhoods.

Effects of gated communities

This section explores whether empirical research into gated communities, both in England and abroad, has found their physical and sociolegal characteristics to be effective in tackling crime and ASB.

Crime

Only one study thus far has tested whether the promise of greater security held out by gated communities is, in fact, fulfilled. In a comparison of perceived safety and actual crime rates between gated and non-gated areas in high-income neighbourhoods and in public housing projects in Newport Beach, California, no significant differences were found between these paired neighbourhoods (Wilson-Doenges, 2000). More recently, in South Africa, 'No statistics could be found to prove or disprove the effect road closures and boom gates have on the crime rate', and, in fact, some of the 'information from the South African Police Services indicated an increase in crime levels' (SAHRC, 2005, p 24).

More practically, one police respondent in the ODPM research in England commented that when 'the development rings to call out the police [the response rate is slower because] the gates are locked and we need to get the security codes to gain access' (Atkinson et al, 2004, p 33). Most community police officers in the case study areas were confident that crime was rare within gated communities, but some of the residents seemed to suffer from increased sensitisation to crime and consequent greater anxiety. An anthropological study of gated communities in the US has highlighted concerns about the effect on residents, particularly children, of living in such insulated and homogeneous environments that they can 'feel quite threatened just being out in normal urban areas' (Low, 2003, p 9).

Anti-social behaviour

There has been no research into the effectiveness of gated communities in dealing with ASB, but the potential can be explored by aligning the characteristics of gated communities with the results of the 2003/04 BCS. Gating could indeed prevent some problems caused by through traffic; however, arguments over allocated parking spaces, and whether or not to build speed bumps, appear to be common among the residents of gated communities (Atkinson et al, 2003; Blandy and Lister, 2005).

Potentially troublesome non-resident young people would be prevented from coming into a gated development, unless of course a resident invited them in. If it was young residents of the gated community themselves, or their invited guests, 'hanging around', could the internal rules deal with this? Analysis of legal documents for gated communities shows that they typically mirror the tenancy agreements of social landlords, for example in forbidding immoral or illegal use of the property (some make specific reference to illegal drugs), and noise between 11pm and 8am. Some restrict children from playing in any communal areas except the designated play areas, which are unlikely to be attractive to teenagers (Atkinson et al, 2003; Blandy and Lister, 2005).

Although these covenants seem designed to deal with common types of ASB, it should be remembered that they are not negotiated by the gated community's residents themselves, but drafted by lawyers acting for the developer. They are a legal representation of behavioural norms, designed to maintain property values. In common with Diane Lister's findings in the private rented sector reported in Chapter Six (this volume), most gated community residents are not aware of the details of these covenants when they purchase their property, so it is debatable whether they amount to a common code of behaviour which would strengthen community resolve in tackling ASB (see also Blandy and Lister, 2005). Further, if breaches occur, it is the residents' association or residents' management company that is responsible for enforcing the covenants, which might ultimately mean court action to forfeit the perpetrator's lease. In practical terms, the enforcement of covenants against owner-occupiers poses the same difficulties as enforcing clauses in tenancy agreements, with potentially additional problems caused by a group of neighbours, rather than an external landlord, taking action against another resident.

Collective efficacy

The analysis of the 2003/04 BCS uses the term 'collective efficacy' to describe the ability and will of a community to deal with local problems. Lack of collective efficacy in an area was found to be a strong predictor of ASB; generally, the vast majority of incidents were neither reported nor resolved through an informal approach (Wood, 2004). Thus a further question about gated communities is whether residents' collective management responsibilities provide more possibilities for interaction, leading to new networks of sociability and the creation of neighbourhoods with effective informal social controls. Atkinson et al (2003) found a variety of types of social interaction and collective efficacy in the case study areas. One respondent illustrated her preference for formal over informal social controls ('eyes on the street'), when she commented that she valued her gated community's internal CCTV cameras as providing protection for her children from paedophiles. In some of the case study gated communities, the lack of through traffic contributed to a pleasant, open neighbourhood where children felt safe to play in the streets, and most residents knew each other. In others, a more closed atmosphere prevailed. This diversity means that no general conclusion can be reached on whether English gated communities in general encourage a collective efficacy capable of dealing with ASB.

The national ODPM study found that in some gated communities the arrangements for self-management by residents were working well. In others, there was frustration that firmer action was not taken on breaches of covenant, or, alternatively, allegations made that a 'power-hungry' group of residents had taken control and were running the development with 'a rod of iron' (Atkinson et al, 2003, p 30). At the time when residents decided to purchase, the majority were unaware that they were signing up to collective management. Evidence also indicates that participation follows much the same pattern as in social rented tenants' associations, with a small minority of active residents filling positions in the residents' management company, while the majority are not interested or are resentful of the power exercised by the minority (for further discussion, see Blandy and Lister, 2005). Thus the self-management arrangements in gated communities are no guarantee of harmonious relationships between residents, nor is there evidence that they necessarily lead to more social interaction and increased collective efficacy. Indeed, in gated communities where the residents have become divided over management issues, the opposite is true.

In terms of the wider impact of gated communities, there is some research evidence (Blandy and Lister, 2005, p 299) that they can even lead to anti-social acts by residents of the surrounding area, with one gated community resident reporting that 'just on a wall, some idiot had daubed: "This way to the middle-class ghetto"'. This incident took place in an affluent suburb; the next section considers the effect of gated communities built within more deprived neighbourhoods.

Gating and the regeneration of deprived neighbourhoods

It has been argued that the security which gating offers might persuade owner-occupiers to move into less desirable areas, thus contributing to government policies on regeneration and mixed tenure neighbourhoods (Manzi and Smith-Bowers, 2005). However, the limitations of this approach are that it seems only a small proportion of more affluent owner-occupiers genuinely want to live in mixed areas. Most are driven primarily by high property prices to consider purchasing in cheaper neighbourhoods, and will only do so on condition that physical barriers are provided to divide 'them' from 'us'. These inferences are borne out by Butler's (2001) work on gentrified areas of London, which concludes that many respondents want to live with 'people like us', as a strategy for coping with the demands of modern life and with under-resourced public services. In two of the four case study areas, gentrifying residents had adopted 'an "enclavist" approach to middle class urban living' (Butler, 2001, p 4). One developer of gated communities, interviewed for the study by Blandy and Lister (2005), commented that 'the home-buying public ... they don't have a social conscience, they're worried about their car being stolen, so they will say: "yes, I will buy on the edge of a council estate or an area of deprivation, but I will want a six foot high wall"'.

Castell's (1997) study of a gated community in Tower Hamlets provides an example of these 'inserted' gated developments, where the socioeconomic profile of the residents inside is very different from that of residents in the area surrounding the gated community. This particular walled development had its own shop and leisure facilities. Unsurprisingly, over half of its residents never went into the surrounding area at all, except to shop at a big supermarket, to go to the bank, to visit the park some distance away, or to travel through it on their way to work. There was virtually no contact between the two populations living in close proximity, which can create further divisions rather than social integration. In the ODPM study a tenant representative from a social housing estate said in interview that it felt as if the affluent gated community next door was 'rubbing our noses in it' (Atkinson et al, 2004, p 31).

Manzi and Smith-Bowers (2005, p 357) argue that gated communities can 'present opportunities for urban renewal'. Yet their case study of a gated development within a larger mixed tenure development, inside another set of walls, does little to explain the benefits. The residents of this gated community, while insulated from the problems faced by residents of the surrounding non-gated housing estate, remained fearful of their renting neighbours. The researchers were told, for example, that owner-occupiers had installed further security measures to their properties, and that the 'gates are a necessity. When they were broken (by the kids [from the estate] of course) cars were getting broken into' (Manzi and Smith-Bowers, 2005, p 353). Thus the proximity of valuable cars and property to a deprived area may in fact attract crime and ASB. Gated community residents said they tended not to walk around the estate, and one commented that 'I very rarely go to the shop....They can tell ... that you are not from the housing association flats. It is aggressive' (Manzi and Smith-Bowers, 2005, p 352).

It may be that inserting fortified developments for more affluent residents does 'reduce residential segregation in areas that otherwise would have accommodated ... multi-deprived households exclusively' (Manzi and Smith-Bowers, 2005, p 357), but there is no evidence from the studies cited that this leads to real social integration between the two groups of residents. Acknowledging this, the recent national guidance for planning authorities on design for crime prevention states that:

> Gated communities may increase the sustainability and social mix of an area where problems of crime and image could otherwise lead to the development's failure. The Government believes, however, that it is normally preferable for new development to be integrated into the wider community and that the gating of developments should only be considered as a last resort. (ODPM and the Home Office, 2004, p 30)

Conclusion

Gated communities in England are currently primarily marketed at owner-occupiers who are comfortably off. It can be assumed that a proportion of these residents have moved to a gated community as a reaction to their fear, or experience, of crime and disorder. This response cannot be dismissed as an insignificant and irrelevant attempt by the affluent to insulate themselves from the world outside, because gated communities have a considerable effect on the social and built environment. Fear of others has led to what Reich (2000, p 197) describes as the 'sorting mechanism' by means of which North American citizens are, according to Putnam (2000, p 209), moving 'into more and more finely distinguished "lifestyle enclaves", segregated by race, class, education, life stage, and so on'. Further, the physical exclusiveness of gated communities has a particular impact, reducing both public space and the permeability of the town or cityscape.

It must therefore be questioned whether the spread of gated communities should be allowed to continue, particularly when the research findings considered in this chapter do not support the proposition that they can offer an effective solution to ASB. The evidence is also equivocal on whether gated communities encourage a sense of collective identity among residents; if so, it risks being a 'destructive, negative cohesion ... [based on] a nervous determination to exclude people seen as outsiders' (Urban Design Alliance, 2003). The internal tensions found in gated communities are a useful indication that analogous tensions may result from wider government aims in relation to governance in other housing tenures, and to social and urban policies more generally.

If England follows North America's lead in allowing more gated communities to be built for a wider socioeconomic range of residents, such developments might come to represent 'the spaces of consumption and civility', with the perpetrators of ASB exiled to 'the savage spaces on the margins' (Rose and Valverde, 1998, p 549). Such a dystopian image hardly represents the collective efficacy and social integration measures best suited to tackling ASB.

Notes

[1] The definition of a gated community adopted here is 'a walled or fenced housing development to which public access is restricted, often guarded using CCTV and/or security personnel, and characterised by legal agreements which tie the residents to a common code of conduct and involvement in management of the development' (Atkinson et al, 2003, p 3).

The phrase 'gated communities' will be used as it is the accepted English language term, although whether or not such developments can be described as 'communities' is contested. It should be noted that, for example, in South America the terms *condominios* (implying a degree of common ownership) or *barrios* (neighbourhoods) are used, further defined by the adjectives *exclusivos*, *privados* or *cerrardos*, meaning 'exclusive', 'private' or 'closed'.

[2] In the majority of housing developments, internal roads are constructed by the developer but later, when the scheme is complete, these roads are 'adopted' by the local highways department, which takes over responsibility for maintaining them.

[3] One example is the Cromer Street estate near Kings Cross, London, where enclosure and restricted access were successfully introduced to protect residents from the high crime rates of the surrounding area (for further details, see ODPM and the Home Office, 2004, Annex 1, pp 54-5).

References

Atkinson, R., Blandy, S., Flint, J. and Lister, D. (2003) *Gated Communities in England*, London: ODPM.

Blakely, E.J. and Snyder, M.G. (1997) *Fortress America: Gated Communities in the United States*, Cambridge, MA/Washington, DC: Lincoln Institute of Land Policy/Brookings Institution Press.

Blandy, S. and Lister, D. (2005) 'Gated Communities: (Ne)gating Community Development?', *Housing Studies*, vol 20, no 2, pp 287-301.

Blandy, S., Green, S. and McCoulough, E. (2004) *Boundary Building in NDC Areas*, London: Neighbourhood Renewal Unit.

Blandy, S., Lister, D., Atkinson, R. and Flint, J. (2003) *Gated Communities: A Systematic Review of the Evidence*, London: ODPM.

Blunkett, D. (2004) Speech to New Local Network Annual Conference, 22 January (available at www.nlgn.org.uk/nlgn.php).

Butler, T. (2001) *The Middle-classes and the Future of London*, A summary of findings from the ESRC Cities: Competitiveness and Cohesion Programme, Swindon: ESRC.

Caldeira, T. (2000) *City of Walls: Crime, Segregation and Citizenship in Sao Paulo*, Berkeley, CA: University of California Press.

Castell, B. (1997) 'An Investigation into Inward-looking Residential Developments in London', Unpublished MPhil thesis, London: University College, University of London.

Cohen, S. (1985) *Visions of Social Control: Crime, Punishment and Classification*, Cambridge: Polity Press (in association with Basil Blackwell, Oxford).

Crawford, A. (1998) *Crime Prevention and Community Safety*, London: Longman.

Dodd, T., Nicholas, S., Povey, D. and Walker, A. (2004) *Crime in England and Wales 2003/2004*, Home Office Statistical Bulletin 10/04, London: Home Office.

Forster, M. (2000) *Trends and Driving Factors in Income and Inequality in the OECD Areas*, OECD Labour Market and Social Policy Occasional Paper No 42, Paris: Organisation for Economic Co-operation and Development.

Garland, D. (2002) *The Culture of Control: Crime and Social Order in Contemporary Society*, Oxford: Oxford University Press.

Glasze, G., Webster, C. and Frantz, K. (eds) (2005) *Private Cities: Global and Local Perspectives*, London: Routledge.

Gooblar, A. (2002) 'Outside the Walls: Urban Gated Communities and Their Regulation within the British Planning System', *European Planning Studies*, vol 10, no 3, pp 321-34.

Guardian, The (2005) 'Swearing In Public May Cost Tenants Their Home', 5 April.

Jacobs, J. (1961) *The Death and Life of Great American Cities*, New York, NY: Random House.

Landman, K. (2003) 'Alley-Gating and Neighbourhood Gating: Are they Two Sides of the Same Face?', Paper presented at the 'Gated Communities: Building Social Division or Safer Communities?' Conference, University of Glasgow, 18-19 September.

Low, S. (2003) *Behind the Gates: Life, Security and the Pursuit of Happiness in Fortress America*, London: Routledge.

McKenzie, E. (1994) *Privatopia: Homeowner Associations and the Rise of Residential Private Government*, New Haven, CT and London: Yale University Press.

Manzi, T. and Smith-Bowers, B. (2005) 'Gated Communities as Club Goods: Segregation or Social Cohesion?', *Housing Studies*, vol 20, no 2, pp 345-59.

Millie, A., Jacobson, J., McDonald, E. and Hough, M. (2005) *Anti-social Behaviour Strategies: Finding a Balance*, York: Joseph Rowntree Foundation.

Newman, O. (1972) *Defensible Space: Crime Prevention Through Urban Design*, New York, NY: Macmillan.

ODPM (Office of the Deputy Prime Minister) and the Home Office (2004) *Safer Places: The Planning System and Crime Prevention*, London: The Stationery Office.

ODPM and the Home Office (2005) *Citizen Engagement and Public Services: Why Neighbourhoods Matter*, London: ODPM.

Putnam, R.D. (2000) *Bowling Alone: The Collapse and Revival of American Community*, New York, NY: Simon and Schuster.

Reich, R.B. (2000) *The Future of Success: Working and Living in the New Economy*, New York, NY: Vintage.

Rose, N. (2000) 'Government and Control', *British Journal of Criminology*, vol 40, pp 321-39.

Rose, N. and Valverde, M. (1998) 'Governed by Law?', *Social and Legal Studies*, vol 7, no 4, pp 541-51.

SAHRC (South African Human Rights Commission) (2005) *Report on the Issue of Road Closures, Security Booms and Related Measures*, Houghton, South Africa: SAHRC.

Soja, E.W. (2000) *Postmetropolis: Critical Studies of Cities and Regions*, Oxford: Blackwell.

Urban Design Alliance (2003) *Design for Cohesive Communities*, Memorandum in Evidence to the Select Committee on ODPM, SOC 09 Session 2002/03, London: The Stationery Office.

Wilson–Doenges, G. (2000) 'An Explanation of Sense of Community and Fear of Crime in Gated Communities', *Environment and Behaviour*, vol 32, no 5, pp 597-611.

Wood, M. (2004) *Perceptions and Experiences of Antisocial Behaviour*, Home Office Findings 252, London: Home Office.

Part 4
Studies of housing and anti-social behaviour from an international perspective

THIRTEEN

Housing and anti-social behaviour in Australia

Kathy Arthurson and Keith Jacobs

Introduction

Since the 1980s social housing in Australia has, as in the UK, increasingly become the tenure for individuals with limited incomes and high levels of social need. Further, the growing residualisation of social housing has meant that the poorest sections of the community are concentrated into smaller geographical localities. As several of the chapters on Britain in this volume describe, contemporary social housing estates accommodate disproportionately large numbers of households suffering from mental illness and exhibiting characteristics associated with poverty and stress. The intensive needs of many tenants result in a new set of challenges for housing managers in terms of supporting sustainable tenancies. This chapter explores the theoretical and policy implications of one of these challenges, that of addressing anti-social behaviour (ASB) on social housing estates. The chapter's aims are threefold: firstly, to provide an overview of the different perceptions of ASB and the emergence of new discourses linked to housing in Australia; secondly, to offer a comparative discussion on Australian and UK approaches, drawing on a recent research project examining key issues and questions facing policy makers and housing organisations in the Australian context; and thirdly, the chapter explores the implications of the current findings for future research on housing and ASB.

Policy context

In Australia funding for social housing is provided under the Commonwealth State Housing Agreement (CSHA), an agreement made between the federal government and state and territory governments. Under the terms of the Agreement, the federal government pursues national objectives to support individuals and communities while state and territory governments are responsible for implementing and administering the delivery of social housing. Overall, Australian governments have provided greater support for home ownership, resulting in a small social rental tenure in comparison with the UK and Europe. At the present time in Australia, 66.2% of households are homeowners/purchasers, 21.8% are private renters, 4.5% are public renters, 2.8% are in other tenures and 0.4% reside in community housing (Productivity Commission, 2004, p 16.4).

Recent evidence from within Australia (Judd et al, 2002; Shield, 2002; Jacobs and Arthurson, 2003, 2004) has highlighted the extent to which ASB has become a significant concern of residents living in social housing, and the correlated expectation that housing agencies will respond to these concerns. Despite the increase in publicity and expectations of a housing agency response, the absence of definitional clarification about what ASB encompasses and apprehension about what consequences can ensue following intervention has acted as a barrier to policy innovation (see Chapter Seven, this volume). Furthermore, for many Australian welfare professionals, since the problems associated with ASB are viewed as a consequence of structural inequality and poverty, they are best addressed by increasing resources and material benefits. Until recently, this view was prevalent within the context of the Australian housing profession, primarily because an overt focus on 'problem' tenants was viewed not only as discriminatory but also because such a focus might accentuate stigmatisation. However, ASB issues have increasingly gained greater prominence, first and foremost, because many tenants now expect individualised, targeted action from state housing authorities (see Darcy et al, 2000; Peel, 2003) and, second, because social housing organisations like other welfare agencies are under increasing pressure to adopt more interventionist practices in areas of crime and social order. However, as we show in this chapter, compared to the UK and the US, Australian housing policies on ASB have yet to become fully embedded in housing service delivery, although there are signs that this situation could soon change. In addition, as ASB has only recently emerged as a policy issue, key federal and state legislation specifically focused on ASB, such as ASB Bills, which are used in the UK context, are not in place in Australia.

The fact that ASB has only recently emerged as a major policy issue also explains why there has been a paucity of research in the Australian context. The research that does examine ASB is often subsumed within the wider context of crime-related concerns (see Judd et al, 2002). Also, within the academic research community, the very term 'anti-social behaviour' is viewed with suspicion, primarily because of a fear that the identification of ASB as an issue legitimises those perspectives that have sought to apportion responsibility on individuals without recourse to the social and political context. It also likely, although difficult to verify, that there is a reluctance to raise some of the issues associated with ASB because the experience of the UK and US suggests that everyday perceptions are commonly intertwined within the rubric of racial stereotypes and social class (as explored by Pauline Card in Chapter Two, Judy Nixon and Sadie Parr in Chapter Four and Rowland Atkinson in Chapter Five, this volume). In the Australian context there is a concern on the part of some that publicity in respect of ASB might reinforce negative perceptions towards specific groups such as young people or Indigenous peoples.

Nevertheless, there are indications that ASB is beginning to feature more prominently in Australian housing discourse. For example, Martin et al (2002) and Westacott (2002) have highlighted the pressures that are accentuated by residualisation processes including ASB and crime. It is now recognised even by those who might feel uncomfortable with the term ASB that tenant behaviours can generate conflict and create additional demands and costs for housing agencies. Evidence from the UK in particular suggests that a failure to address ASB can result in enduring and difficult legacies (SEU, 1998; Home Office, 2005), and undermine policies aimed at advancing social cohesion and community empowerment (Flint, 2002; Stokoe and Wallwork, 2003).

Emergence of anti-social behaviour discourses in housing

The lack of Australian-focused research has encouraged researchers with an interest in ASB and housing to engage with the literature from the UK (for example, Scott and Parkey, 1998; Haworth and Manzi, 1999; Goodchild and Cole, 2001; Hunter and Nixon, 2001; Flint, 2002, 2004; Garland, 2002; Jacobs et al, 2003; Stokoe and Wallwork, 2003; Deacon, 2004). These studies reveal how housing management practices reflect and inform wider ideological debates about the nature of the welfare state. Haworth and Manzi's (1999) work is especially pertinent in the Australian context. They argue that policy prescriptions entailing commitment to addressing inequality by increasing resources have been jettisoned in favour of policies focusing more and more on individual behaviour. Housing management practices by ideologies that emphasise social control and enforcement, and policies to address

ASB are predicated on the assumption that tenants living in social housing require strict rules and sanctions for any transgression of tenancy rules. Likewise, Goodchild and Cole (2001) argue that housing management policies which address ASB are symptomatic of wider developments in social policy that foreground individual responsibility. These perspectives, drawing on governmentality theories developed by the work of Rose (1996), inform the contributions of John Flint and Helen Carr and Dave Cowan (see Chapters One and Three, respectively) in this volume (see also Raco and Imrie, 2000; Arthurson, 2002). In Australia Dean (1999) has articulated similar arguments, and portends that welfare policies are increasingly used to impose sanctions on those who transgress rules and norms of behaviour.

The dominant view articulated within academic literature portrays the emergence of ASB as a symptom of structural factors such as unemployment and poverty, accentuated by the adoption of neoliberal government policies. Within the context of housing studies, structuralist critiques argue that the concern with ASB is symptomatic of the government's incapacity to address inequality. Structuralist explanations of ASB emphasise the growing social exclusion of housing estates, with the poorest sections of the community being concentrated into increasingly smaller enclaves. Social housing has, in essence, become residualised, accommodating the least well off and those who have little choice in where they live. The very composition of these areas and housing estates (for example, characterised by disproportionately high numbers of those suffering from mental illness) is such that 'nuisance neighbours' are much more likely to be evident than otherwise might be the case in more socially heterogeneous neighbourhoods (Burney, 2000). The factors that are often cited to explain this situation include government promotion of home ownership and curbs on expenditure set aside for social housing, accompanied by targeting of social housing to only the most high-need tenants.

However, other viewpoints have been influential, especially in the realm of policy making in the UK and the US and, more recently, Australia; in particular theories that have sought to emphasise individual pathology as a cause of ASB. For example, Murray (1994) has argued that anti-social behaviours are a feature of a cultural underclass which requires appropriate sanctions and regulation if their behaviour is be modified. For Murray, the term 'underclass' denotes individuals and families with poor educational and vocational skills who choose not to seek employment and eschew training opportunities. In the Australian context, Murray's 'underclass' theories have been developed by writers such as Sullivan (2000) and Saunders and Tsumori (2002), who have sought to influence policy debate by maintaining that the most effective responses are those aimed at the level of the individual and challenge attempts to devise modes of intervention focused at the structural level. Rather, they maintain that the imposition of rules is the most appropriate response.

A distinction can therefore be drawn between two competing perspectives to explain the emergence of ASB policies in the context of Australian housing management. The first perspective is informed by a social justice perspective that seeks to explain the *causes* of ASB as a consequence of neoliberal economic policies and the residualisation of the social housing stock. Those who adopt this perspective tend to emphasise the need for more resources for social housing and the need for community-based initiatives that seek to empower residents (although see Rowland Atkinson, Chapter Five, this volume, for an alternative articulation of these arguments). Housing management strategies based on this perspective tend to adopt more holistic approaches, emphasising community renewal strategies and partnership arrangements through tenant participation practices and neighbourhood forums that encourage tenants to collaborate with housing providers. The alternative perspective focuses on the *symptoms* of ASB to highlight issues of individual responsibility as the primary cause of ASB. Those who adopt this perspective often draw on US literature and advance policies that promote sanctions, linked to notions of an underclass that have been particularly influential in the promotion of housing management practices that seek to impose regulations and containment, for example, probationary tenancies, Antisocial Behaviour Orders (ASBOs) and eviction policies (Jacobs and Arthurson, 2004).

The evidence from international practice in countries such as the UK and the US illustrates how these competing ideological perspectives inform housing management policies. In the US the focus of many housing management policies is on individual responsibility, with a propensity to engage in law enforcement and surveillance activities as a way of combating ASB. Feins et al (1997) and Grogan and Proscio (2001) provide examples of these types of policies involving warden schemes and additional police monitoring activities and reveal an emphasis on social control and the use of legal sanctions to target perpetrators of ASB.

The focus of many of the most innovative housing management policies within the UK involves social interventions (see Chapters Nine and Ten). These policies are often predicated on an assumption that structural inequality and poverty exacerbate both dysfunctional social relationships and ASB. For this reason, they seek to address the underlying source of ASB and can include the organisation of social activities, self-esteem projects and specialist service provision to address issues such as family violence and drug abuse (Armitage, 2002). The philosophy behind many of these forms of interventions is that a combination of material improvements, dialogue and understanding can ameliorate some of the problems surrounding ASB. Recent research by the UK Home Office (Home Office, 2005) highlighted how support programmes such as better parenting workshops, money advice, school truancy schemes and drugs and alcohol services are more effective in the long term than draconian punitive policies such as evictions and ASBOs.

The research study

In order to address the research lacunae on housing management practices in relation to ASB in Australia, the Australian Housing and Urban Research Institute (AHURI) funded an empirical study by the authors (Jacobs and Arthurson, 2003) in two states (South Australia and Tasmania) which explored the emergence of new discourses relating to ASB in Australia and their impact on housing practice. The case study investigations were undertaken in two localities: Bridgewater in Hobart, Tasmania, and Christie Downs in Adelaide, South Australia. The aim was to capture empirical data on how ASB is perceived and what interventions were appropriate. The study entailed semi-structured interviews with housing staff (24 in total) and other relevant stakeholders, including law enforcement, social services and community workers (16 in total). Two focus groups were conducted with tenants, one in each locality. The study explored how ASB was perceived, examined the scope for developing community-based responses to ASB and assessed how wider discourses around ASB were impacting on housing management practice.

The case study areas

The Bridgewater area just outside the city of Hobart is an area of high social need. In recent years it has been the location for a community renewal programme known as BURP (Bridgewater Urban Renewal Program). A feature of the renewal programme is that local tenants and community groups orchestrate the management of services. It therefore provides a valuable example of tenant-centred policies and a proactive approach to ASB concerns at the neighbourhood level. The population of the area at the time of the last Census was 3,867, the median age 29 years and the unemployment rate 23.6%; the median weekly household income was between $400 and $499. There were a total of 1,438 dwellings in the locality of which over 45% were rented from the state housing authority at a median rent of $50-$99 per week (ABS, 2001a).

The Christie Downs area is located in the southern region of Adelaide. Christie Downs is also characterised by a high concentration of public housing. At the last Census, there were a total of 2,091 dwellings of which 28% were rented from the state housing authority. There are large numbers of elderly residents and a significant proportion of the population have special needs associated with housing stress, including victims of domestic violence, residents with mental health issues and ex-offenders (ABS, 2001b). In 2001, the total population was 4,934 and the unemployment rate was 17.3%. The median weekly household income was between $400-$500 per week. The median weekly rent was $50-$99 per week (ABS, 2001b).

Perceptions of anti-social behaviour and emergence of new discourses

What constitutes anti-social behaviour?

Since ASB is a contested term and subject to competing definitions (see Jacobs et al, 2003), it was necessary to gauge the ways in which ASB is understood by public housing tenants and welfare professionals. The study revealed that ASB is viewed as a term that covers a wide spectrum of different behaviours including noise from parties and visitors coming and going, car burnouts and dogs barking. At the more extreme end, ASB activity cited by professionals and tenants included harassment of, and disputes between, neighbours (overhearing domestic violence incidents, people leaving rubbish, verbal abuse, trashing of lawns and backyards, graffiti and throwing items at cars or over backyard fences). While ASB was generally articulated in these terms, there was also recognition that subjectivity is an important factor in determining whether or not ASB is perceived to be a problem. For instance, it was recognised that what one person might find acceptable another might find insufferable. As one housing manager explained:

> It's anything that a tenant or neighbour finds upsets them, that isn't the norm. Music, wheelies on the road, or people coming and going at one or two o'clock in the morning.

> Some people can tolerate that, others can't. So if it upsets
> them and affects their right to quiet peace then its anti-
> social behaviour. (housing manager, Bridgewater)

However, at the more extreme end of the spectrum, ASB is often
construed in more definitive terms:

> We have kids who are harassing neighbours, throwing rocks
> on their roof, smashing their letterboxes. There is general
> harassment where if someone is standing out the front they
> will say 'what the hell are you looking at?' and may make
> threats. A lot of time the attacks don't actually take place
> but they do threaten. (housing manager, Christie Downs)

It is evident that the term 'anti-social behaviour' accommodates a
range of behaviours that impact negatively on individuals and the
wider community and that reactions to ASB are formed by a
combination of subjective values and wider social discourses, in
particular, media portrayals (see Mee, 2004; Palmer et al, 2004). As we
discuss in the conclusion to this chapter, the contested nature of ASB
makes it difficult to provide a clear ostensive definition, although there
is evidence that in Australia, as in other parts of the industrialised
world, policy makers are putting in place measures to embed
management practices to address the concerns of tenants and that
media discussions of ASB continue to have a detrimental impact on
perceptions of ASB.

Effects of anti-social behaviour

Our study explored the practical effects of ASB, both on communities
as a whole and on individuals subject to ASB management practices.
The focus group discussions revealed that the impact of ASB on tenants
varied from case to case, depending on the severity of the behaviour
and whether or not the behaviour was habitual. A significant secondary
impact of ASB identified by tenants was the sense of induced
powerlessness felt by the victim. Specifically, many tenants faced the
dilemma between not reporting incidents and therefore continuing
to experience the ASB, or reporting the problem and risking retributive
acts of ASB. This fear of retaliation appears to be a factor that deters
people from making any complaint (see Chapter Eight, this volume),
as described by tenants:

If you do become involved by reporting them to the police or the housing department you become a bigger target because you've had the guts to stand up for yourself. We've got an old lady in our street who is too terrified to say anything because she's frightened of the reprisals that will happen. (tenant, Christie Downs)

We had 28 girls on our lawn baying for blood because one of their boyfriends had been arrested and they blamed us for it. One of them threatened to burn our house down and screamed at me through the window 'I hope your children squeal when they burn!' The police stood there and did nothing, I reported it to housing and housing did nothing. (tenant, Bridgewater)

This problem of fear of retaliation was confirmed in comments made by a housing manager:

Putting things in writing can actually aggravate the situation because, 'that person dobbed me in…'. Then there'd be retaliation against that person by slashing their tyres, targeting their cars. Then we'd have to transfer them because it was a dangerous situation. (housing manager, Bridgewater)

This evidence of fear of reprisal acting as a major deterrent in the reporting of ASB activity suggests that problems experienced by victims may not necessarily come to the attention of housing managers. It also provides evidence that some tenants fear action by housing agencies can actually exacerbate problems if not carefully managed.

Causes of anti-social behaviour

Our exploration of how housing managers and tenants perceive the causal factors of ASB revealed that interviewees quite often framed their understanding of ASB within a context of interpersonal dynamics reflecting not just interactions between individuals, but a framework of family or group interactions:

Disputes between people, neighbour disputes, domestic violence, spreading out and involving other people in the community. Often a lot of the ASB is between families and

> between families or groups of relatives and the whole family
> is on this side or that side. (school professional, Bridgewater)

While the focus group participants consistently identified young people, especially 13- to 16-year-old males, as culpable for ASB, some tenants attributed a lack of parenting skills as a factor, echoing the findings of Judy Nixon and Sadie Parr in Chapter Four (this volume), and resonating with some of the underclass explanations of ASB referred to earlier:

> The parents have been brought up like it and they don't
> know so the children grow up like that. They're out on the
> street and their mother doesn't know where they are. (tenant,
> Bridgewater)

Other explanations focused on the physical environment and, in particular, environmental design factors:

> You walk out of our front door and you're looking at their
> back door. It's the way the houses are built and positioned
> on the blocks. There's no screening, no protection for you.
> It's a matter of better insulation or different structure. (tenant,
> Bridgewater)

But by far the most common perception was that ASB is a consequence of the limited opportunities available for young people:

> I think a lot of the issues we have around Christie Downs
> and other suburbs are due to the impact of
> deinstitutionalisation and the high concentration of young
> people. Currently, thirty per cent of young people between
> 15 and 19 in this region are unemployed. Young people
> who don't go to school are often considered to be
> intimidating as they don't have anything to do but just
> hang around. (housing manager, Christie Downs)

The range of explanations for ASB proffered by interviewees and focus group discussants include both pathological and structural explanations. The pathological interpretations emphasise the difficulties faced by many individuals under stress and with only limited personal resources to develop effective strategies. The structuralist interpretations emphasise contextual causal factors, such as poverty, poor housing and unemployment. The divergence of viewpoints reflects the contested nature of ASB and the influence of competing ideologies on the discourses that inform both housing staff and tenant perceptions of ASB.

Housing intervention strategies

So far in this chapter we have made use of interviews and focus groups with tenants and welfare professionals to show how issues of ASB are conceptualised. In this section, we turn our focus to how ASB is engaged with by setting out some of the interventions that have been advanced to address the problem. Our research showed that the practices identified by staff and tenants included: sensitive allocation policy; probationary tenancies; communication strategies; working directly with tenants; collaboration between law enforcement agencies; and mediation services. Policies perceived as draconian, including evictions, were also endorsed by some interviewees, although it was recognised that such policies were unlikely to tackle the underlying causes of the problem.

Allocation policies

In both case study localities housing managers and staff pointed out that a sensitive allocation policy makes it possible to prevent potential problems. For example, the introduction of a more flexible allocation policy in the Bridgewater locality, although originally intended to reduce the number of empty properties, had a positive impact by conveying to the residents that there was a demand for properties in the locality. Nevertheless, while problems can to some extent be avoided by a careful allocation policy, this is not always possible when the overriding policy objective is to address housing need. In Bridgewater, the scope for innovation was possible because of the previous low occupancy rate in the area that allowed flexibility in allocating properties and matching neighbours. As demand in the area has increased, and the availability of properties has declined, there is less scope for this sort of intervention.

This tension between utilising sensitive allocation policies and addressing housing need was also evident in Christie Downs. Recent changes in allocation policies have involved tighter targeting and taking on more Category 1 (higher need) clients, as a housing manager describes:

> There's more complex people nowadays. This is it. Where do you put them? It is extremely difficult. (housing manager, Christie Downs)

Thus tighter targeting effectively limits the possibility of using allocation policy as an effective policy instrument.

Probationary tenancies

Another practice that was seen as useful by housing managers is probationary tenancies (see Chapter Seven, this volume, for a UK comparison). In South Australia, new tenants are placed in conditional six-month tenancies and if these are successfully completed they are given ongoing tenure. The housing managers described these conditional tenancies as positive in developing relationships between tenants and housing staff:

> They provide a structure so that if you have somebody on a conditional tenancy it means we can focus on them and the relationship you have as tenancy manager with the tenant is established at the front end of the process. People accept it and it helps lay the ground rules, what the expectations are and the ramifications if the expectations aren't met. (housing manager, Bridgewater)

However, some tenants viewed probationary tenancies as less effective, and questioned the efficacy of probationary tenancies as an instrument to tackle ASB in the long term:

> Lots of people can be good for three months and then its hell for leather and they show their true colours. In the first three months you're just getting to know your neighbours and the lay of the land. Once they've signed up for twelve months that's when it starts. (tenant, Bridgewater)

Communication strategies

Housing staff felt that the management of ASB could be enhanced by a communication strategy that publicises good news stories about the locality. While landlords may do this, a key theme emerged that the most effective approach is for community-based agencies to undertake this task. In the Bridgewater area, the Bridgewater Urban Renewal Project (BURP) was instrumental in the promotion of positive stories about the locality in an attempt to address stigma. While the connection between communication strategies and ASB might not be immediately obvious, staff and tenants viewed effective communication as instrumental in facilitating an enhanced sense of community well-being, as a tenant actively involved in BURP highlights:

> We got some positive news stories out so that the general population got the view that something was happening in Bridgewater that was good. We orchestrated that and we had more people that were prepared to come and live in the area. (tenant, Bridgewater)

However, such communication strategies are not in themselves a sufficient condition for effecting change and they require considerable resources and commitment from staff and tenants.

Working directly with tenants

All of the housing staff involved in the study emphasised that an individual, more personal approach between tenants and housing staff worked best. This meant working with those engaged in ASB, assessing the nature of the problem, referring tenants on to appropriate agencies and generally taking an interest in what was happening in the community:

> You need to let them know that we will help them because a lot of the time the frustration and anti-social behaviour is due to other problems and sometimes you can get to the bottom of it and sometimes you can't. We're not social workers and we haven't got a lot of time to deal with them but it does take up a lot of our time. Because we deal with it in the best way in the long run it's less work and more effective. (housing manager, Bridgewater)

Collaboration between housing and law enforcement agencies

Housing managers and the police emphasised the importance of collaboration. In Bridgewater collaboration occurred through the 'Officer Next-Door' programme, which was established in 1998 with the aim of providing a visible police presence on the estate. Police officers and their families are offered a house to rent for $2 per week in return for producing a six-monthly report. Housing staff that have worked in the area for some time described the relationship with police as 'fantastic' but acknowledged that, like any relationship, work has to be undertaken by both parties for ongoing success:

> They'd help us out and vice versa without going too far. In order to make something work you need to know more and they've got the knowledge about how many times the police went out to that address, who was involved. It was really wonderful to have that. (housing manager, Bridgewater)

Mediation services

If tenants were amenable, housing managers quite often deployed mediation services to resolve disputes. In general, housing staff and tenants felt that mediation with an outside facilitator was a useful way of resolving certain disputes:

> We had a problem with young boys in our street and they were targeting the school a lot. The father was brought in for mediation. He really saw there were a lot of neighbours that didn't like what they were doing and it worked. I haven't heard from them, they've been very quiet and the school hasn't been targeted as much. (tenant, Bridgewater)

However, mediation was seen as effective only in certain situations and there were limitations where individuals have literacy problems or mental health issues, where serious disputes have escalated and where there is a fear of recrimination. The evidence suggests that mediation can be effective in particular circumstances and when both parties are willing to accept responsibility for their actions. For particularly vulnerable people with a high degree of special needs, mediation is likely to provide less effective intervention.

In summary, the findings suggest that the most effective policies and practices are those that are sensitive to both the causes and symptoms of ASB. There was a general consensus that the most effective forms of intervention were practices sensitised to the needs of the local community, which prevented problems taking place or managed problems to ensure that the effects were contained early and at the source. These findings concur with recent evidence provided by the

UK Home Office (2005). At this juncture, Australian housing policy makers have resisted pressures to introduce retributionist policies and have sought more holistic interventions. However, as we discuss in the following section, for persistent perpetrators of ASB practices, such solutions are not necessarily immediately effective.

Policies for persistent perpetrators of anti-social behaviour

In our research it was evident that although holistic types of housing management practices and multiagency working are invaluable as policy instruments for dealing with ASB, a different range of policies are required for addressing more intractable problems, in particular, persistent offenders. This section focuses on specific policies that are used as a last resort when other forms of intervention have proved ineffective.

Dealing with persistent anti-social behaviour offenders

Persistent offenders over the age of 16 years can be arrested by the police, dealt with through the courts and, depending on the crime, removed from the locality. Housing managers reported that, often, persistent offenders are served with warning letters and notices but this process was frequently an insufficient deterrent, especially in serious cases of ASB. One housing manager suggested:

> We should pursue the Leeds model [UK] where warning letters to disruptive tenants are sent out under the joint police and housing authority logos. This makes sure that the tenant realises that the agencies mean business. (housing manager, Christie Downs)

However, it was recognised that it is more difficult to deal with young persistent offenders (minors) for whom there are no criminal sanctions. For housing staff it means intensifying the involvement they already have in working with this group:

> We do as much as we possibly can by working with them and calling in other assistance where possible. When we see broken windows in houses we always say it only takes one child with rocks rather than 15 and I think that is correct. (housing manager, Christie Downs)

Some measures suggested by housing managers for dealing with minors included imposing Supervision Orders and sanctions on parents if their children were out of control. However, in contrast to the UK, where ASBOs are an option for housing agencies, in Australia these modes of intervention have yet to be developed. In common with the UK, housing agencies are using evictions as a last resort for the most difficult and intractable problems.

Legal procedures and eviction notices

In conducting our research we were struck by how the challenge for respondents of dealing with serial offenders who do not respond to strategies to change their behaviour led directly to discussions of eviction (which in Australia is the principal legal procedure that can be deployed when other policies are ineffectual). Housing staff stipulated that eviction is enacted as a last resort. However, in certain circumstances, some housing managers felt that evictions had to be carried out to serve as a deterrent and to indicate to tenants that the landlord was serious in their intent to address the problems of ASB when other measures had failed:

> In the past if there had been clear involvement in three anti-social behaviour incidents then in Tasmania the tenant was automatically evicted. Housing staff saw both the usefulness and difficulties with this. On the one hand it meant that eviction was a real threat.... It helped us immensely. The police could say 'You've had two warnings, this is your third, I'll be letting the housing department know tomorrow' and we would act on that. (housing manager, Bridgewater)

In practice, however, most respondents in Tasmania could not remember the last time there was an eviction for ASB. There is a notice of intention to vacate if the conditions of the lease are broken, but this is rarely issued. In South Australia, eviction is pursued but it was reiterated by housing staff that it is used only as a last resort. Housing managers are committed to working with persistent offenders but sometimes circumstances make eviction inevitable:

> We work really hard to keep people in housing. It's not our job to evict and we try very hard. But when you have got a violent person next to an aged person that's eviction

and it should be immediate, not mucking about. (housing manager, Christie Downs)

Housing managers in both the localities recognised that eviction is not a satisfactory long-term solution and that it would only result in moving the perpetrator elsewhere and 'just perpetuates the cycle'. This view among Australian housing professionals that eviction does not address underlying causes and is not a long-term solution, even at a local level, is supported by evidence in the UK (Local Government Association, 2002), where evicted tenants regularly end up in the same community, but in private tenure, where little action can be taken to curtail the problem.

While housing staff were generally reluctant to use eviction, many tenants interviewed supported pursuing eviction policies, in the belief that this would act as a deterrent for ASB, once people realised that the housing authority was serious in its intent to evict:

> I think with some families tough is the only thing they understand. They don't understand the softly, softly approach. But then you end up at a point where kids don't know any different. They've said there's a tougher penalty and the behaviour is still continuing. (tenant, Bridgewater)

Conclusion

What conclusions can be drawn about the different perceptions of ASB and discourses in Australia, and how does Australian practice compare to other countries, such as the UK and the US? The findings from our study suggest that the term ASB remains contested ideologically and politically, both in terms of its causes and the solutions proffered. Managers of social housing are often requested by tenants to respond to incidents of ASB and to take action against offenders. In this respect, the discourse surrounding ASB stems from the demand of tenants for effective action and reflects a pathological discourse foregrounding individual responsibility as a causal factor for poverty and crime.

Thus far in the Australian context, housing managers and other professionals in general terms eschew more stringent sanctions or legally based punitive measures, such as those adopted in the US and to a lesser extent in the UK. Instead they support more community-focused responses seeking to endorse forms of intervention that address the root causes of ASB. However, there is pressure from some tenants to adopt a more punitive response, particularly when the more serious or repeat incidents of ASB occur.

It seems that Australian policy is very much at a critical juncture. Policies can continue to advance progressive innovations or they can follow policies similar to those adopted in the US that tend to be more punitive. Clearly, the way in which the media report issues of ASB has provided succour to those advancing draconian interventions and the degree to which housing officers can resist the changes to 'act tough' will play a large part in determining the success of future policy intervention in this area. The limited research undertaken on ASB in the Australian context makes it difficult to fathom future policy development.

In relation to the implications for future research our empirically informed study suggests that it is important to pay closer attention to the views of individual actors about the problems of ASB than has hitherto been the case. Although, indeed, ASB practices are symptomatic of neoliberalism, there has been a tendency for writers drawing from Foucauldian perspectives to undervalue the demand for action by local residents or other individual actors. Where local resident responses are not foregrounded in research (see Chapter Four, this volume, which does attempt this), their demands for a housing management response can appear reactionary and such responses therefore do not fit with most Foucauldian perspectives aimed principally at critiquing neoliberalism. Hence, it is important that debates about ASB do not slip into the abstract world of discourse, the 'other' and ideology, but are grounded in empirical data and take account of tenant perceptions.

References

ABS (Australian Bureau of Statistics) (2001a) *Census Basic Community Profile SSC61041 Bridgewater (Suburb)*, Canberra: ABS.

ABS (2001b) *Census Basic Community Profile SSC41221 Christie Downs (Suburb)*, Canberra: ABS.

Armitage, R. (2002) *Tackling Anti-Social Behaviour: What Really Works*, London: Crime and Social Policy Section, NACRO.

Arthurson, K. (2002) 'Creating Inclusive Communities through Balancing Social Mix: A Critical Relationship or Tenuous Link?', *Urban Policy and Research*, vol 20, no 3, pp 245-61.

Burney, E. (2000) 'Ruling Out Trouble: Anti-Social Behaviour And Housing Management', *The Journal of Forensic Psychiatry*, vol 11, no 2, pp 268-73.

Darcy, M., Randolph, B. and Stringfellow, J. (2000) *Social and Behavioural Issues in Housing Estates: An Overview of Research Questions and Policy Issues*, Sydney: University of Western Sydney.

Deacon, A. (2004) 'Justifying Conditionality: The Case of Anti-social Tenants', *Housing Studies*, vol 19, no 6, pp 911-26.

Dean, M. (1999) *Governmentality: Power and Rule in Modern Society*, London: Sage Publications.

Feins, J.D., Epstein, J.C. and Widom, R. (1997) *Solving Crime Problems in Residential Neighbourhoods: Comprehensive Changes in Design, Management and Use*, Report prepared for the US Department of Justice, Newark.

Flint, J. (2002) 'Social Housing Agencies and the Governance of Anti-social Behaviour', *Housing Studies*, vol 17, no 4, pp 619-38.

Flint, J. (2004) 'Reconfiguring Agency and Responsibility in the Governance of Social Housing in Scotland', *Urban Studies*, vol 41, no 3, pp 151-72.

Garland, D. (2002) *The Culture of Control: Crime and Social Order in Contemporary Society*, Oxford: Oxford University Press.

Goodchild, B. and Cole, I. (2001) 'Social Balance and Mixed Neighbourhoods in Britain Since 1979: A Review of Discourse and Practice in Social Housing', *Environment and Planning D: Society and Space*, vol 19, no 1, pp 103-21.

Grogan, P.S. and Proscio, T. (2001) *Comeback Cities: A Blueprint for Urban Revival*, Boulder, CO: Westview Press.

Haworth, A. and Manzi, T. (1999) '"Managing the Underclass": Interpreting the Moral Discourse of Housing Management', *Urban Studies*, vol 36, no 1, pp 153-66.

Home Office (2005) 'Findings of the Neighbourhood Nuisance Expert Panel' (available at www.together.gov.uk/article.asp?aid=3280&c=408).

Hunter, C. and Nixon, J. (2001) 'Taking the Blame and Losing the Home: Women and Anti-social Behaviour', *Journal of Social Welfare and Family Law*, vol 23, no 4, pp 395-410.

Jacobs, K. and Arthurson, K. (2003) 'Can Effective Housing Management Policies Address Anti-Social Behaviour', Final Report for the Australian Housing and Urban Research Institute (AHURI) (available at www.ahuri.edu.au).

Jacobs, K. and Arthurson, K. (2004) 'Public Housing and the "Problem" of Anti-Social Behaviour', Joint Edition of *Housing Works and Parity, The Journal of the Australasian Housing Institute*, November.

Jacobs, K., Kemeny, J. and Manzi, T. (2003) 'Power, Discursive Space and Institutional Practices in the Construction of Housing Problems', *Housing Studies*, vol 18, no 4, pp 429-46.

Judd, B., Samuels, R. and O'Brien, B. (2002) 'Linkages between Housing, Policing and Other Interventions for Crime and Harassment Reduction on Public Housing Estates: AHURI Positioning Paper' (available at www.ahuri.edu.au).

Local Government Association (2002) *Tackling Anti-social Behaviour: Information and Case Studies about Local Authority Work*, London: Local Government Association.

Martin, C., Mott, P. and Landles, Z. (2002) 'Marginalising Public Housing Tenants: From the "Good Neighbourhood Policy" to "Renewable Tenancies"', Paper presented at the Australian Housing and Urban Research Institute (AHURI)/Australian Institute of Criminology (AIC) Housing, Crime and Stronger Communities Conference, Melbourne, 6-7 May.

Mee, K. (2004) 'Necessary Welfare Measure or Policy Failure: Media Reports of Public Housing in Sydney in the 1990s', in K. Jacobs, J. Kemeny and T. Manzi (eds) *Social Constructionism in Housing Research*, Aldershot: Ashgate, pp 117-41.

Murray, C. (1994) *Underclass: The Crisis Deepens*, London: Institute of Economic Affairs.

Palmer, C., Ziersch, A., Arthurson, K. and Baum, F. (2004) 'Challenging the Stigma of Public Housing: Preliminary Findings from a Qualitative Study in South Australia', *Urban Policy and Research*, vol 22, no 4, pp 411-26.

Peel, M. (2003) *The Lowest Rung: Voices of Australian Poverty*, Melbourne: Cambridge University Press.

Productivity Commission (2004) *Report on Government Services: Housing*, Steering Committee Report, Canberra: AGPS.

Raco, M. and Imrie, R. (2000) 'Governmentality and Rights and Responsibilities in Urban Policy', *Environment and Planning A*, vol 32, no 12, pp 2187-204.

Rose, N. (1996) 'The Death of the Social? Refiguring the Territory of Government', *Economy and Society*, vol 25, no 3, pp 327-56.

Saunders, P. and Tsumori, K. (2002) *Poverty in Australia: Beyond the Rhetoric*, CIS Monograph 57, Sydney: Centre for Independent Studies.

Scott, S. and Parkey, H. (1998) 'Myths and Reality: Anti-social Behaviour in Scotland', *Housing Studies*, vol 13, no 3, pp 325-45.

SEU (Social Exclusion Unit) (1998) *Bringing Britain Together: A National Strategy for Neighbourhood Renewal*, London: The Stationery Office.

Shield, J. (2002) 'Reducing Crime and Anti-social Behaviours in Public Housing Environments', Paper presented at the AHURI/AIC Housing Crime and Stronger Communities Conference, Melbourne, 6-7 May.

Stokoe, E. and Wallwork, J. (2003) 'Space Invaders: The Moral Spatial Order in Neighbourhood Dispute Discourses', *British Journal of Social Psychology*, vol 42, no 4, pp 551-69.

Sullivan, L. (2000) *Behavioural Poverty*, Sydney: Centre for Independent Studies.

Westacott, J. (2002) 'Keynote Address', at the AHURI/AIC Housing, Crime and Stronger Communities Conference, Melbourne, 6-7 May.

FOURTEEN

Testing urban forms: city, control and 'urban violence' in France

Olivier Ratouis and Jérôme Boissonade

Introduction

The prolonged riots and disturbances in several French cities in October and November 2005 focused attention on urban tensions and disorder among young people, and particularly minority ethnic groups, living in deprived peripheral housing estates; while President Chirac's response calling for renewed 'respect' mirrored the language of Prime Minister Tony Blair in the UK (Henley, 2005). The term 'urban violence' is one of the dominant contemporary expressions used in France to describe and define society and the deviant behaviour of some of its members in particular locations. It offers a suitable conceptual framework for understanding the specific nature of national approaches to addressing issues of disorder and anti-social behaviour (ASB). This chapter examines the historical development of conceptualisations of urban violence in France and links these to changing urban environments, the cultures and circumstances of young people and evolving city policies and urban governance structures.

The concept of urban violence

The concept of urban violence, like the concept of ASB discussed in other contributions to this volume, combines numerous categories of sometimes very different phenomena[1]. This concept ascribes a category of actions to a category of locations, reactivating the Babylonian myth of the city as the place of evil and all vices. 'Violence, from time immemorial, was known as new, upward and urban' (Chesnais, 1981, p 431). To understand current French politics, they must be looked at in this context, because they represent a moment within longer historical dynamics which have in large part led to a redefining of the social questions previously concerned with 'exploited workers' to a set of new urban questions based on 'zones of exclusion' (Donzelot and Mongin, 1999).

Viewing the transformations of French society at the end of the 1970s, Castells, looking back to the words of Marx, posed the question 'a new spectre haunts the world: will the urban crisis become an urban revolution?' (Castells et al, 1978, p 7). Since the Second World War, France has experienced radical transformation. The rise in the power of state town planning and development activity including the construction of new housing schemes resulted in the replacement of existing society by an urban one that exceeded all the hopes of social reformers at the beginning of the 20th century (Magri and Topalov, 1987). These developments forged a brand new coalition of part of the working classes and the new middle classes, mobilised around urban questions including quality of transport, liveability, the environment and urban renovation.

These urban struggles in France signal the emergence of a new political force rising out of this middle class (the 'second left'). It relates specifically to a new way of organising society in areas of social space, centred on the problems of everyday life. The actions and proposals arising from these struggles directly articulate lifestyle and the use of urban space, through, for example, Municipal Action Groups and Public Town Planning Studios.

Having brought its (largely municipal) elite to power, this multiform and decentralised movement came to an end with the shock of the first urban riots occurring at Les Minguettes in the suburbs of Lyon at the beginning of the1980s, shortly after the Brixton troubles in England. These events fall within the framework of the end of the welfare state. Spontaneous and deprived of political development, the riots called into question the capability of the preceding movements, which have been gradually institutionalised, to deal with the evolution of society. More profoundly, these events were the forerunners of a persistent uncertainty about the ability of the city to ensure a certain social cohesion if society itself did not have the means to do so. This uncertainty was in evidence during the riots that occurred less than 10 years later at the Mas du Taureau, a housing scheme that had, in fact, just been the subject of major urban restoration works. It was on this basis, however, that an economic and political 'realism' developed, and a rise to prominence of what became known as the 'policy of the city'. In an article entitled 'The New Urban Question', Jacques Donzelot (1999) argued that this twofold trend did not succeed in stopping the passing from a civil society, the basis of the urban struggles of the 1970s, to an 'uncivil society' whose urban riots formed the future outlook, predicting the events of autumn 2005.

'Young people' and urban areas: the structure of the problem

Nowadays, in France daily portrayals of 'uncivil society' are no longer made from the image of the proletariat, but from 'groups of young people'. This evolution, and its study, has a long history, which we will try to trace back through the work of F. Dubet and D. Lepoutre in particular. Such processes may be dated back to at least the late 19th and early 20th centuries, where concerns were raised about 'apaches': groups of young people from working-class backgrounds who had populated the suburbs following the economic recession of 1880 and were pushed out of the working world by the new regulations on child protection. They responded to the new environments in which they lived through accessing 'employment' in theft, violence and prostitution (Pierret, 2003); similar contemporaneous processes were identified in US cities by the Chicago School, showing the importance of the urban environment in the development of gangs (Thrasher, 1963 [1927]).

With the massive increase in salaried employees after the Second World War, juvenile delinquency distanced itself from organised crime to establish itself more clearly in the processes of adolescent socialisation, with the figure of the 'hooligan'. While competing directly with middle-class 'dandies', the Teddy Boys clearly asserted their popular connections. The former were the sons of the middle class, of aesthetes. Hooligans were the children of the working class whose relationships were founded on the permanency of local ties, with some lapsing into minor delinquency. J. Monod, among others, tried to understand and account for the violence that occurred in gangs of young people. Like Frederick M. Thrasher, he noted that 'to exist, the hooligan needs a victim' (Monod, 1968, p 349), whether a member of the group that they are trying 'to hustle' or a common enemy that they are fighting. Brawls with others outside of the gang represented a positive alternative to an internal fission and provided a pretext to evaluate the degree and the extent of the solidarity of group members. Monod was interested in particular in the 'ritualisation' of situations of violence. This ritualisation consists of protagonists adhering to the same value system in order to evade conflict. Tensions are ritualised by jokes that denigrate others to advantage those who show off exuberantly. This amounts to a transformation by words from a state of latent conflict to obvious ritual conflict.

The evolution of different groupings of young people accompanied massive urban development. The years of growth after the Second World War, very significantly known as 'thirty glorious years' (Fourastié, 1979), were characterised by an initial period of rebuilding of French cities and their centres destroyed by the war, and then a new phase emerging in the mid-1950s, and linked to industrialisation, involving massive urbanisation on the periphery of the cities. The Priority Urban Development Zones (ZUPs) were developed as an alternative to the traditional town (Vayssière, 1988). Lying on a level plateau and built on agricultural land available at low cost, located far away from city centres, they gave their name to the great visions of social utopia after the war, which Kaës (1963) described as the project of a classless society, one of the 'français moyen'. The housing was equipped with modern comforts; everything was 'new', including the vocabulary of the developers (Ratouis, 2005).

ZUPs gave rise within this context to important questions about lifestyles. In fact, the ZUPs gathered together populations of multiple origin (French and immigrant labour from the new industrial basins, repatriates from North Africa, as well as the middle classes, and so on). However, Chamboredon and Lemaire (1970) showed that this utopia of a classless society was actually characterised by spatial proximity but also by social distance. Various forms of localised segregation were in operation, and the middle classes did nothing but pass through the ZUPs on their way to relocating elsewhere in the small suburbs (Béhar, 1997). With the progressive evolution of these spaces, the processes of socio-spatial segregation and stigmatisation were thus at work (see Chapters Two and Five, this volume, for analogous developments in the UK). The ZUP appeared to be a type of 'Fordist residential space' (Ascher, 1995), to whose future these populations are linked. Within these areas of housing appeared 'gangs of teenagers'.

Lascoumes and Robert (1974 [1966], p 429) showed that the gang is 'not the inescapable grouping of abnormal children, but the shutting out of a social group by the effect of reciprocal segregation'. In general, trigger acts such as an attack or fight mark the birth of the gang. Such a 'feat', continuously embellished by the gang members, is universally disparaged by the adults in the surrounding environment. From this critical incident, the disparate gathering structures itself and finds coherence in its defensive attitude. In a work entitled *La Galère*, Dubet (1987), writing from a class-based perspective, described undefined young people in France plunged into a situation of personal violation. *La Galère* developed with de-industrialisation, its corollary being concentrations of mass unemployment, especially in districts of social housing, and their segregation from more affluent populations resulting from the growth of suburban housing.

Twenty years after the construction of these housing estates, the phenomenon of gangs of young people decreased and changed in nature (Dubet and Lapeyronnie, 1992). From then on the absence of any regulation of violence linked to the 'galley' (*la galère*) would build the image of the gang. The gang, 'a small island of warmth and solidarity, of emotional safety' (Dubet, 1987, p 69), which would make it possible for members to rebel against the damaged world of a society without future, was replaced by a 'group of pals', a core of three or four individuals with tenuous links. The galley makes it impossible to form a hierarchy of homogeneous groups like those described by F.M. Thrasher. They all share three characteristics: disorganisation, exclusion and rage. The first, with its two sides of 'rotten world' and personal problems, the second, with alienation through a lack of power ('destiny') and frustrated conformism (they would like to live 'like everybody', see Chapter Four, this volume) and the third, based on nihilism and the strength that results from the absence of class relationships. Jubilant but not heroic, the galley does not rely on any already established group structuring. It is 'violence without object' (Dubet, 1987, p 103), banal and explosive, malicious and free, provocative and nihilist. The galley is precisely this non-regulation of violence, which comes from disorganisation, rage and frustration with which these young people are confronted. The young are 'enraged', incapable of registering a marginal action within the positive significance of social action, not because they are dominated, 'but because this domination prohibits conflict, because this action is moulded in institutional images and techniques which prohibit their perception as forms of domination' (Dubet, 1987, p 431).

Nowadays, while flexibility of work destabilises social contexts among the working classes, urban violence is redefined from the psychological categorisation of 'the evil of the housing schemes' and the pathology supposed to affect its inhabitants towards sociological and ethnological studies aiming to understand the phenomena of violence (Collovald, 2001). Lepoutre (1997) used his ethnographic investigation of adolescent society in the suburbs to denounce the disorganisation–exclusion–rage trilogy because it defined this population of young people by its problems and its failings. He argues (1997, p 20) that there 'are no human groups, so disorganized as they are, without an ideology, a vision of the world, a unified system of personal attitudes, in short, a culture'. He confines the study of this method of sociability to the age bracket between 12 and 16 years. After these ages, young people then either integrate within the dominant standards conveyed by the middle class or alternatively adhere to a delinquent subculture, a degradation of the culture of the streets.

For Lepoutre (1997), city space is stigmatised not only for objective physical reasons (towers, roads and concrete) but also by the violence that is symbolic of certain practices (the dirtying of common spaces, throwing dustbins through the windows and the stoning of buses) that relate to offences directed against oneself. He shows that groups of young people are particularly affected, insofar as it is they who are the privileged carriers of this stigma, although denying it by affecting detachment; or more rarely by accepting it, and even asserting this negative image. Such findings have clear resonance with the discourse around young people and environmental degradation that dominates ASB discourses in the UK.

The space of the city is often the place and the context for conflict. Lepoutre (1997) again looks at the lesson of the Chicago School and shows in particular that the feeling of belonging develops mainly on a basis of the 'deathly practice' of conflict and violence. An aggressive ethos is culturally determined, in particular by the values transmitted during early childhood. The popular ideals of virility, strength, hardness (which are its negative side), honour or physical violence are inculcated by the family in which the father plays a central repressive role and in the street where training is given by example. To fight is to defend one's person against aggression from outside. Strength here is both a legitimate means of power and a privileged way of managing and resolving conflicts. Superiority depends on the network that can be mobilised by each individual in a solidarity of agony that requires reciprocity and balance. Such a concept of violence arises from three dominations suffered by young people: their youth, being low on the social scale and their position as outsiders. It is opposed to the social standard which school, in particular, transmits, where violence must give way to justice. In the same way, young people are pulled between two systems of standards: the dominant social culture and a 'culture of the streets', which would favour group conscience over other concerns. Based on the domination of the strongest, according to honour codes, personalities and reputations are assured.

This concept of a culture of the streets, with its system of codes, rituals and languages (Lepoutre, 1997), previously called a subculture, misses, however, what Lascoumes and Robert (1974 [1966]) had already noted in the previous period: that the violence of 'young suburban people' represents less an aggression against the dominant social norms than an unfiltered, roundabout search for conformity. It is this adhesion to common values that causes firstly frustration, then violence in proportion to the economic and social exclusion that they suffer. In recent years, the increasing significance of concepts of collective subcultures re-legitimised an urban policy focus on urban space as the essential means to confront the 'pathologies' specific to the 'youth from the localities', in particular through the processes of redesigning residential housing, and more recently those of demolition and redevelopment. As cities have reorganised their public and private spaces, public spaces are subject to various forms of controlling the movements of users, while private spaces are protected and are subject to access controls. However, as the rules for areas of public movement become increasingly ambiguous in, for example, commercial galleries or on public transport, certain portions of the population, and young people in particular, are driven to confine themselves to the only public spaces available (see also Chapters Five and Twelve, this volume).

From social violence to urban violence

It is the relationship that society maintains with urban space, and in particular public space, which in the long term affects our attitude with respect to the violence of youth. Whereas the rural migration of the end of the 19th century in France produced disorganisation marked by the violence of the 'apaches', the rural migration impelled by the massive requirement for immigrant manpower from the early 1960s witnessed the emergence, less than 20 years later, of the 'galley' of the 'young people of the suburbs' (Dubet, 1987). The earlier shift of identities from rural migrants to urban dwellers was accompanied by a discourse of social disorganisation (that is, lumpen proletariat, orphans) and of social violence. More recent migrations transform rural dwellers from the Maghreb and the south of Europe into urban dwellers who must above all fit into a process of industrial production. The return of these populations to their countries of origin appears impossible for many. Transient facilities (transit cities, shanty towns) are set up, a situation which would justify the 'urban violence' shown by the second generation, while continuing its work of acculturation at the same time, as highlighted in the events of autumn 2005.

In the contemporary context of de-industrialisation and the restructuring of the labour market, the 'disaffiliation'[2] of these populations favours an abstract economy, a carrier of all types of traffic and violence (Kokoreff, 2000). The contributors to a recent collection (Muchielli, 2001) have shown how these situations of violence are gradually made known in terms of insecurity. This shift from the term of 'violence' to that of 'insecurity' has further evolved into 'feeling of insecurity', with a final semantic shift replacing 'of insecurity' with 'of uncivility' (see Roché, 2002a). This shift seems to result from a conflict around definitions of the issues that public policies have a need to resolve. The earlier approach that focused on the violence of youth related to educational and psychological action and was aimed at understanding and addressing social circumstances. This has been replaced by an approach that addresses disorder in terms of incivilities and relies on authority and morals; it aims at the rules of society being respected through the prevention of situations developing. The shift from the dread of the violence of youth, from social violence to urban violence, in terms of insecurity and then incivility, has had several consequences in the way in which we approach these phenomena.

The first shift from the terms of violence to that of insecurity has been described in terms of personal isolation (Dubet and Lapeyronnie, 1992). However, researchers are not all in agreement on the character of personal isolation[3]. Baudry (1988, p 11) prefers to speak of 'ruined rituals' and Lepoutre (1997, p 20) of 'significant violence, codified, controlled and given shape; in short, a cultivated violence'. The concept of a 'feeling of insecurity' accentuates the unpredictable nature of this chaotic violence. It shows especially that the phenomena described under these terms are constructions increasingly independent of the actual acts of violence (see also Chapter Three, this volume). More attention is given to security concerns and less to what is supposed to cause them. However, Pottier and Robert (2004, p 16) have shown that the feeling of insecurity is not a simple transfer of the risks involved[4]. In addition, by setting distinctions between uncivil youths and the 'average' inhabitant, this discourse does not account for the fact that the majority of the victims of these acts of violence are also those most likely to commit them.

The necessary quantification of this 'insecurity' has led in France to a reliance on research from the police and judicial sources, carried out in particular by the Institute of Higher Studies for Interior Safety (Ministry for the Interior), and its review, *Les Cahiers de la Sécurité Intérieure*. One issue stands out: 'Town planning and safety: Towards an urban project?: New definitions of space, new forms of control' (IHESI, 2001). This focus on controlling public space fails to recognise that often the places where conduct labelled urban violence occurs are not public places of obvious movement (Kokoreff, 2000), and 'calm' districts are ignored, even if the cause of this apparent quietude is in fact the presence of very significant movement.

Space becomes both the framework and the cause that generates manifestations of deviant behaviour. One finds the radical expression of this idea in, for example, *Les Cahiers de la Sécurité Intérieure*, the Ministry for the Interior's magazine: 'In any location, there exist the germs of disorder, of insecurity, of violence: these germs, in certain individuals or groups who, belonging to networks of delinquency are likely to contaminate their environment in different ways, and in the place itself which, by its characteristics, lends itself to more or less noxious behaviour' (Akrich et al, 2001, p 83). In the face of a perception of the city as a dangerous medium, the district or neighbourhood may appear as a 'universe' that is simultaneously 'village', 'security' and 'territory' (Bachmann and Le Guennec, 1997).

However, violence and insecurity are at the same time the product of a socio-spatial medium and an institutional product – a socio-spatial product because violence is a component of the culture of the young people of the suburbs, characterised by its visibility (if one compares it with the hazing/ragging within the elite, for example). It is also a violence of representation and an institutional product, the fruit of the daily work of the 'contractors of morals' (Becker, 1985 [1963]). Violence and insecurity which emanate from a simple dispute between young people in a city and police officers show that violence and insecurity are the product of specific interactions which one finds in the contact between police officers and young people, but also at school and, more generally, in all 'mixed contacts'[5].

In the interest of safety, the French state responded by eliminating the apparent disorders in public spaces (incivilities), with the aim of reducing the feeling of insecurity and the probability of violence. However, at the same time, Lagrange (2003) shows that the representatives of the state, in particular via the public services, gave up a regular presence in these districts. The police force moved from preventive monitoring and dissuasion by presence to reactive monitoring, detection and punishment of committed acts of disorder. Moreover, the personnel entrusted with reducing 'urban violence' have multiplied, each one with a legitimacy and a specific status, including, for example: municipal police forces, gendarmerie, private watchmen, social workers, the national police force and youth employment agencies (see Chapter Eleven, this volume).

City policy: towards public space or a space of control?

The 1970s witnessed the experimental dimension of 'urban struggles' in the make-up of the city: 'an excessively warlike expression by which it was agreed to indicate ... the action of associations specialising in the denunciation of the excesses of land speculation, the shortages of facilities in the recently urbanised zones and, generally, the exercise of patronage of technology in the practice of power by the local councillors' (Donzelot and Estèbe, 1994, pp 37-8). The objective was a social and political recovery of local areas (Wolf and Osselin, 1979). However, according to the Marxist rhetoric then fashionable, the importance given to the urban question 'originates in the initiative of the dominant classes, rather than the new struggles of the dominated classes' (Castells et al, 1978, p 8).

The 'city policy' ('*politique de la ville*') that really began in France with the arrival of the Left in power in 1981 was aimed at a transformation of the way in which the state acts. The administrative culture, traditionally divided into autonomous technical sectors, was opened up to project-based groups capable of gathering together a variety of actors and sources of finance (Donzelot and Estèbe, 1994). One can thus understand the policy of the city as an alternative to the theme of urban struggle and as a way to urban reform.

The policies of urban zoning during the 'thirty glorious years' fragmented the planning of urban space. But the city policy fell under an urban philosophy that continued to be that of zoning: it aimed to rectify the zoned areas (ZUPs) and it maintained their perimeters (these were continually reduced progressively throughout these years by new ministerial directives). Thus, the 'dormitory towns' were transformed little by little into 'districts of exclusion' (Touraine, 1991) or of 'relegation' (Delarue, 1991), requiring a policy 'of vigorous integration'. Within the framework of the policy of the city, the old ZUPs were renamed with the euphemised term 'districts'. Thus, in the 1980s, the first 22 DSQ districts (social development neighbourhood areas) included the most distressed ZUPs, a measure known as 'anti-ghetto'. The ZUPs were finally ended in October 1991, with the 'Law of Orientation on the City' (LOV). This policy legitimised the renovated developments that emerged all over France during the 1980s (Anselme, 2000). The innovative social experiments that this policy initiated, based on the participation (and confrontation) of the various urban participants, were used as a reference point for a whole generation of social workers and social science researchers. It showed the limits of city policies that tried to respond to the problems of the 'zones of lawlessness' by a form of 'positive discrimination' which was primarily territorial (Béhar, 1999), as well as of an urban policy combining demolitions and re-housing aimed at 'separating' localities and allocating them to clearly identified managers.

The city policy also developed a new political initiative, that of ensuring safety in these areas. The most significant development appeared in 1997 when, at the initiative of the Ministry for the Interior, Local Safety Contracts (CLSs) were created, with the aim of giving a clear framework to partnerships linked around safety (Bauer and Raufer, 1998, p 85). A CLS can focus on one district or several, one or more towns or even an urban grid system. It thus aims to remove territorial limits (spatial, functional or jurisdictional). Local areas and the division of governance roles are in fact the creators of cracks into which 'disorders slipped' and 'delinquency made its nest' (Roché, 2002b, p 20). It is interesting to apply this argument to the neighbourhood governance processes in the UK discussed by John Flint in Chapter One (this volume).

Far from being initiatives without a definite origin, the CLS can be understood as the result of a historical reflection (Landauer, 1999) with its roots in the town planning ideas of Jane Jacobs (1961), the concept of 'defensible space' developed by Oscar Newman (1973) and the charges brought by Alice Coleman (1985) against 'Utopia', the Le Corbusier and functionalist town planning considered to be directly responsible for the behaviour of individuals, returning to the theme of the 'Sarcellite'[6] or the 'evil of housing schemes'.

In France, the 'Law of Orientation and Programming Relating to Safety' (LOPS) of January 1995 included the idea of an evaluation of areas arranged according to their capacity to be supervised. Article 11 expressed limitations to the idea that when faced with uncivil behaviour, security is no longer only a question of state law and order and for the police force but is the business of everyone. The installation of councils for the prevention of delinquency on various levels, and especially the Community Councils for the Prevention of Delinquency (CCPDs), which became CLSs and which were 'territorialized authorities of dialogue', framed the involvement of the mayors in local safety required by them (Montain-Domenach and Froment, 1999).

This extension-rationalisation of urban security policies appeared at the same time as the concept of residentialisation emerged, reversing urban concepts of fluidity and movement. Rather, residentialisation consisted of systematically making a clear distinction between public and private areas[7]. It is applied in social housing schemes in the shape of a whole panoply of marks of separation including hedges, barriers and entry doors with codes (Dunoyer de Segonzac, 2004), and is posed as representing the only alternative to the degradation of districts of social housing and to the feeling of dereliction among their inhabitants (see Chapter Twelve, this volume). The residentialisation operations already carried out show the homogeneity of the urban and architectural answers which were brought in to rectify situations which at the beginning could be regarded as quite different, ranging from the old social housing integrated into an existing urban fabric, to flagstoned residences and the housing schemes of the 1960s (Tabet, 1999). If the responses are similar despite these different contexts, it is because the aims pursued by these operations were often limited to the question of insecurity. The same conclusions can be raised concerning CLS (Akrich et al, 2001), and the subsequent demise of public space through reduction, closure and privatisation.

According to Milburn, the evolution of public policies in France after 1981 attempted to defuse 'the effects of social control aiming at standardizing society within disciplinary dynamics' (Milburn, 2004, p 139). These policies were based on the principle of a democratic exercise of power where citizens (users, professionals, local councillors and experts) take part in public policies through partnership authorities, like the DSQ. However, recently, in local policies, including those relating to security, it is no longer a question of maintaining an established social order but of preserving the principles of a fragmented and complex society, to be achieved by introducing support for victims and systems of punishment quantitatively proportional to the damages suffered.

By regarding uncivility as being 'provocative behaviour without embarrassment, a source of disturbance and aggravation in the everyday life of cities' (Balduyck and Lazerges, 1998, p 78), public policies directly refer to the idea of urbanity. However, does managed residency undermine the anonymous meetings and associations of crowds that make the metropolises urban (Simmel, 1979 [1903])? While the term 'ghetto' tirelessly returns to the mouths of the elected officials and media experts, Wacquant (1992) shows that one cannot compare the black districts of the South Side of Chicago to the 'difficult' districts of the Parisian suburbs, due to different ethnic concentrations. Nevertheless, a number of 'poor districts' are afflicted with racial stigma (Kokoreff, 2003). This reputation often goes hand in hand with a geographical distance from the city centre, poor communal transport, a lack of public services, and a lack of choice as regards trade, services and other meeting places which the traditional city provides, as highlighted in the 2005 disturbances.

Supposedly inspired by the model of the traditional city in order to initiate processes of 'gentrification', doesn't the step of managed residency of the housing schemes participate in a wider shift concerning urban space as a whole, with the closed-circuit television monitoring of the great cities as well as that of the subway or the theme parks? Linked to the European Community, the European Committee for Standardisation (CEN) potentially outlaws any street corner, and prohibits 'the existence of blind zones making it possible for attackers to hide and also making it likely to reinforce a feeling of insecurity' (Garnier and Moreau de Saint-Martin, 2001, p 13)[8]. It recommends cul-de-sacs self-monitored by the residents. However, the police force and fire services reject the cul-de-sacs in general for reasons of safety (Vayssière, 2001).

In order to understand the range of these dynamics, it becomes interesting to look again at the categories worked out by Foucault (1975) and in particular the idea of the passage from a disciplined society, based on the generalised supervision through public works (for example, schools or asylums) to a society of control. The philosopher Gilles Deleuze explains that, according to Foucault, the disciplined society in which individuals do not stop moving from one closed environment to another (schools, barracks or hospitals), is today in full crisis. Rather, what is at play is a movement to societies of control 'that function not by imprisonment, but by continuous assessment and instantaneous communication' (Deleuze, 1990, p 236), based on new models which advocate opening 'ceaseless control in an open environment' (Deleuze, 1990, p 236). The old model was the panoptical prison; the new one is electronic tagging. The chain has dematerialised. Each individual today is called on to demonstrate constraint. One last distinction made by Foucault between discipline and security is crucial here insofar as it qualifies the relationship to space. While discipline organises complete constructions in empty spaces, security rests on material information, such as the sites and shapes already there. While 'discipline structures a space, security will try to deal with an environment' (Foucault, 2004, p 22). Indeed, whereas discipline seeks to rectify dangerous individuals, in the society of control each one of these individuals is likely to undermine its fragile balance.

The term 'co-veillance', or shared monitoring, whose influence in France is similar to that of 'situational prevention' or 'defensible space' (Newman, 1972) on the other side of the Channel, consists of instantaneously broadcasting the information captured by the cameras to all of the resident population. It relates here, no longer to a location, but to a security environment. Moreover, this practice is coordinated by a focusing of interest on certain locations, the most obvious being perhaps the apartment hall and stairwell that were the subject of surveys of gathering places (Law Sarkozy, 2003)[9].

Conclusion

Throughout the 20th century, the phenomena of social segregation and violence were perceived sometimes as overwhelming and at other periods as unimportant. In addition to the fact that 'the spectacle of dereliction' of the districts of social housing have continued despite more than 20 years of city policy, Beaud and Pialoux (2003, p 342) insist on one essential factor: 'The closing of the future, the shrinking of possible societies that young people from the districts with poor school and social resources became more and more aware of earlier and earlier'.

In debates about insecurity, it is the state that is summoned to set a dividing line between disorder and the respect of order. To be able to live together assumes not perceiving your neighbour as an 'enemy within' and being able to differentiate yourself from them in order to exist as an individual. However, the coexistence of inhabitants in district housing areas (HLMs) arises from administrative decisions over which they have no control, but which gives them the right to be there. Accordingly, the rental relationship functions as a social relationship where each person must differ from their neighbour. It is this right to be there which also explains, we believe, both the constant discussion on the feeling of insecurity and relatively peaceful coexistence that finally characterises the majority of HLM districts (Anselme, 2000).

City policy, like any other public policy, requires a representation of reality likely to be useful as a reference point. The concept of 'mix' ('*mixité*') nowadays plays this role of generating a direction and mobilising the public actors. It is generally regarded that a 'state of equilibrium' should be reached between social classes and ethnic categories. With the term 'mix', the actors place themselves in a symbolic register over a long time period. The various laws issued include many direct references to 'mixed urban functions', 'social mix of districts' and 'diversity of the offer available'[10]. They no longer aim at an urban model, but at a mobilisation of the urban actors through a collective 'putting in place' based on these mix–development rules (Local Housing Programmes, great City Projects, National Agency for Urban Renewal). It is thus a new model of public intervention that emerges through these procedures.

However, mix, far from being a problem of residential balance to be respected between categories of population, proves to be a 'process of permanent friction between the social groups, that must be driven and guaranteed' (Béhar, 1997, p 284) through the social activities and public places where they occur. If one regards social mix as a process of friction between social groups, it is no longer a question of urbanising, but of producing 'urban' situations (Boissonade, 2001). Suddenly, public intervention is centred around strategic objects of producing social integration in urban territory, including public spaces and collective transport. This emphasis on links rather than places leads us from the language of a city model and urban forms to that of a focus on ensuring the safe movement of city dwellers through urban spaces.

Acronyms
CCPD   Conseil communal de Prévention de la Délinquance
CEN   Conseil européen de normalisation
CLS   Contrat local de sécurité
DSQ   Développement social de quartiers
HLM   Habitation à loyer modéré
LOV   Loi d'orientation sur la ville
LOPS   Loi d'orientation et de programmation sur la sécurité
ZUP   Zone à urbaniser en priorité

Notes

[1] The Ministry for the Interior gives a definition of urban violence that includes degrees of violence, from 'day-to-day' vandalism to full-blown guerrilla riots (Bui-Trong, 1998).

[2] Beyond the dwindling of family links, the disaffiliated individual no longer fits into any network. He is thus no longer attached to any of the chains whose entanglement constitutes social fabric; he is 'useless in the world' (Castel, 1995, pp 90-6).

[3] Personal isolation, according to Emile Durkheim (1967 [1893], pp 343-65), is the absence or the insufficiency of regulation making it possible to ensure the cooperation between various specialised social functions, such as those ensured by capitalists and workers. Regulations also make it possible to calm individual aspirations whose disproportion could lead to suicide if they are controlled too little or not regulated in the case of personal isolation.

[4] The progression from the term 'violence' to that of 'insecurity', then 'incivility' can mean that 'the more an unpleasant phenomenon decreases, the more of what remains is perceived or experienced as unbearable' (Tocqueville, in Pottier and Robert, 2004, p 213).

[5] A mixed contact, in Goffman's sense, is a contact with a stigmatised person. The singularity of this situation comes as a result of the fact that stigmatisation disturbs any readable structure which can or may give rules to be followed in this precise situation and guide the interactions (Goffman, 1973).

[6] Sarcelles, located in Paris and its suburbs, is one of the very large French ZUPs.

[7] A handbook edited by the federation of the district housing area (HLM) companies and intended for social financial backers, specifies the reasons for these actions: 'The building, originally placed in areas with unspecified purposes, frequently became the cause of conflicts of use and technical dysfunctions, generating a feeling of insecurity, can become [thanks to residentialisation] an object where ownership is created on the part of its inhabitants; the inhabitants know where their "at home" starts and who manages what.... "Who makes what where" is thus the first question that managers are asked which clarifies the rules of each location' (Launay and Royer-Vallat, 1992).

[8] CEN has a technical committee: Prevention of Ill Will by Town Planning and the Design of Buildings.

[9] 'Acts of violence or the threat of committing violence against a person, or an obstacle deliberately made to the access and freedom of movement of people or the correct operation of safety and safety devices, when they are carried out jointly with several others or accomplices, in the entrances, stairwells or other common parts of housing apartment buildings, are punished with two months of imprisonment and a fine of 3,750 Euros' (Article 61, Law Sarkozy, 2003).

[10] 'Law of Social Cohesion', 'Law of Orientation on the City', 'Law of Solidarity and Urban Renewal'.

References

Akrich, M., Meadel, C., Frenay, J. and Ocqueteau, F. (2001) 'Désordres en Territoires Urbains. Pour une Confrontation de Positions', *Les Cahiers de la Sécurité Intérieure*, no 43, pp 81-99.

Anselme, M. (2000) *Du Bruit à la Parole. La Scène Politique des Cités*, La Tour d'Aygues: l'Aube.

Ascher, F. (1995) *Métapolis*, Paris: Odile Jacob.

Bachmann, C. and Le Guennec, N. (1997) *Autopsie d'une Émeute*, Paris: Albin Michel.

Balduyck, J.P. and Lazerges, C. (1998) *Mission Interministérielle sur la Prévention et le Traitement de la Délinquance des Mineurs*, Rapport au Premier Ministre, Paris: La Documentation Française.

Baudry, P. (1988) 'Approche Sociologique de la Violence', *Cahiers Internationaux de Sociologie*, vol LXXXIV, pp 6-16.

Bauer, A. and Raufer, X. (1998) *Violences et Insécurité Urbaines*, Paris: Presses Universitaires de France.

Beaud, S. and Pialoux, M. (2003) *Violences Urbaines, Violence Sociale*, Paris: Fayard.

Becker, H. (1985 [1963]) *Outsiders*, Paris: Métailié.

Béhar, D. (1997) 'De la Modélisation à la Mobilisation: La Mixité dans les Politiques Urbaines', in A. Obadia (ed) *Entreprendre la Ville. Nouvelles Temporalités, Nouveaux Services*, Colloque de Cerisy, La Tour d'Aigues: l'Aube.

Béhar, D. (1999) 'En Finir avec la Politique de la Ville?', *Esprit*, no 2581, Paris: Seuil, November, pp 209-18.

Boissonade, J. (2001) 'Agrégations Juvéniles et Dynamiques du Proche', *Les Annales de la Recherche Urbaine*, no 90, pp 173-81.

Bui-Trong, L. (1998) 'Sur Quelques Secrets de Fabrication. Entretien avec Lucienne BuiTrong', *Les Cahiers la Sécurité Intérieure*, no 33, pp 217-33.

Castel, R. (1995) *Les Métamorphoses de la Question Sociale*, Paris: Fayard.

Castells, M., Cherki, E., Godard, F. and Mehl, D. (1978) *Crise du Logement et Mouvements Sociaux Urbains*, Paris: Mouton.

Chamboredon, J.C. and Lemaire, M. (1970) 'Proximité Spatiale et Distance Sociale. Les Grands Ensembles et leur Peuplement', *Revue Française de Sociologie*, vol 11, no 1, pp 3-33.

Chesnais, J.C. (1981) *Histoire de la Violence*, Paris: Robert Laffont.

Coleman, A. (1985) *Utopia on Trial: Vision and Reality in Planned Housing*, London: Hilary Shipman.

Collovald, A. (2001) 'Des Désordres Sociaux à la Violence Urbaine', *Actes de la Recherche en Sciences Sociales*, nos 136-7, pp 104-13.

Delarue, J.M. (1991) *Banlieues en Difficulté. La Relégation*, Paris: Syros.

Deleuze, G. (1990) 'Contrôle et Devenir', *Pourparlers*, Paris: Minuit.

Donzelot, J. (1999) 'La Nouvelle Question Urbaine', *Esprit*, no 258, November, pp 87-114.

Donzelot, J. and Estèbe, P.H. (1994) *L'Etat Animateur. Essai sur la Politique de la Ville*, Paris: Esprit.

Donzelot, J. and Mongin, O. (1999) 'De la Question Sociale à la Question Urbaine', *Esprit*, no 258, November, pp 83-6.

Dubet, F. (1987) *La Galère*, Paris: Fayard.

Dubet, F. and Lapeyronnie, D. (1992) *Les Quartiers d'Exil*, Paris: Seuil.

Dunoyer de Segonzac, P. (2004) *De la Cité à la 'Résidence'. Repères pour la Résidentialisation*, Paris: Union Sociale pour l'Habitat.

Durkheim, E. (1967[1893]) *De la Division du Travail Social*, Paris: Presses Universitaires de France.

Foucault, M. (1975) *Surveiller et Punir. Naissance de la Prison*, Paris: Gallimard.

Foucault, M. (2004) *Sécurité, Territoire, Population. Cours au Collège de France, 1977-1978*, Paris: Gallimard-Seuil.

Fourastié, J. (1979) *Les Trente Glorieuses, Ou la Révolution Invisible de 1946 à 1975*, Paris: Fayard.

Garnier, A. and Moreau de Saint-Martin, L. (2001) 'Sur la Normalisation de la Prévention de l'Insécurité par l'Urbanisme', *Les Cahiers de la Sécurité Intérieure*, no 43, pp 9-17.

Goffman, E. (1973) *La Mise en Scène de la Vie Quotidienne. T.2: Les Relations en Public*, Paris: Minuit.

Henley, J. (2005) 'Chirac Calls for Calm as Violence Spreads Through Capital's Suburbs', *The Guardian*, 3 November.

IHESI (Ministry for the Interior) (2001) *Cahiers de la Sécurité Intérieure. Urbanisme et Sécurité: Vers un Projet Urbain? Nouvelles Définitions de l'Espace, Nouvelles Formes de Contrôle*, IHESI, Ministère de l'Intérieur, no 43.

Jacobs, J. (1961) *The Death and Life of Great American Cities*, New York, NY: Random House.

Kaës, R. (1963) *Vivre dans les Grands Ensembles*, Paris: Les éditions ouvrières.

Kokoreff, M. (2000) 'Faire du Business dans les Quartiers. Eléments sur les Transformations Socio-historiques de l'Économie des Stupéfiants en Milieux Populaires. Le Cas du Département des Hauts-de-Seine', *Déviance et Société*, vol 24, no 4, pp 403-23.

Kokoreff, M. (2003) *La Force des Quartiers*, Paris: Payot.

Lagrange, H. (2003) *Demandes de Sécurité: France, Europe, Etats-Unis*, Paris: Seuil.

Landauer, P. (1999) 'Introduction à la Lecture d'Alice Coleman, Espace et Sécurité', *Les Cahiers de la Recherche Architecturale et Urbaine*, no 1, pp 51-2.

Lascoumes, P. and Robert P. (1974 [1966]) *Les Bandes d'Adolescents. Une Théorie de la Ségrégation* (édition remaniée), Paris: Les éditions ouvrières.

Launay, O. and Royer-Vallat, R.M. (1992) *Résidentialisation*, Paris: Fédération Nationale des Sociétés Anonymes et Fondations d'HLM, Caisse des Dépôts et Consignations.

Law Sarkozy (2003) *Loi no 2003-239 du 18 mars 2003 pour la sécurité intérieure*, Paris: Assembleé Nationale.

Lepoutre, D. (1997) *Cœur de Banlieue: Codes, Rites et Langages*, Paris: Odile Jacob.

Magri, S. and Topalov, C. (1987) 'De la Cité-jardin à la Ville Rationalisée. Un Tournant du Projet Réformateur 1905-1925', *Revue Française de Sociologie*, no 28, pp 417-51.

Milburn, P.H. (2004) 'Le Panoptisme Nouveau est-il Arrivé? Les Politiques Sociales et Sécuritaires Actuelles à l'Épreuve de la Théorie de Foucault', *Le portique*, Metz, pp 137-47.

Monod, J. (1968) *Les Barjots*, Paris: Julliard.

Montain-Domenach, J. and Froment J.-Ch. (1999) 'Sécurité et Urbanisme. Propos sur la Loi du 21 Janvier 1995 Relative à la Sécurité', *Les Cahiers de la Recherche Architecturale et Urbaine*, no 1, pp 19-34.

Mucchielli, L. (2001) *Violences et Insécurité. Fantasmes et Réalités dans le Débat Français*, Paris: La Découverte.

Newman, O. (1972) *Defensible Space: Crime Prevention Through Urban Design*, New York, NY: Macmillan.

Pierret, R. (2003) 'Les Apaches, 1900-1914, Premier Acte de Violence des Jeunes en Milieu Urbain', in M. Bouchel and A. Vulbeau (eds) *Emergences Culturelles et Jeunesse Populaire. Turbulences ou Médiations*, Paris: L'Harmattan, pp 215-27.

Pottier, M.-L. and Robert, P. (2004) 'Les Préoccupations Sécuritaires: Une Mutation?', *Revue Française de Sociologie*, vol 45-2, pp 211-42.

Ratouis, O. (2006) 'La Fonction Crée-t-elle le Nom? Obsolescence et Renouveau du Vocabulaire Urbanistique des Aménageurs Français des Trente Glorieuses', in B. Marin (ed) *La Ville: Les Catégories de l'Urbain*, MSH – Unesco, Paris, à paraître.

Roché, S. (2002a) *Tolérance Zéro? Incivilités et Insécurité*, Paris: Odile Jacob.

Roché, S. (2002b) 'Délinquance des Jeunes: Des Groupes Actifs et Éphémères', *Sciences Humaines*, no 129, July, pp 16-20.

Simmel, G. (1979 [1903]) 'Métropoles et Mentalités', in Y. Grafmeyer and I. Joseph (eds) *L'école de Chicago*, Paris: Aubier, pp 61-78.

Tabet, J. (1999) 'La Résidentialisation du Logement Social', *Annales de la Recherche Urbaine*, no 83-84, pp 155-63.

Thrasher, F.M. (1963 [1927]) *The Gang: A Study of 1313 Gangs in Chicago*, Chicago, IL: University of Chicago Press.

Touraine, A. (1991) 'Face à l'Exclusion', *Esprit*, no 169, pp 7-13, February.

Vayssière, B. (1988) *Reconstruction, Déconstruction. Le Hard French Ou l'Architecture Française des Trente Glorieuses*, Paris: Picard.

Vayssière, B. (2001) 'Regard sur l'Urbanisme et l'Architecture Face aux Tentations Sécuritaires', *Les Cahiers de la Sécurité Intérieure*, no 43, pp 19-30.

Wacquant, L. (1992) 'Pour en Finir avec "le Mythe des Cités-ghettos"', *Annales de la Recherche Urbaine*, Paris: Ministère de l'Équipement, pp 20-30.

Wolf, M. and Osselin, J. (1979) *Les Ascenseurs de la ZUP. Contrôle Populaire et Autogestion Communale, l'Expérience Municipale de Mons-en-Baroeul*, Paris: François Maspero.

FIFTEEN

Residential stability among adolescents in public housing: a risk factor for delinquent and violent behaviour?

Timothy O. Ireland, Terence P. Thornberry, and Rolf Loeber

Introduction

The private housing market exposes working tenants to great instability. Private housing residents are shuttled around by rezoning, redevelopment, renewal, evictions, and slumlord neglect. Residents flee intolerable sanitary conditions, rats that bite their children, and other domestic hazards. In this context public housing remains an oasis of stability not simply for the dependent single-parent families, but also for the poor and working households who at the very least can rely on their housing status when all else is in flux. (Venkatesh, 1997, p 36)

Renewed interest in understanding the links between public housing and crime is evidenced by recent research in Australia (Weatherburn et al, 1999), Canada (DeKeseredy et al, 2003), the UK (Bottoms and Wiles, 1986; Bottoms et al, 1992; Flint, 2002), and the US (Popkin et al, 2000; Santiago et al, 2002; Ireland et al, 2003). The general consensus is that areas where public housing is located have higher rates of official crime or reported victimisation. The opinion that public housing is crime-ridden is reflected in several local and federal initiatives in the US that are directed at controlling crime and drugs in and around public housing, including local police actions in public housing (Popkin et al, 1999; Barbrey, 2004), the Public Housing Drug Elimination Program (for example, Popkin et al, 1995), and the One-Strike and You're Out initiative (Dzubow, 1996; Hellegers, 1999), as well as efforts to disburse assisted housing out of the most impoverished areas of the city via HOPE VI[1] (Naparstek et al, 2000; Popkin, 2003) and the Moving to Opportunity Demonstration Project (Briggs, 1997; Popkin et al, 2002).

However, Ireland et al (2003) found that self-reported involvement in property and violent crime among adolescents residing in public housing in Rochester, New York and Pittsburgh, Pennsylvania was not statistically significantly higher than among adolescents not in public housing. Their cross-sectional study did, however, find that in large developments or high-rise units in Pittsburgh the level of self-reported violence was quite high, particularly during late adolescence.

In this chapter we attempt to ascertain whether living in public housing for a relatively long period of time is more behaviourally detrimental than living in public housing for a relatively short period of time. According to Newman and Harkness (1999, p 6; 2002) with the exception of their work 'there is no empirical work on the residential stability of children in assisted housing'. This chapter attempts to address this research gap.

Public housing and policy in the United States

Federally supported public housing in the US was formalised in the US Housing Act of 1937 (Fisher, 1959; Wendt, 1983). The term 'public housing' refers to multiple federal programmes that in some way subsidise housing in the US; however, the focus here is on conventional public housing developments that are operated by local housing authorities and are subsidised by federal tax dollars (Fisher, 1959). To date no clear consensus exists on what objectives were being initially pursued by the federal government in setting housing policy, whether those objectives were met, and whether the federal public housing initiative represents a success or a failure (Meehan, 1979; Wendt, 1983; Bratt, 1989). Bratt (1989, p 55) argues that federally subsidised housing was driven by a desire to (a) reduce unemployment arising from the Great Depression; (b) clear the urban slums; and (c) provide 'safe and sanitary dwellings for families of low income'. Whatever the initial goals of federally subsidised housing were, by 1957 'the federally aided public-housing inventory consisted of more than half a million active dwellings' (Fisher, 1959, p 12). By 1998, federally subsidised housing had evolved into several different programmes including Public Housing, Section 8 Certificates and Vouchers, Section 8 Moderate Rehabilitation, Section 8 New and Substantial Rehabilitation, as well as other US Department of Housing and Urban Development (HUD) subsidy programmes. The total number of federally subsidised households in 1998 was close to five million, of which about 1.3 million were conventional public housing units[2].

Despite this expansion in provision, debates over the fundamental purpose of housing assistance for the poor persist (Newman and Harkness, 1999, 2002; de Silva and Harris, 2004). One argument suggests that the purpose of public housing is to provide decent and affordable housing. To this end, any assessment of public housing should focus on how many families were helped, how many units were occupied, and the relative quality and cost of the public housing stock (Newman and Harkness, 2002). Length of time in public housing should not be a major concern. Indeed, quite the opposite: a long tenure in public housing would confirm the need for such housing in a particular community.

However, prolonged stays in public housing are often viewed as problematic because public housing somehow – because of how it is designed (Newman, 1972; Merry, 1981), where it is located (Newman and Harkness, 2002), or who resides there (Weatherburn et al, 1999) – has a criminogenic effect on those who stay too long. In this model, the longer a family stays in public housing, the greater the risk for involvement in criminal activity. For example, Newman and Harkness (2002, p 23) suggest that children and adolescents growing up in public housing may be 'negatively affected by the degree of concentrated poverty in their residential environment ...'. To the degree that such neighbourhood effects exist then the developmental trajectory of adolescents in public housing may be disrupted and their life chances diminished. Therefore, while public housing may provide necessary housing for families caught in the net of poverty, living in public housing over time is considered problematic because of the possible criminogenic effect.

An alternate view is that public housing should act as a temporary way-station that provides affordable housing for families experiencing economic hardship while they work to re-establish economic self-sufficiency, which in turn enables them to leave assisted housing (HUD, 1996; Naparstek et al, 2000). From this perspective, government handouts like housing assistance can create dependency and apathy, as well as learned helplessness, which may be passed on across generations. This position is exemplified by welfare strategies currently in place in the US that limit benefits and require some level of work or job training (Blank, 1997; Boo, 2001). For example, those in public housing, according to the Quality Housing and Work Responsibility Act of

1998, are required to perform 96 hours of unpaid community service during each year and '[s]upporters say that the volunteer work [sh]ould instill a greater sense of discipline and responsibility among public housing residents' (Chen, 2004, p 1A). Additionally, the Chicago Housing Authority, in dismantling Cabrini-Green and creating a mixed-income community, has mandated a goal of self-sufficiency for those families moving into the mixed-income community by requiring employment, participation in job training or pursuit of education (Paulson, 2004). This broadly defined objective of family self-sufficiency would celebrate high rates of mobility among those residing in public housing. In addition, limited time in public housing should be a protective factor by limiting exposure to the criminogenic nature of public housing.

Residential mobility versus residential stability

Tracking mobility among public housing families over time has proven difficult, and little is known about the long-term effects, including any criminogenic effects, on children raised in public housing (de Silva and Harris, 2004). The only longtudinal study of the long-term consequences of residential stability in public housing found that 'public housing enhanced children's long-term outcomes' (Newman and Harkness, 2002, p 34), including increasing the probability of employment and self-sufficiency and thereby reducing the likelihood of receiving welfare. Contrary to concerns about the detrimental effects of living in public housing, Newman and Harkness (2002) find that long-term residence in public housing during adolescence may help facilitate rather than hinder self-sufficiency in adulthood.

While evolving public housing policy appears focused on the issue of self-sufficiency, which encourages mobility, the issue of residential stability has long been a theoretical and empirical staple in the disciplines of sociology (for example, Kasarda and Janowitz, 1974; Sampson, 1988, 1991) and criminology (for example, Krohn, 1986; Sampson and Groves, 1989; Sampson et al, 1997; Taylor, 1997; Sampson and Raudenbush, 1999; Kowaleski-Jones, 2000; Triplett et al, 2003).

In considering residential stability, Kasarda and Janowitz (1974, p 330) argued that the 'systemic model focuses on length of residence as the key exogenous factor influencing community behavior and attitudes ... [and] residential mobility operates as a barrier to the development of extensive friendship and kinship bonds and widespread local associational ties'. The alternate hypothesis is that community size and population density, *not residential stability*, are key contributors to the absence or presence of local associational ties – the larger the community population and the higher the density the lower the level of associational ties in the community. Kasarda and Janowitz (1974) and more recently Sampson (1988, 1991) have found support for the systemic model such that an individual's increasing period of residence in a particular community increases individual-level community attachment, while controlling for community size and population density.

In the early days of North American criminology Clifford Shaw and Henry McKay (1942) collected data on Chicago neighbourhoods and found that communities with limited mobility, limited racial/ethnic heterogeneity and limited poverty tended to have lower crime rates, although they did not explore mediating mechanisms (Sampson and Groves, 1989). Criminologists have drawn on the systemic model of associational ties in the community to explain the process by which residential mobility increases crime both at the macro-level and the micro-level (for example, Sampson and Groves, 1989; Sampson et al, 1997; Sampson and Raudenbush, 1999; Kowaleski-Jones, 2000). Sampson et al (1997) found that communities high in *collective efficacy*, defined as 'social cohesion among neighbors combined with their willingness to intervene on behalf of the common good' (Sampson et al, 1997, p 918), tend to have lower rates of perceived violence, lower rates of violent victimisation and lower rates of homicide. Furthermore they found that collective efficacy partially mediates the relationship between residential stability and crime at the neighbourhood level.

Broken windows

Along similar lines, Wilson and Kelling (1982) argued that communities in disrepair with clear evidence of graffiti and poorly maintained property are at increased risk for untended persons and quite possibly for serious crime. Accordingly, a broken window left unrepaired will soon result in multiple broken windows in the building as '... one unrepaired broken window is a signal that no one cares, and so breaking more windows costs nothing' (Wilson and Kelling, 1982, p 31). 'Likewise, when disorderly behavior, say, rude remarks by loitering youths, is left unchallenged, the signal given is that no one cares [and] the disorder escalates' (Wilson and Kelling, 1982, p 48).

'Broken windows' hypothesised that untended property and untended people in a community make a particular neighbourhood or block unappealing and at risk for crime and may foster a desire for families to leave, thereby exacerbating the downward spiral into decay, disorder and crime.

Policies derived from the broken windows perspective have been far-reaching in policing (Wilson and Kelling, 1989; Kelling and Coles, 1996) and public housing policy (Briggs, 1997; Popkin, 2003). For example, the HUD-sponsored HOPE VI programme focuses on the demolition of severely distressed public housing and creation of revitalised mixed-income residents in the hope of reducing both social and physical disorder and crime (Naparstek et al, 2000; Popkin, 2003)[3].

While both collective efficacy and broken windows focus on community characteristics, a similar argument can be proposed at the micro-level as it pertains to family mobility, community ties and involvement in delinquency or crime. One would expect families that move frequently to have weaker community ties, and for those weaker community ties to increase the likelihood that they or that their children are involved in criminal activity. For example, Kowaleski-Jones (2000) found that community residential stability is related to reduced levels of aggressive behaviour at the individual level, after controlling for individual and community variables. Furthermore, when a family measure of residential stability was included in the estimated equation, the macro-level measure of residential stability remained a significant protective factor for aggressive behaviour, and also 'individual-level residential stability significantly predicted lower levels of aggressive behavior' (Kowaleski-Jones, 2000, p 460).

Evolving HUD public housing policy focuses on family self-sufficiency and thus requires departure from public housing when self-sufficiency is attained. Therefore, longevity in public housing is a liability not an asset. However, this is in conflict with theory and empirical research in sociology and criminology that views residential stability as both a family and community asset that can reduce crime and delinquency by, in part, increasing collective efficacy.

We actually know little about what might be influencing the behaviour of adolescents in public housing – especially the large developments that often house hundreds of families in rather confined areas. This chapter reports findings from a study of the relationship between residential mobility in public housing and the involvement in crime among adolescents in Rochester, New York, and Pittsburgh, Pennsylvania.

The research study

The data for this analysis is drawn from the Rochester Youth Development Study (RYDS) and the Pittsburgh Youth Study (PYS). The RYDS is an ongoing multiwave panel study that interviewed young people every six months for nine consecutive waves, and their primary caregiver for eight consecutive waves. After a hiatus in data collection, three additional annual interviews were conducted with subjects during emerging adulthood. The RYDS initially had a panel of 1,000 adolescents whose average age was 13.9 at the start of the project. Males are over-represented in the sample, and African-Americans comprise 68%, Hispanics 17% and Whites 15%. The PYS is also an ongoing panel study, which initially comprised 1,517 male adolescents, their parents and teachers. Sampled boys, their parents and teachers were followed up at half-yearly intervals for six consecutive waves of data collection. After the sixth wave of data collection interviews occurred on an annual basis for another five years for a total of 11 waves of data that are used in this analysis. Just over half the sample was African-American and just under half was White. Although the Pittsburgh study sampled three cohorts of boys (6 year olds, 9 year olds, and 12 year olds), only the oldest sample of boys is used in the analysis presented here to closely parallel the age distribution and time frame for data collection in the Rochester study.

This research identifies residence in public housing at each wave and assesses the length of residence in public housing over time. It then relates time in public housing to three constructed crime measurement categories cumulated across waves: property crime, violent crime and gun carrying, based on self-reporting from survey participants (see Table 15.1). The cumulative measures of delinquency across the two study sites contain the same delinquency items from each interview and are therefore comparable. For a more detailed account of the studies and the research methodology, including the sampling framework and list of individual measurement items, see Stouthamer-Loeber and van Kammen (1995), Loeber et al (1998), Krohn and Thornberry (1999), Ireland et al (2003) and Thornberry et al (2003).

Overall, among Rochester respondents, 66.3% reported involvement in violent crime during adolescence and 27.1% reported violent crime in emerging adulthood. Property crime is similarly high during adolescence (45.6%) and decreases in emerging adulthood (17.6%). About 20% of the Rochester sample admits to carrying a gun at least once in adolescence, but the question was not asked in emerging

Table 15.1: Descriptive statistics (%)

	RYDS		PYS	
	Adolescence	Emerging adulthood	Early adolescence	Late adolescence
Time in public housing				
Never	89.5	94.3	81.0	81.1
Sometimes	6.7	3.3	7.3	10.1
Always	3.8	2.4	11.7	8.8
n	906	786	494	476
Property crime				
No	54.4	82.4	41.1	44.4
Yes	45.6	17.6	58.9	55.6
n	880	833	445	381
Violent crime				
No	33.8	72.9	26.7	39.6
Yes	66.3	27.1	73.3	60.4
n	880	833	445	381
Gun carrying				
No	80.1	na	89.8	79.0
Yes	19.9	na	10.2	21.0
n	880	na	440	414

Note: RYDS adolescence ranges on average from about 14 to 18 years old, and emerging adulthood ranges on average from about 21 to 23 years old; PYS early adolescence ranges from about 13 to 16 years old, and late adolescence ranges from about 17 to 20 years old.

adulthood. Among Pittsburgh respondents in early adolescence the prevalence of violence is quite high (73.3%) and comparable to the levels of violence reported among the Rochester respondents. The prevalence of violent crime among Pittsburgh respondents also decreases as they move into later adolescence (60.4%). The prevalence of property crime among Pittsburgh respondents is 58.9% in early adolescence and 55.6% during late adolescence. About 10% of the Pittsburgh sample admits to carrying a gun in early adolescence and this doubles to 21% by late adolescence (it is important to note that, unlike the Rochester sample, the Pittsburgh sample contains only males and that the age ranges are not perfectly aligned between the studies). The descriptive statistics presented in Table 15.1 are unweighted, although the sampling strategies in both studies resulted in the over-sampling of high-risk adolescents. In the following bivariate analyses both samples are weighted to reflect the characteristics of the underlying population from which each sample was drawn.

The Rochester study has 95 respondents (about 11%) who spent at least some time in public housing during adolescence (see Table 15.1). Of those 95 respondents, the majority (64%) did not remain in public housing for the entire four-and-a-half years' duration of the first waves of the study. The later RYDS interviews with subjects in emerging adulthood revealed 45 individuals as living in public housing, and 58% did not remain in public housing for the entire three-year study period. In Pittsburgh, there is less mobility among those in public housing. Across the first six interview waves (early adolescence), a total of 94 subjects (19%) lived in public housing and only 38% of these did not spend the entire three years in public housing. The later interview waves (late adolescence) indicate a somewhat higher rate of mobility among public housing residents. Of the 90 public housing residents, 53% were not in public housing for the entire time[4].

Public housing in the research localities

Rochester is located in western New York state along the southern shore of Lake Ontario. In 1990 it had a population of approximately 230,000 (US Census Bureau, 2005). The Rochester Housing Authority manages approximately 6,500 housing units for the greater metro-region (RHA, 1990; HUD, 2000a). The largest family public housing development in Rochester has only 130 units (RHA, 1996). There is a substantial waiting list for both conventional and Section 8 public housing units in Rochester (HUD, 2000b).

Pittsburgh is located in western Pennsylvania and in 1990 had a population of approximately 370,000 (US Census Bureau, 2005). Pittsburgh has about 22,000 public housing units operated by two housing authorities (HUD, 2000a). Pittsburgh has a greater proportion of conventional public housing stock than Rochester and also has some larger developments. For example, Allequippa Terrace consists of 77 buildings and over 1,700 units (Fitzpatrick, 1997). Pittsburgh, unlike Rochester, also has several high-rise public housing developments.

Research findings: public housing residence and delinquency

Table 15.2 examines the relationship between length of time in public housing and prevalence measures of cumulative property crime, violent crime and gun carrying using contingency table analysis and a chi-square test of independence.

The first column of Table 15.2 reveals that among Rochester adolescents it is not those in public housing who are at greatest risk for offending. Rather, those who move into and out of public housing

Table 15.2: Prevalence of property and violent crime among those always, sometimes and never in public housing (%)

	RYDS		PYS	
	Adolescence	Emerging adulthood	Early adolescence	Late adolescence
Property crime				
Always in public housing	28.0*	10.0	59.2	48.1
Sometimes in public housing	52.4	26.1	56.7	54.8
Never in public housing	40.9	16.1	48.7	50.2
Violent crime				
Always in public housing	53.8***	22.2ª	73.5	82.1***
Sometimes in public housing	79.4	27.3	74.2	61.3
Never in public housing	60.6	27.0	68.3	52.6
Gun carrying				
Always in public housing	4.0	NA	12.8*ª	23.3***
Sometimes in public housing	17.5	NA	17.2	39.5
Never in public housing	14.7	NA	6.8	16.0

Notes:

* $p<0.10$

** $p<0.05$

*** $p<0.01$

ª At least one cell has an expected count of less than 5.

have the highest prevalence rates of property crime, violent crime and gun carrying. While all relationships implicate mobility into and out of public housing, the relationships between public housing mobility and self-reported property crime, and public housing mobility and self-reported violent crime are statistically significant. A total of 79.4% of the transient adolescents report engaging in violence compared to 53.8% of adolescents always in public housing, and 60.6% for those never in public housing. A similar pattern is found for property crime where those who move into and out of public housing report the highest rates, while those always in public housing report the lowest rates. Although the findings from emerging adulthood do not provide statistically significant findings, again individuals moving into and out of public housing have the highest prevalence rates of offending.

However, in Pittsburgh there appears to be very little, if any, relationship between length of time in public housing and offending patterns during early adolescence. Only the prevalence of gun carrying indicates a statistically significant relationship, with adolescents who are transient public housing dwellers being more than twice as likely to carry a gun compared to those never in public housing and about a third more likely compared to those always in public housing. The results from late adolescence produce no statistical differences for property crimes, although the transient public housing adolescents report the highest prevalence rate. For violent crime those always in public housing are the most involved; in excess of 80% of those always in public housing admit to such behaviour. For gun carrying, however, the transient group exceeds those always in public housing and those never in public housing and the differences are statistically significant.

The fact that the transient group apparently is more involved in crime in Rochester and more likely to carry a gun in Pittsburgh but that in Pittsburgh and particularly in late adolescence those reporting the highest prevalence rates of violence are respondents who are always in public housing may be, to some degree, an artefact of the decision to collapse the duration variable into three broad categories: never, sometimes, always. We conducted a more detailed examination of the relationship between length of residence and crime (Table 15.3). If there is a 'dose' effect – the longer the exposure to public housing the greater the violent behaviour – one would expect increasing involvement in self-reported delinquency as the time in public housing increases.

The results from both Rochester and Pittsburgh consistently indicate the absence of an increasing relationship between period of residence in public housing and offending behaviour[5]. Rather, the data suggests that fairly short periods of time in public housing may be more behaviourally detrimental than longer periods of residency. Nevertheless, the results indicate, to some degree, that rates of violent crime in Pittsburgh are higher among those in public housing when compared to the broader community of respondents not in public housing.

One possible explanation might be the presence of several large public housing developments and the inclusion of family units in high-rise buildings in Pittsburgh. While the pattern of results in small public housing developments like those in Rochester might not show a dose effect of living in public housing, the dose effect might be more evident when the analysis is restricted to only large developments or those developments that house families in high-rise buildings. No clear rules exist to define large developments (see Holzman et al, 1996). We stratified the Pittsburgh public housing residents into three categories – not in large developments, in developments that have 500 or fewer units without high-rise buildings, in developments that have either more than 500 units or high-rise buildings – and developed

Table 15.3: Prevalence of property and violent crime among those never, transiently and always in public housing (%)

	Never in public housing	More than never and less than a third of the time in public housing	Between one third and two thirds of the time in public housing	Between two thirds of the time and less than always in public housing	Always in public housing
Rochester					
Property crime					
Adolescence	40.9	60.5	40.0	45.5	28.0
Emerging adulthood	16.1	44.4	15.4	na	10.0
Violent crime					
Adolescence	60.6	86.8	73.3	63.6	53.8
Emerging adulthood	27.0	22.2	30.8	na	22.2
Gun carrying					
Adolescence	14.7	13.2	33.3	9.1	4.0
Emerging adulthood	na	na	na	na	na
Pittsburgh					
Property crime					
Early adolescence	48.7	50.0	66.7	62.5	59.2
Late adolescence	50.2	83.3	43.8	55.6	48.1
Violent crime					
Early adolescence	68.3	71.4	90.0	57.1	73.5
Late adolescence	52.6	85.7	62.5	37.5	82.1
Gun carrying					
Early adolescence	6.8	7.1	37.5	14.3	12.8
Late adolescence	16.0	62.5	36.8	30.0	23.3

measures of residing in large developments for none of the time, some of the time, or all of the time during both early and late adolescence (Table 15.4).

The prevalence comparisons indicate that there are no significant differences across groupings in terms of property crime, but those who move into or out of large public housing developments in early adolescence are significantly more likely to carry a gun. However, in late adolescence those always in large public housing developments are significantly more likely to be involved in violent crime. In fact, all respondents in large developments reported involvement in violent crime in late adolescence. However, a slightly greater percentage of the transient group reports carrying a gun compared to those always in a large development during late adolescence. In all of the comparisons in Table 15.4, only self-reported violence in late adolescence reflects a dose effect. Those never in public housing report the lowest prevalence rate (53.7%), those sometimes in public housing

Table 15.4: Prevalence of property and violent crime among those always, sometimes and never in large developments or high-rise buildings (Pittsburgh only) (%)

	Early adolescence	Late adolescence
Property crime		
Always in large developments	62.1	54.5
Sometimes in large developments	46.2	62.5
Never in large developments	49.7	49.7
Violent crime		
Always in large developments	75.9	100.0***
Sometimes in large developments	65.4	66.7
Never in large developments	69.3	53.3
Gun carrying		
Always in large developments	14.8**a	30.8*a
Sometimes in large developments	19.2	33.3
Never in large developments	6.9	17.1

Notes:

* p<0.10

** p<0.05

*** p<0.01

[a] At least one cell has an expected count of less than 5.

For early adolescence there were 36 respondents who always lived in a large development, 30 respondents who sometimes lived in large developments and 440 who never lived in large developments. For late adolescence 20 respondents always lived in a large development; 37 sometimes lived in large developments and 433 never lived in large developments. In analysis not presented, if a person ever lived in a small low-rise development they were excluded and the results were re-estimated. Findings remained substantively unchanged.

report greater involvement in violence (66.7%), and those always in public housing report the highest prevalence rate (100%).

A more detailed examination of the link between size of development and offending behaviour (Table 15.5) again reveals no clear pattern suggesting that longer periods of time in large public housing developments are more behaviourally detrimental. The only pattern that comes close to paralleling a dose response effect is among those in late adolescence who engage in violent crime.

Conclusion

This study represents the first step in considering the relationship between the length of time in public housing and involvement in delinquency, violent crime and gun carrying. We recognise that the data and analysis presented here have several limitations. Firstly, more analysis is required to explore mediating factors between public housing residence and risk of delinquency. Secondly, we do not know the reason behind the residential mobility of those moving into and out of public housing. These may include households no longer meeting the eligibility criteria for public housing assistance due to improved family economic circumstances or a change in family composition, while others may leave because of lease termination or eviction (de Silva and Harris, 2004). Thirdly, these findings are based on a relatively small number of subjects identified in public housing for each city.

Nevertheless, there are several intriguing patterns in the data. First, mobility into and out of public housing is fairly high. Blank (1997) argues that there is a general concern in the US with the notion of welfare dependence or addiction creating dependency and learned helplessness which may be passed across generations (see Chapters One, Two and Three of this volume for UK debates). However, according to Blank (1997, p 151), 'about half of those who ever receive AFDC [Aid to Families with Dependent Children] at any time in their life receive assistance for three years or less', and that among the long-term users of AFDC most will cycle on and off the programme several times. It is interesting to note that we find a similar pattern with regard to housing assistance. Over half of those in public housing at some time during the period of late adolescence in Pittsburgh did not remain in public housing for the entire period of time, and similar results were found in Rochester. The view that public housing is a long-term multigeneration condition of living for most of those who utilise public housing is simply not supported by data from either

Table 15.5: Prevalence of property and violent crime among those never, transiently and always in large developments or high-rise buildings (Pittsburgh only) (%)

	Never in large developments or high-rise buildings	More than never and less than a third of the time in large developments or high-rise buildings	Between one third and two thirds of the time in large developments or high-rise buildings	Between two thirds of the time and less than always in large developments or high-rise buildings	Always in large developments or high-rise buildings
Property crime					
Early adolescence	49.7	45.5	44.4	50.0	62.1
Late adolescence	49.7	50.0	54.5	85.7	54.5
Violent crime					
Early adolescence	69.3	63.6	77.8	40.0	75.9
Late adolescence	53.3	66.7	70.0	62.5	100.0
Gun carrying					
Early adolescence	6.9	8.2	22.2	20.0	14.8
Late adolescence	17.1	22.2	38.5	37.5	30.8

Note: See the note for Table 15.4.

study site, and supports Blank's (1997) conclusions about other forms of assistance as well.

Second, it appears that transient families who move into and out of public housing may create the most risk for their children in terms of violent offending, gun carrying and possibly property crime. While the results are far from definitive, they indicate that it is not adolescents who experience the stability of living in public housing for long periods of time who are consistently at greatest risk for engaging in violent crime but, rather, those whose families move into and out of public housing during relatively short periods of time. The pattern of results in Rochester further suggests that adolescents always in public housing may be the least at risk for violent behaviour even when compared with adolescents never in public housing, although these results are not consistently replicated in Pittsburgh.

When the analysis is restricted to only large developments (Pittsburgh), the finding of higher rates of violence among those always in a large development persists and there seems to be somewhat of a dose effect pattern in the data – the longer an adolescent stays in a large development, the greater the risk of involvement in violence, particularly during late adolescence. Therefore, it appears that there is something unique about living in large public housing developments for extended periods of time and violent crime, particularly during late adolescence. However, we cannot determine the causal factors of the high rates of violence among the adolescents in the large developments in Pittsburgh, which may include environmental or structural problems inherent in the design of large public housing developments, concentrated poverty, or characteristics of the families that are placed into these developments[6].

Overall, the results parallel the criminological and sociological literature on residential stability at the individual level. In Rochester residential stability in public housing resulted in lower rates of involvement in property crime and violent crime compared with residential mobility into and out of public housing. Therefore, the risk of living in public housing for several years, at least in terms of delinquency and violent crime, does not appear to exceed the risk of short-term stays in public housing or never residing in public housing.

Our results offer the possibility of important insights as they pertain to the relevant literature on public housing policy. In their study of Chicago neighbourhoods, Sampson and Raudenbush (1999) found that collective efficacy was an important factor in the control of crime at the community level irrespective of the level of physical disorder in the community, and that residential stability was a primary contributor to collective efficacy. Furthermore, Venkatesh's (1996, 2000) ethnographic study among the residents of the Robert Taylor Homes in Chicago found social cohesion in a setting of serious physical disorder, observed community kinship and friendship networks amidst grinding poverty, and identified a variety of informal networks springing up throughout a huge public housing development. Both he and Paulson (2004) found people living in public housing who were unwilling to leave their community, regardless of all the crime, violence and disorder. In the context of what we have found in this analysis, and we want to be careful not to overstate the case, it appears that stability in public housing, especially in small developments where families do not reside in high-rise buildings, may have an important positive effect on adolescent behaviour compared to those who move into and out of public housing. The possible reasons for this pattern of results are numerous and remain unexplained here, but it is conceivable that smaller developments foster the emergence of associational ties and collective efficacy in the community.

Acknowledgements

This research was supported by the National Science Foundation grant (SBR-9513040) to the National Consortium on Violence Research (NCOVR). Prepared under Subagreement No 541162 from the NCOVR, H. John Heinz III School of Public Policy and Management, Carnegie Mellon University, Pittsburgh, PA. Additional support was provided from the Office of Juvenile Justice and Delinquency Prevention, Office of Justice Programs, US Department of Justice (86-JN-CX-0007 [S-3] and 86-JN-CX-0009), National Institute on Drug Abuse (5 R01 DA05512-02), the National Institute of Mental Health (MH48890 and MH50778) and the National Science Foundation (SBR09123299). Work on this project was also aided by grants to the Center for Social and Demographic Analysis at the University at Albany (NICHD P30 HD32041 and NSF SBR-9512290). Any opinions, findings, and conclusions or recommendations expressed in this material are those of the authors and do not necessarily reflect the views of the funding agencies. The authors would like to thank Karen Mizelle who coordinated and produced the public housing databases from the PYS.

Notes

[1] HOPE VI is a HUD programme focused on transforming public housing in the US. HOPE VI focuses on several key elements including (a) revitalising the housing stock of severely distressed public housing, (b) establishing avenues for self-sufficiency, and (C) reducing concentrated poverty by developing mixed-income communities (Naparstek et al, 2000).

[2] We use descriptive data from the 1990s instead of more contemporary data on public housing assistance because the data utilised in this analysis are primarily drawn from the late 1980s and the early to mid-1990s.

[3] 'Broken windows' as a cause of crime is not without its critics as empirical support for the perspective is often anecdotal or based on case studies. Miller (2001) raises several concerns with the perspective and argues that contemporary research seems to suggest that social disorder, physical disorder and crime may all be manifestations of underlying conditions of living.

[4] Because Section 8 addresses were not available in Pittsburgh, anyone not in conventional public housing was classified as not in public housing. In Rochester Section 8 addresses were available but are coded here as not in public housing to parallel the analysis in Pittsburgh. At the same time this strategy focuses our attention on conventional public housing that has been the primary focus of much of the research to date.

[5] In Rochester in emerging adulthood there is no 'two thirds to less than always' category because none of the public housing residents fell into this category.

[6] Meehan (1979), for example, argues that the Pruitt-Igoe Development in St Louis quickly became an undesirable place to live and families with the greatest economic need tended to reside there.

References

Barbrey, J.W. (2004) 'Measuring the Effectiveness of Crime Control Policies in Knoxville's Public Housing', *Journal of Contemporary Criminal Justice*, vol 20, February, pp 6-32.

Blank, R.M. (1997) *It Takes a Nation: A New Agenda for Fighting Poverty*, Princeton, NJ: Princeton University Press.

Boo, K. (2001) 'After Welfare: Working Two Jobs, Elizabeth Jones Does Her Best for Her Family. But Is It Enough?', *New Yorker*, 9 April, p 93.

Bottoms, A.E. and Wiles, P. (1986) 'Housing Tenure and Residential Community Crime Careers in Britain', in A.J. Reiss Jr and M. Tonry (eds) *Communities and Crime*, Chicago, IL: University of Chicago Press, pp 101-63.

Bottoms, A.E., Claytor, A. and Wiles, P. (1992) 'Housing Markets and Residential Community Crime Careers: A Case Study from Sheffield', in D.J. Evans, N.R. Fyfe and D.T. Herbert (eds) *Crime, Policing, and Place: Essays in Environmental Criminology*, London: Routledge, pp 11-35.

Bratt, R.G. (1989) *Rebuilding a Low-income Housing Policy*, Philadelphia, PA: Temple University Press.

Briggs, X.D. (1997) 'Moving Up Versus Moving Out: Neighborhood Effects in Housing Mobility Programs', *Housing Policy Debate*, vol 8, no 1, pp 195-234.

Chen, D.W. (2004) 'In Public Housing, It's Work, Volunteer or Leave', *The New York Times*, Late Edition, 15 April, A2, p 1.

DeKeseredy, W.S., Schwartz, M.D., Alvi, S. and Tomaszewski, E.A. (2003) 'Crime Victimization, Alcohol Consumption, and Drug Use in Canadian Public Housing', *Journal of Criminal Justice*, vol 31, no 4, pp 383-96.

de Silva, L. and Harris, L.E. (2004) *Where Are They Now? A Study to Identify, Locate, and Survey Former Residents of Subsidized Housing*, Washington, DC: US Department of Housing and Urban Development, Office of Policy Development and Research.

Dzubow, J. (1996) 'Fear Free Public Housing? An Evaluation of HUD's "One Strike and You're Out" Housing Policy', *Temple Political & Civil Rights Law Review*, vol 6, Fall 1996, pp 55-74.

Fisher, R.M. (1959) *20 Years of Public Housing: Economic Aspects of the Federal Program*, Westport, CT: Greenwood Press.

Fitzpatrick, D. (1997) 'Public housing, private struggles', *Pittsburgh Business Times* (available at www.bizjournals.com/pittsburgh/stories/1997/09/08/story2.htm).

Flint, J. (2002) 'Social Housing Agencies and the Governance of Anti-social Behaviour', *Housing Studies*, vol 17, no 4, pp 619-38.

Hellegers, A.P. (1999) 'Reforming HUD's "One-strike" Public Housing Evictions Through Tenant Participation', *Journal of Criminal Law and Criminology*, vol 90, no 1, pp 323-61.

Holzman, H.R., Kudrick, T.R. and Voytek, K.P. (1996) 'Revisiting the Relationship between Crime and Architectural Design: An Analysis of Data from HUD's 1994 Survey of Public Housing Residents', *Cityscape: A Journal of Policy Development and Research*, vol 2, no 1, pp 107-26.

HUD (US Department of Housing and Urban Development) (1996) 'Promoting Self-sufficiency in Public Housing', *Urban Policy Brief*, no 3, 19/6/05 (available at www.huduser.org/publications/urbaff/upb3.html).

HUD (2000a) 'Housing Authority Profiles', 20/2/00 (available at www.hud.gov/pih/pha/pha_stat.html).

HUD (2000b) 'Affordable Housing Shortage in Metro Rochester, New York'.

Ireland, T.O., Thornberry, T.P. and Loeber, R. (2003) 'Violence Among Adolescents Living in Public Housing: A Two Site Analysis', *Criminology and Public Policy*, vol 3, no 1, pp 3-38.

Kasarda, J.D. and Janowitz, M. (1974) 'Community Attachment in Mass Society', *American Sociological Review*, vol 39, June, pp 328-39.

Kelling, G.L. and Coles, C.M. (1996) *Fixing Broken Windows*, New York, NY: Touchstone.

Kowaleski-Jones, L. (2000) 'Staying Out Of Trouble: Community Resources and Problem Behavior Among High-risk Adolescents', *Journal of Marriage and the Family*, vol 62, no 2, pp 449-64.

Krohn, M.D. (1986) 'The Web of Conformity: A Network Approach to the Explanation of Delinquent Behavior', *Social Problems*, vol 33, no 6, pp 581-93.

Krohn, M.D. and Thornberry, T.P. (1999) 'Retention of Minority Populations in Panel Studies of Drug Use', *Drugs and Society*, vol 14, nos 1/2, pp 185-207.

Loeber, R., Farrington, D.P., Stouthamer-Loeber, M. and Van Kammen, W.B. (1998) *Antisocial Behavior and Mental Health Problems: Explanatory Factors in Childhood and Adolescence*, Mahwah, NJ: Lawrence Erlbaum Associates.

Meehan, E. (1979) *The Quality of Federal Policymaking: Programmed Failure in Public Housing*, Columbia, MO: University of Missouri Press.

Merry, S.E. (1981) 'Defensible Space Undefended: Social Factors in Crime Control Through Environmental Design', *Urban Affairs Quarterly*, vol 16, no 4, pp 397-422.

Miller, D.W. (2001) 'Poking Holes in the Theory of "Broken Windows"', *The Chronicle of Higher Education*, vol 47, no 22, pp A14-A16.

Naparstek, A.J., Freis, S.R., Kingsley, G.T., Dooley, D. and Lewis, H.E. (2000) *HOPE VI: Community Building Makes a Difference*, Washington, DC: US Department of Housing and Urban Development.

Newman, O. (1972) *Defensible Space: Crime Prevention through Urban Design*, New York, NY: Macmillan.

Newman, S.J. and Harkness, J. (1999) *The Long-term Effects of Housing Assistance on Self-sufficiency: Final Report*, Washington, DC: US Department of Housing and Urban Development.

Newman, S.J. and Harkness, J. (2002) 'The Long-term Effects of Public Housing on Self-sufficiency', *Journal of Policy Analysis and Management*, vol 21, no 1, pp 21-43.

Paulson, A. (2004) 'Chicago Raises the Bar for Living in Public Housing', *The Christian Science Monitor*, 5 October, p 3.

Popkin, S.J. (2003) 'Beyond Crime Prevention: How The Transformation of Public Housing has Changed the Policy Equation', *Criminology and Public Policy*, vol 3, no 1, pp 45-52.

Popkin, S.J., Harris, L. and Cunningham, M. (2002) *Families in Transition: A Qualitative Analysis of the MTO Experience. Final Report to the US Department of Housing and Urban Development, Office of Policy Development and Research*, Washington, DC: Urban Institute.

Popkin, S.J., Gwiasda, V.E., Olson, L.M., Rosenbaum, D.P. and Buron, L. (2000) *The Hidden War: Crime and the Tragedy of Public Housing in Chicago*, New Brunswick, NJ: Rutgers University Press.

Popkin, S.J., Olson, L.M., Lurigio, A.J., Gwiasda, V.E. and Carter, R.G. (1995) 'Sweeping Out Drugs and Crime: Residents' Views of the Chicago Housing Authority's Public Housing Drug Elimination Program', *Crime and Delinquency*, vol 41, no 3, pp 73-100.

Popkin, S.J., Gwiasda, V.E., Rosenbaum, D.P., Amendolia, J.M., Johnson, W.A. and Olsen, L.M. (1999) 'Combating Crime in Public Housing: A Qualitative and Quantitative Longitudinal Analysis of the Chicago Housing Authority's Anti-drug Initiative', *Justice Quarterly*, vol 16, no 3, pp 519-57.

RHA (Rochester Housing Authority) (1990) *Addressing the Needs of Our Community*, Rochester, NY: Rochester Housing Authority.

RHA (1996) *Rochester Housing Authority Inventory*, Rochester, NY: Rochester Housing Authority, August.

Sampson, R.J. (1991) 'Linking the Micro- and Macro-level Dimensions of Community Social Organization', *Social Forces*, vol 70, no 1, pp 43-64.

Sampson, R.J. (1988) 'Local friendship ties and community attachment in mass society: A multilevel systemic model', *American Sociological Review*, vol 53, no 5, pp 766-79.

Sampson, R.J. and Groves, W.B. (1989) 'Community Structure and Crime: Testing Social Disorganization Theory', *American Journal of Sociology*, vol 94, no 4, pp 774-802.

Sampson, R.J. and Raudenbush, S.W. (1999) 'Systematic Social Observation of Public Spaces: A New Look at Disorder in Urban Neighborhoods', *American Journal of Sociology*, vol 105, no 3, pp 603-51.

Sampson, R.J., Raudenbush, S.W. and Earls, F. (1997) 'Neighborhoods and Violent Crime: A Multilevel Study of Collective Efficacy', *Science*, vol 277, pp 918-24.

Santiago, A.M., Galster, G.C. and Pettit, K.L.S. (2002) 'Neighbourhood Crime and Scattered-site Public Housing', *Urban Studies*, vol 40, no 11, pp 2147-63.

Shaw, C.F. and McKay, H.D. (1942) *Juvenile Delinquency and Urban Areas*, Chicago, IL: University of Chicago Press.

Stouthamer-Loeber, M. and van Kammen, W.B. (1995) *Data Collection and Management: A Practical Guide*, Newbury Park, CA: Sage Publications.

Taylor, R.B. (1997) 'Social Order and Disorder of Street Blocks and Neighborhoods: Ecology, Microecology and the Systemic Model of Social Disorganization', *Journal of Research in Crime and Delinquency*, vol 34, no 1, pp 113-55.

Thornberry, T.P., Krohn, M.D., Lizotte, A.J., Smith, C.A. and Tobin, K. (2003) *Gangs and Delinquency in Developmental Perspective*, New York, NY: Cambridge University Press.

Triplett, R., Gainey, R.R. and Sun, I.Y. (2003) 'Institutional Strength, Social Control and Neighborhood Crime Rates', *Theoretical Criminology*, vol 7, no 4, pp 439-67.

US Census Bureau (2005) 'United States Population Finder' (available at http://factfinder.census.gov).

Venkatesh, S.A. (1996) 'The Gang in the Community', in C.R. Huff (ed) *Gangs in America* (2nd edn), Thousand Oaks, CA: Sage Publications, pp 241-56.

Venkatesh, S.A. (1997) 'An Invisible Community: Inside Chicago's Public Housing', *The American Prospect*, vol 34, September/October, pp 35-40.

Venkatesh, S.A. (2000) *American Project: The Rise and Fall of a Modern Ghetto*, Cambridge, MA: Harvard University Press.

Weatherburn, D., Bronwyn, L. and Simon, K. (1999) 'Hotbeds of Crime? Crime and Public Housing in Urban Sydney', *Crime and Delinquency*, vol 45, no 2, pp 256-71.

Wendt, P.F. (1983) *Housing Policy – The Search for Solutions: A Comparison of the United Kingdom, Sweden, West Germany, and the United States since World War II*, Westport, CT: Greenwood Press.

Wilson, J.Q. and Kelling, G. (1982) 'Broken Windows', *The Atlantic Monthly*, vol 249, no 3, pp 29-38.

Wilson, J.Q. and Kelling, G. (1989) 'Making Neighborhoods Safe', *The Atlantic Monthly*, vol 263, no 2, pp 46-52.

SIXTEEN

Conclusion

John Flint

This concluding chapter identifies the key themes that have emerged across the contributions in this book and sets out an agenda for future research into housing, urban governance and anti-social behaviour (ASB).

Key themes

Analysing the construction of anti-social behaviour

The concept of ASB is constructed by a large number of actors working through various mechanisms. Much of the current policy emphasis is on operationalising ASB, both through providing legally and practically applicable definitions and through attempts to quantify the extent of such conduct and trends in its growth or reduction. However, some of the difficulties that government and professional bodies have faced in these attempts reflect, firstly, the sheer range of behaviours that it may encompass and, secondly, how ASB, linked to concepts of normality, deviance, duty, obligation, conditionality and responsibility, is an inherently contested and shifting notion, subject to constant reinterpretation and negotiation. Through such processes a dominant discourse is discernable, driven in a cyclical process by powerful media and government rhetoric, diffused, interpreted and subsequently reconfigured by intermediary agencies such as social landlords and also by individual citizens, who as tenants or owner-occupiers subsequently perceive a growing social problem and demand further action, reinforcing and legitimising government discourse as arising from the demands of the general population. A key feature of definitions of ASB in government discourse and legislation has been the blurring of criminal and non-criminal conduct and an expanding range of behaviours that are regarded as anti-social (see Rowlands, 2005; Scraton, 2005).

This dominant discourse has been remarkable for its historic consistency in being founded on the juxtaposition of (undefined) norms and values, ethical standards and respectable forms of behaviour among the majority of 'ordinary' people with the deviant and morally deficient conduct of marginalised 'others'. Engagement in ASB is in a literal sense conceived as being 'against society', and necessitates that society be defended through a range of disciplinary sanctions, with or without a rehabilitative element. Judy Nixon and Sadie Parr in Chapter Four demonstrated that such discourses play out at individual and neighbour levels. In Chapter Thirteen, Kathy Arthurson and Keith Jacobs present evidence from Australia, importantly showing, however, that such discourse is not inevitable, either at government or community levels.

Arenas of anti-social behaviour

Governance processes of classification, surveillance and disciplinary interventions have always been targeted at particular groups and places. A common argument in this book is that social housing tenants as individuals, and laterally council or social housing estates as collective communities, have, since the 19th century, been subject to both categorisation as deviant and dangerous, to classifying processes between the 'deserving' and 'undeserving' or the respectable and unrespectable, and a tier of government and governance mechanisms that have not been applied to other housing tenures. In part this reflects the fact that social housing is managed housing, enabling a range of legal and conditionality techniques to be applied to its inhabitants. ASB is therefore, in part, a construction of social housing management. This has been reinforced by the residualisation of social housing that has increased the concentration of ASB in the tenure. However, there is a noticeable shift in recent policy discourse away from the previous conceptualisation of ASB as largely specific to the social rented tenure.

One of the interesting findings presented in this book is that the arenas of governance appear to be expanding beyond the social housing tenure. A number of chapters have identified how the traditional individual tenant–landlord relationship has widened to include increasing obligations on tenants in relation to their families, guests and neighbours, and on social landlords to govern non-tenants and wider localities, so that the focus of the housing governance of ASB has moved from tenants to neighbours to neighbourhoods. The growing expectation on social landlords to provide mediation services that regulate the relations and interactions *between* residents, rather than the behaviour of individuals, are indicative of this trend. Furthermore, the role of private landlords in tackling ASB is increasingly falling within the scope of government rationales. Mechanisms such as Antisocial Behaviour Orders (ASBOs) are equally applicable to owner-occupiers (indeed, this was one of the premises for their introduction), and through the emergence of gated communities and the purchasing of additional security patrols there is an increasing governance of ASB within the owner-occupied and affluent private rented sectors. As Rowland Atkinson describes in Chapter Five, ASB is no longer conceived as confined to housing estates. Rather, the policy focus has turned towards city centres as the sites of conduct that become newly defined as ASB including begging, street homelessness and binge drinking. Just as the policy response to ASB in residential areas was to increase the responsibilities of housing agencies and residents, so the governance of city centre ASB extends new roles and responsibilities to private businesses including public house landlords. It is also the case that ASB policies have increasingly focused on an age group (young people) rather than a specific housing tenure.

A new disciplinary governance of anti-social behaviour?

One of the recurring messages of this book is that a state focus on policing the deviant, a role for social landlords in regulating the behaviour of tenants and indeed the very techniques of governance deployed to achieve this are not new, but have existed since the very beginning of public urban governance and housing. However, there is a wealth of evidence that supports arguments suggesting that the contemporary governance of ASB by the state, and social landlords in particular, is characterised by an increasing use of an expanded range of punitive legal sanctions including strengthened eviction powers and injunctions. ASBOs and Dispersal Orders not only increase legal mechanisms of social control, but also expand the scope of, often non-criminal, behaviours that are subject to prohibition. Acceptable Behaviour Contracts (ABCs) and Parenting Orders extend the surveillance of formerly private spheres of conduct, while tenancy agreements, good neighbour agreements and tenant reward schemes increasingly define required positive behaviours in relation to duty and obligations to communities, rather than requiring desistance from prohibited behaviours.

It has also been argued that the governance of ASB has increased the professional power of housing practitioners, and that ASB is now regarded primarily as a housing, rather than policing, issue (Brown, 2004). While housing has always been a more conditional element of the welfare state than education or health, conditionality is being pushed further through the introduction of probationary tenancies, the removal of the Right to Buy and the proposals to cut Housing Benefit payments for anti-social tenants. Timothy Ireland and colleagues, in Chapter Fifteen, illustrate how, in the US, this conditionality has been extended to requiring active citizenship and volunteering as a condition of access to public housing.

This intensification and broadening of the governance of conduct is not confined to social housing. Analogous processes are apparent in the regulation of behaviour in gated communities and the increasing presence in residential areas of both state and non-state authority manifested in record numbers of police officers, community support officers, neighbourhood wardens and private security patrols. The chapters have also identified a proliferation of actors in the governance of ASB, including attempts to incorporate citizens, through, for example, enabling them to apply for ASBOs and the use of publicity strategies to 'name and shame', partly to empower residents in the surveillance and policing of ASBO conditions.

There are, however, also counter-arguments that are apparent here that suggest a more ambiguous picture. Brown (2004) argues that the emphasis on punitive sanctions, the focus on removing disorder from public spaces, the reliance on social landlords and the appeal to residents and communities to 'take a stand' against ASB reveal the limitations as much as the expansion of state power. Indeed as I outline in Chapter One, policy rationales are explicit in indicating that government cannot effectively tackle ASB without the active engagement of local 'communities'. The emphasis on actuarial governance may be argued to reflect a reduction in the state's (and society's) ambition to rehabilitate individuals, to 'reform the souls' of the 'deviant', and to tackle the causal structural social and economic processes underlying much ASB. This may indicate a proactive revanchist attack on the poor or a political assumption that government action is unable to resolve such issues, and similar processes are also apparent in urban governance rationales in France (see Chapter Fourteen).

A different argument is also put forward in this book, which suggests that the state and social landlords are indeed engaged in a range of techniques which aim to provide support and rehabilitation to alleged perpetrators of ASB, as set out by Hal Pawson and Carol McKenzie in Chapter Eight and most powerfully illustrated in the resettlement projects evaluated in Chapters Nine (Anwen Jones et al) and Ten (Suzie Scott). Furthermore, Caroline Hunter, in Chapter Seven, has shown the wide variation among social landlords in utilising legal mechanisms, which partly reflects technical problems in their implementation, but is also illustrative of different perspectives about the utility and appropriateness of such sanctions within the housing profession. While many of the chapters here identify the paucity of discussions about causes and personal circumstances in ASB discourse, it is apparent that in many examples of localised practice, these issues are indeed at least being addressed, and, importantly, the evidence here suggests with some success.

One further element of ambiguity is inherent in the emergence of community and neighbourhood governance. In tandem with increasingly disciplinary powers and a visible authority presence, there is an increasing empowerment of citizens. Again there is validity in the argument made in Chapters Three (Helen Carr and Dave Cowan) and Five (Rowland Atkinson) that this represents an abdication of responsibility by the state and more affluent sections of society for resolving social problems that are increasingly concentrated in deprived communities. However, there are also clearly emancipatory elements to the devolution of powers to local neighbourhoods and communities, for example, allowing them to increase the accountability of the police and to assume ownership of communal facilities. Again social housing is at the forefront of these new forms of government, both through the long-standing promotion of tenant participation and, ultimately, through the facilitation of stock transfer as a means to securing community ownership of houses and local service delivery. As Pauline Card (Chapter Two) also reminds us, the increasing rights achieved by tenants during the 20th century meant that, at least until recently, some surveillance technologies were no longer open to housing management, necessitating the use of new legal mechanisms of control. This book suggests that, as Dean (1999, p 33) has identified: 'Governance has ... become more multiple, diffuse, facilitating and empowering, it is however, strangely more disciplinary, stringent and punitive'.

Anti-social behaviour, housing and urban governance

A further theme of this book has been to place the role of housing and the governance of ASB in the context of wider trends in contemporary rationales and processes of governance. These include the emphasis on governing at a distance through the self-regulated conduct of subjects and the linking of citizenship rights to personal and communal responsibility. This is linked to the rise of contractual governance identified by many chapters in this book. Rented housing, through the mechanism of the tenancy agreement, provides the most established arena for this technique of regulating conduct, and we are witnessing an increasing emphasis of contractual governance in both housing and ASB policy and practice, including lengthening tenancy agreements, more prominence given to tenancy signings, probationary tenancies, good neighbour agreements and ABCs.

The emergence of neighbourhood governance and governing through community is evident in ASB policy and practice and is symbolised most prominently in housing governance, both through the encouragement of tenant participation and community ownership in social housing and in the emergence of gated communities and common interest developments in the owner-occupied sector which, to some extent, represent forms of parochial governance that both recast the roles and responsibilities of the state, communities and individuals and narrow the horizons of policy interventions. If such developments do indeed indicate the death of 'social' governance (Rose, 1996), they also raise important questions about the continuing function of 'public' policing, housing provision and the crime management function of local authorities. The influence of communitarian ideas on these new rationales of governance remind us of the centrality of communitarianism to the very beginnings of social housing in the 19th century.

Towards a research agenda

This book started with a call by Tony Blair for respect. There is clearly scope for far more respect in debates about ASB. This book has sought to expose the false dichotomy between those who support the present direction of ASB discourse, policy and practice and those who are alleged to condone all forms of anti-social behaviour and to minimise the impacts that ASB has on individual victims, witnesses and perpetrators. Many of the chapters have identified the social damage ASB causes and Chapters Five and Thirteen in particular are explicit in criticising liberal commentaries that suggest that ASB is not a significant problem requiring action.

The book has also sought to identify the very real challenges facing individuals involved in ASB – local communities, police and housing officers, policy makers and politicians. However, if there is a new politics of conduct (Rose, 1999), then competing notions of what causes and constitutes ASB, negotiations about the legitimate rights and responsibilities of individuals, different groups in society, communities, voluntary, private and state sectors and differing perspectives and priorities about how the problem should be tackled are inherently valid and should not be readily dismissed.

There is, secondly, a strange irony among academic commentaries that criticise ASB discourse and policy because of its failure to recognise the diversity of voices and the different ethical interpretations of norms and values while simultaneously dismissing alternative theoretical perspectives. This book applies a diverse range of theoretical insights. In particular, a Foucauldian framework is evident in the opening four chapters. However, there are a number of alternative theoretical approaches that have been usefully applied to studies of housing and ASB, including Marxism, social constructionism and critical realism (see, for example, Clapham, 1997; Damer, 2000; and the collection edited by Sommerville and Sprigings, 2005), and there is also a role for contributions from a wide range of academic disciplines. Nor should the more controversial contributions of commentators such as Murray (1990) and Field (2003) be lightly dismissed. Not only have they been very influential in current policy and practice, but their ideas are also required to be engaged with and challenged through the construction of alternative interpretations that should lead, importantly, to alternative policy solutions. Finally, there is a need for the recognition of the validity of both independent theoretical approaches and empirical research, including research funded by government and other public agencies. Much of the evidence presented in this book, which has informed our theoretical commentaries, has arisen through such research.

Before turning to specific lines of future enquiry, it should be emphasised that there is a pressing need for a much more robust evidence base in relation to ASB policy interventions. A key theme of this book is to challenge the appeals to 'common sense' that characterise ASB discourse and policy rationales (see Chapter Three). This is exemplified in the Home Office's promotion of naming and shaming of individuals subject to ASBOs while simultaneously admitting that the consequences of such strategies are unknown (Commons Select Committee on Anti-social Behaviour, 2005; Home Office, 2005). Similarly, in Chapter Eight, Hal Pawson and Carol McKenzie have exposed the lack of evidence that ASB is actually a growing phenomenon. Research is required at both wider national scales (see Chapters Seven and Eight) and also at much smaller local levels (see, for example, Chapters Four, Six, Nine, Ten and Fifteen). This research should both evaluate particular policy interventions and initiatives on their own terms and link such evaluations to wider discussions about the overall scope, direction and impacts of ASB policy and practice.

This research should not be confined to academics, but should be the remit of a wide range of policy makers, practitioners and individuals working in voluntary and community groups. What is also required is a policy framework that is responsive to findings that challenge assumptions and consensus (for example, the apparent success of the projects in Chapters Nine and Ten in addressing ASB among families facing eviction; the perspectives and personal circumstances of alleged 'neighbours from hell' in Chapter Four, and the mixed findings about public housing and rates of offending among adolescents in Chapter Fifteen).

This book has identified the need for future research, including the following:

- Research into the personal circumstances, social contexts and perspectives of those engaged in ASB.
- Research that identifies the range of support needs required by different perpetrators of ASB at different life stages.
- Research that continues to focus on the underlying causes of ASB, including the impact of actions in more affluent neighbourhoods.
- Research that explores the extent to which concentrations of ASB are the result of individuals and individual households rather than deficient community processes.
- Explorations of how different communities respond to ASB and in particular the extent to which responses actually differ in relation to tenure and income.
- Further research focused on the nature, extent and governance of ASB in the private rented and owner-occupied sectors.
- Research that examines the impacts of emerging forms of community and neighbourhood governance and policing.
- Research that evaluates the appropriate ASB governance functions and division of responsibilities between the police, social landlords, other agencies and residents.
- Research into the interactions, relationships and accountability mechanisms among the proliferation of actors in the mixed economy of policing and governing ASB.
- Research which looks at the cumulative impact and relationship between a range of intervention mechanisms deployed simultaneously (preventative and reactive, supportive and punitive) rather than evaluating the impact of individual measures in isolation.
- Examinations of the extent to which a balance between support and sanction is actually being enacted in ASBOs, ABCs, Parenting Orders and probationary tenancies.

- Research that explores the impacts of new developments linked to ASB, including ASBOs, Dispersal Orders and gated communities, on other government aims including social inclusion, community cohesion and an enhanced public realm.
- Longitudinal studies that assess the longer-term impacts of a range of interventions including intensive rehabilitation initiatives, ASBOs and mediation.
- Exploring the consequences of the blurring of boundaries between civil and criminal legal processes in the governance of ASB.
- Research into the efficacy of the increasing conditionality of welfare entitlement related to ASB.
- Research into the emergent emphasis on defining a sense of 'Britishness' though commonly shared 'traditional' values.
- Continuing research into the governance of ASB in city centres.
- Comparative international research that explores how ASB is constructed and the efficacy of policy interventions in other countries and also reveals international perspectives on what is happening in the UK.

This list is far from exhaustive and it should be acknowledged that this book has not addressed other important dimensions of ASB. These include the gender basis of constructions of deviant behaviour, in particular related to notions of inadequate parenting (although see Chapter Four), and also links between ASB and ethnicity, although interestingly much of the imagery and discourse around ASB has focused on white working-class communities, in contrast to the explicit linking of street robbery with young black males, for example (Hall et al, 1978).

Arguing for the importance of further research returns us to the most important theme of this book: that debates about ASB, and the role for housing and urban governance in tackling it, are embedded in much more fundamental conceptions of the causes of exclusion, marginalisation and social conflict and the roles and responsibilities of different sections of society in ameliorating their impacts. The concept of 'anti-social' behaviour requires us to reassess the fundamental underpinnings of our society and social conduct.

References

Brown, A. (2004) 'Anti-social Behaviour, Crime Control and Social Control', *Howard Journal of Criminal Justice*, vol 43, no 2, pp 203-11.

Clapham, D. (1997) 'The Social Construction of Housing Management Research', *Urban Studies*, vol 34, no 5, pp 761-74.

Commons Select Committee on Anti-social Behaviour (2005) *Report of the Commons Select Committee on Anti-social Behaviour*, London: House of Commons.

Damer, S. (2000) '"Engineers of the Human Machine": The Social Practice of Council Housing Management in Glasgow, 1895-1939', *Urban Studies*, vol 37, no 11, pp 2007-26.

Dean, M. (1999) *Governmentality: Power and Rule in Modern Society*, London: Sage Publications.

Field, F. (2003) *Neighbours from Hell: The Politics of Behaviour*, London: Politico's.

Hall, S., Critcher, C., Jefferson, T., Clarke, J. and Roberts, B. (1978) *Policing the Crisis*, London: Macmillan.

Home Office (2005) *Working Together: Guidance on Publicising Anti-social Behaviour Orders*, London: Home Office.

Murray, C. (1990) *The Emerging British Underclass*, London: Health and Welfare Unit, Institute of Economic Affairs.

Rose, N. (1996) 'The Death of the Social? Refiguring the Territory of Government', *Economy and Society*, vol 25, no 3, pp 327-56.

Rose, N. (1999) *Powers of Freedom: Reframing Political Thought*, Cambridge: Cambridge University Press.

Rowlands, M. (2005) 'The State of ASBO Britain: The Rise of Intolerance', ECLN Essay No 9, European Civil Liberties Network (available at www.ecln.org).

Scraton, P. (2005) 'The Denial of Children's Rights and Liberties in the UK and the North of Ireland', ECLN Essay No 14, European Civil Liberties Network (available at www.ecln.org).

Sommerville, P. and Sprigings, N. (eds) (2005) *Housing and Social Policy: Contemporary Themes and Critical Perspectives*, London: Routledge.

Index

A

ABCs, *see* acceptable behaviour contracts
abuse
  alcohol 89, 90, 105, 121, 161, 186, 204,
    208, 212, 244
  child 104, 204
  domestic 60, 93, 104, 204, 265, 267; *see*
    also domestic violence *and* family
    violence
  drug 84, 89, 90, 104, 105, 121, 158, 161,
    179, 186, 204, 212, 232, 264, 301
  neighbour spatial 87
  of welfare state 4
  verbal 170, 265
acceptable behaviour contracts (ABCs) 2,
  11, 14, 31, 81, 85, 149, 155, 171-2,
  180, 184, 327, 330, 332
active citizenship 25, 29, 40, 46, 66, 96,
  328
adolescents 13, 69, 283, 285, 301-17, 332;
  see also children *and* minors
advanced liberal democracy 8, 19, 40, 41
AFDC, *see* Aid to Families with
  Dependent Children
affiliation 41, 108-9, 111, 114, 287
affluence 64, 109
affluent areas/neighbourhoods 10, 108-9,
  111, 239, 249, 332
affluent citizens 34
affluent common interest developments
  32
affluent developments 125
affluent households 44
affluent owner-occupiers 243, 249
affluent private rented sector 327
affluent tenants 102
after-school groups 200
agencies
  addressing causes of anti-social
    behaviour 121
  attitudes of to Shelter Inclusion Project
    185, 211
  circulation of contact details of 168
  community-based 270
  community safety 93
  cooperation between 209-11, 215, 216
  devolution of powers to 157
  entitled to apply for ASBOs 28
  failure of 121
  for prevention of anti-social behaviour
    171
  funding 331
  housing 81, 260, 261, 267, 274, 327

  impact of Dundee Families Project on
    213, 216
  impact of Shelter Inclusion Project on
    181, 194
  inappropriate referrals to Shelter
    Inclusion Project by 185
  increased profile given to anti-social
    behaviour by 2
  law enforcement 103, 104, 191, 269,
    271-2; *see also* police
  liaison with Shelter Inclusion Project
    188
  local 27
  of social control 72, 110, 114
  partnerships with wardens 228
  political 41
  problems with referral to Dundee
    Families Project 215
  public 33
  referral to 190, 194, 271
  social housing 81
  state 2, 23, 37
  statutory 86, 95, 96, 190, 194
  voluntary 180, 203
  wardens as channel of communication
    with 228
  welfare 260
  youth employment 289
aggression 84, 96, 99, 103, 108, 250, 286,
  306; *see also* anger management
AHURI, *see* Australian Housing and
  Urban Research Institute
Aid to Families with Dependent
  Children (AFDC) 314
alcohol
  abuse 89, 90, 103, 105, 121, 158, 161,
    204, 208, 212, 244
  dependence 186, 187
  support services 264
alienation 285
Allequippa Terrace 309
alley gating 33, 245
allocation
  of funds for security 234
  of housing 33, 43-5, 269-70
ALMOs, *see* arm's-length management
  organisations
anger management 187, 200, 208; *see also*
  aggression
anonymous evidence 69
anti-ghetto 290
anti-social behaviour
  arenas of 326-7
  as consequence of neoliberalism 263

as contested 265, 266, 275
as housing issue 327
as national problem 155
as personal problem 85
as product of housing management 24
as vehicular idea 57
audit of 59
Blair on 1
causes 7, 24, 112, 133, 236, 263, 267-9,
  275, 329, 330, 332
community ties and 13
complaining about/reporting 159, 166,
  266-7
complex nature of 95
construction of 3, 8, 9, 79-96, 119,
  325-6, 333
contractual relationships and 124
converging expertise and 67-74
costs of 201, 213
crime and 6, 21, 49, 52, 57, 79, 99, 121,
  156, 162, 261
debates about 330
definition of 5-6, 8, 20, 53, 58-64, 83,
  156-8, 325
delegation of responsibility for
  managing 29
discourses of 12, 62, 80, 82, 91, 261-9,
  326, 329-31
ecology of 105
effects of 8, 88, 120, 201, 213, 266-7,
  330
effects of residential stability on 13,
  301-17
effects of tenant support on 188-9
engagement with 269-73
epistemic underpinnings 57
eviction for 66, 81, 179, 202, 274
failure to address 261
gated communities and 239-52
generic approach to 162
geography of 100
governance/management of 2, 3, 6-8,
  12, 19-34, 64-6, 70-2, 103, 119,
  149-50, 199-216, 219-36, 327-33
housing and 2, 3, 6-8, 19-34, 49, 71,
  100, 104-5, 155-74, 220, 259-76, 326
Housing Act (1996) and 138
housing intervention strategies 25,
  269-73
identification of 49
in Australia 12, 259-76
'increase' in 5, 11, 156, 158-60, 173, 331
in rural areas 142
law and 65, 155, 263
liberal treatments of 108
lists of 61
local communities and strategy
  development 27

local government and 52, 162
measurement of 59
mixed economy governance of 9, 19,
  24, 32-4, 219-36
new developments linked to 333
new powers to control 145
non-legal measures 155, 161, 165, 170-2
operationalisation of 325
parallels with terrorism 99
perception of 264-9
perpetrators 10, 11, 89-91, 161, 166,
  172, 179-96, 199-216, 273-5, 288,
  330, 332
persistent 52, 85, 165, 229, 273-6
personal circumstances and 329
policy 24, 110, 112, 149-50, 327-31
poverty and 58, 99, 105-8
power of lack of definition 6, 9, 58, 74
prevention 119, 125, 129
prioritisation of 20
proactive approach to 264
problematic of 49-53
public concern about 19, 79
research into 260-1, 325
responses to 8, 10, 12, 64, 113, 141, 199,
  239-52, 259, 261, 263, 264, 281
shallowness of concept 57
shaping of agenda 10, 100
social exclusion and 48
social geography of 100
specialist response to 11, 162, 173
statistics 159-60
tenancy agreements and 24, 119-33
tenures affected by 63
three-pronged approach to 180
witnesses of 9, 86-9
Anti-social Behaviour Act (2003) 2,
  66-7, 138, 142-7, 150, 223
Antisocial Behaviour etc (Scotland) Act
  (2004) 156
antisocial behaviour orders (ASBOs)
  application for 28, 158, 246
  as adjunct to possession proceedings
    148
  as individualistic solution 85
  as mechanism of state policing 32
  as 'young person's injunction' 167
  balance between support and sanction
    in 332
  complexity of decision to seek 70
  costs associated with 171
  criticisms of 6, 120, 121, 174, 246
  description 121-2
  discretionary use 112
  effectiveness of 120, 121, 174, 246
  enforcement 28, 124
  evidence required for 6, 169

housing associations and 148
Human Rights Act (1998) and 68
increased use of 127, 327
individualised policy and 263
interim 169
introduction of 2, 138
monitoring compliance with 168, 328
needed to control behaviour 54
non-criminal behaviour and 6
owner occupiers and 327
perceived as empowering 173
research into 333
social landlords and 11, 24, 33, 148-9,
155, 157, 158, 162, 166-8, 223
social renters and 103, 163, 164
take-up 148
used where self-regulation fails 81
Antisocial Behaviour Units (ASBU) 1, 26,
58
anti-welfare discourses 54
apaches 283
area effects 102
arm's-length management organisations
(ALMOs) 25, 29, 182
arson 160, 184, 204
ASBOs, *see* antisocial behaviour orders
ASBU, *see* Antisocial Behaviour Unit
assault 108, 158, 168, 204
associational ties 304, 305
assured tenancies 138-40
Australia 8, 12-13, 111, 259-76, 301
Australian Housing and Urban Research
Institute (AHURI) 264

B

bad parenting 10, 85, 91, 94
balanced communities 48
barrios 252
BCS, *see* British Crime Survey
begging 10, 61, 83, 99, 103, 167, 224, 327
benefits
dependency 13, 22, 46, 47, 102, 204,
303, 314
entitlement to 32
fraud 4
help with claiming 187, 188, 193
levels of 39
proposals to cut for anti-social tenants
328
universalistic provision of 39
whether 'deserved' 43
Best Value reviews 161
better parenting workshops 264
Blair, Tony 1, 27, 30, 47, 48, 281, 330
Blunkett, David 80, 83, 85, 245
bounded autonomy 20
Bournville 23

Bridgewater 264-74
Bridgewater Urban Renewal Programme
(BURP) 264, 271
British Crime Survey (BCS) 5, 243, 247
British Security Industry Association
(BSIA) 221, 230-1, 236
broken windows 105, 305-6, 318
budgets
for private security patrols 230, 234
public service 111
Shelter Inclusion Project 181
Building Communities, Beating Crime 3, 27,
223
Bullingdon Club 100
BURP, *see* Bridgewater Urban Renewal
Programme

C

capacity building 20
categorisation of individuals/estates 9, 43,
326
CCPD, *see* Community Councils for the
Preventation of Delinquency
CCTV 33, 72, 230, 232, 245, 248, 252,
292
CDRPs, *see* crime and disorder reduction
partnerships
CEN, *see* European Committee for
Standardisation
Centre for Housing Policy 181
Centre for Research in Social Exclusion
195
Chartered Institute of Housing 6
Chicago 111, 292, 305, 316, 317
Chicago Housing Authority 304
Chicago School 283, 286
child abuse 104, 204
child neglect 204
child protection 190, 283
Child Protection Register 187
children
accusations of anti-social behaviour
against 95, 161, 170
as victims of anti-social behaviour 89
assessment of behaviour 95
dysfunctional families and 85
effects of anti-social neighbours on 87
effects of noise on 88
effects of poverty on 303
effects of residential mobility/stability
on 302, 304, 316
housing inspectors' role to ensure care
for 44
in Bridgewater 268
in Dundee Families Project 11, 204-10,
213, 214, 216
in gated communities 245, 247-8
in Shelter Inclusion Project 181-94

local authority conditions regarding behaviour of 125
out-of-control 84, 94, 161, 274
parents of problematic 74, 81
positive effects of home ownership on 47
use of ASBOs with 6, 167, 168
with special educational needs 95
Children's Fund 181
Chirac, Jacques 281
Christie Downs 264-75
circuits of exclusion 49
citizen governors 24
citizens, *see also* citizenship
as part of wider policing family 27
categorisation of 43
community governance and 24
increasing empowerment of 329
obligations to act against crime, etc. 29-31
provision of benefits to 39
relationship with society 38
reshaping behaviour of 7, 19
responsible 38
role in enforcement of antisocial behaviour orders 28
role in governance of conduct 33
citizenship, *see also* citizens
active 25, 29, 40, 46, 66, 96, 328
acts of 30
basis of 4
compounded 10, 101, 109-14
rights 26, 39, 46-9, 53, 329
social 40, 46
training in 23
city centres 327, 333
city centre wardens 103
city competitiveness 10, 104
city policy 281, 282, 289-94
City Projects 294
civil action 52
civil association 126
civil liberty 126
civil rights 39, 46, 86
civil society 20, 282
civil state 126
classification 326-7
Cleaner Neighbourhoods Bill (2004) 28
Clingham v. Kensington and Chelsea RLBC 68
CLS, *see* Ministry for the Interior Local Safety Contracts
codes 286
collective efficacy 12, 248-9, 305, 306, 316, 317
collectivisation 82
colonisation 239

commercialisation 221
commodification 124, 133, 234
common space 286
Commons Select Committee on Anti-social Behaviour 331
Commonwealth State Housing Agreement (CSHA) 259-60
communal areas 171
communal responsibility 329
communication strategies 269, 270-1
communitarianism 12, 24, 26, 48, 72, 108, 111, 155, 173
communities
balanced 48
challenges facing 330
empowerment 27, 107
gated 239-52
involvement of 27, 328
police inability to protect 52
self-governing 32
self-policing 32
sustainable 48
therapeutic 70
community activity 22
community advocacy 28
community-based agencies 270
community-based housing organisations 29
community-based initiatives 263
community cohesion 107, 333
Community Councils for the Prevention of Delinquency (CCPD) 291
community-focused interventions 13
community-focused responses 275
community governance 7, 9, 19, 24-6, 34, 40, 329, 332
community groups 103, 107
community of strangers 125
community ownership 26, 329, 330
community policing 220-1, 232
community relations 3, 7
community renewal 263
community reparation orders 29
community safety officers 28
community safety schemes 223
community size 304, 305
community spirit 110
community support officers 2, 32, 223-8, 236, 328
community ties 13
competitiveness 10, 104
compounded citizenship 10, 101, 109-14
compulsory competitive tendering 65
concentration effects 102, 220
concentration of poverty 101, 220
concierges 240, 245

conditionality 7, 31, 325-8, 333
condominios 252
Connexions 187
contracts 12, 30, 31, 38, 66, 73, 119,
    122-5, 164, 171-2, 289-92; *see also*
    acceptable behaviour contracts
contractual governance 9, 24, 31-2, 329,
    330
contractualisation 10, 124, 125, 133
control, *see also* social control
  city policy and 289-94
  disciplinary 54, 327-9
  informal 108
  of crime 19
  of working class 21, 103
  spaces of 99-114
  techniques 149
  technology of 53
core block 199, 207
council estates 48, 52
council housing; *see also* public housing
    and social housing
  as safety-net tenure 47
  changing role of 54
  Labour government's approach to 40
  management of as control technique 37
  roles of 9
  translational discourses and 43-5
  unpopular 51, 220
courts
  common knowledge and 58
  demotion orders and 142
  eviction and 67, 139, 147
  fast-track actions in 85
  persistent offenders and 273
  repossession and 164
  use of ASBOs 121
co-veillance 293
CRASBOs, *see* criminal anti-social
    behaviour orders
crime
  anti-social behaviour and 6, 21, 49, 52,
    57, 79, 99, 156, 261
  broken windows theory 305
  collective efficacy and 305
  control of 19, 24, 25, 26, 31, 63, 65, 101,
    155, 157, 220
  decline in 221-2
  designing out 242
  displacement of 109
  effect of Dundee Families Project on
    216
  fear of 12, 219, 222, 223, 225, 232, 236,
    241, 242, 243, 251
  gated communities and 2, 240-52
  HOPE VI programme and 306
  local authorities and 52, 65, 330

media reports on 99, 104, 241
  neighbourhood wardens and 228
  networks and 107
  organised 283
  perceptions of 221
  policy 19, 25
  prevention 105, 219, 224, 226, 228, 233,
    234, 242
  property 302, 307-17
  protection from 109, 242
  public/social housing and 13, 48, 220,
    301, 303
  residential mobility and 305
  residential stability and 305, 306
  residualisation and 261
  serious 196, 305
  social exclusion and 48
  statistics 159
  trends 160
  US initiatives 301
  violent 241, 302, 307-17
Crime and Disorder Act (1998) 2, 65, 68,
    121, 138, 148, 222
crime and disorder plan 65
Crime and Disorder Reduction
    Partnerships (CDRPs) 1, 2, 25, 222,
    235
crime complex 241, 242
crime-free neighbourhoods 110
criminal anti-social behaviour orders
    (CRASBOs) 6
criminal ASBOS, *see* criminal anti-social
    behaviour orders
criminal damage 159, 184
criminalisation 112
criminalising discourse 92
criminal justice system 241
criminogenic effects 303, 304
criminology 7, 304, 305, 306
critical realism 331
Cromer Street estate 252
CSHA, *see* Commonwealth State
    Housing Agreement
cultural capital 235
cultural responses 13
culture 26, 81, 159, 209, 285, 289
curfews 2, 103, 110

D
damage to property 204
debt 186, 192
defensible space 242, 291, 293
dehumanisation 82, 91
de-industrialisation 284, 287
deinstitutionalisation 64, 268
Deleuze, Gilles 293
delinquency 283, 286, 291, 301-17

democracy
advanced liberal 8, 19, 40, 41
property owning 46, 65
democratisation of ideas 64
demolition 287, 290, 306
demonisation 9, 81, 82, 84, 89, 91, 92, 96, 112
demotion 50, 66, 70, 142
de-municipalisation 46
dependence
on alcohol 186, 187
on benefits 13, 22, 46, 47, 102, 204, 303, 314
on drugs 161, 179, 208
depression 186-8, 193, 205
deprived areas 79, 102, 109-12, 114, 244-6, 249-51
dereliction 291, 294
'deserving' individuals 7, 9, 43, 44, 53
design 51, 242, 268, 303, 316
designing out crime 242
deviance 4, 9, 21, 29, 50, 57, 70, 81-3, 325
deviancy amplification 4
difficult tenants 37-54
disability 186
disaffiliation 287
discipline 20, 54, 58, 75, 113, 293, 326-9
discourses
anti-social behaviour 12, 62, 80, 82, 91, 261-9, 326, 329-31
anti-welfare 54
criminalising 92
dominant 325
government 325
interaction between 49
'lawless Britain' 4
moral underclass 45-8
neoliberal 10, 104
new 265-9
of deserving and undeserving poor 53
of deviance 70
official 80
of marginalisation 70
of morality 20 21
of National Efficiency 53
of poverty 51, 53
of social exclusion 51, 53
policy 5, 12, 81
political 83-6, 96
private 80, 82, 91-3
public 91-3
redistributional 45
shifts in 53
social integrationist 45, 47, 48
translation 37
discretionary practices 45
discrimination 45, 260, 290

dispersal orders 2, 32, 81, 85, 232, 327, 333
displacement of problems 93, 109, 180, 202, 214
disrespect 1
distancing 82
districts of exclusion 290
domestic abuse 60, 93, 104, 204, 265, 267; *see also* domestic violence *and* family violence
domestic violence 264; *see also* domestic abuse *and* family violence
domination 285, 286
Donzelot, Jacques 282
dreadful enclosures 50-1
drugs
abuse 84, 89, 90, 104, 105, 121, 158, 161, 179, 186, 204, 212, 232, 264, 301
dealing 84, 164, 165, 204, 244
support services 264
Dundee City Council 199, 200, 202, 205, 209, 210
Dundee Families Project 11, 93, 166, 172, 180, 194, 199-216
Durkheim, Emile 295
dysfunctional families 10, 85, 91, 105

E

ecology of anti-social behaviour 105
employment 64, 262, 304
empowerment 20, 27, 29, 30, 34, 65, 105, 111, 173, 261, 329
enforcement 73, 120, 124, 150, 171, 195, 227, 228, 261, 263
ethnicity 182, 333; *see also* minority ethnic groups
ethopower 20
eugenics 50
European Committee for Standardisation (CEN) 293, 295
European Community 293
eviction
as deterrent 274
as individualistic solution 85
as show of sovereign force 70
convictions as grounds for 146
cost of 213, 214
effects of 179, 264, 269, 275
effects of tenant support on rates of 207, 215
for anti-social behaviour 66, 81, 179, 202, 274
frequency of use 50
in Australia 274
in private housing market 301
increased powers of 52
judges reluctance to use 67

landlords and 2, 45, 138, 144
not solution to anti-social behaviour
180, 201
of assured/secure tenants 139
of victims of harassment 146
punishment for non-conformity 50
restriction by 1980 Housing Act 51
risk of 199
starter tenancies and 139, 141
strengthened powers of 22, 327
support for among tenants 275
tendency to displace problems 214
threat of 73, 168
use of 81, 164-6
eviction notices 274
evidence
anonymous 69
hearsay 68, 166
witnesses' 169
exclusion 12, 13, 80, 82, 85, 96 194, 285,
333; *see also* social exclusion
ex-slum dwellers 43, 45, 49, 50, 53

F

family breakdown 47
family stress 179
family values 48
family violence 264; *see also* domestic
violence
fast-track court action 85
fear
about security 68
in gated communities 109
neighbourhood 4
of crime 12, 219, 222, 223, 225, 232,
236, 241, 242, 243, 251
of eviction 45
of immigration 4
of intervening 111
of intimidation 86
of retaliation 86, 159, 169, 201, 266,
267, 272
of social housing tenants 250
of terrorism 4
of the 'other' 84, 235, 251
of violence 170
politicisation of 106
Field, Frank 20
fines 85
fire authorities 236, 293
fireworks 244
fixed penalty notices 226, 227, 246
flexible allocation 269
flight of capital 220
flight of people 220
focus groups 269
folk devils 4, 82

Fordism 284
foster care 213, 214
Foucault, Michel 64, 75, 81, 276, 293, 331
fragmentation 125
français moyen 284
France 13, 82, 281-96, 328
freehold documents 127
freehold property 125
friendship networks 317
fun days 188, 189
funding
central government 225
for community support officers 225,
227
for Dundee Families Project 199, 203,
212
for security 224, 234
local initiatives adapted to fit 226
to combat anti-social behaviour 1

G

galley 285
gangs 83, 84, 161, 284, 285
gardens 60, 72, 86, 87, 125, 158, 187, 191,
193
gated communities 239-52
academic interest in 240, 242-3
anti-social behaviour and 239-52, 327
anxieties in 109
contractualised social control and 12
emergence of 3
growth of 109
in deprived areas 244-6, 249-51
legal considerations 239, 241, 247-8
management of 7, 249
neighbourhood governance and 330
regulation of behaviour in 125, 328
research into 333
social control and 241
tensions associated with 12
gender 54, 182, 333
gentrification 250, 292
geographical lottery 113
geographical mobility 113
geography
of anti-social behaviour 100
of social housing 109
ghettoisation of the affluent 109
globalisation 241
good customer schemes 72
good neighbour agreements 2, 11, 120,
125, 127, 327, 330
governance
at a distance 19, 329
community 7, 9, 19, 332
contractual 9, 19, 31-2, 329, 330
empowerment through 34

extending beyond social housing 326
neighbourhood 2, 7, 19, 27-9, 239, 330, 332
of anti-social behaviour 2, 3, 6-8, 12, 19-34, 64-6, 70-2, 103, 119, 149-50, 199-216, 219-36, 327-33
of conduct 328
of tenants 37-54
panoptic 20
policing and 24
shift from social to communal 235
techniques of 23, 327
urban 7, 325, 328
government discourse 325
grammars of living 20
group identity 111
gun carrying 307-17
G v. Harrow LBC 148

H

harassment 59, 88, 146, 158, 159, 165, 170, 244, 265
hard-pressed areas 244-5
health
  mental 93, 121, 158, 161, 166, 179, 186, 187, 205, 259, 265, 272
  physical 7, 25, 26, 38, 47, 95, 183, 188, 205
  public 6, 21, 39
healthcare provision 38
Helping Others to Enjoy Yourself (HOTEY) 233
high-rise accommodation 302, 309, 311, 317
Hill, Octavia 21, 22, 37, 43, 50, 71, 72
Hollingdean Estate 245-6
homelessness 10, 12, 183, 184, 194, 213, 214
Homeless Persons Service 202
Homeless to Home 180
home ownership 46, 260, 262
homicide 305
homophobic attacks 60
honour codes 286
HOPE VI 302, 306, 318
HOTEY, see Helping Others to Enjoy Yourself
housebreaking 204
housekeeping 50, 53
housing; see also council housing, public housing and social housing
  access to 21, 26, 31
  allocation 33, 43-5, 269-70
  anti-social behaviour and 2, 3, 6-8, 19-34, 49, 71, 100, 104-5, 155-74, 220, 259-76, 326
  as social control 2, 3, 22, 145-50

community ownership of 239
community relations and 3
conditionality of access to 7
contractual governance in 31
cost 303
design 33, 51, 242, 268, 303, 316
diluting of state role in policy 25
  in Australia 13, 259-76
location 303
neighbourhood decline and 25
new 282
poor 47, 268
providers 263
quality of 303
temporary 202
Housing Act (1980) 22, 51, 52, 73, 138
Housing Act (1985) 138
Housing Act (1988) 139
Housing Act (1996) 52, 66, 138, 139, 143, 145, 146, 147
housing action trusts 223
housing advocacy 188
housing assistance 303, 314, 318
housing associations 63, 103, 139-42, 144, 148-51, 167, 172
housing benefit 32, 328
Housing Corporation 139, 140, 144, 145, 150
housing inspectors 44
housing management
  anti-social behaviour and 24, 25
  as control technique 30, 37, 43, 50
  effect of anti-social behaviour discourses on 264
  ideological considerations 261
  in Australia 264-5
  intensive 44
  neighbourhood management and 25
  policies in the UK 263
  risk communications and 70
  slum dwellers and 49
  strategies 263
  surveillance of tenants' conduct and 21, 22
  zero tolerance 58
housing managers 13, 33, 45, 113, 271-5
housing market 39
housing needs 269
housing officers 103, 111, 167, 170, 185
housing organisations 22, 52
Housing Plus 26
housing quality 51
housing schemes 285, 292
housing stress 265
housing visitors 137
Human Rights Act (1998) 68

I

ideologies 57, 65, 261,269, 285
immigrants 284, 287
immigration 4
implicit agreements 123
inclusive society 82
incomplete agreements 123
Indigenous peoples 261
individualisation 10, 82, 85, 92, 263, 275
industrialisation 284
informal networks 317
injunctions 2, 11, 22, 52, 66, 74, 81, 113, 137, 138, 142-5, 148, 151-2, 161, 164, 168-9, 180, 201, 327; *see also* interdicts
Institute of Higher Studies for Interior Safety 288
instrumental behaviour 120
inter-agency cooperation 209-11, 215, 216
interdicts 169, 201; *see also* injunctions
intergenerational poverty 108
interim antisocial behaviour orders 169
interpretative ventriloquism 9; *see also* judicial ventriloquism
intimidation 86, 88, 158
intolerance 106, 107, 195
introductory tenancies 11, 66, 137-42; *see also* probationary tenancies *and* starter tenancies
Irwell Valley Housing Association 72
Islington London Borough Council 171

J

Jacobs, Jane 291
Joseph Rowntree Housing Trust 231, 233
judges
    hearsay evidence and 166
    reluctance to evict 67
judicial knowledge 67
judicial review 140
judicial ventriloquism 67-70; *see also* interpretative ventriloquism

K

Kensington and Chelsea RLBC v. Simmonds (*Simmonds* case) 66, 67
kinship 241, 304, 317
kitemarking 236
knowledge, of the law 127

L

labelling 4, 45, 57-76
labour market 287
La Galère 284
landlords; *see also* private landlords *and* social landlords
    approaches to enforcement 73

increased powers of 66
investigative role 72
liaison with 188
more proactive role 10
non-housing powers 148-9
of public houses 327
personality of 133
powers of 150
publicising actions of 162
relationship with tenants 11, 119-33, 326
role in controlling behaviour 120
use of acceptable behaviour contracts 171-2
use of evictions 81, 164-6
views of tenancy agreements 129
land speculation 290
law; *see also* legislation
    antisocial behaviour and 65, 155, 263
    as idealised form of social relations 119
    as repressive 75
    blurred civil/criminal boundary 156, 157, 325, 333
    civil 10, 52
    civilising effect 127
    gated communities and 239, 241, 247-8
    individual behaviour and 120-2
    limitations of 126-7
    property 119
    role of wardens in enforcing 228
    social landlords and 137-51, 219, 328
    technicality of 69
    use of 9, 163-70, 201
law enforcement agencies 269, 271-2; *see also* police
Law of Orientation and Programming Relating to Safety (LOPS) 291
Law of Orientation on the City 290, 296
Law of Social Cohesion 296
Law of Solidarity and Urban Renewal 296
lawless Britain discourse 4
learned helplessness 303, 314
learning difficulties 121
Le Corbusier 291
Leeds model 273
legal aid 4
legal expenses 213
legal sanctions 13
legislation
    changes in 11, 137-51
    civil association and 126
    homeless persons 202
    in Australia 260
    increase in 155
    interpretations of 119
    priority given to anti-social behaviour in 1

public health 39
punitive 92
recent history 66
responses to anti-social behaviour 65
to control behaviour 2
legitimacy gap 111
length of residence 301-17
Les Cahiers de al Sécurité Intérieure 288, 289
levies 224
lifestyle clashes 158, 159, 170
lifestyle enclaves 251
literacy problems 272
liveability 282
local associational ties 304, 305
local authorities
  allocation of housing by 44
  as providers of social housing 51
  crime management function 52, 65, 330
  delegation of housing management functions 29
  formation of pressure group 64
  housing associations and 149
  in Scotland 1
  legal action and 52
  powers of 1, 6, 28, 138, 144
  regulation of 150
  rent arrears and 141, 165
  responses to anti-social behaviour 52, 162
  responses to public anxieties 225
  selection of tenants by 44
  use of antisocial behaviour orders 149
  use of contracts 125
  use of injunctions 144
  use of tenancy agreements 73
local councillors 290
Local Government Association 149
Local Government Information Unit 5
Local Housing Programmes 294
localism 25, 26
locality 147, 151
local renewal strategies 25
local sanctions 108
local state 25, 109
lone-parent families 79, 183, 204; *see also* single-parents
longitudinal studies 333
LOPS, *see* Law of Orientation and Programming Relating to Safety

M
Major, John 47
Manchester City Council 143
Manchester City Council v Cochrane 140
Manchester City Council v Lee 67-8, 147,
marginalisation 41, 48, 64, 70, 95, 333

Marxism 290, 331
Marx, Karl 282
Mas de Taureau 282
material improvements 264
McKay, Henry 305
media 3, 19, 20, 52, 79-80, 96, 101, 104-5, 109, 113, 155, 158, 159, 195, 241, 266, 276, 292, 325
mediation 3, 11, 120, 155, 161, 165, 170-1, 180, 269, 272-3, 326, 333
mental health problems 93, 121, 158, 161, 166, 179, 186, 187, 205, 259, 265, 272
middle classes 104, 282-6
Mill, John Stuart 67
Ministry for the Interior (French) 295
Ministry for the Interior Local Safety Contracts (CLSs) 291, 292
minority ethnic groups 281; *see also* ethnicity
minors 168, 273-4; *see also* adolescents *and* children
mix 294
mixed contacts 296
mixed economy of anti-social behaviour governance 9, 19, 24, 32-4, 219-36
mixed economy of policing 7, 9, 12, 219-36, 332
mobility 10, 107, 301-17
money management 188
monitoring 293
moral behaviour, social exclusion and 26
moral cleansing 71
moralisation 21, 33, 102, 103
moral order 91
moral panics 4, 52, 53, 75, 113
moral underclass discourse 45-8
Moving to Opportunities Demonstration Project 302
multiagency approach 25
multiagency cooperation 209-11, 215, 216
multiagency meetings 74
multiagency partnerships 150
multiagency working 273
municipal action groups 282
mutuality 32

N
naming and shaming 28, 162, 168, 328, 331
National Agency for Urban Renewal 294
National Association of Prison Officers 113
National Crime Reporting Standard 159
National Efficiency 39, 50, 53
natural liberty 126
natural surveillance 221

NCH Action for Children Scotland 199, 200, 209
neighbour disputes 80, 184, 204, 244, 265, 267
neighbourhood agreements 245
neighbourhood-based policing 2, 22
Neighbourhood Charters 27, 246
neighbourhood decline 25
neighbourhood forums 263
neighbourhood governance 7, 19, 24-9, 34, 239, 291, 329, 330, 332
neighbourhood renewal 21, 25, 222
Neighbourhood Renewal Fund 181
neighbourhood wardens 2, 12, 32, 33, 103-6, 170, 220-4, 228-30, 236, 328
neighbour nuisance 91, 214
'neighbours from hell' 10, 81, 84, 93-6, 105-8, 332
neighbour spatial abuse 87
neoliberal discourses 10, 104
neoliberalism 10, 65, 104, 262, 276
New Deal 47
New Earswick 231-4
New Institution for the Formation of Character 23
New Labour 1, 23, 24, 48, 65, 80, 96, 173
New Lanark 23
New Local Government Network 244-5
Newman, Oscar 242, 291
noise 87, 88, 91, 94, 99, 124, 125, 158, 170, 184, 244, 245
Noise Abatement Notices 180
non-legal remedies 155, 161, 165, 170-2
non-tenants 145-6, 326
normalising gaze 81
notice of seeking possession (NSP) 165, 124, 183, 195
NSP, *see* notice of seeking possession
nuisance 5, 51, 66, 91, 94, 124, 125, 141, 143, 146, 159, 184, 196, 201, 262

O

occupation contract, *see* tenancy agreement
occupier-managers 72-4
occupiers' rights 73
odours 87
ODPM, *see* Office of the Deputy Prime Minister
Office of the Deputy Prime Minister (ODPM) 155, 166, 195, 236, 242, 249, 250, 252
Officer Next-Door Programme 271
off-the-shelf agreements 123, 129
older people 89, 233
one-day count 5, 60
One-Strike and You're Out initiative 301

operational costs 212-13
Operation GateIT 245
orphans 287
othering 82
otherness 85
'other', the 62, 64, 84
outreach 199, 203
Owen, Robert 22
owner occupancy 63, 243, 249, 260, 330, 332

P

paedophiles 4
pamper days 189
panoptic governance 20
parenting
    bad 10, 85, 91, 94
    classes 85, 92, 264
    orders 2, 81, 85, 92, 327, 332
    skills 95, 208
    support 187, 189
parents
    control strategies 92
    duties 85
    sanctions on 274
park attendants 111, 221
parking disputes 170, 247
pathology 81, 86, 262, 268, 285, 287
patrols 219-36, 327
patronage of technology 290
pauperisation 58, 71
perpetrators
    constructions of anti-social behaviour 89-91
    vulnerability of 11, 161, 166, 172, 179, 190, 204
personal autonomy 107
personal isolation 288, 295
physical environment 268
Pittsburgh 302, 306-18
Pittsburgh Youth Study (PYS) 307
planning policy 112
planning system 240
plural policing personnel 12
police *see also* law enforcement agencies
    British Transport 236
    challenges facing 330
    collaboration with housing managers 271-2
    contact with young people 289
    housing associations and 149
    inability to protect communities 52
    inability to protect witnesses 69
    inadequacy of responses to calls 224
    local presence of 111
    monitoring activities 27, 263
    moral panic and 113

need to remodel stations 112
not monopolistic guardians of safety
    220, 291
numbers of officers 1, 2, 12, 32, 222,
    328
persistent offenders and 273
powers 60
public housing and 301
public lack of confidence in 4, 221, 224
recording practices 159
rejection of cul-de-sacs 293
role in governance of conduct 33
senior officers' attitudes 225
support reduces complaints to 213
use of dispersal orders 32
use of eviction threat 274
Police and Magistrates Court Act (1994)
    222
police authorities 236
Police Reform Act (1992) 148
Police Reform Act (2002) 2, 138, 223,
    236
policing 219-36
    blurring of boundaries 24
    citizens role in 2, 27
    commodification of 234
    community 220-1
    emerging forms of 332
    housing management and 7
    mixed economy of 7, 9, 12, 219-36, 332
    neighbourhood-based 2, 27
    of anti-social behaviour 103
    of antisocial behaviour orders 328
    policy 19, 222-4, 306
    reassurance 2
    reforms 2
    social landlords and 33
policy
    anti-social behaviour 24, 110, 112,
        149-50, 327-31
    city 281, 282, 289-94
    communitarian drive 111
    crime 19, 25
    development 1
    disciplinary enforcement measures in 24
    discourse 5, 12, 81
    for persistent perpetrators 273-5
    in Australia 12-13, 259-62, 276
    individualised 263
    in France 292
    in the UK 262
    in the US 263
    limiting of role of state in 25
    little knowledge of outcomes 174
    narratives 20
    planning 112
    policing 19, 222-4, 306

progressive 276
public housing 306
punitive 276
rationales for 3
research 332
responses to anti-social behaviour 8
retributionist 273
social 39
social theories and 7
urban 12
welfare 262
policy makers 3, 104, 107, 111, 273, 330
political discourses 83-6, 96
political rationalities 37-41
political rights 39
politics of behaviour 8, 20, 22
politics of conduct 20, 33
politique de la ville, *see* city policy
pollution 86, 87, 92
positive discrimination 290
possession 52, 54, 142-5, 148, 161, 165,
    179; *see also* repossession
possession orders 142, 145, 169
posters 60, 62
primary care trusts 236
priority urban development zones
    (ZUPs) 13, 284, 290
private housing 71, 260, 301
private landlords
    anti-social behaviour and 3, 327
    legal techniques used by 8
    licensing of 124
private rental sector 3, 8, 124, 43, 63-4,
    128, 202, 260, 327, 332
private security 12, 33, 220, 223-6, 230-1,
    328
Private Security Industry Act (2001) 223
private space 87, 287
privatisation 12, 13, 46, 292
probationary tenancies 2, 31, 63, 66, 269,
    328, 330, 332
problem of many hands 226
professional witnesses 169-70
programme translation 41-2
property crime 302, 307-17
property law 119
property managers 43
property-owning democracy 46, 65
property prices 242, 249
prostitution 103, 164, 167, 283
protection rackets 204
Pruitt-Igoe Development 318
public health departments 21
public health legislation 39
public housing 6, 13, 38, 113, 302-4, 306,
    332; *see also* social housing

Public Housing Drug Elimination
Program 301
publicity 261, 270, 328
public landlords 53; *see also* social
landlords
public opinion 96
public order 92
public services 107, 221, 292
public space 13, 242, 287-93, 328
public town planning studios 282
punishment 86
punitive measures 275, 332

Q
Quality Housing and Work
Responsibility Act (1998) 304
quality of housing 51
quality of life 122, 208, 214, 222

R
racial stereotypes 261
racial stigma 292
rage 285
ragging 289
rationality 23
reaffirmation of normality 9, 82, 89
reassurance 219-23, 227, 232
reassurance paradox 221
reassurance policing 2, 32, 223
recording practices 159, 173
redevelopment 287, 301
redistributional discourse 45
reflexivity 120
regeneration 99, 249-52
regulation 150, 295
rehabilitation 44, 49-53, 85, 92-3, 150,
194-5, 214, 326, 328, 333
rehabilitation projects 3
re-housing 45, 188, 207, 208, 290
relegation 290
rent arrears 141, 164, 165, 179
repossession 155, 164; *see also* possession
representation 100
reprisals 86, 201, 267
research 7, 8, 13, 200-1, 259-61, 264-5,
276, 288, 301, 306-17, 325, 330-3
Research Development and Statistics
Directorate 58
resettlement 3, 180, 328
residentialisation 291
residential mobility 10, 301-17
residential stability 13, 301-17
residents' associations 107, 224
residualisation 7, 41, 47-8, 51, 53, 101-2,
105, 108, 137, 220, 259, 262-3, 326
responsible authorities 236
responsible citizens 38

retaliation 266, 267; *see also* retribution
retraining 74
retribution 86, 169; *see also* retaliation
retro-gating 240
rights
citizenship 26, 39, 46-9, 54
civil 39, 46, 86
in tenancy agreements 31, 123, 129, 131
occupiers' 73
of individuals 330
political 39
shift to responsibilities from 72
social 38, 39, 40, 46
tenants' 22, 54, 142
understanding of 127
Right to Buy 46, 65, 102, 220, 328
riots 52, 123, 125, 186, 281, 282, 295
risk communications 70
risk theorists 120
rituals 283, 286, 288
Robert Taylor Homes 317
Rochdale 11, 120, 166, 183, 192
Rochdale Borough-wide Housing 182,
183
Rochdale Metropolitan Borough Council
180
Rochester 302, 306-16, 318
Rochester Youth Development Study
(RYDS) 307, 309
Royal Institute of Chartered Surveyors
242
ruined rituals 288
rules 262, 263
rural migration 287
RYDS, *see* Rochester Youth Development
Study

S
safety 99, 122, 219-36, 235, 288, 289, 291,
302
sanctions 21, 105, 114, 126, 326-9, 332
sanitary conditions 301
sanitation 302
Sarcelles 296
school attendance 189
school exclusion 179, 187, 205
school truancy schemes 264
Scotland 1, 11, 22, 33, 148, 152, 156, 164,
167, 169, 171, 224
Scottish Executive 27, 155
Scottish Office 203
'second left', the 282
Second World War 282-4
Secure by Design housing 33
secure tenancies 66, 138, 139
security
commercialisation of 221

investment in 242
mechanisms 3
patrols 219-36, 327
personnel 103
privatised 241
segregation 41, 48, 70, 112, 234, 250-1,
    284, 285, 294
self-esteem projects 264
self-governing communities 23, 25, 29, 32
self-policing communities 32
Serious Organised Crime and Police Act
    (2005) 2, 28, 224
shanty towns 287
Shaw, Clifford 305
Shelter 166, 181, 196
Shelter Inclusion Project 11, 120, 166,
    179-96
shoplifting 204
SIA, *see* British Security Industry
    Association
Simmonds case, *see* Kensington and Chelsea
    RLBC v. Simmonds
single mothers 46, 66, 93
single parents 66, 161; *see also* lone-parent
    families
sink estates 45
skateboarding 28-9
skills 47, 262
SLCNG, *see* Social Landlords Crime and
    Nuisance Group
slum clearance 44, 49, 50, 302
social activities 264
social capital 26, 229, 236
social citizenship 39, 40, 40, 46
social class 100, 261, 282, 284-6, 294
social cohesion 106, 107, 113, 114, 261,
    282, 305, 333
social constructionism 331
social control, *see also* control
    agencies of 72, 110, 114
    formalisation of 241, 248
    gated communities and 125, 241
    good neighbour agreements as 125
    housing management policies and 30,
    . 43, 261, 263
    informal 10, 72, 107, 111, 248
    in France 292
    legal mechanisms of 327
    new forms of 33, 80
    of tenants 219
    residents' unease with 113
    through contractualisation 10, 12
    tools of 246
social diversity 102, 112
social exclusion 9, 26, 45-9, 51, 53, 79, 86,
    137, 287
Social Exclusion Unit 59, 60, 179

social geography 100
social housing; *see also* council housing,
    housing *and* public housing
    access to 31, 137
    agencies 81
    anti-social behaviour and 259-76
    as managed housing 7, 9, 57-8, 71, 75,
    326
    as safety-net accommodation 47, 64
    as site and process 101
    as spatial segregation of the
    marginalised 41
    birth of 9
    classification of tenants 326-7
    clustering 108
    colonisation of 239
    compounded citizenship of 109-14
    concentration of vulnerable individuals
    in 51
    control and 45, 75, 103, 137
    curbs on expenditure for 262
    discipline as role of 103
    environmental problems 114
    geography of 109
    governance of conduct and 328
    governing through crime 220
    in Australia 259-76
    management 7, 11, 21, 22, 24, 75
    reproductive nature of 64
    residualisation of 7, 47-8, 51, 53, 101,
    102, 105, 108, 137, 220, 259, 262-3,
    326
    role in promoting moral frameworks
    22-3
    social exclusion and 48-9
    social inclusion and 64
    stigmatisation of 108
    surveillance as role of 103
    withdrawal of middle-income groups
    from 108
social hygienism 45
social inclusion 64, 333
social insurance 38
social integrationist discourse 45, 47, 48
social interaction, disadvantage and 26
social intervention 263
social justice 38, 263
social landlordism 138, 219
social landlords
    antisocial behaviour orders and 11, 24,
    33, 148-9, 155, 157, 158, 162, 166-8,
    223
    CDRPs and 2
    contracts as tools of 73
    legal powers of 6, 8, 9, 11, 150-1, 219
    neighbourhood wardens and 229
    policing and 147, 219-36

power of eviction 45, 52
private security and 230
use of ABCs 31
use of injunctions 143, 145, 168-9
use of law 137-51, 219, 328
use of probationary tenancies 2, 31, 63,
    66, 269, 328, 330, 332
Social Landlords Crime and Nuisance
    Group (SLCNG) 2, 14, 64, 144
social mobility 111
social need 259, 264
social networks 107
social rights 38, 39, 40, 46
social skills 187, 188
social solidarity 38, 40, 125
social theories 7
social ties 107, 108
social violence 287
social workers 44, 202, 203, 205, 213
socioeconomic change 220
special constables 236
special education 186
specialist anti-social behaviour teams 11,
    162, 173
special schools 205
speed bumps 247
speed cameras 28
starter tenancies 11, 139-42
state, the
    abdication of responsibility by 329
    duties of 110
    intervention in housing market 39
    limitations of 34
    local 25, 109
    reduced role of 25, 29
state of nature 126
statutory agencies 86, 95, 96
Steyn, Lord 68, 69
stigmatisation 45, 63, 79, 84, 91, 102, 108,
    110, 113, 260, 284, 286, 292, 296
street wardens 103, 236
stress 187, 193, 259
subcultures 286, 287
supervision orders 274
support 3, 120, 133, 166, 179-96,
    199-216, 328, 332
Supporting People 122, 133, 180, 181
supportive intervention 12
Sure Start 187
surveillance
    as feature of governance of conduct 33
    as role of social housing 103
    deviancy amplification and 4
    electronic monitoring and 2
    extension of 20
    ghettoisation and 51
    in early 20th century 241

in French cities 13
in poor neighbourhoods 105
intensive deployment of 45
mechanisms 32
of problematic families 44
of public space 242
of re-housed slum dwellers 50
of working class 21, 103
poverty and 110
technology 53, 54, 329
varied deployment of 44
suspended possession order 168
sustainable communities 48
sustainable tenancies 259

T
Tackling Anti-social Behaviour 63
Take a Stand prizes 108
target hardening 245
technical knowledge 63
Teddy Boys 283
teenage parenthood 49
temporary housing 202
tenancies
    assured 138, 139, 140
    establishment of 119
    introductory 11, 66, 137-42
    precontractual phase 128
    probationary 2, 31, 63, 66, 269, 328,
        330, 332
    secure 66, 138, 139
    starter 11, 139-42
    sustainable 259
tenancy agreement 10, 22, 24, 31, 73,
    119-33, 162, 247, 327, 330
tenancy signings 330
tenancy support, *see* support
tenant participation 26, 30, 263, 329, 330
tenant reward schemes 2, 327
tenants
    affluent 102
    agreements with landlords 119-33
    assured 138, 139
    classification of 326
    collaboration with housing providers
        263
    conduct of 137
    contributors to decline of estates 51
    demotion of 142
    difficult 37-54, 260
    effects of landlords' powers on 66
    empowerment of 30
    evicted 275
    expectations 260
    governance of 37-54
    labelling as underclass 52
    obligations 326

of housing associations 139, 140
problematisation of 4
reconfiguration of identities 22
reduction in security of 151
relationship with landlords 119-33, 326
rights of 22, 54, 142
secure 138, 139
shifting perceptions of 53
single mothers as 46
social control of 219
support for eviction among 275
training in citizenship 23
work with 271
Tenants Rights Act (1980) 22
Thatcherism 48
Thatcher, Margaret 47, 65
theft 184, 204, 283
therapeutic communities 70
therapeutic intervention 73
Third Way 24, 57
Thrasher, Frederick M. 283
'three-pronged approach' 180
tidiness 72
TOGETHER campaign 1-2
town planning 282, 288, 291
tracking 85
Trade Union and Professional Association
    for Family Court and Probation Staff
    121
traditional values 333
traffic wardens 236
training 42, 188, 262, 304
transit cities 287
translation 41-5
translation discourses 37
transport 282, 287, 292
traveller communities 103
truancy 49, 179, 193
'tyranny of the radio' 227

U

uncivil society 283
underclass 4, 9, 45-8, 52-3, 100, 137,
    262-3, 268
'undeserving' individuals 7, 43-5, 50,
    53-4
unemployment 38, 46, 47, 183, 262, 265,
    268, 269, 284, 302
United Kingdom
    housing management in 263
    research in 301
United States 8, 13, 263, 283, 301
urban forms 281-96
urban governance 7, 325, 328
urbanisation 112, 284
urban regeneration/renewal 21, 219, 250,
    282

urban space 287, 292
urban struggles 282, 289-93
urban tensions 281
urban violence 281-96

V

vandalism 51, 171, 184, 244, 295
vehicle nuisance 61
vernacular knowledge 63
victimisation 219, 234, 301, 305
victims 80, 330
victim support 169
violence 88, 89, 93, 158, 165, 170, 274,
    281-96, 302-17
    residential stability and 301-17
    social 287
    urban 13, 281-96
violent crime 241, 302, 307-17
visible patrols 219-36
visual pollution 87
vocabulary of irresponsibility 79
voluntary agencies 180, 203
vulnerability
    as cause of anti-social behaviour 10
    of new tenants 121
    of perpetrators of anti-social behaviour
        11, 166, 172 179, 190, 204
    of witnesses to ASB 86
vulnerable individuals 6, 51, 166, 228, 272

W

wardens 2, 12, 32, 33, 103-6, 170, 220-4,
    228-30, 236, 328
warnings 192, 195, 273, 274, 304
welfare
    conditionality in provision 31
    dependence 13, 22, 46, 47, 102, 204,
        303, 314
    neoliberal attack on 65
    rights-based approach 138
welfare state 4, 7, 38-40, 43, 261, 282, 328
windows, broken 105, 305-6, 318
witnesses 69, 80, 103, 169-70, 201, 330
witness protection 169
workplace insecurity 107

Y

yob culture 4
young offenders institutions 121
youth nuisance 184, 196

Z

zero tolerance 58, 92, 120
zones of exclusion 282
zoning 290
ZUPs, *see* priority urban development
    zones